DEVELOPING
PRACTICE GUIDELINES
FOR SOCIAL WORK INTERVENTION

DEVELOPING

PRACTICE GUIDELINES

FOR SOCIAL WORK INTERVENTION

ISSUES, METHODS, AND RESEARCH AGENDA

Aaron Rosen and Enola K. Proctor, Editors

COLUMBIA UNIVERSITY PRESS • NEW YORK

COLUMBIA UNIVERSITY PRESS

Publishers Since 1893

New York   Chichester, West Sussex

Library of Congress Cataloging-in-Publication Data

Developing practice guidelines for social work intervention : issues, methods, and research
  agenda / Aaron Rosen and Enola K. Proctor, editors.
      p. cm.
  Includes bibliographical references and index.
  ISBN 0-231-12310-8 (cloth : alk. paper)—ISBN 0-231-12311-6 (pbk. : alk. paper)
  1. Social service. 2. Social service—Research. I. Rosen, Aaron. II. Proctor, Enola Knisley.

  HV40.35.D48 2003
  361.3'2—dc21

                                                                                        2003051634

∞

Columbia University Press books are printed
on permanent and durable acid-free paper.
Printed in the United States of America
c 10 9 8 7 6 5 4 3 2 1
p 10 9 8 7 6 5 4 3 2 1

CONTENTS

Preface VII

1. Practice Guidelines and the Challenge of Effective Practice
   AARON ROSEN AND ENOLA K. PROCTOR 1

   PART I Precursors of Guidelines: Intervention Research
   and Evidence-Based Practice

2. Intervention Research in Social Work: A Basis for Evidence-Based
   Practice and Practice Guidelines MARK W. FRASER 17

3. Evidence-Based Practice: Implications for Knowledge Development and
   Use in Social Work EILEEN GAMBRILL 37

4. Empirical Foundations for Practice Guidelines in Current Social Work
   Knowledge WILLIAM J. REID AND ANNE E. FORTUNE 59

   PART II Practice Guidelines for Social Work: Need, Nature,
   and Challenges

5. Clinical Guidelines and Evidence-Based Practice in Medicine,
   Psychology, and Allied Professions
   MATTHEW OWEN HOWARD AND JEFFREY M. JENSON 83

6. The Structure and Function of Social Work Practice Guidelines
   ENOLA K. PROCTOR AND AARON ROSEN 108

7. Social Work Should Help Develop Interdisciplinary Evidence-Based
   Practice Guidelines, Not Discipline-Specific Ones BRUCE A. THYER 128

8. The Role of Diagnostic and Problem Classification in Formulating
   Target-Based Practice Guidelines STUART A. KIRK 140

9. Constructing Practice: Diagnoses, Problems, Targets, or Transactions?
   MARK A. MATTAINI 156

PART III Responsiveness of Practice Guidelines to Diversity in Client Populations and Practice Settings: The Idiographic Application of Normative Generalizations

10. Accounting for Variability in Client, Population, and Setting Characteristics: Moderators of Intervention Effectiveness LYNN VIDEKA 169

11. Service-Delivery Factors in the Development of Practice Guidelines
    LUIS H. ZAYAS 193

12. Performance Standards and Quality Control: Application of Practice Guidelines to Service Delivery
    WILMA PEEBLES-WILKINS AND MARYANN AMODEO 207

PART IV Practitioner, Organizational, and Institutional Factors in the Utilization of Practice Guidelines

13. Practitioner Adoption and Implementation of Practice Guidelines and Issues of Quality Control EDWARD J. MULLEN AND WILLIAM F. BACON 223

14. Organizational and Institutional Factors in the Development of Practice Knowledge and Practice Guidelines in Social Work JEANNE C. MARSH 236

15. Social Work Practice Guidelines in an Interprofessional World: Honoring New Ties That Bind NINA L. ARONOFF AND DARLYNE BAILEY 253

PART V Conclusion

16. Advancing the Development of Social Work Practice Guidelines: Directions for Research ENOLA K. PROCTOR AND AARON ROSEN 271

Index 291

PREFACE

We consider as axiomatic the view that social work practice must be based on empirically tested and verified knowledge. Yet the empirical basis of support for interventions is all but absent from practitioners' considerations as they make clinical decisions in routine practice. The premise of this book is that social work must redouble its efforts to devise ways to ensure that the best available empirically tested knowledge is used in practice. We believe that one means to facilitate utilization of such knowledge by practitioners is to incorporate it into readily available, accessible, and professionally sanctioned practice guidelines. The need for empirically supported guidelines for intervention has become all the more pressing with the advent of managed care and the associated demands throughout the practice environment for greater accountability, effectiveness, and efficiency.

Practice guidelines for a variety of practice tasks are already in use by service organizations and other professions, and they are increasingly entering the public discourse in social work. Convinced that social work needs to develop research-based guidelines, we invited some of the key scholars in social work practice to focus on the challenge of developing practice guidelines for social work. Accordingly, this book explores a number of critical conceptual, methodological, and organizational issues that are related to the development by social work of research-based practice guidelines for intervention and their use in practice.

We first floated the ideas for this volume with our colleagues Eileen Gambrill, of the University of California at Berkeley; Jeanne Marsh, of the University of Chicago; and Lynn Videka, of the State University of New York at Albany. We thank them for their enthusiastic support and acknowledge their early influence on the planning of this project. On the basis of the book's conception, authors were selected and invited to prepare chapters, first versions of which were presented at a working conference on social work practice guidelines hosted in May 2000 by the George Warren Brown School of Social Work at Washington University in St. Louis. The conference provided a forum for presenting and discussing the ideas expressed here and for shaping the agenda for advancing social work guidelines. The contributions to this volume represent revised and updated versions of the works originally presented at the conference, many of which had to be appreciably abbreviated to meet the length limitations of this volume.

We are grateful to the authors, who viewed the project as timely and propitious, enthusiastically accepted our invitations, and devoted their scholarly efforts to the various topics addressed here. We particularly appreciate the authors' gracious, thoughtful, and repeated responsiveness to our editorial comments and those of the Columbia University Press reviewers. Their grace and forbearance significantly enhanced our task as editors.

We are deeply grateful to Shanti Khinduka, dean of the George Warren Brown School of Social Work, who encouraged and supported us in this undertaking. He enthusiastically endorsed, sponsored, and hosted the initial conference, committing the necessary resources for its success.

We express our appreciation to our faculty colleagues at the George Warren Brown School of Social Work for their support of the practice guidelines conference and, more significantly, for their conviction that social work practice and education should be evidence based. This conviction was exemplified by a unanimous faculty decision in May 2000 to advance evidence-based education throughout the M.S.W. curriculum.

We also acknowledge the financial support for the conference on practice guidelines by the National Institute of Mental Health. We are particularly grateful to the late Dr. Kenneth Lutterman and to Dr. Juan Ramos of the institute for their advice, consultation, and facilitation of the conference. George Warren Brown's Center for Mental Health Services Research also provided resources in support of the conference and for the preparation of this volume.

We thank George Warren Brown's doctoral program graduates Drs. Chaie-Won Rhee, Catherine Striley, and Violet Horvath, who shared our enthusiasm, stimulated our thinking, and contributed to the fruitfulness of the conference and the focus of this book.

Last, but certainly not least, we express our gratitude to Cindy Betz, who has made our task pleasant and manageable. She orchestrated the logistics of the conference; organized and facilitated our communication with the authors; cheerfully, patiently, and accurately tracked and compiled the revisions to the chapters in this volume; and was instrumental in seeing it to publication.

Aaron Rosen and Enola K. Proctor
February 5, 2003

CONTRIBUTORS

MARYANN AMODEO, PH.D., Associate Professor, Associate Dean for Academic Affairs, Boston University

NINA L. ARONOFF, PH.D., Assistant Professor, Social Work Program, Wheelock College

WILLIAM F. BACON, PH.D., Associate Vice President, Research and Evaluation, Planned Parenthood of New York City, Inc.

DARLYNE BAILEY, PH.D., Vice President of Academic Affairs, Dean of the College Teachers College, Columbia University

ANNE E. FORTUNE, PH.D., Professor, Associate Dean for Academic Programs, School of Social Welfare, State University of New York

MARK W. FRASER, PH.D., John A. Tate Distinguished Professor, Associate Dean for Research, School of Social Work, University of North Carolina, Chapel Hill

EILEEN GAMBRILL, PH.D., Hutto Patterson Professor, School of Social Welfare, University of California, Berkeley

MATTHEW OWEN HOWARD, PH.D., Associate Professor, George Warren Brown School of Social Work, Washington University

JEFFREY M. JENSON, PH.D., Professor, Graduate School of Social Work, University of Denver

STUART A. KIRK, PH.D., Professor, Marjorie Crump Chair, Department of Social Welfare, University of California, Los Angeles

JEANNE C. MARSH, PH.D., Professor, School of Social Service Administration, The University of Chicago

MARK A. MATTAINI, DSW, Associate Professor, Director, PhD Program in Social Work, Jane Addams College of Social Work, University of Illinois, Chicago

EDWARD J MULLEN, DSW, Wilma & Albert Musher Chair Professor, School of Social Work, Columbia University

WILMA PEEBLES-WILKINS, PH.D., Dean and Professor, School of Social Work, Boston University

ENOLA K. PROCTOR, PH.D., Frank J. Bruno Professor of Social Work Research, Associate Dean for Research, Director, Center for Mental Health Services Research, George Warren Brown School of Social Work, Washington University

WILLIAM J. REID, PH.D., Distinguished Professor, School of Social Welfare, State University of New York, Albany.

AARON ROSEN, PH.D., Barbara A. Bailey Professor Emeritus of Social Work, George Warren Brown School of Social Work, Washington University

BRUCE A. THYER, PH.D., Dean and Professor, School of Social Work, Florida State University

LYNN VIDEKA, PH.D., Professor, School of Social Welfare, Director, Center for Human Services Research, University at Albany-State University of New York

LUIS H. ZAYAS, PH.D., Shanti K. Khinduka Distinguished Professor of Social Work, George Warren Brown School of Social Work, Washington University

DEVELOPING
PRACTICE GUIDELINES
FOR SOCIAL WORK INTERVENTION

1

PRACTICE GUIDELINES AND THE CHALLENGE OF EFFECTIVE PRACTICE

AARON ROSEN AND ENOLA K. PROCTOR

This book addresses what we believe is the most basic challenge facing the profession of social work—ensuring the effectiveness of social work practice. This complex and multifaceted task has two primary dimensions: (1) ensuring the availability of tested knowledge that is relevant to and can inform effective practice and (2) ensuring that social work practitioners have access to, understand, and properly use that knowledge in their work. This book examines these two dimensions through the concept of practice guidelines.

Practice guidelines, which have been the subject of considerable developmental work in allied professions, are also being discussed with increasing frequency within social work (cf. Howard and Jenson 1999, chapter 5, this volume). In general, across all professions espousing them, practice guidelines are viewed as a means to ensure that practitioner behaviors conform to desirable standards. Explicit adherence to guidelines of desirable practice is intended to promote the effectiveness of practice, reduce variability in implementing best practice, increase the predictability of practice behaviors, and enhance client confidence in treatment as meeting professional standards.

Practice guidelines are meant to assist practitioners in decision making; potentially, they can address any aspect of practice in which decisions and resultant behaviors are likely to vary among practitioners—determining eligibility for service, performing assessment and diagnosis, selecting and implementing interventions, and evaluating treatment results, for example. In this volume we focus on practice guidelines for selecting and implementing interventions. Our working definition of *practice guidelines* is that they are a set of systematically compiled and organized statements of empirically tested knowledge and procedures to help practitioners select and implement interventions that are most effective and appropriate for attaining the desired outcomes. We believe that this definition is applicable to all the contributions in this volume.

Practice guidelines that meet this definition serve as an indispensable tool for confronting the two basic challenges of social work practice—enhancing practitioner use of tested and appropriate knowledge and encouraging further knowledge development that is attuned to and addresses the needs of practice. These two themes are further developed in the following chapters. The volume concludes with a singular focus on the knowledge needed for effective practice and an attempt to evolve and suggest the format and substance of a research agenda to guide further development and use of practice guidelines.

PREMISES UNDERLYING OUR APPROACH TO SOCIAL WORK PRACTICE

This volume, its content, and its organization are rooted in a number of premises that we see as basic and necessary for responsible social work practice. Although some are widely espoused among social workers, we realize that they may not be universally endorsed—in substance or in emphasis. These premises are so basic to practice that they merit full discussion. But because their analysis and the advocacy of their pros and cons appear throughout the social work literature, we will mention here only those principles that are most germane to explicating the assumptive framework of our approach (Rosen 1993).

First, like most professional endeavors, social work practice is utilitarian and goal directed, with improvement in the clients' welfare being its ultimate purpose. That is, social work practice must be justified by the pursuit of worthwhile goals for its clientele. Accordingly, the primary criterion for undertaking service and for selecting practice methods should be evidence of their potential to achieve the desired goals for clients. Second, since social work is a profession with a public mandate, its sanction to practice is conditioned on a number of expectations (which are also shared by other professions). The expectations most pertinent to this discussion are the following:

1. Social work practice is not random but is guided by a body of knowledge and skills that are discernible and transmittable and that facilitate attainment of its socially worthwhile and publicly sanctioned goals.

2. Social work is responsible for maintaining the institutions necessary to update its knowledge base, to train its practitioners, and to oversee the proper and ethical discharge of its services.

3. Practicing as part of a publicly sanctioned profession, social workers must be accountable—to clients, to peers, and to a variety of sanctioning bodies. Accountability is most rudimentarily expressed by a commitment to and a responsibility for demonstrating that practice is effective and efficient.

Demonstrating the effectiveness of practice requires *evidence* that service goals have been achieved and that goal attainment was causally linked to the activities (programs, methods) undertaken to reach the goals. Demonstrating efficient practice also requires evidence that service goals are attained with the least possible cost—in time, money, effort, and client suffering. Thus, in order for social work practice to be accountable it must be subject to scrutiny according to acceptable evidentiary standards.

4. A fourth basic premise is that professional knowledge in general, and knowledge that guides intervention in particular, must be tested and supported by empirical evidence obtained and evaluated according to prevailing scientific standards. Such standards must include, at the minimum, an explicit and systematic procedure for defining, gathering, and analyzing relevant evidence.

5. Finally, human behavior, individually and in the aggregate, as well as the process of behavior change, is complex and multi-determined. Hence, interventions cannot be viewed as or expected to be uniformly applicable or universally effective. Their effectiveness is likely to vary in relation to the outcomes that are pursued, to the problem and other client characteristics, and to factors of the helping and in vivo situation.

LACUNAE IN PRACTICE AND RESEARCH

Unfortunately, the correspondence between these basic premises and day-to-day, real-world practice cannot be assumed. Indeed, the gap between some of the premises and the realities of practice is considerable. We believe, however, that through the development and use of practice guidelines the gap can be appreciably narrowed. In this section we note instances in which practice, as well as efforts to develop practice knowledge, diverges from some of these premises.

Social work has long vacillated between approaches to practice that are intuitive, relying on implicit considerations, and those that advocate greater explicitness of and transparency for the rationales that guide practice decisions (cf. Rosen, Proctor, and Livne 1985; Rosen 1993; Zeira and Rosen 2000). Particularly as they pertain to the process of clinical treatment, the implicit and ad hoc nature of practice decisions has been defended and even extolled (Kondrat 1992). Such an orientation to practice necessarily compromises the standards of accountability and evidence, as well as rendering practice non-amenable to systematic evaluation and study (Rosen 1994).

Another departure from the basic premises of practice, which is likely reinforced by a nonsystematic and implicit approach to decision making, is the extremely low utilization in practice of the products of research—and hence of interventions whose effectiveness has been empirically tested (Rosen 1994; Rosen et al. 1995). Not only is there little actual utilization of research products in practice, but studies have also found little practitioner exposure to practice-relevant research, as well as reluctance to use systematic approaches to practice, such as single-system designs (Cheatham 1987; Fischer 1993; Kirk and Penka 1992; Richey, Blythe, and Berlin 1987).

Compounding these trends has been social work's relative neglect of undertaking the kind of research that aims to develop and test the effectiveness of interventions. As we found in a recent survey of research studies published in social work journals, research focusing on development and testing of interventions to influence and change human conditions has been meager compared with research devoted to description and explanation of existing conditions (Rosen, Proctor, and Staudt 1999). These findings reinforce the by-now-prevalent calls for social work to intensify its efforts and investment in intervention research (Austin 1999; Fortune 1999; Fortune and Proctor 2001; Schilling 1997; Task Force on Social Work Research 1991).

Research devoted to development and testing of effective interventions has also been justly criticized for insufficiently taking into consideration and investigating possible moderators of effectiveness, such as different conditions and settings of practice and diverse characteristics of client populations. Interventions tested under selective or optimal conditions (efficacy studies) are not similarly or necessarily effective when applied to different populations under a variety of service conditions (Chambless and Hollon 1998; Newman and Tejeda 1996; Seligman 1996). There is undoubtedly a need to intensify and improve basic intervention research and efficacy studies using randomized clinical trials (RCT), but further research is also needed to test the effectiveness of interventions across different clienteles and settings, and with more appropriate designs (see Fraser, chapter 2, this volume).

The extent to which practice uses research is undoubtedly related to the availability of research that is relevant to and capable of guiding interventions. Nonutilization, however, cannot be attributed simply to the relatively low volume of relevant research. Results of intervention research relevant to guiding practice are available both from within and from outside social work (Nathan and Gorman 1998; Reid and Fortune, chapter 4, this volume; Reid and Hanrahan 1982; Thyer and Wodarski 1998). Additionally, an interdisciplinary effort spearheaded by the Campbell Collaboration (Campbell Collaboration Steering Committee 2001) is conducting and compiling systematic reviews of research on intervention with the potential of informing practitioner decision making.

Assuming the availability of at least a modicum of relevant research on intervention, proponents of evidence-based practice (EBP) advocate its use in practice decisions, supplemented as necessary by nonresearch evidence. Practicing according to EBP tenets requires, in addition to adherence to the premises of responsible professional practice as described above, espousal of a critical attitude regarding practice decisions, involvement of and commitment to clients, and other practice attributes (Gambrill 1999, chapter 3, this volume). We concur with the objectives and premises underlying EBP, but we believe that it places too heavy a burden on practitioners, exceeding their capacity to systematically process and judiciously integrate research results from disparate studies (or critical reviews) and to then apply those results to treatment decisions for individual clients (Gigerenzer and Goldstein 1996; Janis and Mann 1977; Tversky and Kahneman 1974; Wilson and Brekke 1994). We think that in order to base decisions for individual clients on the best available evidence, practitioners must also be equipped with a means of organizing, synthesizing, and judiciously using empirically based probabilistic evidence to guide practice decisions. We view practice guidelines, as we conceive their function and structure (see Proctor and Rosen, chapter 6, this volume), as a requisite tool for implementing evidence-based practice.

PRACTICE GUIDELINES AND THE PRACTITIONER

Our position is that practice guidelines for social work intervention, particularly those having the features that we advocate and consider to be essential (see Proctor and Rosen, chapter 6, this volume), can enhance the correspondence between practice and the basic premises that underlie it. In particular, we believe that practice guidelines for intervention will aid practitioners in overcoming some of the hurdles that are inherent in everyday practice and will contribute to more responsible and empirically supported practice decisions. But a number of dilemmas need to be considered.

By their very nature, practice guidelines aim to increase the predictability of practice around a set of standardized "best practices" and reduce the variability between practitioners in departing from such practices. That intent brings to the fore a fundamental assumption that underlies the use of guidelines—and perhaps the use of all professional knowledge: In spite of its diversity and complexity, human behavior has significant commonalities, and interventions can have applicability across clients and situations. Thus, empirically supported principles warrant cautious generalization to clients and situations other than those that were directly studied. This assumption notwithstanding, we recognize that practice situations also have idiosyncratic elements and that in order to be maximally effective with different individuals and conditions, interventions need to be developed and tested for relevant groupings of clients and situations and carefully applied accordingly.

We acknowledge the uniqueness of individuals and of practice situations, but we disagree with extant particularistic notions of practice that view treatment as not amenable to appropriate use of preformulated interventive principles (Kondrat 1992). In that, we differ from such views as those of Witkin and Harrison, who, in a purportedly dispassionate discussion of EBP and the concept of evidence, argue the fallibility of all evidence for capturing the true existential meaning of practice, particularly the experiences of clients from diverse groups (Witkin and Harrison 2001). Although they state that preformulated interventions may be appropriate for problems that "are believed to exist stably across time and context," they proceed to reject such a possibility "for a world characterized by shifting, multiple identities and relational constructions, in which an 'outcome' is at most the beginning of something else" (Witkin and Harrison 2001:294). Such characterizations of the realities of social work practice—highlighting the transitory, unique, and ephemeral in human behavior—serve only to place it outside the realm of responsible professional practice as we outlined it above.

Our position is that beyond their unique characteristics, individuals, problems, situations, and their associated behaviors can be distinguished along certain treatment-relevant dimensions or variables (e.g., age, ethnic origin, personality type, health status, service auspices). Individuals and situations with similar placement on a given dimension have some common characteristics and may be grouped by such. Development of practice guidelines must capitalize on such group-specific commonalities, for they permit formulation of better-targeted interventions than those based only on the more universal commonalities of human behavior. Description and understanding of commonalities and variability of behavior, within and across groupings, are important elements in the knowledge base of professions. This base of descriptive and explanatory knowledge must in turn be used for the development and testing of interventions that are effective for attaining the desired outcomes of service (Rosen, Proctor, and Staudt 1999). Thus, interventive knowledge should be based on both the universal and the group-specific commonalities in human behavior.

To apply that knowledge appropriately and be ultimately helpful to the individual client, practitioners need first to determine a client's (often intersecting) memberships in the relevant groupings (the tasks of assessment and diagnosis). The next step is to select and apply critically the best-fitting preformulated (standardized) interventions for these groupings, always recognizing the client's uniqueness beyond the established commonalities, in a manner that is amenable to correction and adjustment on the basis of feedback from evaluation. The rationale and some of the procedures of single-system designs (SSD) (Bloom, Fischer, and Orme 1995), as well as those embodied in systematic planned practice (SPP) (Rosen 1992; Rosen et al. 1993) are examples of means for aiding practitioners in application of standardized knowledge while particularizing the individual client. In fact, the conception of practice guidelines advanced in this volume (Proctor and Rosen, chapter 6, this volume) may be viewed as an integration of evaluation principles from SSD and systematic practice of SPP in applying evidence-based practice to an individual client (Rosen 2002). Hence, it is our position that practice guidelines, to be useful to practitioners, must help in selection and proper use of preformulated interventions, as well as guide practitioners through a recursive, self-correcting process that addresses the unique situation of the particular client.

Practitioners have expressed considerable resistance to practice guidelines, as well as to other forms of systematic and explicit practice. Much of their resistance to guidelines in particular may derive from the fear that they lead to "cookbook" or formulary-driven practice, with few degrees of freedom left for practitioner discretion and judgment, and for individualizing clients. As the preceding discussion should indicate, however, we see many degrees of freedom for practice to vary within the context of guidelines, albeit with explicit and well-defined choice junctures. That is, use of practice guidelines can help practitioners cope with the uncertainty inherent in making practice decisions in a more explicit and structured manner, rather than through a largely intuitive and unsystematic process. With guidelines, the practitioner is not only aware of specific decisions that must be made at certain points of the treatment process but also is provided with the information and tools needed to support making these decisions. Regardless of the extent to which practice decisions are supported by standardized guidelines, however, practitioners still face the task of particularizing and creatively meeting the needs of the individual client. As will become clear from our conception of practice guidelines (Proctor and Rosen, chapter 6, this volume), the use of guidelines necessitates, rather than supplants, the need for creativity and innovation, and the exercise of professional judgment and practice wisdom.

Approaches to EBP recognize that available empirical evidence is often lacking and practitioners must critically exercise considerable choice and creativity in combining knowledge from theory, research, and personally acquired practice wisdom to address client needs properly (Gambrill 1999 and chapter 3, this volume). This is true also when using guidelines for most practice tasks, such as assessment, deciding on the outcomes to pursue, and selecting and implementing interventions. Guidelines do not preclude creativity, use of theory, or capitalizing on practitioners' wisdom and experience. Rather, guidelines call forth all these qualities and harness them in a more systematic and critical manner for the benefit of the individual client. Proper use of practice guidelines requires and encourages the practitioner to adopt an active, critical, and innovative stance.

As will be discernible from contributions to this volume, guidelines are not cure-alls for the uncertainty that characterizes practice, nor can guideline statements be construed as dictums. Although their primary function is to help select pretested interventions that have been found effective, guidelines also serve as a means for acknowledging and dealing with the uncertainty that is inherent in making practice decisions. Containing statements about what is known, practice guidelines also qualify and point to the gaps in that knowledge, signaling caution to practitioners on the one hand and contributing to the generation of needed research for further reductions in uncertainty on the other (Proctor and Rosen, chapter 6, this volume). Importantly, in addition to aiding in making decisions and taking action, practice guidelines help to demystify the process of practice and thereby encourage further systematic efforts to reduce its uncertainty. But practice guidelines are only as good as the knowledge that undergirds their formulation. If they are not to mislead, they should not be offered prematurely or without a relatively solid evidentiary basis. We hope that this volume will enhance the development of such a basis.

FUNCTION OF GUIDELINES FOR THE SOCIAL WORK PROFESSION

In the preceding section we outlined some of the presumed advantages of practice guidelines for practitioners, while also acknowledging possible reservations for their use. Because of the advantages for both practitioners and clients that we see as inherent in guidelines, we consider their use to be essential from a profession-wide perspective. As a publicly sanctioned profession, social work has the responsibility to develop, organize, and elucidate its practice knowledge. Whenever possible, such knowledge must include empirically tested formulations of substantive standards that can be applied discriminately to guide its members in successfully addressing the varying demands of practice. Without such standards, practice may be viewed by the public as—and might actually be—largely dependent on the individual worker, with clients having no clear protection from incompetence, arbitrariness, and malpractice (Myers and Thyer 1997; Thyer 1995). Knowledge consisting of empirically tested substantive standards for practice must be applied, of course, in a manner that is consistent with a professional code of ethics that is value-derived and universal in application (Rosen 1994). Practice guidelines, or standards of best practice to which the profession is committed, are thus inherent in the very essence of a responsible and accountable profession. How social work has survived—and perhaps thrived—these many years without such a tool is a question to ponder.

The deliberate use of practice guidelines, their ongoing evaluation, and continuous work to improve their effectiveness will materially contribute to the development and refinement of the profession's knowledge base and its stature as a profession based on scientifically derived and tested knowledge. Efficient use of practice guidelines requires that they be coherently organized for ready access and retrieval. The merits of organizing guidelines according to classifications or taxonomies of the targets of intervention—the outcomes to be achieved—are further addressed in following chapters (see Proctor and Rosen; Kirk; and Mattaini—chapters 6, 8, and 9, respectively, this volume). Development of such taxonomies in tandem with guidelines for intervention will have added benefits for social work. They could serve to portray the products that social work intervention can produce, signaling and highlighting its potential contributions as an independent profession among other human helping professions (Rosen, Proctor, and Staudt 2003).

As one of the helping professions in our society, however, social work need not ignore, and in fact should be engaged in, formulating and articulating its points of contact and its role in relation to the other human helping professions (see Aronoff and Bailey, chapter 15, this volume). An obvious and most important concern in that context is whether, and to what extent, social work should utilize, rely upon, and collaborate with other professions in the research and compilation of a scientific knowledge base to guide its practice (see also Thyer, chapter 7, this volume). The commonality of the subject matter of social work—human behavior and transactions in the social environment (Mattaini, chapter 9, this volume)—with other human helping professions, as well as with that of the behavioral and social sciences, is obvious. Hence, much of the knowledge developed within these disciplines is potentially relevant and valuable to social work as well. Nonetheless, social work has an inescapable responsibility to ascertain that its practitioners' knowledge base and repertoire of potent interventions fully address the service needs of its own diverse clienteles.

The development and compilation of social work's knowledge should be as economical and efficient as possible—utilizing, reformulating, testing, and collaborating in all relevant research, irrespective of disciplinary origin. But it is amply clear to us that social work's knowledge needs cannot be fully satisfied by the mere transportation of empirical studies and practice guidelines from other fields. Social work's service-delivery settings, professional functions, clientele and their service goals also require knowledge that is not usually addressed by other professions. Even for social workers in mental health, a field that we share with other professions, extant intervention knowledge and guidelines developed by psychiatry and psychology have limited applicability, since those professions are relatively silent with respect to certain domains, like prevention, family and caregiver, and community-based aspects of care—the domains of most social work mental health treatment, as well as with respect to their applicability to diverse client populations. Social work practice must be guided by knowledge about the differential effectiveness of interventions for clients of various ethnic, minority, and cultural groups, who receive services for a variety of conditions and in a variety of settings.

Accordingly, social work needs its own research agenda for developing practice guidelines, not to preclude utilization of developments and collaboration with initiatives in allied fields. Without an organized and public research agenda, social work's progress toward meeting its needs for practice guidelines will lag behind the needs of practice (see Proctor and Rosen, chapter 6, this volume). A research agenda that is adopted and enunciated by the profession can stimulate, organize, and advance the conduct of intervention studies. Further, it can focus researchers' attention on such issues as how findings can be accumulated, synthesized, disseminated, and utilized in actual practice.

ORGANIZATION OF THE BOOK

Beyond the introductory and concluding chapters, this volume is organized thematically into four sections. Starting from the premise that social work practice should be informed by an empirically supported knowledge base, contributions in part I focus on precursors to and foundations for the development of practice guidelines. Mark Fraser introduces the section in chapter 2 with discussion of intervention research in social work from a methodological perspective. Eileen Gambrill presents in chapter 3 a critical and comprehensive appraisal of evidence-based practice (EBP) and highlights its unique contributions to social work, including serving as a means for acknowledging the uncertainty in practice knowledge and moving away from an authority-based practice model. Chapter 4, by William Reid and Anne Fortune, surveys and organizes a ten-year accumulation of empirical research devoted to testing and evaluation of social work intervention programs that can serve as a foundation for developing practice guidelines.

Part II addresses the need for practice guidelines in social work, as well as their functions, structure, and components. Matthew Howard and Jeffrey Jenson introduce the section in chapter 5 by tracing the development of practice guidelines in medicine and psychology, drawing implications for social work. Enola Proctor and Aaron Rosen (chapter 6) offer a conception of the desirable function and structure of practice guidelines, designed to facilitate the use of empirically tested knowledge in practice and to stimulate the continued development of such knowledge. In chapter 7, Bruce Thyer, who favors the development of practice guidelines yet takes a different course, rejects development of guidelines by or for social work and argues for social work's participation in an interdisciplinary process of guidelines development, as well as for exclusive reliance on interdisciplinary guidelines.

Concluding part II, chapters 8 and 9, by Stuart Kirk and Mark Mattaini, respectively, critically assess the merits of organizing practice guidelines for intervention using outcome-based target taxonomies, as proposed by Proctor and Rosen in chapter 6. In his analysis Kirk highlights the indispensable roles that knowledge of such factors as client problem and diagnosis play in selection of appropriate interventions, and he advocates that they be considered in tandem with the outcomes to be pursued. Mattaini evaluates critically the appropriateness of anchoring practice guidelines in the targets of intervention in relation to social work's mission and values. Adopting a transactional perspective, he advocates formulation of outcome-based targets according to interpersonal transactions rather than individual behavior.

One dilemma that social work and other science-based helping professions face is the "idiographic application of normative generalizations" (Rosen 1994:562). In order to be useful in practice, generalizations need to be applicable to situations that are different from the instances (situations, people, and behaviors) from which they were derived. Also, because empirical generalizations usually are based on study of variability in only a subset of the factors involved in a given phenomenon, their applicability to a particular situation is often questionable (Rosen 1994). This dilemma is especially evident in the use of practice guidelines, which are, in essence, generalizations. All three chapters of part III address aspects of this issue. In chapter 10, Lynn Videka discusses methodological issues that bear on means of accounting for factors that moderate generalized formulations of interventions, addressing thereby efficacy and effectiveness study designs. Then, in chapter 11, Luis Zayas focuses on the treatment process, highlighting the need for practice guidelines to address clients' cultural factors as potent moderator variables that impinge on service accessibility and utilization. And finally (chapter 12), Wilma Peebles-Wilkins and Maryann Amodeo address issues related to guidelines development and adoption, particularly from the perspective of quality control in the managed care environment, viewing practice guidelines as means of differentially and appropriately addressing clients' cultural diversity while still ensuring unbiased quality care through standardization.

Conducting the research and formulating purportedly effective guides for practice are necessary prerequisites, but unfortunately these tasks are not sufficient to ensure the use of intervention guidelines by practitioners. Although this volume's primary focus is on the activities necessary for developing empirically based practice guidelines, issues related to their eventual utilization in practice must also be addressed. The three chapters that constitute part IV deal with different aspects of this complex issue. Edward Mullen and William Bacon (chapter 13) address challenges to the use of guidelines by practitioners at the agency level, basing their discussion also on a recent survey of practitioners' attitudes. Jeanne Marsh applies theories of professions to social work professional organizations as legitimating bodies for utilization of guidelines by practitioners (chapter 14). Marsh's focus is complemented by Nina Aronoff and Darlyne Bailey's discussion in chapter 15 of the role of social work in an interprofessional environment and its relation to the use of systematized knowledge by practitioners.

The volume concludes with a presentation of our conception of the research activities and scholarly work needed for advancing the development of practice guidelines for social work (chapter 16).

REFERENCES

Austin, D. M. (1999). A report on progress in the development of research resources in social work. *Research on Social Work Practice, 9,* 673–707.

Bloom, M., Fischer, J., and Orme, J. G. (1995). *Evaluating Practice: Guidelines for the Accountable Professional.* Englewood Cliffs, N.J.: Prentice Hall.

Campbell Collaboration Steering Committee (2001). *Guidelines for the Preparation of Review Protocols* (version 1.0). Philadelphia: University of Pennsylvania.

Chambless, D. L., and Hollon, S. D. (1998). Defining empirically supported therapies. *Journal of Consulting and Clinical Psychology, 66,* 7–18.

Cheatham, J. M. (1987). The empirical evaluation of clinical practice: A survey of four groups of practitioners. *Journal of Social Service Research, 10,* 163–177.

Fischer, J. (1993). Empirically-based practice: The end of ideology. *Journal of Social Service Research, 18,* 19–64.

Fortune, A. E. (1999). Intervention research (Editorial). *Social Work Research, 23,* 2–3.

Fortune, A. E., and Proctor, E. K. (2001). Research on social work interventions. *Social Work Research, 25,* 67–69.

Gambrill, E. (1999). Evidence-based practice: An alternative to authority-based practice. *Families in Society, 80,* 341–350.

Gigerenzer, G., and Goldstein, D. G. (1996). Reasoning the fast and frugal way: Models of bounded rationality. *Psychological Review, 103,* 650–669.

Howard, M. O., and Jenson, J. M. (1999). Clinical practice guidelines: Should social work develop them? *Research on Social Work Practice, 9,* 283–301.

Janis, I. L., and Mann, L. (1977). *Decision Making: A Psychological Analysis of Conflict, Choice, and Commitment.* New York: Free Press.

Kirk, S. A., and Penka, C. E. (1992). Research Utilization and MSW Education: A Decade of Progress? In A. J. Grasso and I. Epstein (Eds.), *Research Utilization in Social Services* (pp. 407–421). Binghamton, N.Y.: Haworth.

Kondrat, M. E. (1992). Reclaiming the practical: Formal and substantive rationality in social work practice. *Social Service Review, 66,* 237–255.

Myers, L. L., and Thyer, B. A. (1997). Should social work clients have the right to effective treatment? *Social Work, 42,* 288–298.

Nathan, P. E., and Gorman, J. M. (1998). *A Guide to Treatments That Work.* New York: Oxford University Press.

Newman, F. L., and Tejeda, M. J. (1996). The need for research that is designed to support decisions in the delivery of mental health services. *American Psychologist, 51,* 1040–1049.

Reid, W. J., and Hanrahan, P. (1982). Recent evaluations of social work: Grounds for optimism. *Social Work, 27,* 328–340.

Richey, C., Blythe, B., and Berlin, S. B. (1987). Do social workers evaluate their practice? *Social Work Research and Abstracts, 23,* 14–20.

Rosen, A. (1992). Facilitating clinical decision making and evaluation. *Families in Society, 73,* 522–532.

———. (1993). Systematic planned practice. *Social Service Review, 67,* 84–100.

———. (1994). Knowledge use in direct practice. *Social Service Review, 68,* 561–577.

———. (2002). "Evidence-Based Social Work Practice: Challenges and Promise." Invited address at the Society for Social Work and Research, San Diego, California, January.

Rosen, A., Proctor, E. K., and Livne, S. (1985). Planning and direct practice. *Social Service Review, 59,* 161–177.

Rosen, A., Proctor, E. K., Morrow-Howell, N., Auslander, W., and Staudt, M. (1993). *Systematic Planned Practice: A Tool for Planning, Implementation, and Evaluation.* St. Louis, Mo.: George Warren Brown School of Social Work, Washington University.

Rosen, A., Proctor, E. K., Morrow-Howell, N., and Staudt, M. (1995). Rationales for practice decisions: Variations in knowledge use by decision task and social work service. *Research on Social Work Practice, 5,* 501–523.

Rosen, A., Proctor, E. K., and Staudt, M. (1999). Social work research and the quest for effective practice. *Social Work Research, 23,* 4–14.

———. (2003). Targets of change and interventions in social work: An empirically based prototype for developing practice guidelines. *Research on Social Work Practice, 13,* 208–233.

Schilling, R. F. (1997). Developing intervention research programs in social work. *Social Work Research, 21,* 173–180.

Seligman, M. E. P. (1996). Science as an ally of practice. *American Psychologist, 51,* 1072–1079.

Task Force on Social Work Research. (1991). *Building Social Work Knowledge for Effective Services and Policies: A Plan for Research Development.* Washington, D.C.: NASW Press.

Thyer, B. A. (1995). Promoting an empiricist agenda in the human services: An ethical and humanistic imperative. *Journal of Behavior Therapy and Experimental Psychiatry, 26,* 93–98.

Thyer, B. A., and Wodarski, J. S. (Eds.). (1998). *Handbook of Empirical Social Work Practice* (Vols. 1–2). New York: Wiley.

Tversky, A., and Kahneman, D. (1974). Judgment under uncertainty: Heuristics and biases. *Science, 185,* 1124–1131.

Wilson, T. D., and Brekke, N. (1994). Mental contamination and mental correction: Unwanted influences on judgment and evaluation. *Psychological Bulletin, 116,* 117–142.

Witkin, S. L., and Harrison, W. D. (2001). Whose evidence and for what purpose? *Social Work, 46,* 293–296.

Zeira, A., and Rosen, A. (2000). Unraveling "tacit knowledge": What social workers do and why they do it. *Social Service Review, 74,* 103–123.

PART I

PRECURSORS OF GUIDELINES: INTERVENTION
RESEARCH AND EVIDENCE-BASED PRACTICE

INTERVENTION RESEARCH IN SOCIAL WORK: A BASIS FOR EVIDENCE-BASED PRACTICE AND PRACTICE GUIDELINES

MARK W. FRASER

I n 1949 seventy-three clinicians gathered at Regents Hall in Boulder, Colorado, to discuss training for practice in psychology. The concept of the "scientist-practitioner" emerged from this conference. It consisted of the idea that practice should be founded on research and that training for practice should be based on significant exposure to social science methods plus content on human development and social intervention (Raimy 1950). Although the use of research to guide practice was not a new concept in social work (for a review, see Fraser, Jenson, and Lewis 1993), the ideas from the Boulder Conference influenced a generation of postwar social workers who sought concomitantly to reform training and practice in the profession (Boehm 1959; Briar and Miller 1971).

While the scientist-practitioner model is a keystone of training for practice in psychology (Benjamin and Baker 2000), it and its corollary—the empirically based practitioner model—never gained a significant toehold in social work. To be sure, the emergence of social work doctoral programs has enlarged the research capabilities of the profession, and recent support from federal agencies—most noticeably the National Institute of Mental Health (NIMH) and the National Institute on Drug Abuse (NIDA)—holds promise for strengthening the profession's knowledge base. But the National Association of Social Workers (NASW) and the Council on Social Work Education (CSWE) have not embraced research, and few M.S.W. programs appear to provide adequate training in social science methods (Fraser 1994; Fraser, Jenson, and Lewis 1993). On balance, practitioners make little use of research (Rosen et al. 1995). The migration of research knowledge to practice is

Thanks to Maeda J. Galinsky, Kenan Professor, School of Social Work, University of North Carolina at Chapel Hill, for helpful comments on drafts of this chapter. James K. Nash, Assistant Professor, School of Social Work, Portland State University, developed figure 2.1. Special thanks also to Carlton Craig and Patricia Cook, who developed findings for table 2.1

attenuated, more anecdotal than systematic. At best, practice in social work is distally related to research. It is rooted instead in weakly substantiated claims, well-intended beliefs, policy-related programmatic criteria, and reference to authority (Gambrill 1999). In medicine, where a somewhat similar state of affairs regarding the utilization of research exists, a new concept has arisen—evidence-based practice (Sackett et al. 1996).

A concept with European roots, evidence-based practice (EBP) is characterized by a process of systematically identifying and employing the strongest evidence in making practice decisions (Jaeschke, Guyatt, and Meade 1998). It is "the conscientious, explicit and judicious use of current best evidence in making decisions about the care" of individuals, families, or other clients (Sackett et al. 1996:71). This perspective acknowledges and incorporates the wide range of information that practitioners use routinely in developing understandings of problems and devising intervention plans. Accumulated expertise—practice wisdom—and consumer preferences are integrated with current research findings.

EBP requires a knowledge base on the effectiveness of interventions, mechanisms for the translation of research knowledge into practice resources, and organizational contingencies for promoting the use of the "best evidence" in programs. The movement to establish practice guidelines—systematically organized sets of "knowledge statements that . . . enable practitioners to find, select, and use the interventions that are most effective and appropriate"—is a linchpin of EBP (Proctor and Rosen, chapter 6, this volume). This chapter explores the intersection of practice guidelines, EBP, and intervention research. First, I review basic tenets of EBP. Then, because practice guidelines depend on research, I consider the status of intervention research in the profession. Building on the work of Gambrill (chapter 3, this volume), Reid and Fortune (chapter 4, this volume), and others, I describe briefly the findings from a study of research papers nominated for Outstanding Research Awards by members of the Society for Social Work and Research (SSWR). The characteristics of these papers provide clues to both the status of intervention research in the profession and the kinds of knowledge-building enterprise valued by social work researchers. Finally, I discuss criteria for declaring interventions to be effective or empirically supported—a prerequisite for developing practice guidelines—and methodological challenges, which must be confronted if intervention research is to become more informative.

EVIDENCE-BASED PRACTICE

The EBP perspective differs from the empirically based practitioner model in the sense that a social worker is not expected to conjoin day-to-day practice with research methods involving data collection and analysis. Rather, the practitioner is expected to understand and use research knowledge in defining practice problems and selecting interventions that optimize outcomes. Using the "best available" information suggests that selected interventions will represent the best current thinking and will be rooted in research. By extension, it implies that in the absence of research related to a specific problem or issue, the worker is expected to use theory with a research basis, knowledge of the etiology of social and health problems, knowledge derived from clinical supervision, and knowledge from practice experience.

EBP is collaborative in the sense that the client or consumer is involved in defining the problem, selecting and tailoring practice strategies, and assessing outcomes. The process may be summarized in steps that include:

1. defining the problem collaboratively with the client
2. identifying with the client a set of practice questions ("What outcomes do we want to observe?")
3. selecting and searching appropriate resources to answer the questions ("What interventions are associated with the desired outcomes?")
4. integrating and applying the evidence to the design of an initial practice strategy ("Which interventions seem most appropriate for the current situation?")
5. modifying the initial practice strategy on the basis of client preference and practice expertise ("What does the client want? How can the best available interventions be tailored on the basis of consumer preference and practice experience?")
6. applying a tailored practice strategy ("Is there a practice guideline that clearly specifies the central elements of the best available strategy?")
7. evaluating outcomes with the client ("What measures can be used to assess desired outcomes—both proximal and distal?")

EBP places control in the hands of the practitioner; it is not a top-down or paint-by-the-numbers perspective (Sackett et al. 1997). Practitioners involve consumers in defining the problem and determining the relevance of evidence. They integrate consumer preferences with practice experience and evidence to form a strategy. They manage how and when a strategy is implemented. The assessment of the validity of knowledge lies with the practitioner, who must have skills in searching, critically appraising, and giving meaning to the literature. Because practitioners rarely have access to the range of information in the literature, practice guidelines and other practice resources must be developed to bring EBP to fruition.

The publication of practice resources—from literature syntheses to practice guidelines and, more programmatically specific, to treatment manuals—is an arena in which the NASW, the CSWE, and the Society for Social Work and Research (SSWR) could exert leadership. Assessments and integrative studies of available evidence that are compiled routinely across fields of practice are the building blocks of practice guidelines. They, in turn, can be compiled only if a profession has a fertile research culture. Thus, developing practice guidelines places a premium on both the conduct of research and the generation of research syntheses, meta-analyses, practice protocols, treatment manuals, and other scholarly products that integrate, summarize, and distill research. The challenge of consolidating findings from discrete studies into a rich array of practice resources looms large for social work.

KNOWLEDGE BASES FOR PRACTICE: EXPLANATORY, INTERVENTIVE, AND LOCAL KNOWLEDGE

To create these resources, at least two types of knowledge are needed. The first, explanatory knowledge, describes factors associated with social problems. The second, interventive knowledge, describes change strategies—services or programs designed to alter risk factors, i.e., the conditions giving rise to a problem or set of problems. Explanatory research seeks to discover patterns where none seem to exist (Fraser 1997). It builds explanatory models or theory by identifying causes and describing causal mechanisms. As a result of increased federal and foundation funding for longitudinal research, significant advances have been made in explaining problems. For example, we have increasingly clear understandings of developmental sequences that produce youth violence (Loeber et al. 1998; Patterson 1995). Moreover, we have increasingly useful understandings of the ways in which contextual factors—for example, school and neighborhood conditions—contribute to social problems (Coulton, Korbin, and Su 1999). In the past fifteen years, more than 29,000 children have participated in more than one hundred longitudinal studies from which more than sixty risk factors have been identified (Burns, Hoagwood, and Mrazek 1999). The incorporation of these risk factors in studies designed to build interventive knowledge should be a high priority in social work research.

INTERVENTION RESEARCH AND CHANGE STRATEGIES

For professions such as social work, the needs of practitioners are only partially met by explanatory research. As many argue (Rubin 2000; Thyer 2000), intervention research—studies of the efficacy and effectiveness of systematic change strategies—should be the basis of social work practice. Intervention research is rooted in the integration of epidemiological (incidence and prevalence), etiological (explanatory), and "control" knowledge. Knowledge fills a control function "when it is capable of guiding practitioners in the selection and implementation of interventions that successfully attain the desired outcomes" (Rosen, Proctor, and Staudt 1999:5). From a direct practice perspective, this means—arguably—that a sufficient number of the risk and protective factors affecting desirable outcomes are subject to manipulation *and* that practitioners can successfully implement change strategies (Fraser and Galinsky 1997).

Intervention research is requisite for a profession because professions are committed to change. Even at the theory level, explanatory research is insufficient because it provides little knowledge regarding the means to change social problems and conditions. Although it identifies risk factors, explanatory research provides no information about which factors may be subject to change or the nature of the effort needed to create change. Moreover, it sometimes identifies risk factors that are not subject to control. Gender, for example, is correlated with aggressive behavior, but gender is not subject to change in a social intervention. It has interventive value only when research begins to articulate the developmental sequences that produce differential outcomes for boys and girls (Crick 1996) and when change strategies related to these sequences are shown to produce desirable outcomes. In this sense, explanatory research is helpful because it maps risk mechanisms that may be subject to intervention and provides a range of possible points of intervention. Yet it is when researchers and practitioners attempt to alter risk mechanisms that research rises to its full potential, when it focuses on change.

The relationships among epidemiological, etiological, and interventive knowledge can be portrayed. As shown in figure 2.1, epidemiological knowledge (e.g., incidence and prevalence data) and explanatory research (e.g., structural equation models based on longitudinal cohort studies) contribute to the conceptualization of social problems. They can even specify the means by which one risk factor may interact with another to elevate a problem condition. Both, however, must be combined with interventive knowledge to produce an experimental program. Once designed, new interventions are pilot-tested in controlled settings—efficacy testing—where researchers and practitioners may refine change strategies sequentially over the course of many small studies. Ideally, it is only after a schedule of rigorous development and refinement that programs are exposed to effectiveness testing, where they are brought to scale as community services and then evaluated. After several effectiveness trials, a program or elements related to it may be published in the form of practice guidelines and treatment manuals. Dissemination begins.

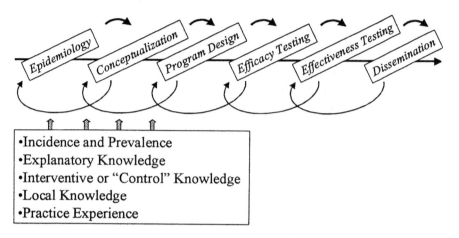

FIGURE 2.1. Intervention Research: Building Knowledge for Practice.

CONDITIONING ROLE OF LOCAL KNOWLEDGE

As suggested in figure 2.1, effective practice relies on both systematic and idiographic information. It is based on accumulative, recursive, and iterative processes of integrating a broad range of sources of knowledge, including what might be called "local" knowledge (Fraser and Galinsky 1997). Local knowledge describes restricted individual, family, and community influences that affect problem levels. It is case- and community-specific knowledge accessed through careful assessment and refined by a keen understanding of culture and context. To be sure, local knowledge is subject to systematic study; however, extreme distributions and temporal instability militate against its discovery. For example, the untimely illness of a local medicine man in a tribal community may increase the risk of depression for a woman whose husband was recently killed in a traffic accident. A savvy tribal social worker might readily understand this, but time-varying measures of access to traditional faith healers are rarely included in explanatory models. Research—especially quantitative research—is unlikely to be an information source for this type of knowledge. In EBP, case-specific strategies are devised by drawing on the best available current information—some of which is derived from research and developed into practice guidelines and some of which may be derived from understanding local conditions and engaging in careful assessment. *Comprehensive assessment and understanding the local cultural and contextual bases of problems are integral to EBP, and they condition the use of practice guidelines.*

INTERVENTIVE KNOWLEDGE IN SOCIAL WORK

In the context of local knowledge, the development of practice guidelines requires a base of research that can be readily accessed by practitioners. Recognizing that the research bases of social work are interdisciplinary, one might ask, Does the profession have a body of knowledge that can contribute to practice guidelines? In spite of advances in doctoral training, the growth of federal research development programs, and greater numbers of social workers with federal research awards, it is not clear whether social work researchers are producing more research knowledge. Rosen, Proctor, and Staudt (1999) recently found that about 47 percent of articles in social work journals reported research findings. This percentage is comparable to that of studies of social work research in the late 1980s (Fraser et al. 1991; Glisson 1995).

The characteristics of articles nominated for research awards for the 1997–2000 meetings of the SSWR provide another clue as to the state of research knowledge in the profession. The intent of the SSWR Outstanding Research Awards program is to honor outstanding scholarly contributions to the peer-reviewed research literature. Articles that are nominated for an award must report the design and results of a qualitative or quantitative study related to social work practice, policy, or a social problem. In addition, at least one of an article's authors must possess a graduate social work degree, *or* be a faculty member, staff member, or student in a social work education program, *or* be a member of the SSWR. An awards committee is charged with the task of nominating articles from approximately ninety journals in which social workers are thought to publish. Each nominated article is matched to reviewers on the basis of subject matter and methodology. And each is then independently reviewed on the basis of (a) social significance of the problem; (b) suitability of research design; (c) appropriateness of data or text analysis and interpretation; (d) potential for replicability; (e) clarity of applications to social work; and (f) attention to gender, race, socioeconomic status, and other issues of difference.

Though nominated articles do not represent all research articles published by social workers (for some articles and research reports are published in unreviewed journals and in books), these nominating and rating processes should produce a pool of articles that represents much of the profession's finest research scholarship. Between 1997 and 2000, 264 articles were nominated. Using a scoring protocol similar to that of Reid and Fortune (chapter 4, this volume), the core characteristics of these articles are shown in table 2.1 (for a more extensive description, see Craig, Cook, and Fraser 2001). Most (194, 73.5%) of the studies reported in these articles were quantitative. Less than 30 percent of the articles with quantitative designs used experimental (33, 14.5%) or quasi-experimental (32, 14.1%) methods, with either control or comparison groups respectively. Ten (4.4%) additional articles used pre-experimental designs, including single-group and single-subject designs. Across the 264 nominations, 73 (27.7%) of the studies focused on intervention in which a systematic change strategy was tested (Craig, Cook, and Fraser 2001). Coupled with earlier work (Fraser et al. 1991; Glisson 1995), these data—and findings from Reid and Fortune (chapter 4, this volume)—suggest that social work has a base of research knowledge that could contribute to the development of practice guidelines. But the findings suggest also that social work research is disproportionately focused on explanation. Control knowledge, which focuses on the effectiveness and efficacy of interventions, is developed in slightly more than one in four studies. It is no wonder that fewer than one percent of the practice decisions made by social workers are influenced by research findings (Rosen et al. 1995). If practice guidelines are to be developed from social work scholarship, the profession must rise to the challenge of conducting more intervention research.

DEVELOPING PRACTICE GUIDELINES: WHAT CONSTITUTES "STRONG" EVIDENCE?

Practice guidelines and other resources such as treatment manuals are an important aspect of making the best current information available to practitioners (Howard and Jenson 1999). Guidelines can be thought of as "systematically developed statements to assist practitioner and patient decisions about appropriate care for specific clinical circumstances" (Institute of Medicine 1990:27). They are rooted in intervention studies and are usually devised by panels of experts who interpret research and determine acceptable treatment alternatives within fields of practice (see, e.g., American Psychiatric Association 1996, 1997; Division 12 Task Force of the American Psychological Association 1998).

TABLE 2.1 Characteristics of Articles Nominated for Outstanding Research Awards by the Society for Social Work and Research, 1997–2000

VARIABLE	PERCENTAGE	NUMBER
Type of research method ($N = 264$)		
Quantitative	73.5	194
Qualitative	12.1	32
Mixed	11.4	30
Literature review	1.9	5
Meta-analysis	1.1	3
Designs of quantitative, mixed, and meta-analysis articles only ($N = 225$)		
Experimental	14.5	33
Quasi-experimental	14.1	32
Pre-experimental	4.4	10
Survey—cross-sectional or longitudinal	65.6	149
Meta-analysis	1.3	3

Commonplace in intervention research, treatment manuals are more specific than guidelines. Manuals usually describe a single program and often include brief literature reviews, general guidelines for establishing therapeutic relationships (e.g., tips for working with groups), descriptions of specific techniques and content (sometimes in the form of a curriculum), suggestions for sequencing activities, examples of successful, difficult, and failure cases, and strategies for dealing with special problems, implementation issues, and termination (Fraser et al. 2000; Henggeler et al. 1998). Although treatment manuals can be unwieldy in practice, they contribute to replication of programs. A challenge in using a manual is finding a balance between the prescribed structure in a manualized program and the flexibility needed in meeting the unique needs of clients. While good manuals do not replace supervision and training, they do provide substantial content and encourage practitioners to tailor services on the basis of local knowledge. Not subjected to peer or panel review in the same way as guidelines are, some treatment manuals are available only from authors, while others are published by such presses as NASW Press, Guilford, Plenum, Pergamon, and Castalia.

WHEN IS THE EVIDENCE SUFFICIENTLY STRONG?

Both guidelines and treatment manuals require a substantial body of intervention research in which programs have been pilot-tested, revised, tested again, and—ideally—evaluated in a large-scale effectiveness trial. If a program has been shown to be effective, it is often appropriate to estimate the impact of various components of the program by using a components-analysis or dismantling design in which elements of the intervention are contrasted with one another (Hunsley and Rumstein-McKean 1999). Promising programs can also be tested on different populations or in different contexts. Finally, cost-benefit analyses can be used to assess the short- and long-term costs of service relative to routine services or no services. Because such a research agenda is time-consuming, one might wonder how to determine the point at which evidence becomes so compellingly strong that it warrants drafting practice guidelines and publishing treatment manuals.

The decision that a program is sufficiently empirically supported to warrant publishing a treatment manual or when a set of programs is sufficiently tested to warrant developing practice guidelines (which focus on the intervention-outcome linkage across numerous interventions) is a value judgment. The criteria used to declare an intervention to be "empirically tested" are far from clear. In a world replete with research, interventions should be rooted in explanatory and intervention research. That is, they should focus on key risk mechanisms, promote protection, and employ change strategies that work. Moreover, studies of interventions that have been deemed validated should consistently demonstrate clinically significant findings, findings of practical import over and above those observed in routine services. In social work, we should expect research in which African American, Latino, and other racial and ethnic groups are recruited and randomly assigned to treatment and control or routine services groups, in which language- and culture-sensitive instruments are used to assess outcomes, and in which findings are replicated. But in fact few, if any, studies meet such criteria. What criteria should be used?

As a starting point, it will not be possible, nor is it advisable, to rely solely on randomized, blind studies in the social work or other literatures. At least initially, it may be necessary to broaden criteria to reflect the nascent character of intervention research in the profession. Reid and Fortune (chapter 4, this volume) required an intervention "to be tested through an experimental or quasi-experimental design," including single-system designs with controls and at least six subjects. Similarly, the American Psychological Association (Chambless et al., n.d.) recently set the criteria for empirically validated treatments as at least two between-group design experiments conducted by different investigators who use treatment manuals, with findings demonstrating efficacy in one or more of the following ways:

- superior to pill or placebo or another treatment; or
- equivalent to an already established treatment (with adequate power of about thirty participants per group); or
- single case studies with multiple participants (n > 8) and controls

SAMPLING ADEQUACY AND CULTURALLY SENSITIVE MEASUREMENT: RACE, ETHNICITY, GENDER, AND OTHER ISSUES OF DIFFERENCE

While randomized trials are important, sampling adequacy and culturally sensitive measurement must be taken into account in developing practice resources for the profession. A single experiment might be valued highly if it were based, say, on explanatory research that involved adequate sampling of African American, Latino, and other children at risk. It might sustain even higher value if the researchers used culturally sensitive procedures—e.g., translating and back-translating instruments—and addressed contextual factors. Social information processing theory, for example, was developed in part by studying minority children (Crick and Dodge 1994; Graham and Hudley 1994; Graham, Hudley, and Williams 1992). A successful quasi-experimental study of an intervention that employed social information processing theory might enjoy greater salience because its research base included careful measurement of children who are often at greater risk of poor developmental outcomes. In addition to design criteria such as those used by the American Psychological Association, the inclusion of sampling and measurement criteria is central to establishing credible social work practice guidelines.

STRENGTHENING INTERVENTION RESEARCH IN SOCIAL WORK

To provide a base of interventive research from which to develop practice guidelines, a more extensive research enterprise is needed in the profession. Developing and testing practice-relevant programs is a major undertaking that—from a purely pragmatic perspective—requires exceptional resources. As Reid and Fortune imply, the conduct of intervention research is often associated with a program of study requiring years of development. Similar to figure 2.1, Rothman and Thomas (1994) describe intervention research as consisting of six phases:

1. information gathering, where the conditions generating a problem are enumerated
2. the distillation of information into causal processes that are subject to intervention
3. the design of a prototype program to address the causal processes
4. pilot testing and a preliminary assessment of effects under controlled conditions
5. testing a revised program under real-world conditions
6. taking a program to scale through dissemination

Intervention research requires skill, patience, support, collaboration, and perseverance. It is often undertaken in the context of a team of affiliated researchers who may have different kinds of expertise—knowledge of the etiology of problems (i.e., explanatory knowledge), knowledge of clinical or community change strategies, knowledge of special populations, skill in research design (including culturally sensitive measurement), skill in building community partnerships, skill in training and supervising practitioners, and skill in data collection and analysis. The creation of teams requires a collegial organizational climate and unusual fiscal support. Funding is often needed both to support research staff and to support the delivery of experimental services, services that usually cannot be provided through existing funding at agencies. The lack of funding for intervention studies probably contributes to the low level of intervention research in the profession. Suggesting that the funding problem is being recognized, recent program announcements at NIMH and NIDA provide many new mechanisms for intervention research (see, e.g., PAR-01-090, Developing Centers for Interventions and Services Research at http://www.nimh.nih.gov).

In light of such renewed interest in intervention research at the federal level and to strengthen the base of practice-central research that will be critical in developing practice guidelines, researchers will have to confront significant methodological challenges. These challenges are, perhaps, more pesky in intervention research than in explanatory research. They include developing and measuring clinical change models, selecting measures that are sensitive to change sequences, assessing change continuously, controlling reactivity in raters, and dealing with method variance (for a more extensive discussion of these ideas, see Eddy, Dishion, and Stoolmiller 1998).

DEVELOPING AND MEASURING TECHNIQUES THAT ENHANCE CLINICAL CHANGE MODELS

Intervention is based on two kinds of theoretical modes: explanatory models and clinical change models. Explanatory models, described above, focus on developmental sequences of risk factors—risk chains—that produce social or health problems. On balance, intervention attempts to identify and target principal risk factors and, to the extent that they are known, identify and strengthen protective factors (Fraser 1997). Explicitly or implicitly, most intervention research is based on a clinical change model, a model that specifies the precise means used to alter risk or protective factors. A common clinical change model, the psychoeducational change model, usually involves the idea that changes in knowledge and skills will produce changes in behavior or beliefs. Often interventions based on this model are time limited and involve mixing didactic content with modeling, role play, and practice. Knowledge, skills, behavior, and beliefs are constructs within the psychoeducational clinical change model. While these constructs are often measured in intervention research, factors that engage, enhance, and empower the change model are largely ignored.

Change is almost always interactive. The environment, what the worker says (or does—or more distally, her mannerisms), and what the client says (or does—or more distally, her mannerisms) engage emotions and shape perceptions (risk and benefit appraisal) that, in turn, relate to positive expectations for change (including hope), willingness to collaborate, motivation to change, and engagement in change-related activities. At the simplest level, we acknowledge this when we discuss the matching of client and worker on the basis of gender, race, ethnicity, language, age, and other sociodemographic characteristics (Orrell-Valente et al. 1999). Clinical change models are dependent on interpersonal interactions. To be more central to practice, intervention research must begin to articulate the latent strategies that energize the psychoeducational and other models (Eddy, Dishion, and Stoolmiller 1998). This might involve, for example, monitoring the behaviors of practitioners who are successful in engaging clients and in producing socially desirable outcomes. As practitioners and practice researchers, we need to understand the techniques—providing concrete assistance (food or housing assistance), tracking (using lexicals and local knowledge), and mimesis (matching pace, body language, and mannerisms)—that produce positive interactions and that create environments supportive of change (Robbins and Szapocznik 2000). To heighten the utility of common clinical change models for practice guidelines, measurement models must begin to include factors related to engagement and retention.

SELECTING MEASURES THAT ARE SENSITIVE TO CHANGE SEQUENCES DERIVED FROM EXPLANATORY KNOWLEDGE

Effective treatments usually are based on sequencing content and activities. Activities and events are timed so that change accrues in steps, sometimes little steps. Consequently, measures should be sensitive to changes planned during the provision of a service. As opposed to global measures of change ("How often does your child argue with you?"), specific measures that are sensitive to small changes in treatment-sequenced outcomes are more likely to show change ("In the past 24 hours, did your child _____? In the past 24 hours, did you _____?").

The case for clinical significance is made on the basis of matching specific outcomes to patterns of change that are relevant to explanatory knowledge. Proximal outcomes then are linked to explanatory knowledge, and explanatory knowledge is used to show the relative impact of an intervention. For example, in showing that by participating in a family-centered intervention parents reduced their nagging and nattering, one might begin to demonstrate that coercive parenting is decreased. Because coercion theory involves nagging and nattering as features of parenting that increase delinquency, an argument for delinquency prevention begins to accrue (Patterson 1995; Patterson et al. 1998).

ASSESSING CHANGE CONTINUOUSLY

Change occurs incrementally and sometimes nonlinearly during and after treatment, thus traditional pretest and posttest group designs may miss theoretically important patterns of change. In a study of thirty-nine physically abused children and their parents who were randomly assigned to cognitive-behavioral or family therapy conditions, Kolko (1996) measured weekly changes in parental anger, physical discipline, and family problems. He found that between-group differences emerging early in treatment predicted final differences between groups—levels of parental anger and use of physical discipline/force were lower in the cognitive-behavioral treatment condition. That is, a significant percentage of the treatment effect emerged in the first several weeks of intervention. With the advent of event history analysis and growth curve modeling, it is possible to measure weekly changes in knowledge and skill (assuming, for example, a psychoeducational clinical change model in which knowledge and skill are proximal outcomes) and, further, to relate such changes to more distal, socially relevant outcomes, e.g., substance abuse. Though costly, continuous measurement of this nature has the added advantage of permitting examination of changes that are lagged—so-called "sleeper effects" where changes emerge at unexpected points in time.

CONTROLLING REACTIVITY: SENSITIVITY TO CHANGE VERSUS REACTIVITY IN "NATURAL" RATERS

Parent and teacher ratings, like the ratings from neighbors, relatives, friends, and others who are informed about the behaviors of clients, are used often by intervention researchers to increase the sensitivity of measurement to change. But the very familiarity that makes such ratings attractive also makes them problematic. Scores from "natural raters" are at once slow to react to recent changes in behavior and quite subject to suggestion that occurs through repeated measurement or knowledge that a client is involved in an innovative service (Stoolmiller, Eddy, and Reid 2000). The first can produce low sensitivity to change on scales—such as scales that invite raters to score child attributes (e.g., "never true of child," "sometimes true of child," "almost always true of child"). This tends to underestimate a true treatment effect. The second creates the expectation of change and tends to inflate treatment effects. This can be controlled by using a Solomon four-group design or reduced by using measures that are not sensitive to expectancy effects. These include physiological measures (e.g., saliva tests), measures by raters who are blind to treatment condition, moment-by-moment behavioral observation, and official reports such as arrests, births, and hospitalizations. But each of these poses complications that elevate the difficulty and cost of intervention research.

DEALING WITH METHOD VARIANCE

As suggested above, the combined problems of sensitivity to change and expectancy of change usually compel intervention researchers to adopt multi-method, multi-source measurement models. That is, one hopes the truth lies somewhere in the approximation of treatment effects based on different sources and methods of estimation. This approach often leads to a situation where some measures produce significant findings and other measures do not (Fraser, Pecora, and Haapala 1991; Grossman et al. 1997). *Method variance* refers to variation in scores because of the reporting source (e.g., parent versus teacher), setting (e.g., home versus school), measurement procedure (e.g., observation versus self-report), scoring and scaling protocols, and length of recall required of raters. Eddy, Dishion, and Stoolmiller (1998:61) found that "a full 30% of the variance . . . (across parent, child, and worker ratings of parental monitoring, problem-solving, reinforcement, and child attachment) . . . was due to method." If they are stable over time, method variances will not bias estimates within methods. But they may be responsible for different findings across methods. If they are unstable (influenced, say, by changing neighborhood conditions or the cycle of a disease or disorder), they may produce quite different findings within and across methods. Method variance often produces findings that are equivocal and not given to the authority orientations of many practitioners. In short, the exigencies of research lead to findings that practitioners are unlikely to use.

PRACTICE GUIDELINES AND CROSS-CULTURAL INTERVENTION RESEARCH: WHITHER CONSTRUCT VALIDITY?

The capacity of social work research to inform the development of practice guidelines rests not just with increasing the number of studies that test interventions but also with increasing the sensitivity of research to the day-to-day exigencies of practice. This will involve measuring techniques that enhance change, matching change strategies and measures to risk mechanisms, assessing change continuously, controlling reactivity, and interpreting findings in the context of method variance. Because risk varies from population to population, sampling adequacy and construct validity will continue to complicate the design of intervention studies and the distillation of findings into practice guidelines.

Although explanatory research is increasingly informative, the degree to which constructs and relationships between constructs are valid across race/ethnicity, gender, language, religion, and other factors is unclear. For example, the construct of *familism* (*familismo*) is widely thought to affect the beliefs and behaviors of Latino children (Vega 1990; Vega and Gil 1999; Zayas 1992). Familism represents the support, pride, cohesion, respect, guidance, and nurturance that characterize the strong kinship networks of many Latino families, especially immigrant families. In a recent study of approximately two thousand U.S.-born and immigrant Latino males attending middle schools in South Florida, Gil, Wagner, and Vega (2000) found that the influence of acculturation and acculturation stress on alcohol use was mediated by familism. The findings clearly indicate that familism should be considered in studies focusing on Latino children and families.

Such findings lead inevitably to a knotty question: To what degree does a culturally specific construct like familism have cross-cultural construct validity? To answer this question, studies of the influence of familism on adolescent alcohol use in other populations are needed. Lacking direct evidence of cross-cultural applicability in the field of alcohol studies, one might turn to studies using familism as an explanatory variable for other child and family problems. For example, in a case-control study of 35 abusive Latino, 35 nonabusive Latino, 51 abusive European American non-Latino, and 51 nonabusive European American non-Latino families in Chicago, Coohey (2001) found that nonabusive Latino families had the highest levels of familism. However, high levels of familism distinguished nonabusive from abusive families within ethnic groups, i.e., familism appears to have both culturally specific and cross-cultural relevance. It distinguishes Latino families from other families, and it distinguishes abusive from nonabusive families within ethnic groups.

Findings from studies such as these advance explanatory knowledge and call attention to the importance of sampling and measurement. Practice guidelines must be developed in the context of an array of studies representing the diversity of the populations with whom social workers work. The issue of sampling adequacy is related to construct validity in the sense that some constructs may be culturally specific and some may be more generalized. The degree to which constructs such as familism operate differently across cultures is still being explored and poses continuing challenges in research design. But findings already suggest that practice guidelines may need to address both culturally specific and cross-cultural constructs and risk processes.

In summary, a base of intervention research in social work holds the potential to contribute to the development of practice guidelines, but this base is clearly inadequate. The cultivation of both a greater number of intervention studies and an interpretive body of integrative scholarship that translates research into literature syntheses, practice guidelines, and treatment manuals must be assigned a high priority (Boyer 1990). This will require locating the responsibility for developing practice resources with professional and other organizations, and it will involve establishing design, sampling, and measurement criteria for assessing research. It will involve also specifying universally applicable key constructs and risk mechanisms, which are targeted in all interventions related to particular problems, and culturally specific key constructs and risk mechanisms, which are targeted in interventions focused on problems within special populations. In psychology, medicine, and nursing, practice guidelines and other types of practice resources are beginning to emerge (Bollini et al. 1999; Burns, Hoagwood, and Mrazek 1999), and NASW Press, suggesting that professional organizations in social work are rising to the challenges presented by evidence-based practice, has recently undertaken a Practice Resources Book Series. But foundational in the task of developing practice guidelines in social work is the challenge of developing new infrastructures to strengthen the profession's intervention research.

REFERENCES

American Psychiatric Association. (1996). Practice guideline for the treatment of patients with nicotine dependence. *American Journal of Psychiatry, 153* (10, supplement), 1–31.
———. (1997). Practice guideline for the treatment of patients with schizophrenia. *American Journal of Psychiatry, 154* (4, supplement), 1–63.

Benjamin, L. T., and Baker, D. B. (2000). Boulder at 50. *American Psychologist, 55* (2), 233–236.

Boehm, W. W. (1959). *Objectives of the Social Work Curriculum of the Future* (Vol. 1). New York: Council on Social Work Education.

Bollini, P., Pampallona, S., Tibaldi, G., Kupelnick, B., and Munizza, C. (1999). Effectiveness of antidepressants: Meta-analysis of dose-effect relationships in randomised clinical trials. *British Journal of Psychiatry, 174,* 297–303.

Boyer, E. L. (1990). *Scholarship Revisited: Priorities of the Professoriate.* Princeton, N.J.: Carnegie Foundation for the Advancement of Teaching.

Briar, S., and Miller, H. (1971). *Problems and Issues in Social Casework.* New York: Columbia University Press.

Burns, B. J., Hoagwood, K., and Mrazek, P. J. (1999). Effective treatment for mental disorders in children and adolescents. *Clinical Child and Family Psychology Review, 2* (4), 199–254.

Chambless, D. L., Sanderson, W. C., Shoham, V., Johnson, S. B., Pope, K. S., Crits-Christoph, P., Baker, M., Johnson, B., Woody, S. R., Sue, S., Beutler, L., Willams, D. A., and McCurry, S. (n.d.). Update on empirically validated therapies. Division 12 of the American Psychological Association. http://www.apa.org/divsions/div12/est/newrept.html

Coohey, C. (2001). The relationship between familism and child maltreatment in Latino and Anglo families. *Child Maltreatment, 6* (2), 130–142.

Coulton, C. J., Korbin, J. E., and Su, M. (1999). *Child Abuse and Neglect, 23* (11), 1019–1040.

Craig, C. D., Cook, P. G., and Fraser, M. W. (2001). The best of the best: An analysis of articles nominated for research awards by the Society for Social Work and Research. Manuscript in preparation.

Crick, N. R. (1996). The role of overt aggression, relational aggression, and prosocial behavior in the prediction of children's future social adjustment. *Child Development, 67,* 2317–2327.

Crick, N. R., and Dodge, K. A. (1994). A review and reformulation of social information-processing mechanism in children's social adjustment. *Psychological Bulletin, 115,* 74–101.

Division 12 Task Force of the American Psychological Association. (1998). Update on empirically validated therapies: II. *Clinical Psychologist, 51,* 3–16.

Eddy, J. M., Dishion, T. J., and Stoolmiller, M. (1998). The analysis of intervention change in children and families: Methodological and conceptual issues embedded in intervention studies. *Journal of Abnormal Child Psychology, 26* (1), 53–69.

Fraser, M. W. (1994). Scholarship and research in social Work: Emerging challenges. *Journal of Education in Social Work, 30,* 252–266.

Fraser, M. W. (Ed.) (1997). *Risk and Resilience in Childhood: An Ecological Perspective.* Washington, D.C.: NASW Press.

Fraser, M. W., and Galinsky, M. J. (1997). Toward a resilience-based model of practice. In M. W. Fraser (Ed.), *Risk and Resilience in Childhood: An Ecological Perspective* (pp. 265–275). Washington, D.C.: NASW Press.

Fraser, M. W., Jenson, J. M., and Lewis, R. E. (1993). Research training in social work: The continuum is not a continuum. *Journal of Social Work Education, 29* (1), 46–62.

Fraser, M. W., Nash, J. K., Galinsky, M. J., and Darwin, K. E. (2000). *Making Choices: Social Problem-Solving for Children.* Washington, D.C.: NASW Press.

Fraser, M. W., Pecora, P. J., and Haapala, D. A. (1991). *Families in Crisis.* New York: Aldine.

Fraser, M., Taylor, M. J., Jackson, R., and O'Jack, J. (1991). Social work and science: Many ways of knowing? *Social Work Research and Abstracts, 27* (4), 5–15.

Gambrill, E. (1999). Evidence-based practice: An alternative to authority-based practice. *Families in Society: The Journal of Contemporary Human Services, 80* (4), 341–350.

Gil, A. G., Wagner, E. F., and Vega, W. A. (2000). Acculturation, familism, and alcohol use among Latino adolescent males: Longitudinal relations. *Journal of Community Psychology, 28* (4), 443–458.

Glisson, C. (1995). The state of art of social work research: Implications for mental health. *Research on Social Work Practice, 5,* 205–222.

Graham, S., and Hudley, C. (1994). Attributions of aggressive and nonaggressive African-American male early adolescents: A study of construct accessibility. *Developmental Psychology, 30,* 365–373.

Graham, S., Hudley, C., and Williams, E. (1992). Attributional and emotional determinants of aggression among African American and Latino young adolescents. *Developmental Psychology, 28* (4), 731–740.

Grossman, D., Neckerman, H., Koepsell, T., Liu, P., Asher, K., Beland, K., Frey, K., and Rivara, F. (1997). Effectiveness of a violence prevention curriculum among children in elementary school. *JAMA, 277,* 1605–1611.

Henggeler, S. W., Schoenwald, S. K., Borduin, C. M., Rowland, M. D., and Cunningham, P. B. (1998). *Multisystemic Treatment of Antisocial Behavior in Children and Adolescents.* New York: Guilford.

Howard, M. O., and Jenson, J. M. (1999). Clinical practice guidelines: Should social work develop them? *Research on Social Work Practice, 9* (3), 283–301.

Hunsley, J., and Rumstein-McKean, O. (1999). Improving psychotherapeutic services via randomized clinical trials, treatment manuals, and component analysis designs. *Journal of Clinical Psychology, 55* (12), 1507–1517.

Institute of Medicine. (1990). *Guidelines for Clinical Practice: From Development to Use.* Washington, D.C.: National Academy Press.

Jaeschke, R., Guyatt, G., and Meade, M. (1998). Evidence-based practice: What it is, why we need it. *Advances in Wound Care, 11* (5), 214–218.

Kolko, D. J. (1996). Clinical monitoring of treatment course in child physical abuse: Psychometric characteristics and treatment comparisons. *Child Abuse and Neglect, 20* (1), 23–43.

Loeber, R., Farrington, D. P., Stouthamer-Loeber, M., and Van Kammen, W. B. (1998). *Antisocial Behavior and Mental Health Problems: Explanatory Factors in Childhood and Adolescence.* Mahwah, N.J.: Lawrence Erlbaum.

Orrell-Valente, J. K., Pinderhughes, E. E., Valente, Jr., E., Laird, R. D., and Conduct Problems Prevention Research Group. (1999). If it's offered, will they come? Influences on parents' participation in a community-based conduct problems prevention program. *American Journal of Community Psychology, 27* (6), 753–783.

Patterson, G. R. (1995). Coercion as a basis for early age onset for arrest. In J. McCord (Ed.), *Coercion and Punishment in Long-Term Perspective* (pp. 81–105). New York: Cambridge University Press.

Patterson, G. R., Forgatch, M. S., Yoerger, K. L., and Stoolmiller, M. (1998). Variables that initiate and maintain an early-onset trajectory for juvenile offending. *Development and Psychopathology, 10,* 531–547.

Raimy, V. C. (1950). *Training in Clinical Psychology*. Englewood Cliffs, N.J.: Prentice-Hall.

Robbins, M. S., and Szapocznik, J. (2000, April). *Juvenile Justice Bulletin: Brief Strategic Family Therapy*. Washington, D.C.: U. S. Department of Justice, Office of Justice Programs, Office of Juvenile Justice and Delinquency Prevention.

Rosen, A., Proctor, E. K., Morrow-Howell, N., and Staudt, M. M. (1995). Rationales for practice decisions: Variations in knowledge use by decision task and social work service. *Research on Social Work Practice, 5,* 501–523.

Rosen, A., Proctor, E. K., and Staudt, M. M. (1999). Social work research and the quest for effective practice. *Social Work Research, 23* (1), 4–14.

Rothman, J., and Thomas, E. J. (Eds.) (1994). *Intervention Research: Design and Development for Human Services*. New York: Haworth.

Rubin, A. (2000). Social work research at the turn of the millennium: Progress and challenges. *Research on Social Work Practice, 10* (1), 9–14.

Sackett, D. L., Richardson, W. S., Rosenberg, W., and Haynes, R. B. (1997). *Evidence-Based Medicine: How to Practice and Teach EBM*. New York: Churchill Livingstone.

Sackett, D. L., Rosenberg, W. M. C., Gray, J. A. M., Haynes, R. B., and Richardson, W. S. (1996). Evidence-based medicine: What it is and what it isn't. *British Medical Journal, 312,* 71–72.

Stoolmiller, M., Eddy, J. M., and Reid, J. B. (2000). Detecting and describing preventive intervention effects in a universal school-based randomized trial targeting delinquent and violent behavior. *Journal of Consulting and Clinical Psychology, 68* (2), 296–306.

Thyer, B. A. (2000). A decade of Research on Social Work Practice. *Research on Social Work Practice, 10* (1), 5–8.

Vega, W. A. (1990). Hispanic families in the 1980s: A decade of research. *Journal of Marriage and the Family, 52,* 1015–1024.

Vega, W. A., and Gil, A. G. (1999). A model for explaining drug use behavior among Hispanic adolescents. *Drugs and Society, 14* (11/2), 57–74.

Zayas, L. H. (in press). Service delivery factors in the development of practice guidelines. In A. Rosen and E. K. Proctor (Eds.), *Developing Practice Guidelines for Social Work Intervention: Issues, Methods, and Research Agenda*. New York: Columbia University Press.

3

EVIDENCE-BASED PRACTICE: IMPLICATIONS FOR KNOWLEDGE DEVELOPMENT AND USE IN SOCIAL WORK

EILEEN GAMBRILL

P rofessions claim special knowledge and skills to help clients achieve certain ends. The question "What is knowledge?" has been of concern to philosophers throughout the ages. Two developments, evidence-based practice (EBP) and the practice guidelines movement, both of which originated outside of social work, highlight the importance of thinking carefully about what knowledge is, how it can be gained, how it should be used, and what the implications of different views are for clients, professionals, researchers, and taxpayers. This chapter focuses on contributions of EBP in helping practitioners to enhance quality of services and to honor ethical obligations to clients by drawing on research findings related to practice/policy decisions, considering client values and expectations, and involving clients as informed participants.

WHAT IS EVIDENCE-BASED PRACTICE?

Evidence-based medicine (EBM) arose as an alternative to authority-based medicine in which decisions are based on criteria such as consensus among experts, anecdotal experience, or tradition. It is hoped that professionals who consider research findings regarding decisions and inform clients about them will provide better, more ethical care than those who rely on authority. Given the many misperceptions and misrepresentations of EBP (Gibbs and Gambrill 2002; Straus and McAlister 2000) it is important to describe the process of EBP in order to gain its potential benefits to clients and professionals. The definition of evidence-based practice used here originated in the medical and health area. It describes a series of steps and related challenges for using clinical expertise to integrate the best external evidence based on research findings, with information about a client's unique characteristics and circumstances and preferences and actions in a context of limited resources

(Haynes, Devereaux, and Guyatt 2002). It is an evolving process designed to attend to interrelated evidentiary, ethical, and implementation concerns. Evidence-based practice (EBP) "is the integration of best research evidence with clinical expertise and [client] values" (Sackett et al. 2000:1). Clinical expertise refers to the use of practice skills and past experience to rapidly identify each client's unique circumstances and characteristics, "their individual risks and benefits of potential interventions, and their personal values and expectations" (Sackett et al. 2000:1). Practitioners draw on such expertise to integrate information from these varied sources (Haynes, Devereaux, and Guyatt 2002). The term *client values* refers to "the unique preferences, concerns and expectations each [client] brings to a clinical encounter and which must be integrated into clinical decisions if they are to serve the [client]" (Sackett et al. 2000:1). EBP requires locating and critically reviewing research findings related to important practice/policy decisions and sharing what is found (including nothing) with clients. Steps include the following:

1. converting information needs related to practice decisions into answerable questions
2. tracking down, with maximum efficiency, the best evidence with which to answer such questions
3. critically appraising that evidence for its validity, impact (size of effect), and applicability (usefulness in practice)
4. applying the results of this appraisal to practice/policy decisions, which involves deciding whether evidence found (if any) applies to the decision at hand (e.g., Is a client similar to those studied? Is there access to services described?) and considering client values and preferences in making decisions, as well as other applicability concerns.
5. evaluating our effectiveness and efficiency in carrying out steps 1–4 and seeking ways to improve them in the future.

(ADAPTED FROM SACKETT ET AL. 2000:3–4)

Some authors define EBP much more narrowly: "We use evidence-based practice here primarily to denote that practitioners will select interventions on the basis of their empirically demonstrated links to the desired outcomes" (Rosen and Proctor 2002:743). This definition leaves out local implementation concerns, other kinds of practice decisions (e.g., selecting assessment measures), the importance of considering client values and expectations, and involving clients as informed participants. EBP draws on the results of systematic, rigorous, critical appraisal of research related to important practice questions such as "Is this assessment measure valid?" or "Does this intervention do more good than harm?" Efforts are made to prepare comprehensive, rigorous reviews of all research related to questions addressed. Different questions require different kinds of research methods to critically appraise related assumptions (Gray 2001a; Greenhalgh 2001; Guyatt and Rennie 2002; Sackett et al. 2000). Kinds of questions include the following:

- *Effectiveness:* Do job training programs help clients get and maintain jobs? Do such programs have any harmful effects?
- *Prevention:* Do Head Start programs prevent students from dropping out of school?
- *Prediction (risk/prognosis):* Does this measure accurately predict suicide attempts?
- *Description/assessment:* Do self-report data provide accurate descriptions of parenting practices?
- *Harm:* Does (or will) this intervention harm clients?
- *Cost:* How much does this program cost compared to others?
- *Practice guidelines:* Are these practice guidelines valid and are they applicable to my client/agency/community?
- *Self-improvement:* How can I stay up to date, improve my skills, and be more effective and efficient?

Reasons Sackett and his colleagues (2000) suggest for the rapid spread of EBM include four realizations made possible by five recent developments: (1) practitioners' need for valid information about decisions they make, (2) the inadequacy of traditional sources for acquiring this information (e.g., because they are out of date, frequently wrong, overwhelming in volume, and of variable validity), (3) the gap between assessment skills and clinical judgment, "which increase with experience, and our up-to-date knowledge and clinical performance, which decline" (p. 2); and (4) lack of time to locate, appraise, and integrate this evidence. For example, a variety of biases in published research (submission, publication, methodological, abstracting, and framing biases) compromises the accuracy of available material (Gray 2001b). The economic interests of the pharmaceutical industry and fraud also diminish accuracy (e.g., preventing publication of negative findings). Sackett and his colleagues (2000) suggest that five developments have allowed improvement in this state of affairs:

1. The development of strategies for efficiently tracking down and appraising evidence (for its validity and relevance)
2. The creation of systematic reviews and concise summaries of the effects of health care (epitomized by the Cochrane Collaboration)

3. The creation of evidence-based journals of secondary publication . . .
4. The creation of information systems for bringing the foregoing to us in seconds
5. The identification and application of effective strategies for lifelong learning and for improving our clinical performance

(SACKETT ET AL. 2000:3)

EBP is not a method to save money. It consists of using services that "maximize the quality and quantity of life for individual [clients]; this may raise rather than lower the cost of care" (Sackett et al. 1997:4). Sackett and his coauthors argue that EBP is not "old hat." They argue that the belief that everybody already is doing it "falls before evidence of striking variations in both the integration of patient values into our clinical behavior and in the rates with which we provide interventions to our patients" (Sackett et al. 1997:3). Indeed, the more one reads about current practices in the helping professions, the clearer it is that helping efforts do not have characteristics of EBP as envisioned by its originators. Many (most?) practitioners do not search for external research findings related to important practice decisions. The social work literature suggests that social workers do not draw on practice-related research findings to inform practice decisions (Rosen 1994; Rosen et al. 1995). Not keeping up with new research findings related to important practice decisions renders our knowledge increasingly out of date. As a result, decisions may be made that harm rather than help clients (Jacobson, Mulick, and Schwartz 1995). In addition, many professionals do not honor requirements for informed consent (Braddock et al. 1999).

WHAT IS EVIDENCE?

What is evidence? What criteria should be used to identify it? What are underlying assumptions in different views of how to obtain evidence? How much evidence is needed to determine that a treatment is "appropriate," that it should be used, and how it should be paid for? (Eddy 1993:521). How such questions are approached is of central importance to what is done in the name of EBP and who benefits and who does not. Traditional and current criteria include what is "standard or accepted" or what the helper believes is in the client's best interests. However, as Eddy notes, "the credibility of clinical judgement, whether examined individually or collectively, has been severely challenged by observations of wide variations in practices, inappropriate care, and practitioner uncertainty" (Eddy 1993:521) (see also Grove and Meehl's [1996] research comparing clinical and actuarial judgment). Approaches to reviewing evidence related to claims differ in their rigor of critical appraisal

(Oakley and Fullerton 1996; Jüni, Altman, and Egger 2001; Schulz et al. 1995). A justification approach to knowledge (a focus on gathering support for, confirming a certain view) is common. This may result in ignoring contradictory data and alternative views. The effects of confirmation biases are evident in many different areas (Nickerson 1998). Content-area experts produce lower-quality appraisals of research rigor than do reviewers who, although skilled in methodological appraisal, do not work in the area of concern (Oxman and Guyatt 1993). An interest in minimizing common biases and maximizing up-to-date accurate accounts in descriptions of practice-related research, including those in textbooks and professional journals, is a key reason for developing EBP and related enterprises such as the Cochrane Collaboration and the Campbell Collaboration. Thus, one contribution of EBP has been to increase the consistency, rigor, completeness, and transparency of search and appraisal procedures of research reviews.

Popper (1972) argues that we cannot discover what is true by induction (generalizing from the particular to the general). In his view, falsification (attempts to falsify, to discover the errors in our beliefs) via critical discussion and testing is the only sound way to discover knowledge. He uses the criteria of falsifiability to demarcate what is or could be scientific knowledge from what is not or could not be. This view of knowledge suggests that words and phrases such as *well established*, *validated,* and *proven* convey a certainty that cannot be achieved. Use of rigorous methods for evaluating claims (e.g., tests that control for biases) and active search for competing views and evidence decrease the likelihood of inflated claims of knowledge that mislead both clients and professionals, stifle needed inquiry, and overlook promising alternatives. These strategies decrease the likelihood that we mislabel what is in "the package" as evidence. Inflated claims resulting from a justification approach to knowledge may result in overlooking effective methods and using ineffective or harmful practices and policies.

EVIDENCE-BASED PRACTICE COMPARED TO EMPIRICAL SOCIAL WORK PRACTICE

EBP, as described here, differs in a number of ways from empirical social work practice as presented in published sources. EBP describes a step-by-step process for drawing on external research findings and attending to ethical issues, and its proponents have actively pursued creation of tools such as routinely updated electronic databases and professional training programs (e.g., problem-based learning) designed to help practitioners implement this process. Compared to empirical social work practice, there is more attention in EBP to ethical issues such as informed consent—considering client values and expectations (see list of steps in EBP, above, and see Edwards and Elwyn 2001). And there is greater attention in EBP to involving clients in the design, conduct, and interpretation of research (Hanley et al. 2001). There is more attention in EBP to helping practitioners and clients to acquire critical appraisal skills. Another important difference is the greater rigor of critical appraisal of practice and policy-related research findings in EBP and related enterprises such as the Cochrane and Campbell Collaborations (www .cochrane.org and www.campbellcollaborations.org). These are typically more rigorous, more exhaustive in the search for related studies, more transparent in the description of search and appraisal procedures, and less excessive in their claims of knowledge. Authors of research reviews in empirical social work sources often do not describe how they searched, where they searched, or criteria used to appraise different kinds of studies, and they often do not rigorously critique studies. The literature on empirical social work includes many uncritical, incomplete reviews of research regarding important practice questions. For example, Moseley and Deweaver (1995) conclude that case management for the severely and chronically mentally ill is effective, when rigorous reviews of related randomized controlled trials (RCTs) suggest the reverse (Gomory 1999). Quite different conclusions may be made based on incomplete, uncritical reviews compared to rigorous reviews.

Another difference is the greater emphasis on the production of knowledge on the part of practitioners in the empirical social work literature. Practitioners were to draw on practice-related research findings with minimal guidelines and tools for doing so, such as readily accessible electronic databases containing high-quality reviews, and, in addition, were supposed to generate knowledge. There is greater recognition in the EBP literature of obstacles to EBP and planning how to minimize them, including lack of time, knowledge, resources, and training on the part of practitioners needed to locate research findings relevant to important decisions. Both EBP and empirical social work share an interest in integrating practice and research. EPB should carry forward and enrich efforts in empirical social work practice to integrate practice and research and honor ethical guidelines as suggested in the sections that follow.

PRACTICE GUIDELINES AND EVIDENCE-BASED PRACTICE

Proctor and Rosen define practice guidelines as "a set of systematically compiled and organized knowledge statements that are designed to enable practitioners to find, select, and use the interventions that are most effective and appropriate" (2000:1). Practice guidelines, as defined by Proctor and Rosen, focus on intervention questions, leaving out other questions, such as those that concern the validity of assessment measures, prognosis, and causation/harm. Practice guidelines are one component of EBP as illustrated by a review of topics in Sackett et al. (2000). They are discussed in one of nine chapters; other chapters focus on diagnosis and screening, prognosis, therapy, harm, teaching methods, and evaluation. Thus these two enterprises also differ in the comprehensiveness of their efforts to integrate practice and policy related research findings and on-the-job decisions. Other differences include the greater emphasis in EPB on helpers and clients acquiring critical appraisal skills, open recognition of the degree of ignorance about important questions which highlights uncertainty, the promotion of transparency of what is done to what effect, attention to ethical issues (informed consent), and attention given to making practice-related research findings accessible to all involved parties. Although written statements in the practice guideline literature call for aspects of EBP, such as openness to public scrutiny, being based on all relevant empirical evaluation, considering [client] values (e.g., see *Criteria for Evaluating Treatment Guidelines* 1999), related activities are often missing. Criteria appealed to in guidelines include "agreement among experts" (e.g., see draft of Criteria for Evaluating Treatment Guidelines published by the American Psychological Association, August 1999). Recommendations in the EBP literature regarding practice guidelines call for rigorous appraisal of the evidentiary status of each guideline (e.g., see Sackett et al. 2000:173–177), as well as considering the applicability of a guideline to local conditions. Decisions regarding whether practice guidelines are valid are separate from whether they are applicable to a particular client, agency, or community.

CONTRIBUTIONS OF EVIDENCE-BASED PRACTICE FOR KNOWLEDGE DEVELOPMENT AND USE

Given the greater scope of EBP, the emphasis here is on its contributions to the development and use of knowledge in the helping professions, including the development of practice guidelines and the honoring of ethical obligations to clients. These include a call for transparency of what is done to what effect, measured rather than inflated claims of knowledge, and training of helpers and clients to critically appraise the quality of evidence for themselves. A key contribution of EBP is encouraging social work to move from being an authority-based profession to being one in which critical appraisal and honest brokering of knowledge and ignorance thrive (Gambrill 1999, 2000). Indicators of the authority-based nature of social work include large gaps between our obligations and what is done (e.g., our code of ethics and our practice and policy), basing decisions on criteria such as consensus and tradition, inflated claims, lack of informed consent, and trade barriers to the free flow of knowledge (e.g., censorship of certain kinds of knowledge, such as variations in services and their outcomes) (Gambrill 2001). Research, practice, and educational issues are closely intertwined. For example, poor quality reviews of research related to practice and policy questions may result in bogus "practice guidelines," which result in poor quality services for clients. Students may be misinformed about the evidentiary status of practice and policy claims and so may harm rather than help clients or forgo opportunities to maximize the likelihood of achieving hoped-for outcomes.

Interrelated contributions of EBP include the following:

1. *Focuses on client concerns and hoped-for outcomes*

EBP encourages a focus on client concerns and hoped-for outcomes. Most of the practice guideline literature is organized around "psychiatric disorders" rather than specific client-desired outcomes. A perennial concern in the helping professions is a drift away from addressing clients' concerns to a concern with professional or organizational status, income, and personal preferences (Blenkner 1972).

2. *Encourages a comprehensive, systemic approach to provision of effective, efficient, ethical services*

Evidence-based practice involves a systemic approach to improving quality of services, including (1) attending to educating professionals who are lifelong learners, (2) involving clients as informed participants in decisions made, (3) attending to management practices and policies that influence practice (i.e., evidence-based purchase of services), (4) considering the implications of scarce resources on services purchased, and (5) attending to applicability challenges (Gray 2001; Sackett et al. 2000). This is an evolving systemic approach to practice/policy questions designed to help practitioners and clients integrate research findings (if any) and to make practice decisions in which both professionals and clients are involved as informed participants. Attention is given to identifying and helping practitioners to acquire the knowledge, skills, and tools required to deliver services to clients within a helping framework in which related research findings are actively sought and critically appraised and populations as well as individuals are considered. A systemic approach has many advantages, including not overlooking any weak link in the system that could pull down the rest (e.g., administrative and supervisory practices, poor-quality training programs) and involving all parties as informed participants by encouraging the development of critical appraisal skills among both helpers and clients. Quality of services is unlikely to improve in a fragmented approach that does not attend to *all* links in the system of service provision.

3. *Describes a process for integrating evidentiary, ethical, and application concerns*

A key difference between EBP and practice guidelines, even if the latter are defined broadly as encompassing assessment as well as intervention questions, is the greater attention given to describing the steps involved in integrating practice-related research findings, creating needed tools such as access to high-quality reviews, and exploring a framework for professional education (i.e., problem-based learning) that will contribute to EBP (Sackett et al. 2000). I by no means imply that all related problems have been solved (e.g., integration of clinical expertise and external research findings). However, problems are recognized and struggled with.

4. *Promotes transparency and honesty*

Transparency refers to clearly describing variations in services and their outcomes, research methods used and their limitations, and alternative views of topics addressed and related research findings, including data contradictory to preferred views. EBP encourages clear description of variations in services provided and related outcomes and gaps between services provided and what information is available (if any) describing what is needed to attain outcomes pursued (Enkin et al. 1995). This may reveal bogus credentialism (lack of need for professional licenses to provide certain services [Dawes 1994]), futile pursuit of outcomes (they are unattainable), or insufficient staff training or resources. Transparency of what is done to what effect contributes to judicious distribution of scarce resources (Eddy 1994). That is, whenever we fund services of unknown effects, there is less money for services critically tested and found to help clients. Transparency is also important with regard to conceptual views and alternatives and related evidence. Thus, proposed guidelines should be critically appraised not only in relation to their evidentiary base (e.g., is there evidence that they result in better outcomes compared to alternatives such as doing nothing?), but also in relation to the completeness and rigor of their conceptual analysis (e.g., of problems).

5. *Encourages rigorous testing and appraisal of practice/policy-related claims*

A key contribution of EBP is encouraging preparation of research reviews based on an exhaustive search for research findings related to practice and policy questions and rigorous critical appraisal of each study located (Chalmers and Altman 1995; Egger, Smith, and Altman 2001). Critical appraisal may reveal that programs being widely disseminated are not effective or have harmful effects (for example, see review of research regarding psychological debriefing for preventing post-traumatic stress disorder (PTSD) (Rose, Bisson, and Wessely 2001). Evidence-based practice is closely associated with the Cochrane Collaboration (CC), which is a worldwide network of centers designed to prepare, maintain, and disseminate high-quality reviews of the effects of health care (Chalmers, Sackett, and Silagy 1997). Reviews are based on electronic and hand searches for all material related to a question in all relevant languages, both published and unpublished. The Campbell Collaboration, initiated in 1999, was formed to prepare reviews regarding social and educational interventions (Schuerman et al. 2002). Search processes used to locate studies and criteria used to appraise research reports are clearly described. Efforts in systematic reviews and meta-analyses to locate *all* relevant research related to a question, to use and clearly describe rigorous guidelines for appraising what is found, and to disclose any special interests, such as funding sources, distinguish them from incomplete reviews (Oxman and Guyatt 1993).

Different questions require different research methods to critically test assumptions, as discussed earlier. Each method is subject to certain biases (Campbell and Stanley 1963; Greenhalgh 2001). Reliance on experts in an area to prepare reviews may encourage biased reports; research suggests "that experts, on average, write reviews of inferior quality; that the greater the expertise the more likely the quality is to be poor; and that the poor quality may be related to the strength of their prior opinions and the amount of time they spend preparing a review article" (Oxman and Guyatt 1993:129–130). Conceptual critiques are also needed. For example, personal problems may be assumed to have a biochemical cause when little or no evidence exists for such an assumption.

6. *Promotes the preparation and dissemination of critical appraisals of practice/policy-related research findings*

Another contribution of EBP is the design and evaluation of methods to get practice and policy related information into the hands of clients and professionals in timely, user-friendly ways. Preparation and routine updating of research reviews regarding specific practice questions is a key way knowledge is diffused (see Cochrane Library and reviews prepared by the Campbell Collaboration). EBP encourages helping staff and clients acquire critical appraisal skills (for example, for evaluating the quality of meta-analyses), arranging incentives that encourage their use, providing staff with timely access to relevant databases, and exploring the effects of these innovations on client outcomes. EPB has encouraged exploration of the effectiveness of different kinds of diffusion efforts (Edwards and Elwyn 2001; O'Connor et al. 2002). Such efforts will make it more difficult to mislead people about "what we know," it will be more difficult to ignore counterevidence, and alternative views and harm done in the name of helping.

7. Teaches helpers how to rapidly locate and critically appraise research reports

A key focus in EBP is helping clients and practitioners to quickly locate practice and policy related research, especially systematic reviews related to a specific question, and to develop the skills required to critically appraise research findings, including the quality of research reviews (Spittlehouse, Acton, and Enock 2000). EBP encourages the creation of tools and training programs designed to develop and encourage use of critical appraisal skills. Detailed guidelines are available for reviewing the quality of different kinds of studies (e.g., see work of the CONSORT Group, Altman et al. 2001; Greenhalgh 2001; Gibbs 2003; Guyatt and Rennie 2002; evidence-based tool kit on the Internet). The Critical Appraisal Skills Program (CASP) in Oxford has been offering workshops on critical appraisal to a variety of professionals for many years. Reviews may not be available regarding many questions, and professionals should have the skills to locate and critically review the quality of related studies themselves, especially for problems they often address (Guyatt et al. 2000).

8. Highlights applicability challenges

In their discussion of practice guidelines, Sackett and his colleagues (2000) highlight the importance of considering *two* distinct components of practice guidelines: (1) their evidentiary base and (2) application concerns. They emphasize that those who are the experts in deciding whether a guideline is applicable to a given client/practice/agency/community "are the clients and providers at the sharp edge of implementing the application component" (p. 181), *not* the researchers and academics who critically appraised research findings. As Sackett et al. (2002) suggest, the clients and providers are the experts in identifying application concerns that may be present as "killer Bs." These include incompatible *Beliefs* of individual [clients] or communities about the value of services or their consequences. Potential *Barriers* may be geographic (a particular service may not be available in a local community), organizational (a policy may prohibit a service), traditional (that's the way we've always done it), authoritarian (you have always done it my way), legal (concerns about litigation), or behavioral (social workers may fail to apply a guideline or clients may fail to implement it). Opportunity costs of implementing a guideline may be a bad *Bargain* in use of resources. The differing kinds of expertise needed to prepare reviews regarding the evidentiary base of a guideline and to identify implementation potential highlight the inappropriateness of researchers telling practitioners and clients what guidelines to use in the absence of detailed information about local circumstances. The evidence-based literature describes various efforts to encourage implementation of guidelines by addressing barriers (see Watt, Entwistle, and Sowden 1999 and discussion in items 6 and 7 above).

9. *Attends to individual differences*

Step 4 in EBP emphasizes the importance of attending to individual differences regarding clients' actions and preferences and unique characteristics of a client and his or her circumstances. EBP requires asking whether a practice guideline that calls for use of a particular service matches the characteristics, values, and circumstances of a client.

10. *Discourages inflated claims*

A key contribution of EBP is discouraging inflated claims of knowledge that mislead involved parties and hinder the development of knowledge. Consider terms such as *well established* and *validated,* which convey a certainty that is not possible (see earlier section on uncertainty and ignorance). Consider Proctor and Rosen's (2000) definition of practice guidelines as "a set of . . . knowledge statements" rather than, for example, "well-tested but hypothetical claims." Practice guidelines are often recommended as "established" on the basis of two randomized controlled trials. Practice guidelines are often premature, encouraging the belief that more is known than is the case. Often they fail to consider the quality of the helper-client relationship, or apply only to a modest percentage of all clients with a concern (Garfield 1996; Kirk 1999). Drawbacks of premature guidelines include formalizing unsound practices, inhibiting innovation, reducing practice variations to average rather than best practice, overlooking individual differences and implementation concerns (see section on obstacles), and producing undesirable shifts in the balance of power among different professional groups (for example, researchers and practitioners) (Greenhalgh 2001). Bogus claims based on uncritical appraisals of related research hinder exploration and contribute to harmful practices and policies.

11. *Describes and takes proactive steps to minimize errors, accidents, and mistakes*

The history of the helping professions shows that common practices thought to help people were found to harm them. Consider the blinding of 10,000 children by use of oxygen at birth (Silverman 1998). Remarkably little research has been devoted to the study of errors, accidents, and mistakes in social work. Research regarding errors in medicine shows that latent causes (e.g., quality of staff training, agency policy) contribute heavily to mistakes made by helpers (Reason 2001). EBP encourages programmatic research regarding error, both avoidable and unavoidable, its causes and consequences for clients and other involved parties, and exploration of methods designed to minimize avoidable errors, including agency-wide risk management programs (Reason 1997). A careful review of the circumstances related to mistakes allows us to plan how to minimize avoidable ones.

12. *Welcomes criticism*

A key implication of EBP is an openness to criticism (McIntyre and Popper 1983). A willingness and commitment to submit favored views to severe scrutiny is basic to science, distinguishing it from pseudoscience. Criticism is essential to the growth of knowledge. Increased transparency of services and outcomes allows pointed criticism, as does the selection of research methods that can critically test questions and preparation of rigorous reviews of research related to a claim. EBP encourages the exploration of how to encourage critical discussion in professional contexts (for example, norms that minimize groupthink in case conferences) and policies that protect whistle-blowers.

13. *Recognizes our ignorance and consequent uncertainty*

EBP highlights the play of bias and the uncertainty involved in helping clients and attempts to give helpers and clients the knowledge and skills to handle this ethically and constructively. Consider, for example, the attention given to training both clients and helpers in critical appraisal skills and the use of "quality filters" in reviewing research findings related to practice questions (Greenhalgh 2001). Biases intrude both on the part of researchers when preparing research reviews and at the practitioner level when making practice decisions (Gambrill 1990; Hastie and Dawes 2001; Grove and Meehl 1996). Availability and representative biases may interfere with judicious integration of individual expertise, external evidence, and client values and expectations (Gambrill 1990). Many components of EBP are designed to minimize cognitive biases, such as use of "quality filters" when reviewing external research findings related to a question. EBP requires helpers "to accept and deal with uncertainty . . . and to acknowledge that management decisions are often made in the face of relative ignorance" (Haynes 2002).

14. *Honors professional codes of ethics*

Yet another contribution of EBP is honoring obligations to clients described in professional codes of ethics (for example, informed consent and drawing on practice-related research findings). Evidentiary and ethical concerns are closely intertwined (e.g., see Rosenthal 1994). Ignoring practice and policy related research findings and forwarding bogus claims of effectiveness violates our obligation to provide informed consent and may result in wasting money on ineffective services, harming clients in the name of helping them, and decreasing chances of attaining hoped-for outcomes. Considering client preferences, state, and circumstances, and involving clients as informed participants in decision making are hallmarks of EBP (see list of steps). The

Cochrane Collaboration now has a special Web site for consumers (www .cochraneconsumer.com). A variety of different formats for involving clients as informed participants have been explored (Edwards and Elwyn 2001; O'Connor et al. 2002). There are many opportunities to honor opportunities for informed consent even in nonautonomous situations (Faden and Beauchamp 1986). We could, for example, require each staff member to complete and give to each client a written consent form describing the likelihood of success of each recommended service based on critical tests of effectiveness, the agency's track record of success in achieving related outcomes, and the track record of success of the staff member who will offer this service (Entwistle et al. 1998). Another important way to involve clients is to establish accessible, accountable, and timely complaint procedures and make use of findings to improve services (Schwartz and Baer 1991).

15. *Increases use of available knowledge*

Evidence-based practice encourages purchase of services from agencies on the basis of their acceptability to clients and their documented track record of success in helping clients attain desired outcomes. It encourages a free-market knowledge economy in which there is (1) free knowledge flow, knowledge is readily available to those who can use it to decrease (or reveal) uncertainty; (2) good communication among buyers, sellers, and brokers; (3) a well-developed technology for gaining relevant information (e.g., computerized databases); and (4) an agency culture that supports knowledge flow.

16. *Considers populations as well as individuals*

Evidence-based health care involves drawing on external research findings when making decisions about groups of clients or populations. It provides a way to make informed decisions about the distribution of scarce resources by attending to the evidentiary status of services. Saving money by not paying for ineffective services allows more money for providing services found to be effective at a level that maximizes the likelihood of valued outcomes.

17. *Minimizes harm in the name of helping*

The history of the helping professions reveals the frequency of harm in the name of helping (Sharpe and Faden 1998; Valenstein 1986). Currently, concerns about harm done in the name of helping are often ignored. No matter how carefully we plan, there may be unintended consequences. Some will be harmful (Petrosino, Turpin-Petrosino, and Buehler 2002). Blenkner and her colleagues (1971) found that intensive case management *increased* mortality for older clients (see also critiques of this study as well as replies). The potential for harming in the name of helping is a key concern in EBP.

18. *Blows the whistle on pseudoscience, propaganda, quackery, and fraud*

Transparency, rigorous critical appraisal of claims, and honoring ethical obligations to clients call for blowing the whistle on pseudoscience, fraud, quackery, and propaganda in professional contexts.

19. *Creates educational programs that develop lifelong learners*

Providing evidence-based services to clients will require skills in lifelong learning. Research suggests that traditional continuing education programs do not improve clinical performance (Davis et al. 1995). EBP and problem-based learning are closely connected. Problem-based learning has been explored in medicine as a way to encourage lifelong, self-directed learning (Barrows 1994; Sackett et al. 2000).

20. *Explores how to decrease obstacles to evidence-based practice*

Key components of EBP are designed to decrease obstacles to drawing on practice/policy-related research findings, for example by providing access to electronic databases containing up-to-date, critical reviews of research regarding important practice questions (e.g., is this assessment measure valid) and giving both practitioners and clients the critical appraisal skills required to evaluate research studies, including systematic reviews and meta-analyses (e.g., see Greenhalgh 2000). (See also discussion of application problems.)

OBJECTIONS TO EVIDENCE-BASED PRACTICE

Some objections result from misperceptions of EBP. These include beliefs that EBP denigrates clinical expertise, ignores client values and preferences, promotes a cookbook approach to practice/policy, is simply a cost-cutting tool, is an ivory tower concept (can't be done), is limited to clinical research, and leads to therapeutic nihilism when there is no evidence from RCTs (Gibbs and Gambrill 2002; Straus and McAlister 2000, as well as descriptions of EBP in this chapter). Misperceptions and misrepresentations (Webb 2001) distract from attending to the many real challenges of using EBP. Shahar suggests that EBP, at worst, is "a disguise for a new version of authoritarianism in medical practice" (1997:109), the emperor's new clothes (Shahar 1998; Gomory 2000). This is a possible result as shown by those who use the title ("evidence-based") but forgo the substance (for example, publish incomplete, uncritical reviews and forward inflated claims of effectiveness via words such as *proven, established,* and *validated*). But this path is not inevitable.

Although no evidence will be found related to many answerable questions, there are research findings related to many questions (for example, see Cochrane and Campbell Libraries). Another objection is that clients don't want to be informed about the evidentiary status of different alternatives, don't use the information if given, or can't understand the information. Preparation of interactive, user-friendly decision aids should contribute to overcoming such objections. Systematic reviews related to a question may not point to a specific answer. Informed-consent obligations require social workers to share this with clients and to consider their preferences. Here, too, practice theory can be drawn on in considering options. When different reviews arrive at different conclusions, we can compare their rigor. Another objection is that we don't know how to measure outcomes. Clients have real-life concerns allowing identification of related outcomes, both subjective and objective, and tracking of progress indicators (e.g., see Schwartz and Baer 1991). Transparency (clear description of service variations and their outcomes) and involvement of all interested parties should help to clarify and ethically address conflicts concerning what standards should be used. Some object that EBP limits professional autonomy. Shouldn't professionals welcome limits on their discretion if these benefit clients?

OBSTACLES

Sackett and his coauthors suggest three basic limitations universal to science and the helping professions: "The shortage of coherent, consistent scientific evidence; difficulties in applying any evidence to the care of individual [clients]; barriers to any practice of high-quality [helping]" (Sackett et al. 2000:7). Limitations unique to EBP include the need to develop new skills in searching and critical appraisal, limited time to acquire and apply these skills, and inadequate resources for instant access to evidence. And, they note, "Evidence that EBP 'works' has been late and slow to come" (2000:7). There are challenges in applying research findings to individuals. Decisions regarding whether practice guidelines are empirically sound are separate from those dealing with whether they are applicable to a particular client, agency, or community. Here, too, our obligations to inform clients and to consider their preferences provide a guide (for example, helpers should clearly describe limitations in applying research findings in a particular situation). Challenges in combining clinical expertise with external evidence are an ongoing concern. Helping professionals to learn from their experience in ways that improve the accuracy of future decisions is a key priority.

Functions of the helping profession such as social control and professional expansion suggest that helping efforts often serve the interests not of clients but of professionals and professions (Abbott 1988; Szasz 1994). Inflated claims of knowledge regarding methods are used to justify expansion of mental health services. Value judgments are disguised as expert "scientific" opinions about what is healthy or unhealthy (McCormick 1996). Economic interests of the pharmaceutical industry encourage the medicalization of everyday behaviors (Szasz 2001). Transparency of what is done to what effect may be deeply threatening to professionals. There are many pressures on staff to act more certain than they are, including the rhetoric of professional organizations that oversells the feats of professionals and journal articles with inflated claims. Questioning the effectiveness of programs that bring in lots of money may not be welcomed, even in a university setting. Encouraging EPB and related continuing quality improvement programs that reflect an ethos of collective responsibility for mistakes will require changes in organizational culture. Considerable challenges confront helpers who want to practice in an evidence-based manner, such as gaining timely access to external research findings. We are subject to a wide array of persuasion strategies, thinking errors, and defenses against disliked views (Gambrill 1990; Skrabanek and McCormick 1998).

IN SUMMARY

The key contribution of evidence-based practice (EBP) is to move social work and other helping professions from authority-based professions in which decisions are made based on "expert consensus" or individual opinions of helpers uninformed by related research findings to those which do take account of related research findings as well as the unique circumstances and characteristics of clients, including their values and expectations. EBP is designed to encourage practice-related contexts in which critical appraisal flourishes and codes of ethics are honored (e.g., clients are involved as informed participants). EBP should carry forward and enrich efforts within empirical social work practice to integrate research and practice. EBP encourages honest brokering of knowledge and ignorance. This calls for transparency of what is done to what effect, for measured rather than inflated claims of knowledge based on critical appraisal of research reports, and for enabling helpers and clients to critically appraise the quality of evidence including research reviews. EPB highlights the importance of never forgetting our ignorance. It requires helpers to search for evidence and share what is found, including nothing, with clients. It has a close connection with informed consent. It encourages us to avoid words that convey a certainty that is not possible, such as *validated* and *proven*. Inflated claims of knowledge hide ignorance and uncertainty, mislead clients, and waste money on ineffective or harmful services. They mislead both clients and helpers regarding the evidentiary status of theories and methods. Wasting money on research that cannot test questions addressed results in lost opportunities to discover what helps, what is of no effect, and what harms clients. Involving clients as informed participants and making practices and policies and the reasons for selecting them transparent, will help to counter political, social, economic, and psychological pressures to inflate knowledge claims and censor disliked views and contradictory data. EBP provides yet another fork in the road toward a choice of honest brokering of knowledge and ignorance and honoring ethical obligations.

REFERENCES

Abbott, A. (1988). *The System of Professions: An Essay on the Division of Expert Labor.* Chicago: University of Chicago Press.

Altman, D. G., Schulz, K. F., Moher, D., Egger, M., Davidoff, F., Elbourne, D., et al. for the CONSORT Group. (2001). The revised CONSORT statement for reporting randomized trials: Explanation and elaboration. *Annals of Internal Medicine, 134,* 663–694. Available at www.consort-statement.org.

Barrows, H. W. (1994). *Practice-Based Learning: Problem-Based Learning Applied to Medical Education.* Springfield: Southern Illinois University School of Medicine.

Blenkner, M. (1972). Strategies to Identify and Serve the Target Groups. In J. Thorson (Ed.), *Proceedings: Action Now for Older Americans Toward Independent Living.* Athens: University of Georgia, Center for Continuing Education.

Blenkner, M., Bloom, M., and Nielson, M. (1971). A research and demonstration of protective services. *Social Casework, 52* (8), 483–499.

Braddock, C. H., Edwards, K. A., Hasenberg, N. M., Laidley, T. L., and Levinson, W. (1999). Informed decision making in outpatient practice. Time to get back to basics. *Journal of the American Medical Association, 282* (24), 2313–2320.

Campbell, D. T., and Stanley, J. C. (1963). *Experimental and Quasi-Experimental Designs for Research.* Chicago: Rand McNally.

Chalmers, I., and Altman, D. C. (1995). *Systematic Reviews.* London: BMJ.

Chalmers, I., Sackett, D., and Silagy, C. (1997). The Cochrane Collaboration. In A. Maynard and I. Chalmers (Eds.), *Non-Random Reflections on Health Services Research: On the 25th Anniversary of Archie Cochrane's Effectiveness and Efficiency* (pp. 231–249). London: BMJ.

Criteria for Evaluating Treatment Guidelines. (1999). Unapproved draft—for comment. Template Implementation Work Group of the Board of Professional Affairs, Board of Scientific Affairs, Committee for the Advancement of Professional Psychology. Washington, D.C.: American Psychological Association.

Davis, D. A., Thomson, M. A., Oxman, A. D., and Haynes, R. B. (1995). Changing physician performance: A systematic review of the effect of continuing medical education strategies. *Journal of the American Medical Association, 274,* 700–705.

Dawes, R. M. (1994). *House of Cards: Psychology and Psychotherapy Built on Myth.* New York: Free Press.

Eddy, D. M. (1993). Clinical decision making: From theory to practice. Three battles to watch in the 1990s. *Journal of the American Medical Association, 270,* 520–526.

———. (1994). Principles for making difficult decisions in difficult times. *Journal of the American Medical Association, 271,* 1792–1798.

Edwards, A., and Elwyn, G. (Eds.) (2001). *Evidence-Based Patient Choice: Inevitable or Impossible?* New York: Oxford University Press.

Egger, M., Smith, G. D., and Altman, D. G. (Eds.). *Systematic Reviews in Healthcare: Meta-analysis in Context.* London: BMJ Books.

Enkin, M., Keirse, M. J. N., Renfrew, M., and Neilson, J. (1995). *A Guide to Effective Care in Pregnancy and Childbirth* (2d ed.). New York: Oxford University Press.

Entwistle, V. A., Sheldon, T. A., Sowden, A. J., and Watt, I. A. (1998). Evidence-informed patient choice. *International Journal of Technology Assessment in Health Care, 14,* 212–215.

Faden, R. R., and Beauchamp, T. L. in collaboration with King, N. M. P. (1986). *A History and Theory of Informed Consent.* Oxford: Oxford University Press.

Gambrill, E. (1990). *Critical Thinking in Clinical Practice.* San Francisco: Jossey-Bass.

———. (1999). Evidence-based practice: An alternative to authority-based practice. *Families in Society, 80,* 341–350.

———. (2000). Honest brokering of knowledge and ignorance. Editorial. *Journal of Social Work Education, 35,* 387–397.

———. (2001). Social work: An authority-based profession. *Research on Social Work Practice, 11,* 166–175.

Gambrill, E., and Gibbs, L. (2002). Making practice decisions: Is what's good for the goose good for the gander? *Ethical Human Sciences and Services, 4,* 31–46.

Garfield, S. L. (1996). Some problems associated with "validated" forms of psychotherapy. *Clinical Psychology, Science, and Practice, 3,* 218–229.

Gibbs, L. (2003). *Evidence-Based Practice for the Helping Professions.* Pacific Grove, Calif.: Brooks/Cole.

Gibbs, L., and Gambrill, E. (2002). Evidence-based practice: Counterarguments to objections. *Research on Social Work Practice, 12,* 452–476.

Gomory, T. (1999). Programs of Assertive Community Treatment (PACT): A critical review. *Ethical Human Sciences and Services, 1,* 147–163.

———. (2000). "Social Work Practice in the Real World: An Argument for Evidence-Tested Practice." Paper presented at the Conference on Practice Guidelines, George Warren Brown School of Social Work, May, Washington University, St. Louis, Missouri.

Gray, J. A. M. (1998). Where is the chief knowledge officer? *British Medical Journal, 317,* 832.

———. (2001a). *Evidence-Based Health Care: How to Make Health Policy and Management Decisions* (2d ed.). New York: Churchill Livingstone.

———. (2001b). Evidence-Based Medicine for Professionals. In A. Edwards and G. Elwyn (Eds.), *Evidence-Based Patient Choice: Inevitable or Impossible?* (pp. 19–33). New York: Oxford University Press.

Greenhalgh, T. (2001). *How to Read a Paper* (2d ed.). London: BMJ.

Grove, W. M., and Meehl, P. E. (1996). Comparative efficiency of informal (subjective, impressionistic) and formal (mechanical, algorithmic) prediction procedures: The clinical-statistical authority. *Psychology, Public Policy, and Law, 2,* 293–323.

Guyatt, G. H., Meade, M. O., Jaeschke, R. Z., Cook, D. J., and Haynes, R. B. (2000). Practitioners of evidence-based care: Not all clinicians need to appraise evidence from scratch but need some skills. *British Medical Journal, 320,* 954–955.

Guyatt, G. H., and Rennie, D. (2002). *Users' Guide to the Medical Literature: A Manual for Evidence-Based Clinical Practice/The Evidence-Based Working Group.* Chicago: AMA Press.

Hanley, B., Truesdale, A., King, A., Elbourne, D., and Chalmers, I. (2001). Involving consumers in designing, conducting, and interpreting randomised controlled trials: Questionnaire survey. *British Medical Journal, 322,* 519–523.

Hastie, R., and Dawes, R. M. (2001). *Rational Choice in an Uncertain World: The Psychology of Judgment and Decision Making.* Thousand Oaks, Calif.: Sage.

Haynes, R. B. (2002). What kind of evidence is it that Evidence-Based Medicine advocates want health care providers and consumers to pay attention to? *BMC Health Services Research, 2,* March 6. www.biomedcentral.com (pp. 1–15).

Haynes, R. B., Devereaux, P. J., and Guyatt, G. H. (2002). Editorial: Clinical expertise in the era of evidence-based medicine and patient choice. *ACP Journal Club,* March/April.

Jacobson, J. W., Mulick, J. A., and Schwartz, A. A. (1995). A history of facilitated communication: Science, pseudoscience, and antiscience. Science Working Group on Facilitated Communication. *American Psychologist, 50* (9), 750–765.

Jüni, P., Altman, D. G., and Egger, M. (2001). Assessing the quality of controlled clinical trials. *British Medical Journal, 323,* 42–46.

Kirk, S. (1999). Good intentions are not enough: Practice guidelines for social work. *Research on Social Work Practice, 9,* 302–310.

McCormick, J. (1996). Health Scares Are Bad for Your Health. In D. M. Warburton and N. Sherwood (Eds.), *Pleasure and Quality of Life* (pp. 189–199). New York: Wiley.

McIntyre, N., and Popper, K. (1983). The critical attitude in medicine: The need for a new ethics. *British Medical Journal, 287,* 1919–1923.

Moseley, P. G., and Deweaver, K. L. (1995). Empirical Approaches to Case Management. In J. S. Wodarski and B. A. Thyer (Eds.), *Handbook of Empirical Social Work. Vol. 2, Social Problems and Practice Issues* (pp. 393–412). New York: Wiley.

Nickerson, R. (1998). Confirmation bias: A ubiquitous phenomenon in many guises. *Review of General Psychology, 2,* 175–200.

Oakley, A., and Fullerton, D. (1996). The Lamp-post of Research: Support or Illumination? In A. Oakley and H. Roberts (Eds.), *Evaluating Social Interventions: A Report of Two Workshops Funded by the Economic and Social Research Council.* London: Bernardos.

O'Connor, A. M., Stacey, D., Rovner, D., Holmes-Rovner, M., Tetroe J., Llewellyn-Thomas, H., Entwistle, V., Rostom, A., Fiset, V., Barry, M., and Jones, J. (2002). Decision aids for people facing health treatment or screening decisions (Cochrane Review). In *The Cochrane Library,* Issue 4. Oxford: Update Software.

Oxman, A. D., and Guyatt, G. H. (1993). The Science of Reviewing Research. In K. S. Warren and F. Mosteller (Eds.), *Doing More Good Than Harm: The Evaluation of Health Care Interventions* (pp. 125–133). New York: New York Academy of Sciences.

Petrosino, A., Turpin-Petrosino, C., and Buehler, J. (2002). "Scared straight" and other juvenile awareness programs for preventing juvenile delinquency (Cochrane Review). In *The Cochrane Library,* Issue 2. Oxford: Update Software.

Popper, K. R. (1972). *Conjectures and Refutations: The Growth of Scientific Knowledge* (4th ed.). London: Routledge and Kegan Paul.

Proctor, E., and Rosen, A. (2000). "The structure and function of social work practice guidelines." Paper presented at the Conference on Practice Guidelines, George Warren Brown School of Social Work, Washington University, May 5, 2000.

Reason, J. (1997). *Managing the Risks of Organizational Accidents.* Aldershot: Ashgate.

———. (2001). Understanding Adverse Events: The Human Factor. In C. Vincent (Ed.), *Clinical Risk Management: Enhancing Patient Safety* (2d ed.) (pp. 9–30). London: BMJ.

Rose, S., Bisson, J., and Wessely, S. (2001). Psychological debriefing for preventing post traumatic stress disorder (PTSD) (Cochrane Review). In *The Cochrane Library,* Issue 4. Oxford: Update Software.

Rosen, A. (1994). Knowledge use in direct practice. *Social Service Review, 68,* 561–577.

Rosen, A., and Proctor, E. K. (2002). Standards for Evidence-Based Social Work Practice: The Role of Replicable and Appropriate Interventions, Outcomes, and Practice Guidelines. In A. R. Roberts and G. J. Green (Eds.), *Social Workers' Desk Reference* (pp. 743–747). New York: Oxford University Press.

Rosen, A., Proctor, E. K., Morrow-Howell, N., and Staudt, M. (1995). Rationales for practice decisions: Variations in knowledge use by decision task and social work service. *Research on Social Work Practice, 15* (4), 501–523.

Rosenthal, R. (1994). Science and ethics in conducting, analyzing, and reporting psychological research. *Psychological Science, 5,* 127–134.

Sackett, D. L., Richardson, W. S., Rosenberg, W., and Haynes, R. B. (1997). *Evidence-Based Medicine: How to Practice and Teach EBM.* New York: Churchill Livingstone.

Sackett, D. L., Straus, S. E., Richardson, W. S., Rosenberg, W., and Haynes, R. D. (2000). *Evidence-Based Medicine: How to Practice and Teach EBM* (2d ed.). New York: Churchill Livingstone.

Schuerman, J., Soydan, H., MacDonald, G., Forslund, M., DeMoya D., and Boruch, R. (2002). The Campbell Collaboration. *Research on Social Work Practice, 12,* 309–317.

Schwartz, I. S., and Baer, D. M. (1991). Social validity assessment: Is current practice state of the art? *Journal of Applied Behavior Analysis, 24,* 189–204.

Schulz, K. F., Chalmers, I., Hayes, R. J., and Altman, D. G. (1995). Empirical evidence of bias: Dimensions of methodological quality associated with estimates of treatment effects in controlled trials. *Journal of the American Medical Association, 273,* 408–412.

Shahar, E. (1997). A Popperian perspective of the term "evidence-based medicine." *Journal of Evaluation in Clinical Practice, 3* (2), 109–116.

———. (1998). Evidence-based medicine: A new paradigm or the emperor's new clothes? *Journal of Evaluation in Clinical Practice, 4,* 277–282.

Sharpe, V. A., and Faden, A. I. (1998). *Medical Harm: Historical, Conceptual, and Ethical Dimensions of Iatrogenic Illness.* New York: Cambridge University Press.

Silverman, W. A. (1998). *Where's the Evidence?: Controversies in Modern Medicine.* Oxford: Oxford University Press.

Skrabanek, P., and McCormick, J. (1998). *Follies and Fallacies in Medicine* (3d ed.). Whithorn: Tarragon Press.

Spittlehouse, C., Acton, M., and Enock, K. (2000). Introducing critical appraisal skills training in UK social services: Another link between health and social care? *Journal of Interprofessional Care, 14* (4), 397–404.

Straus, S. E., and McAlister, D. C. (2000). Evidence-based medicine: A commentary on common criticisms. *Canadian Medical Journal, 163* (7), 837–841.

Szasz, T. S. (1994). *Cruel Compassion: Psychiatric Control of Society's Unwanted.* New York: Wiley.

————. (2001). *Pharmacracy: Medicine and Politics in America.* Westport, Conn.: Praeger.

Valenstein, E. S. (1986). *Great and Desperate Cures: The Rise and Decline of Psychosurgery and Other Medical Treatments for Mental Illness.* New York: Basic Books.

Watt, I., Entwistle, V., and Sowden, A. (1999). Using Guidelines to Take Evidence Into Practice. In A. Hutchinson and R. Baker (Eds.), *Making Use of Guidelines in Clinical Practice* (pp. 119–134). Abingdon, Oxon: Radcliffe Medical Press.

Webb, S. A. (2001). Some considerations on the validity of evidence-based practice in social work. British Journal of Social *Work, 31,* 57–79.

4

EMPIRICAL FOUNDATIONS FOR PRACTICE GUIDELINES IN CURRENT SOCIAL WORK KNOWLEDGE

WILLIAM J. REID AND ANNE E. FORTUNE

nsofar as possible, practice guidelines in social work should be based on interventions of demonstrated effectiveness. In this chapter we shall present a review of empirically evaluated social work programs that might serve as a basis for the development of such guidelines. In revealing the kinds of practice theories and interventions that are being subjected to empirical scrutiny (as opposed to those that are not), the review will raise issues about the relations between the world of tested programs and the world of ordinary social work practice—an issue that has important ramifications for the development of social work practice guidelines.

REVIEW OF A DECADE OF EMPIRICALLY TESTED SOCIAL WORK PROGRAMS

We surveyed what we defined as empirically tested social work intervention programs that were reported in the literature in the decade 1990–1999. We assumed that this period would be sufficient to provide an adequate base of state-of-the art interventions that had undergone testing. We expected that this criterion would also enable us to retrieve work conducted in the late 1980s but reported in the decade of the 1990s.

Ultimately, of course, practice guidelines in social work need to draw on research-supported interventions that social workers can employ regardless of which discipline produced or tested them. Nevertheless, if we are to develop such guidelines for social workers, we need to pay particular attention to evidenced-based programs that have a social work stamp.

Our unit of attention was the intervention program rather than the individual study. A program was defined as a social work intervention involving direct work with client systems, including caregivers, to bring about changes or alleviate problems in their life situations. We had in mind the kind of social work efforts with clients or client caregivers that might be used as a basis for practice guidelines. This focus resulted in the exclusion of certain tested programs, even though social workers might have been involved in running or evaluating them. Examples included training programs addressed to social work students or practitioners or programs using non–social work interventions, such as change in legal practices for trying delinquents (Risler, Sweatman, and Nackerud 1998).

We used a relatively inclusive definition of what constitutes an empirically tested intervention: An intervention had to be tested through an experimental or quasi-experimental design, in which outcomes for clients receiving the intervention were compared to outcomes in some form of control or comparison condition. We accepted single-system studies if they used some form of control—e.g., multiple baseline or withdrawal designs—and if they involved at least six subjects.

We were thus interested in programs that had undergone testing through some form of experimental design. We confined our search to programs that had been reported in the literature. In operational terms, a program had to meet either of the following criteria: (1) it had to be reported in an article that had as one of its authors a social worker or an employee of a school of social work or other social work organization or (2) it had to be directed by social workers in a social work organization. We confined our search to U.S.-published studies, which could include programs evaluated in other countries but reported in U.S. publications.

SEARCH METHODS

Our search methods consisted of the following: (1) examination of existing research reviews and meta-analyses, such as Gorey (1996), Fraser and Nelson (1997), Rosen, Proctor, and Staudt (1999), Proctor, Rosen, and Staudt (2000), covering programs evaluated during the period; (2) hand searches of the core social work journals identified by Rosen, Proctor, and Staudt (1999); (3) search of databases in the human services, such as PSYCHINFO, MEDLINE, AGELINE, and SWAB, with keywords defining experimental studies with *social work, social welfare,* or *social service* in the authors' address or affiliation field. In this way we could locate programs appearing in a great variety of non–social work journals, so long as the author was identified as being affiliated with a social work organization. (Unfortunately this information was not available on all databases.) A substantial proportion of the programs were in fact reported in non–social work journals. In most instances a program was reported in a single article, which also presented the research evaluation, but in many cases the program was presented in more than one article, which might take the form of additional studies or descriptions of the program.

SEARCH RESULTS: OVERVIEW

Application of these methods yielded a total of 130 separate programs and a larger number of articles relating to them. Although the programs were identified by who did the evaluation, in most cases the evaluators were also involved in program design or implementation; when this was not the case, the programs themselves had to be designed or conducted by social workers or carried out in social work organizations. There were only a few instances of programs that could be considered non–social work programs evaluated by social work authors.

We have undoubtedly missed some programs. Any search method has its limitations, whether it be hand searching by researchers or computer searching by keywords. Moreover, other definitions of the parameters of social work literature or controlled design would have produced a somewhat different set of programs.

The 130 programs were coded through use of a coding schedule covering various characteristics of each program and the research methods used to evaluate them. Intercoder reliability proved to be generally satisfactory.[1]

A brief questionnaire was sent to the senior or corresponding author of the principal evaluation study. We were interested in learning if the practitioners who carried out the intervention made use of written practice protocols and if these protocols were available for use by others. We also asked if the program had been implemented and if protocols had been used in the implementation. Our response rate, helped along with tracking of individuals who had moved, as well as phone follow-ups, was 80 percent.

A SOCIAL WORK FOUNDATION FOR PRACTICE GUIDELINES

Because we wanted to focus on programs that could be viewed as forming a foundation for practice guidelines, we attempted to identify programs that appeared to be effective and that could be replicated. We had in mind here the particular programs cited rather than a generic class or label. For example, many kinds of family preservation programs have been tested, and some have proved more successful than others. The idea was to use as a starting point programs that have demonstrated a degree of effectiveness.

We used two basic criteria for effectiveness and replicability: (1) the evaluation had to report positive outcome findings at termination of service for at least one major variable tested—*positive* was defined as a statistically significant difference between an intervention and comparison group on the variable; (2) there had to be evidence that practice guidelines were available or that the program was described in the evaluation report or other literature in sufficient detail that it could be implemented by others. Of the 130 programs identified, 107 met both of these criteria. Of those that did not, 16 did not report positive findings, and 10 were not considered replicable, with some of these having neither positive findings nor replicability. (Articles reporting on evaluations of the 107 programs are listed in appendix 4.1.)

Some comments on these criteria: Negative findings may tell us what might not be effective, and that is important information. They do not provide much guidance, however, as to what might be effective. We therefore did not include in our formal review the relatively small number of programs that failed to produce a positive outcome as we had defined it, although we take those programs into account in our assessment of interventions that appear to be effective.

Evidence of replicability took two forms. First, we considered an intervention replicable if the author responded on our questionnaire that practice guidelines were used and were currently available. When authors responded in the negative or did not respond, we considered descriptions of the intervention in the evaluation report or other publications. Rosen, Proctor, and Staudt (1999) had already reviewed many of these programs and had coded the interventions described as "replicable" or not, on the basis of the amount and kind of specific detail about the intervention provided by the authors. We accepted their classifications. We applied our approximation of their criteria to programs they did not review. That we report a much higher proportion of replicable studies than Rosen, Proctor, and Staudt (1999) did is mostly the result of our use of direct information from authors about use and availability of guidelines. We concur with Rosen, Proctor, and Staudt (1999) that interventions are too often inadequately described in the literature evaluating them.

In 63 percent of the programs the replicability criterion was met by the authors' response on our questionnaire that protocols were available. Moreover, 46 percent of the authors indicated that their programs had been implemented after testing, and about a third reported use of the guidelines in one or more of these implementations. The good news here is that in a majority of the programs guidelines are available and that in most of those programs the guidelines have been used in one or more program implementations. The sobering news is that we are talking about only a small number of possibly effective programs whose practice guidelines were actually used in implementations, and of course that number is for an entire decade. We have made some progress, but obviously we have a very long way to go.

PROGRAM CHARACTERISTICS

We shall now consider some general features and issues relating to this set of programs, including the kinds of problems addressed, the kinds of interventions used, and evidence for effective practice.

PROBLEM AREAS

Table 4.1 provides a picture of the main problems addressed by the programs. We made arbitrary decisions about the main problem when the program focused on more than one, such as both mentally impaired and chemically addicted clients.

As the table shows, the problem areas span the major fields of social work practice, with the heaviest concentrations in mental illness (especially the more serious forms), child/youth behavior, and substance abuse. More difficult to discern from the data in the table is an emphasis on primary prevention, which accounts for twelve programs, including seven in the area of substance abuse. It should also be noted that the majority of programs in the health area were concerned with HIV or AIDS. Problem areas that seemed not to get as much attention as one might expect given the traditions of social work practice include unemployment, welfare dependency, and marital discord. A relative lack of attention to health issues aside from those relating to AIDS and to aging is also notable.

INTERVENTION CHARACTERISTICS

What can be said about the interventions used in these programs? First we considered what modality the program used to deliver its interventions; individual, family, group, or mixed were the choices here. The dominant modality was some form of group program (58%), typically small groups. Programs centered on the individual constituted 20 percent of the sample, and family programs accounted for 9 percent. In all but thirteen of the programs we were able to determine the approximate duration of intervention. The majority were short-term programs. For 62 percent the duration of intervention was twelve or fewer weeks. Only 12 percent lasted longer than one year.

TABLE 4.1

PROBLEM AREA	PROGRAMS
Mental illness	29
Serious mental illness	14
Stress management	4
Sex abuse survivors	2
Other	9
Child/youth behavior	16
Substance abuse	13
Aging	10
Health	11
Domestic violence	7
Child abuse/placement risk	11
Other	10
Total	107

All the programs were developed to deal with very specific problems or situations—for example, settlement of homeless persons with a mental illness, prevention of unsafe sexual practices among drug addicts, or social skills training for learning-disabled children. We were, however, interested in whether common elements existed among the programs regardless of the specific intent. Thus, we coded the general intervention approach, structure, and specific techniques in each program. Categories were developed empirically, using the descriptions given by authors. We coded an intervention approach or technique only if the authors explicitly mentioned it, but "use of relationship" was coded if the published description explicitly used the terms *relationship, empathy, support from the worker,* or similar phrases.

As already discussed, description of interventions in published research articles is often inadequate, so this approach has obvious drawbacks. Most interventions are undoubtedly underrepresented. Nevertheless, we assumed that authors included terms that they felt were most essential to characterize their interventions. Consequently, the approaches and techniques as we coded them may be considered the distinctive aspects of the programs.

INTERVENTION APPROACH Many programs drew from several intervention approaches to put together a package of interventions—for example, cognitive-behavioral skills training and social networking for families at risk

TABLE 4.2 Intervention Approaches Used in Programs

APPROACH	PROGRAMS USING	
	NUMBER	PERCENTAGE
Cognitive-behavioral	39	37
Learning theory/behavioral	15	14
Problem-solving	15	14
Task-centered	4	4
Combined cognitive-behavioral, learning theory, problem-solving, task-centered		
	54	51
Family or general systems	8	8
Support/mutual aid	9	8
Social support (not group)	5	5
Combined systems (family, systems, social support, mutual aid, generalist)		
	18	17
Psychoeducation/education	23	21
Case management	12	11
Psychodynamic	3	3
Explicitly eclectic	5	5
Empowerment	4	4
No theory base given	10	9
Other theory	22	21

of removal of a child. Consequently, we coded as many approaches as were mentioned explicitly.

As can be seen from table 4.2, cognitive behavioral and related approaches were mentioned most frequently. In more than half of the programs (54%) there was mention of at least one of four related "action-oriented" perspectives—cognitive-behavioral, learning theory, problem-solving, and task-centered. These approaches were offered largely through group formats.

After cognitive-behavioral, the next most frequently mentioned approach was psychoeducation (21% of the programs). Usually psychoeducation described a focus on formal instruction about a topic combined with some individualized support and learning of coping skills. It was mentioned most in programs dealing with health problems and serious mental illness.

All other approaches were mentioned in less than 10 percent of the programs. However, approaches that emphasize functioning in larger systems (e.g., family systems, social support, and mutual aid) were mentioned by nearly one-fifth of the programs. These systemic approaches were mentioned proportionately more in programs dealing with child maltreatment/placement risk and frail elderly. Case management as a perspective was named in 10 percent of the programs, all using either individual or family approaches.

The "other" category included a wide range of approaches such as the strengths perspective, reminiscence, life review, social inoculation, multimodal voice therapy, social exchange, psychodrama, stress theory, eye movement desensitization and reprocessing, family preservation, spirituality, empathic coercion, humanistic psychotherapy, and mediation.

In sum, the intervention methods tested in these programs drew heavily on cognitive-behavioral approaches, some systems theories that included family and other social supports, and a wide array of theories from numerous disciplines. Psychodynamic and other humanistic approaches play only a very minor role in this set of programs, in stark contrast to their popularity in the world of social work practice. Certain approaches that are stressed in social work education, such as generalist and empowerment, were also underrepresented. Finally, there appeared to be much more emphasis on group intervention approaches than is characteristic of social work practice.

STRUCTURE We coded the program descriptions on a continuum of structure and uniformity (table 4.3). At one end were interventions that were highly structured and uniform across individuals, including lecture-like presentations, videos, or reading material. These highly structured programs accounted for nearly a quarter of the programs and were used disproportionately in domestic violence and mental health. Next were programs that had high structure but expectation of individual variation—for example, scripted training programs in which each individual was expected to use his or her own situation as the basis for exercises or discussion. The most frequent programs (43 percent), these were heavily used in alcohol/addictions (ten of thirteen programs) and child or youth behavior problems (twelve of sixteen programs).

Lower on the scale were programs—14 percent of the total—characterized by loose structure and heavy reliance on participants to set the direction—for example, a standard framework for sessions that included an introductory "checking in," presentation, discussion, ending ritual, and homework but varied content by person and session. At the least structured end of the continuum were programs—about a fifth of the total—with no specified interventions, or a menu of interventions from which practitioners

TABLE 4.3 Amount of Structure and Uniformity

	NUMBER	PERCENTAGE
Unstructured	19	18
Loose structure	15	14
Structured with individualization	45	42
High structure, no individualization	26	24
Total	107	100

selected. Each participant's experience was quite different, for example, in case management or family preservation.

Not surprisingly, the amount of structure varied with the intervention approach. For example, the great majority of the cognitive-behavioral and psychoeducational programs tended to be highly or moderately structured, whereas all of the case management programs were relatively unstructured. A higher degree of structure was also found in group programs than in individual or family programs. In sum, the majority of the programs were quite highly structured, although most included some opportunity for individualization of work. This degree of structure is doubtless greater than one would find in most social work programs.

INTERVENTION TECHNIQUES The most commonly mentioned intervention (60 percent of the programs) was formal instruction, such as education, didactic presentations, and training modules (table 4.4). No other intervention was mentioned in even half the programs. Some form of cognitive-behavioral skills training (such as social skills, problem solving, anger management, assertion) was used in 59 percent of the programs.

To determine if interventions were used together, we used hierarchical cluster analysis.[2] The analysis suggested two distinctive clusters. The more clear of the two consisted of case management, concrete services, and the use of relationship. A second cluster was defined by group approaches that made use of skills training, education, and group processes.

SUMMARY These analyses suggest two distinct types of programs. The case management programs use individual or family modalities, are unstructured and individualized, rely on case management interventions, offer concrete services, and use an individual or team interpersonal relationship. These pro-

TABLE 4.4 Frequency of Intervention Techniques

INTERVENTION	PROGRAMS USING	
	NUMBER	PERCENTAGE
Formal instruction	60	56
Homework assignments	36	34
Reinforcement and feedback	36	34
Practice skills in session	36	34
Problem solving skills training	33	31
Discussion	32	30
Use of group process	31	29
Use of relationship	29	27
Networking and social support	28	27
Use of media (tapes, CD-ROMs)	23	22
Modeling by practitioner	22	21
Coping skills training (general)	22	21
Communication skills training	19	18
Cognitive restructuring	17	16
Self-talk	16	15
Case management	16	15
Stress management skills	16	15
Reading assignments	15	14
Anger management training	15	14
Relaxation skills training	14	13
Concrete services	14	13
Socialization to treatment	14	13
Termination rituals	14	13
Social skills training	13	12
Games	13	12
Systematic self-monitoring (log, diary)	11	10
Conflict resolution skills training	10	19
Assertion skills training	10	19
Arts like storytelling, music, etc.	9	8
Parenting skills training	7	7
Culturally specific interventions	6	6
Other	31	29

grams are typically used in working with the severely mentally ill and with family preservation. A second type is a structured cognitive-behavioral group intervention that includes some type of skills training (such as parenting, assertiveness, anger management, problem solving), instruction, and, often, skills practice, homework, and other cognitive interventions. Such group programs are typically used in mental health, child and youth behavior, and health, both for treatment of acknowledged problems and for prevention of potential problems such as illness or substance abuse.

EVALUATION DESIGNS

The programs were tested through a variety of experimental designs, which on the whole were characterized by a number of strengths. The majority (60%) were evaluated through randomized designs, with an additional 8 percent using strong quasi-experimental designs (natural groups with statistical control for baseline differences). When investigator-created groups, such as wait-list or overflow groups, were used, statistical controls were usually employed to control for baseline differences. The great majority of the studies (63%) had sample sizes greater than fifty; 43 percent had follow-ups of six months or more.

It should be noted that three programs were evaluated through controlled single-system designs, all multiple baselines. As mentioned earlier, we excluded single-system evaluations with fewer than six subjects.

OUTCOMES

As has already been noted, the great majority of programs from the 130 that we retrieved reported positive results at termination of service. These results are encouraging—a far cry from the generally negative findings in the experiments of a generation ago (Kirk and Reid 2001).

Our optimism is tempered, however, by at least three cautions. First, an overwhelming proportion of the presumably effective and replicable evaluations—more than 90 percent—were conducted either by the developers of the program or by investigators who appeared to be supportive of it. Experimental demand or investigator allegiance thus becomes a matter of concern. These kinds of biases can, of course, inflate experimental effects in intervention evaluations, as a good deal of research has demonstrated (Robinson et al. 1990; Smith, Glass, and Miller 1980; Gorey 1996). Second, the most common design (41 percent of the programs) involved simply the comparison of an experimental intervention with some form of no-intervention control condition. Such studies offer little control for common factors, such as the effects of attention. Superior designs in this respect—that is, those that used both alternative interventions and a no-treatment control—were employed in only 17 percent of the evaluations. Finally, there were virtually no replications conducted by independent investigators. Such replications are, of course, necessary to resolve doubts about biases arising from investigator allegiance and other sources in original studies.

—

Most social work programs tested during the past decade have produced positive outcomes, suggesting that the profession has made strides in the creation and identification of effective interventions. It was particularly encouraging to find that a large proportion of the programs made use of protocols that can be made available to others. Protocols used in these and future studies could serve as an important basis for the development of practice guidelines.

One of the issues our study raises concerns two overlapping worlds of practice. The experimental programs we have presented define one of those worlds. The other world consists of the kind of practice in which social workers ordinarily engage. The two worlds have much in common, but they still diverge in important respects. In the world of the experimental programs, it appears that intervention is more structured, more likely to use group methods, more cognitive-behavioral, and more concerned with primary prevention. In the world of everyday practice one finds considerable attention to any number of approaches that are rarely found in these tested programs—for example, generalist, ecological, narrative, and psychodynamic. These estimates are based on our impressions of current practice and its literature rather than on hard data, but they are not inconsistent with what meager information exists on what social workers actually do. (See, for example, Jensen, Bergin, and Greaves [1990]; Teare and Sheafor 1995; Timberlake, Sabatino, and Martin [1997]). In our judgment, the best way of resolving the disparities between these worlds is to have more rigorous testing of approaches that may be valuable but are underevaluated. By this means we may be able to develop empirically based practice guidelines that reflect the broad range of interventions that social workers actually use.

NOTES

1. *Coding and reliability.* A 25 percent random sample of the studies was independently coded. Reliability proved satisfactory for most variables. Percentages of agreement ranged from 52 to 92, with a median of 78. Items with percentages of agreement below 60 all involved three or more values. Cohen's kappa (k) was calculated for each percentage point of agreement. Kappas measure the extent to which agreement between coders occurs beyond chance expectation, with significant kappas in excess of .40 indicating at least fair agreement. Kappas failed to reach significance ($p < .05$) on only three variables. Two were excluded from the analysis, and one was revised by merging categories. The kappa for the revised measure was significant. Significant kappas ranged from .36 to .86, with a median of .73.

2. *Analysis.* Cluster analysis groups items by "agglomerating"—putting together at each step the two items used most together, or by joining items to previously joined clusters (SPSS 1998). Because interventions were coded "mentioned" or "not mentioned," we used hierarchical cluster analysis with the binomial squared Euclidean distance measure and Ward's method for clustering.

REFERENCES

Fraser, M. W., and Nelson, K. E. (1997). Effectiveness of family preservation services. *Social Work Research, 21,* 138–154.

Gorey, K. M. (1996). Effectiveness of social work intervention research: Internal versus external evaluations. *Social Work Research, 20* (2), 119–128.

Jensen, J. P., Bergin, A. E., and Greaves, D. W. (1990). The meaning of eclecticism: New survey and analysis of components. *Professional Psychology: Research and Practice, 21* (2), 124–130.

Kirk, S. A., and Reid, W. J. (2001). *Science and Social Work: A Critical Appraisal.* New York: Columbia University Press.

Proctor, E. K., Rosen, A., and Staudt, M. M. (2000). "Targets of Change and Interventive Methods in Social Work Treatment: An Empirically Based Prototype for Developing Practice Guidelines." Paper presented at the Fourth Annual Conference of the Society for Social Work and Research, January 29–31, Charleston, South Carolina.

Risler, E. A., Sweatman, T., and Nackerud, L. (1998). Evaluating the Georgia legislative waiver's effectiveness in deterring juvenile crime. *Research on Social Work Practice, 8,* 657–667.

Robinson, R. A., Berman, J. S., Neimeyer, R. A., and Morris, P. (1990). Psychotherapy for the treatment of depression: A comprehensive review of controlled outcome research. *Psychological Bulletin, 108,* 30–49.

Rosen, A., Proctor, E. K., and Staudt, M. M. (1999). Social work research and the quest for effective practice. *Social Work Research, 23,* 4–14.

Smith, M. L., Glass, G. V., and Miller, T. I. (1980). The Benefits of Psychotherapy. Baltimore: Johns Hopkins University Press.

Teare, B., and Sheafor, B. (1995). *Practice-Sensitive Social Work Education: An Empirical Analysis of Social Work Practice and Practitioners.* Washington, D.C.: Council on Social Work Education.

Timberlake, E. M., Sabatino, C. A., and Martin, J. A. (1997). Advanced practitioners in clinical social work: A profile. *Social Work, 42,* 374–386.

APPENDIX 4.1 EVALUATIONS OF PROGRAMS MEETING CRITERIA OF EFFECTIVENESS AND REPLICABILITY

Arnold, E. M., Smith, T. E., Harrison, D. F., and Springer, D. W. (1999). The effects of an abstinence-based sex education program on middle school students' knowledge and beliefs. *Research in Social Work Practice, 9,* 10–24.

Bagley, C., and Pritchard, C. (1998). The reduction of problem behaviors and school exclusion in at-risk youth: An experimental study of school social work with cost-benefit analysis. *Child and Family Social Work, 3,* 219–226.

Bagley, C., and Young, L. (1998). Long-term evaluation of group counseling for women with a history of child sexual abuse: Focus on depression, self-esteem, suicidal behaviors, and social support. *Social Work with Groups, 21,* 63–73.

Barber, J. G. (1992). Evaluating parent education groups: Effects on sense of competence and social isolation. *Research on Social Work Practice, 2,* 28–38.

———. (1993). An application of microcomputer technology to the drug education of prisoners. *Journal of Alcohol and Drug Education, 38,* 14–23.

Barber, J. G., and Crisp, B. R. (1995). Social support and prevention of relapse following treatment for alcohol abuse. *Research on Social Work Practice, 5,* 283–297.

Barber, J. G., and Gilbertson, R. (1996). An experiential study of brief unilateral intervention for the partners of heavy drinkers. *Research on Social Work Practice, 6,* 325–336.

———. (1998). Evaluation of a self-help manual for partners of heavy drinkers. *Research on Social Work Practice, 8,* 141–151.

Blanchard, C., Toseland, R., and McCallion, P. (1996). The effects of a problem-solving intervention with spouses of cancer patients. *Journal of Psychosocial Oncology, 14,* 1–21.

Blankertz, L. E., and Cnaan, R. A. (1992). Principles of care for dually diagnosed homeless persons: Findings from a demonstration project. *Research on Social Work Practice, 2,* 448–464.

———. (1994). Assessing the impact of two residential programs for dually diagnosed homeless individuals. *Social Service Review, 68,* 536–560.

Botvin, G. J., Schinke, S. P., Epstein, J. A., Diaz, T., and Botvin, E. M. (1994). Effectiveness of culturally focused and generic skills training approaches to alcohol and drug abuse among minority youths. *Psychology of Addictive Behaviors, 8,* 116–127.

———. (1995). Effectiveness of culturally focused and generic skills training approaches to alcohol and drug abuse among minority adolescents: Two year follow-up results. *Psychology of Addictive Behaviors, 9,* 183–194.

Bradshaw, W. H. (1993). Coping-skills training versus a problem-solving approach with schizophrenic patients. Hospital and Community Psychiatry, 44, 1102–1104.

———. (1996). Structured group work for individuals with schizophrenia: A coping skills approach. *Research on Social Work Practice, 6,* 139–154.

Brannen, S. J., and Rubin, A. (1996). Comparing the effectiveness of gender-specific and couples groups in a court-mandated spouse abuse treatment program. *Research on Social Work Practice, 6,* 405–424.

Brekke, J. S., Long, J. D., and Nesbitt, N. (1997). The impact of service characteristics on functional outcomes from community support programs for persons with schizophrenia: A growth curve analysis. *Journal of Consulting and Clinical Psychology, 65* (3), 464–475.

Carbonell, D. M., and Parteleno-Barehmi, C. (1999). Psychodrama groups for girls coping with trauma. *International Journal of Group Psychotherapy, 49,* 285–306.

Catalano, R. F., Haggerty, K. P., Gainey, R. R., and Hoppe, M. J. (1997). Reducing parental risk factors for children's substance misuse: Preliminary outcomes with opiate-addicted parents. *Substance Abuse and Misuse, 32,* 699–721.

———. (1999). An experimental intervention with families of substance abusers: One-year follow-up of the Focus on Families project. *Addiction, 94,* 241–254.

Cliffone, J. (1993). Suicide prevention: A classroom presentation to adolescents. *Social Work, 38,* 197–204.

Collins, M. E., Bybee, D., and Mowbray, C. T. (1998). Effectiveness of supported education for individuals with psychiatric disabilities: Results from an experimental study. *Community Mental Health Journal, 34,* 595–613.

———. (1999). Establishing individualized goals in a supported education intervention: Program influences on goal-setting and attainment. *Research on Social Work Practice, 9,* 483–508.

Coyne, A. C., Potenza, M., and Broken-Nose, M. A. (1995). Caregiving and dementia: The impact of telephone helpline services. *American Journal of Alzheimer's Disease, 10,* 27–32.

De Anda, D. (1998). The evaluation of a stress management program for middle school adolescents. *Child and Adolescent Social Work Journal, 15,* 73–85.

De Anda, D., Darroch, P., Davidson, M., Gilly, J., and Morejon, A. (1990). Stress management for pregnant adolescents and adolescent mothers: A pilot study. *Child and Adolescent Social Work, 7,* 53–67.

DeMar, J. (1997). A school-based group intervention to strengthen personal and social competencies in latency-age children. *Social Work in Education, 19,* 219–231.

Dhooper, S. S., Green, S. M., Huff, M. B., and Austin-Murphy, J. (1993). Efficacy of a group approach to reducing depression in nursing home elderly residents. *Journal of Gerontological Social Work, 20,* 87–100.

Dhooper, S. S., and Schneider, B. L. (1995). Evaluation of a school-based child abuse prevention program. *Research on Social Work Practice, 5,* 36–46.

Draine, J. (1997). A critical review of randomized field trials of case management for individuals with serious and persistent mental illness. *Research on Social Work Practice, 7,* 32–51.

Dupper, D. R. (1998). An alternative to suspension for middle school youths with behavior problems: Findings from a "school survival" group. *Research on Social Work Practice, 8* (3), 354–366.

Dzigielewski, S. F. (1991). Social group work with the family members of elderly nursing home residents: A controlled evaluation. *Research on Social Work Practice, 1,* 358–370.

Edelson, J. L., and Syers, M. (1991). The effects of group treatment for men who batter: An eighteen-month follow-up study. *Research on Social Work Practice, 1,* 227–243.

Edmond, T., Rubin, A., and Wambach, K. G. (1999). The effectiveness of EDMR with adult female survivors of childhood sexual abuse. *Social Work Research, 23,* 103–116.

El-Bassel, N., and Schilling, R. F. (1992). Fifteen-month follow-up of women methadone patients taught skills to reduce heterosexual HIV transmission. *Public Health Reports, 107,* 500–503.

Feldman, L. H. (1991). Evaluating the Impact of Intensive Family Preservation Services in New Jersey. In K. Well and D. E. Biegel (Eds.), *Family Preservation Services* (pp. 47–71). Newbury Park, Calif.: Sage.

Fraser, M. W., Pecora, P. J., and Haapala, D. A. (1991). *Families in Crisis: The Impact of Intensive Family Preservation Services.* New York: A. de Gruyter.

Gammon, E. A., and Rose, S. D. (1991). The coping skills training program for parents of children with disabilities: An experimental evaluation. *Research on Social Work Practice, 1,* 244–256.

Goldapple, G. C., and Montgomery, D. (1993). Evaluating a behaviorally based intervention to improve client retention in therapeutic community treatment for drug dependency. *Research on Social Work Practice, 3,* 21–39.

Goodman, C. (1990). Evaluation of a model self-help telephone program: Impact on natural networks. *Social Work, 35,* 556–562.

Goodman, C., and Pynoos, J. (1990). A model telephone information and support program for caregivers of Alzheimer's patients. *Gerontologist, 30,* 399–404.

Hall, J., Schlesinger, D., and Dineen, J. (1997). Social skills training in groups with developmentally disabled adults. *Research on Social Work Practice, 7,* 187–201.

Hawkins, J. D., Catalano, R. F., Kosterman, R., Abbott, R., and Hill, K. G. (1999). Preventing adolescent health-risk behaviors by strengthening protection during childhood. *Archives of Pediatric Adolescent Medicine, 153,* 226–234.

Hawkins, J. D., Jenson, J. M., Catalano, R. F., and Wells, E. A. (1991). Effects of a skills training intervention with juvenile delinquents. *Research on Social Work Practice, 1,* 107–121.

Henrickx, H. A., Kinney, R. F., Clarke, G. N., and Paulson, R. I. (1997). Assertive community treatment versus usual care in engaging and retaining clients with severe mental illness. *Psychiatric Services, 48* (10), 1297–1306.

Hepler, J. B. (1994). Evaluating the effectiveness of a social skills program for preadolescents. *Research on Social Work Practice, 4,* 411–435.

———. (1997). Evaluating a social skills program for children with learning disabilities. *Social Work with Groups, 20,* 21–36.

Hogarty, G., Greenwald, D., Ulrich, R., Kornblith, S., DiBarry, A., Cooley, S., Carter, M., and Flesher, S. (1997). Three-year trials of personal therapy among schizophrenic patients living with or independent of family. II. Effects on adjustment of patients. *American Journal of Psychiatry, 154,* 1514–1524.

Hogarty, G. E., Anderson, C. M., Reiss, D. J., Kornblith, S. J., Greenwald, D. P., Ulrich, R. F., Carter, M., and EPICS. (1991). Family psychoeducation, social skills training, and maintenance chemotherapy in the aftercare treatment of schizophrenia. II. Two-year effects of a controlled study on relapse and adjustment. *Archives of General Psychiatry, 48,* 300–347.

Icard, L. D., Schilling, R. F., and El-Bassel, N. (1995). Reducing HIV infection among African Americans by targeting the African American family. *Social Work Research, 19,* 153–163.

Iwaniec, D. (1997). Evaluating parent training for emotionally abusive and neglectful parents: Comparing individual and group intervention. *Research on Social Work Practice, 7,* 329–349.

Jensen, C. (1994). Psychosocial treatment of depression in women: Nine single-subject evaluations. *Research on Social Work Practice, 4,* 267–283.

Johnson, K., Bryant, D. D., Collins, D. A., Noe, T. D., Strader, T. N., and Berbaum, M. (1998). Preventing and reducing alcohol and other drug use among high-risk youths by increasing family resilience. *Social Work, 43,* 297–309.

Klein, A. R., Cnaan, R. A., and Whitecraft, J. (1998). Significance of peer social support with dually diagnosed clients: Findings from a pilot study. *Research on Social Work Practice, 8,* 529–551.

Korr, W. S., and Joseph, A. (1995). Housing the homeless mentally ill: Findings from Chicago. *Journal of Social Service Research, 21,* 53–67.

Larkin, R., and Thyer, B. (1999). Evaluating cognitive-behavioral group counseling to improve elementary school students' self-esteem, self-control, and classroom behavior. *Behavioral Interventions, 14,* 147–161.

Lewis, R. E., Walton, E., and Fraser, M. W. (1995). Examining family reunification services: A process analysis of a successful experiment. *Research on Social Work Practice, 5,* 259–282.

Loneck, B., Garrett, J. A., and Banks, S. M. (1996). A comparison of the Johnson Intervention with four other methods of referral to outpatient treatment. *American Journal of Drug and Alcohol Abuse, 22,* 233–246.

Macgowan, M. J. (1997). An evaluation of a dating violence prevention program for middle school students. *Violence and Victims, 12,* 223–235.

Macias, C., Kinney, R., Farley, O. W., Jackson, R., and Vos, B. (1994). The role of case management within a community support system: Partnership with psychosocial rehabilitation. *Community Mental Health Journal, 30,* 323–339.

Magen, R. H., and Rose, S. D. (1994). Parents in groups: Problem solving versus behavioral skills training. *Research on Social Work Practice, 4,* 172–191.

Mancoske, R. J., Standifer, D., and Cauley, C. (1994). The effectiveness of brief counseling services for battered women. *Research on Social Work Practice, 4,* 53–63.

Marcenko, M. O., Spence, M., and Samost, L. (1996). Outcomes of a home visitation trial for pregnant and postpartum women at-risk for child placement. *Children and Youth Service Review, 18,* 243–259.

McCallion, P., Toseland, R. W., and Freeman, K. (1999). An evaluation of a family visit education program. *Journal of the American Geriatrics Society, 47* (2), 203–214.

McCallion, P., Toseland, R. W., Lacey, D., and Banks, S. (1999). Educating nursing assistants to communicate more effectively with nursing home residents with dementia. *Gerontologist, 39,* 1–12.

McKay, M. M., Gonzales, J., Quintana, E., Kim, L., and Abdul-Adil, J. (1999). Multiple family groups: An alternative for reducing disruptive behavioral difficulties of urban children. *Research on Social Work Practice, 9,* 593–607.

McKay, M. M., Nudelman, R., McCadam, K., and Gonzales, J. (1996). Social work engagement: An approach to involving inner-city children and their families. *Research on Social Work Practice, 6,* 462–472.

McKay, M. M., Stoewe, J., McCadam, K., and Gonzales, J. (1996). Addressing the barriers to mental health services for inner-city children and their caregivers. *Community Mental Health Journal, 32,* 353–361.

———. (1998). Increasing access to child mental health services for urban children and their caregivers. *Health and Social Work, 23* (1), 9–15.

Meezan, W., and McCroskey, J. (1996). Improving family functioning through family preservation services: Results of the Los Angeles experiment. *Family Preservation Journal, 1,* 9–26.

Meezan, W., and O'Keefe, M. (1998). Evaluating the effectiveness of multifamily group therapy in child abuse and neglect. *Research on Social Work Practice, 8,* 330–353.

Mitchell, C. G. (1999). Treating anxiety in a managed care setting: A controlled comparison of medication alone versus medication plus cognitive-behavioral group therapy. *Research on Social Work Practice, 9,* 188–199.

Mittelman, M. S., Ferris, S. H., Steinberg, G., Schulman, E., Mackell, J. A., Ambinder, A., and Cohen, J. (1993). An intervention that delays institutionalization of Alzheimer's disease patients: Treatment of spouse-caregivers. *Gerontologist, 33,* 730–740.

Morrow, D. F. (1996). Coming-out issues for adult lesbians: A group intervention. *Social Work, 41,* 647–657.

Morrow-Howell, N., Becker-Kemppainen, S., and Judy, L. (1998). Evaluating an intervention for the elderly at increased risk of suicide. *Research on Social Work Practice, 8,* 28–47.

Mowbray, C. T., Collins, M., and Bybee, D. (1999). Supported education for individuals with psychiatric disabilities: Long-term outcomes from an experimental study. *Social Work Research, 23,* 89–100.

Mowbray, C. T., Collins, M. E., Plum, T. B., Masterton, T., and Mulder, R. (1997). Harbinger I: The development and evaluation of the first pact replication. *Administration and Policy in Mental Health, 25,* 105–123.

Nugent, W. R., Champlin, D., and Wiinimaki, L. (1997). The effects of anger control training on adolescent antisocial behavior. *Research on Social Work Practice, 7,* 446–462.

O'Connor, R., and Korr, W. S. (1996). A model for school social work facilitation of teacher self-efficacy and empowerment. *Social Work, 41,* 45–51.

O'Donnell, J., Hawkins, J. D., Catalano, R. F., Abbott, R. D., and Day, L. E. (1999). Preventing school failure, drug use, and delinquency among low-income children: Long-term intervention in elementary school. *American Journal of Orthopsychiatry, 65,* 87–100.

Palmer, S. E., Brown, R. A., and Barrera, M. E. (1992). Group treatment program for abusive husbands: Long-term evaluation. *American Journal of Orthopsychiatry, 62,* 276–283.

Patterson, D. A., and Lee, M. S. (1998). Intensive case management and rehospitalization: A survival analysis. Research on Social Work Practice, 8 (2), 152–171.

Peak, T., Toseland, R. W., and Banks, S. M. (1995). The impact of a spouse-caregiver support group on care recipient health care costs. *Journal of Aging and Health, 7,* 427–449.

Pomeroy, E. C., Kiam, R., and Abel, E. (1998). Meeting the mental health needs of incarcerated women. *Health and Social Work, 23,* 71–76.

———. (1999). The effectiveness of a psychoeducational group for HIV-infected/affected incarcerated women. *Research on Social Work Practice, 9,* 171–187.

Pomeroy, E. C., Rubin, A., Van Laningham, L., and Walker, R. J. (1997). "Straight Talk": The effectiveness of a psychoeducational group intervention for heterosexuals with HIV/AIDS. *Research on Social Work Practice, 7,* 149–164.

Pomeroy, E. C., Rubin, A., and Walker, R. J. (1995). Effectiveness of a psychoeducational and task-centered group intervention for family members of people with AIDS. *Social Work Research, 19,* 142–152.

Quadagno, D., Harrison, D. F., Eberstein, I. W., Sly, D. F., Yoshioka, M., and Soler, H. (1996–1997). The development and implementation of a cognitive-based intervention aimed at culturally diverse women at risk for HIV/AIDS. *International Quarterly of Community Health Education, 16,* 271–285.

Reid, W. J., and Bailey-Dempsey, C. (1995). The effects of monetary incentives on school performance. *Families in Society: The Journal of Contemporary Human Services, 76,* 331–340.

Ressler, L. (1991). Improving elderly recall with bimodal presentation: A natural experiment of discharge planning. *Gerontologist, 31,* 364–370.

Richter, N. L., Snider, E., and Gorey, K. M. (1997). Group work intervention with female survivors of childhood sexual abuse. *Research on Social Work Practice, 7,* 53–69.

Rife, J. C., and Belcher, J. R. (1994). Assisting unemployed older workers to become re-employed: An experimental evaluation. *Research on Social Work Practice, 4,* 3–13.

Roffman, R. A., Downey, L., Beadnell, B., Gordon, J. R., Craver, J. N., and Stephens, R. S. (1997). Cognitive-behavioral group counseling to prevent HIV transmission in gay and bisexual men: Factors contributing to successful risk reduction. *Research on Social Work Practice, 7*, 165–185.

Schafer, R., and Erickson, S. D. (1993). Evolving Family Preservation Services: The Florida Experience. In E. S. Morton and R. K. Grigsby (Eds.), *Advancing Family Preservation Practice* (pp. 56–69). Newbury Park, Calif.: Sage.

Schilling, R. F., and El-Bassel, N. (1992). Fifteen-month follow-up of women Methadone patients taught skills to reduce heterosexual HIV transmission. *Public Health Reports, 107*, 297–303.

Schilling, R. F., El-Bassel, N., Schinke, S. P., Gordon, K., and Nichols, S. (1991). Building skills of recovering women drug users to reduce heterosexual AIDS transmission. *Public Health Reports, 106*, 297–303.

Schinke, S. P., Gordon, A. N., and Weston, R. E. (1990). Self-instruction to prevent HIV infection among African-American and Hispanic American students. *Journal of Consulting and Clinical Psychology, 58*, 432–436.

Schinke, S. P., Schilling, R. F., and Snow, W. H. (1987). Stress management with adolescents at the junior high transition: An outcome evaluation of coping skills intervention. *Journal of Human Stress, 13*, 16–22.

Schinke, S. P., Singer, B., Cole, K., and Contento, I. (1996). Reducing cancer risk among Native American adolescents. *Preventive Medicine, 25*, 146–155.

Schinke, S. P., and Tepavac, L. (1995). Substance abuse prevention among elementary school students. *Drugs and Society, 8*, 15–27.

Schwartz, I. M., AuClair, P., and Harris, L. J. (1991). Family Preservation Services as an Alternative to the Out-of-Home Placement of Adolescents: The Hennepin County Experience. In K. Wells and D. Biegel (Eds.), *Family Preservation Services: Research and Evaluation* (pp. 33–46). Newbury Park, Calif.: Sage.

Shepard, M. (1997). Site-based services for residents of single-room occupancy hotels. *Social Work, 42*, 585–592.

Snow, D. J. (1992). Marital therapy with parents to alleviate behavioral disorders in their children. *Research on Social Work Practice, 2*, 172–183.

Solomon, P., and Draine, J. (1995). One-year outcomes of a randomized trial of consumer case management. *Evaluation and Program Planning, 18*, 117–127.

Solomon, P., Draine, J., Mannion, E., and Meisel, M. (1997). Effectiveness of two models of brief family education: Retention gains by family members of adults with serious mental illness. *American Journal of Orthopsychiatry, 67*, 177–186.

Sprang, G. (1997). Victim impact panels: An examination of the effectiveness of this program on lowering recidivism and changing offenders' attitudes about drinking and driving. *Journal of Social Service Research, 22*, 73–84.

Stern, S. B. (1999). Anger management in parent-adolescent conflict. *American Journal of Family Therapy, 27*, 181–193.

Stosny, S. (1994). "Shadows of the Heart": A dramatic video for the treatment resistance of spouse abusers. *Social Work, 39*, 686–693.

Strachan, W., and Gorey, K. M. (1997). Infant simulator lifespace intervention: Pilot investigation of an adolescent pregnancy prevention program. *Child and Adolescent Social Work Journal, 3*, 171–179.

Subramanian, K. (1991). Structured group work for the management of chronic pain: An experimental investigation. *Research on Social Work Practice, 1,* 32–45.

Test, M. A., Knoedler, W. H., Allness, D. J., Burke, S. S., Brown, R. L., and Wallisch, L. S. (1991). Long-term community care through an assertive continuous treatment team. *Advances in Neuropsychiatry and Psychopharmacology, 1,* 239–246.

Thomas, E. J., and Ager, R. D. (1993). Unilateral Family Therapy with Spouses of Uncooperative Alcohol Abusers. In T. J. O'Farrell (Ed.), *Treating Alcohol Problems* (pp. 71–86). New York: Guilford Press.

Thomas, E. J., Yoshioka, M. R., Ager, R., and Adams, K. B. (1990). Experimental Outcomes of Spouse Intervention to Reach the Uncooperative Alcohol Abuser: Preliminary Report. In *Proceedings of the International Society for Bio-medical Research and the Research Society on Alcoholism,* June 17–22, Toronto, Canada.

Tolman, R. T., and Bhosley, G. (1990). A comparison of two types of pre-group preparation for men who batter. *Journal of Social Service Research, 13,* 33–43.

Tolson, E. R., McDonald, S., and Moriarty, A. R. (1992). Peer mediation among high school students: A test of effectiveness. *Social Work in Education, 14* (2).

Toseland, R. W. (1990). Long-term effectiveness of peer-led and professionally led support groups for caregivers. *Social Service Review, 64,* 308–327.

Toseland, R. W., Blanchard, C. G., and McCallion, P. (1995). A problem solving intervention for caregivers of cancer patients. *Social Science Medicine, 40,* 1–21.

Toseland, R. W., Diehl, M., Freeman, K., Manzanares, T., Naleppa, M., and McCallion, P. (1997). The impact of validation group therapy on nursing home residents with dementia. *Journal of Applied Gerontology, 16,* 31–50.

Toseland, R. W., Labrecque, M. S., Goebel, S. T., and Whitney, M. H. (1992). An evaluation of a group program for spouses of frail elderly veterans. *Gerontologist, 32,* 382–390.

Toseland, R. W., O'Donnell, J. C., Englehardt, J. B., Hendler, S., Richie, J. T., and Jue, D. (1996). Outpatient geriatric evaluation and management results of a randomized trial. *Medical Care, 34,* 624–640.

Toseland, R. W., Rossiter, C. M., Peak, T., and Smith, G. C. (1990). Comparative effectiveness of individual and group interventions to support family caregivers. *Social Work, 35,* 209–217.

Toseland, R. W., and Smith, G. C. (1990). Effectiveness of individual counseling by professional and peer helpers for family caregivers of the elderly. *Psychology and Aging, 5,* 256–263.

Tutty, L. M. (1997). Child sexual abuse prevention programs: Evaluating "Who do you tell." *Child Abuse and Neglect, 21,* 869–881.

Umbreit, M. S. (1994). Crime victims confront their offenders: The impact of a Minneapolis mediation program. *Research on Social Work Practice, 4,* 436–447.

———. (1999). Victim-offender mediation in Canada: The impact of an emerging social work intervention. *International Social Work, 42,* 215–227.

Van Noppen, B., Stefetee, G., McCorkle, B. H., and Pato, M. (1997). Group and multi-family behavior treatment for obsessive compulsive disorder: A pilot study. *Journal of Anxiety Disorders, 11* (4), 431–446.

Walton, E. (1998). In-home family-focused reunification: A six-year follow-up of a successful experiment. *Social Work Research, 22,* 205–213.

Walton, E., Fraser, M. W., Lewis, R. E., Pecora, P. J., and Walton, W. K. (1996). An experiment in family reunification: Correlates of outcomes at one-year follow-up. *Children and Youth Services Review, 18,* 335–361.

Wells, E. A., Peterson, P. L., Gainey, R. R., Hawkins, J. D., and Catalano, R. F. (1994). Outpatient treatment for cocaine abuse: A controlled comparison of relapse prevention and twelve-step approaches. *American Journal of Drug and Alcohol Abuse, 20,* 1–17.

Westbury, E., and Tutty, L. M. (1999). The efficacy of group treatment for survivors of childhood abuse. *Child Abuse and Neglect, 23,* 31–44.

Whitfield, G. W. (1999). Validating school social work: An evaluation of a cognitive-behavioral approach to reduce school violence. *Research on Social Work Practice, 9,* 399–427.

Whitney, D., and Rose, S. D. (1990). The effect of process and structured content on outcome in stress management groups. *Journal of Social Service Research, 13,* 89–104.

Wodarski, J. S., and Bordnick, P. S. (1994). Teaching adolescents about alcohol and driving: A two-year follow-up study. *Research on Social Work Practice, 4,* 28–39.

PART II

PRACTICE GUIDELINES FOR SOCIAL WORK:

NEED, NATURE, AND CHALLENGES

5

CLINICAL GUIDELINES AND EVIDENCE-BASED PRACTICE IN MEDICINE, PSYCHOLOGY, AND ALLIED PROFESSIONS

MATTHEW OWEN HOWARD AND JEFFREY M. JENSON

A foolish consistency is the hobgoblin of little minds. —RALPH WALDO EMERSON
If many remedies are prescribed for an illness, you may be certain that the illness has no cure. —ANTON CHEKOV

As social work confronts a new millennium, deficiencies in the production, dissemination, and application of practice-relevant scientific data continue to undermine efforts to foster evidence-based practice. Scientific information facilitating the selection and implementation of effective social interventions has been poorly disseminated and haphazardly utilized. Whereas health professionals routinely scrutinize new research reports, debating their practice implications and practical import, many social workers consider scientific evaluations irrelevant to their professional conduct. Rosen et al. (1995) reported that less than one percent of the practice decisions made by the social workers they studied were justified by reference to empirical findings. They noted that investigations consistently indicate that practitioners "are found to read research literature minimally, to neither know nor apply research methodology, and not to express an appreciation of the value of research to their practice" (1995:502).

In turn, practicing social workers, like clinicians in the health professions, have voiced dissatisfaction with the information generated by researchers. Even practitioners who embrace evidence-based practice acknowledge that potentially useful findings are scattered across a poorly organized, massive, and rapidly growing scientific literature, that few top-flight journals are devoted to the issues and publication types that practitioners find most useful, and that the homogeneous study samples and standardized treatment protocols employed by researchers often do not generalize well to the types of clients and interventions with which they work (Haynes 1990).

Efforts to promote scientific practice in social work have taken many forms but have inevitably encountered significant resistance. Kirk (1999) described four historical movements within social work that aimed to make practice more evidence-based: (1) the evolution of program evaluation methods in response to early reports of social intervention ineffectiveness, (2) efforts to encourage social workers to read, synthesize, and apply the published scientific literature as "scientist-practitioners," (3) R and D—like strategies to strengthen the link between knowledge development and application, and (4) single-case design, which encouraged practitioners to conduct small clinical studies informing their own practices.

Most observers agree that social work practice continues to proceed largely uninformed by current research findings, seriously compromising the profession's perceived credibility. The continued viability of the profession in the increasingly competitive managed care marketplace of the twenty-first century will depend, in large measure, on its ability to generate and apply scientific findings informing practice efforts.

Proponents of guideline development within social work should acknowledge that the profession is currently plagued by systemic problems that seriously limit its efforts to amass a corpus of research findings sufficient to inform practice efforts. These limitations include the small number and low publication rates of doctoral-level scholars, poor research training delivered in most schools of social work, generally poor quality of social work research, and minimal impact of social work journals. These shortcomings will not be directly affected by practice guideline development; thus, guidelines are no panacea for all that ails the profession.

Medical practice guidelines have proliferated over the past decade, and support for a similar guideline movement within professional psychology has also increased recently (Howard and Lambert 1996; Walker and Howard 1996; Walker et al. 1995). Scientifically supported parameters for social work practice are, however, virtually nonexistent. We believe that guidelines are the most promising approach yet developed to bridge the divide between research and practice and to increase the effectiveness of social work practice. Institutional, conceptual, and empirical developments promoting evidence-based medical and psychological practice are relevant to guideline development in social work. A wealth of data and experience has accrued within medicine that should be evaluated by social workers as they develop standards for clinical conduct. Thus, this chapter reviews evidence pertaining to the general acceptance of guidelines by health professionals and trends in clinician use of guidelines and examines characteristics of effective guidelines, promising guideline dissemination strategies, consequences of guidelines, and barriers to guideline utilization, drawing on experience to date in medicine and psychology.

DEFINITIONS

Practice guidelines are recommendations for care based on empirical findings and the consensus of experts who have substantial experience in a given practice area. The Institute of Medicine (IOM) defined practice guidelines as "systematically developed statements to assist practitioner and patient decisions about appropriate care for specific clinical circumstances" (1990:27). The American Academy of Ophthalmology referred to guidelines as "preferred practice patterns" because "no two patients' needs are ever identical [and] 'cook book medicine' cannot ensure quality" (Sommer, Weinter, and Gamble 1990). The phrase *practice parameters* was used by the AMA because it emphasized "the need for flexible guidelines which allow for individualized treatment planning" (Kelly and Swartout 1990). The terms *practice options, protocols, standards, algorithms,* and *critical pathways* are broadly synonymous with the practice guidelines concept.

Although guidelines can take many forms, most definitions emphasize their common goal of improving practitioner decision making by describing appropriate indications for specific interventions. Eddy (1990) distinguished between *practice standards,* which must be followed in nearly all cases, and *practice guidelines,* which allow for greater flexibility. Eddy contended that practice guidelines can be developed when some important health outcomes of an intervention are known, whereas practice standards require greater knowledge of the health and economic consequences of an intervention.

Thousands of guidelines can be found in the allied health literature, but few address issues, populations, or practice methods relevant to social workers. Although guidelines such as the American Psychiatric Association's (APA) recommendations for the treatment of patients with substance use, nicotine dependence, eating, and other disorders (APA 1995) or the American Academy of Child and Adolescent Psychiatry's (AACAP) recently established guidelines for the evaluation of youth who may have been physically or sexually abused (AACAP 1997) are of interest and utility to social workers, the need for guidelines reflecting the unique roles and responsibilities of social workers is pressing.

Guidelines consistent with the IOM's definition are a heterogeneous group with regard to the methods used in their development, dissemination, and evaluation. Some guidelines represent the efforts of small groups with questionable expertise relying largely on informal consensus-driven approaches, whereas others are massive and costly undertakings involving the systematic collection, grading, and synthesis of research findings via meta-analysis, in conjunction with explicit consensus-development methods and weighted treatment recommendations.

ORIGINS OF THE MEDICAL PRACTICE GUIDELINE MOVEMENT

Though more or less formalized guidelines have been used in medicine for more than half a century, the past two decades have witnessed exponential

growth in guideline development and the application of increasingly sophis-
ticated methods and greater monies to guideline construction and dissemination (IOM 1990, 1992).

The early impetus for guideline construction was rooted in three developments that occurred during the 1970s and 1980s. Wennberg's seminal early
studies documented serious and seemingly inexplicable regional variations in
physicians' practices (Wennberg, Freeman, and Culp 1987). Practice variation
was assumed to reflect overuse of medical procedures or therapies in some
regions. Inappropriate under- and overuse of medical interventions were
attributed, in turn, to physicians' uncertainties regarding appropriate indications for selected procedures. Contemporary observers maintain that physicians' uncertainties have continued to increase because medical information
is accruing at an unprecedented rate. The rapid development of medical
technologies and the fact that technologies are applied ever more widely also
contribute to practice variation. Practice trends are currently such that many
patients are treated by physicians who are relatively inexperienced in applying
selected treatments.

Other evaluations called into question the effectiveness of widely used treatments, leading to a growing appreciation of the need for more-comprehensive
outcome assessments and explicit statements of preferred practice approaches
in different practice contexts. Studies documenting inappropriate utilization
of health care interventions also supported the need for more-systematic
recommendations for treatment in relation to specific health conditions (Lohr
et al. 1986). Thus, increasing recognition of inappropriate variation in the use
of health care interventions, many of which were of uncertain value, contributed to the growing demand for practice guidelines.

Proponents of guidelines believe that guidelines decrease physician uncertainty, thereby reducing rates of inappropriate care by codifying knowledge in
particular practice domains. Guidelines provide practitioners with information
in a form that is concise, directive, and easy to use, which is the format many
practicing physicians prefer. Leape (1990:42) observed that "there is poor dissemination of clinically relevant information in a form that is useful to the
practicing physician."

GUIDELINE PROLIFERATION AND THE EMERGENCE OF EVIDENCE-BASED PRACTICE

MEDICINE

Current estimates of the number of practice guidelines range upward of 26,000
(Grimshaw and Hutchinson 1995). Before 1980, only eight medical societies

had developed guidelines. In 1990 Kelly and Swartout reported that twenty-six medical organizations had developed 720 guidelines; by 1992 Kelly and Toepp noted that these figures had increased to forty-five and 1,500, respectively.

A number of new publications reporting guidelines have entered the medical literature recently. The journal *Abstracts of Clinical Care Guidelines* has published scores of medical practice guidelines since its inception. The periodicals *Evidence-Based Medicine* and *Evidence-Based Mental Health* also recently commenced publication. Both journals were founded to counter the tendency of physicians to "rely on custom, hearsay, and dogma in choosing treatments" (Taubes 1996:23).

The federal government is increasingly involved in guideline development. The Agency for Health Care Policy and Research (AHCPR), now the Agency for Healthcare Research and Quality (AHRQ), was, until recently, the leading federal body involved in guideline development. Its mission is to "generate and disseminate information that improves the delivery of health care and to support research that better educates consumers and helps them make informed choices" (Gaus and DeLeon 1995:339). The AHCPR developed approximately twenty guidelines addressing a range of prevalent disorders, but the activities of the agency vis-à-vis guideline development have recently changed (as will be discussed below).

Medical specialty societies have played a major role in developing guidelines. The Council of Medical Specialty Societies and the American College of Physicians are strong proponents of guidelines (White and Ball 1990). Other groups directly involved in guideline development are hospitals and HMOs; insurance, managed care, and utilization review companies; insurance carriers; voluntary organizations such as the American Cancer Society; and research centers, such as the RAND Corporation, the Academic Medical Center Consortium, and the IOM.

Other organizations supporting guideline development include the Joint Commission on the Accreditation of Health Care Organizations. Some states have promoted the development of statutorily imposed guidelines as a means of implementing malpractice reform. Federal involvement in guideline development through agencies of the U.S. Public Health Service, such as the Food and Drug Administration, the National Institutes of Health, the Centers for Disease Control and Prevention, the Health Care Financing Administration, the U.S. Preventive Services Task Force, and the Congressional Office of Technology Assessment, has continued apace.

PSYCHOLOGY

The identification and use of empirically supported treatments in psychology have increased over the past decade. This growing acceptance has led to a cautious endorsement of practice guidelines by many practicing psychologists and researchers.

ORIGINS OF EVIDENCE-BASED PRACTICE Interest in evidence-based practice in psychology can be traced to the 1950s and 1960s when several investigators argued that research evidence from intervention trials should be the basis for the selection of psychological treatments. This early interest in empirically supported treatments contributed to the adoption of the "scientist-practitioner" model, which addressed calls for greater accountability in clinical practice (Hayes, Barlow, and Nelson-Gray 1999). Named after the site of a groundbreaking conference in the late 1940s, the Boulder Model encouraged practicing psychologists to systematically assess their clients' outcomes. Consistent with the model was the recognition that therapists had an obligation to select and implement demonstrably effective therapies.

Adoption of empirically supported treatments and acceptance of the scientist-practitioner model occurred slowly and incompletely in the practice community. Despite a general acceptance of the Boulder Model by prominent schools, effective therapies were inconsistently disseminated and implemented among psychologists. Growing concern about the failure of many therapists to assess client outcomes and use empirically supported treatments led to the formation of the American Psychological Association's Task Force on the Promotion and Dissemination of Psychological Procedures in 1993 (Barlow, Levitt, and Bufka 1999).

DEFINING AND IDENTIFYING EMPIRICALLY SUPPORTED TREATMENTS
The task force was established by the APA's Society of Clinical Psychology to identify efficacious treatments across a range of mental health disorders. Task force members with expertise in diverse therapeutic approaches and populations developed criteria for treatments deemed to be *well-established and empirically validated* and for treatments considered to be *probably efficacious.* Well-established treatments were those therapies that evidenced efficacy in at least two independent and rigorous experimental studies. Probably efficacious treatments were therapies in which only one study supported a treatment's efficacy or therapies that had been tested by a single investigator.

The task force recognized randomized clinical trials (RCTs) as the most rigorous method of identifying empirically supported treatments. In lieu of RCTs and other "group design studies," findings from a large series of single-case studies were considered sufficient to validate a therapy.

The task force initiated a search for efficacious and probably efficacious treatments in 1993. Well-established treatments have since been identified for anxiety and stress-related conditions, depression, marital discord, and a host of childhood and health problems. Probably efficacious therapies have been identified for anxiety and substance-use disorders, depression, marital discord, sexual dysfunction, and prevalent childhood disorders (Chambless et al. 1998).

DEFINITIONAL ISSUES The task force originally referred to *efficacious treatments* as therapies that met criteria sufficient to establish them as empirically *validated.* Garfield (1998) objected to the term *validated* on the grounds that no therapeutic approach could be ever fully validated. Other investigators supported Garfield by noting that treatment efficacy is an ongoing process characterized by constant testing of therapies. Subsequent publications stemming from the task force adopted the phrase *empirically supported* therapies in response to these criticisms.

THERAPIST, CLIENT, AND TREATMENT IMPLEMENTATION MEASURES The task force was criticized for failing to consider the effects of therapist and client variables in relation to treatment effectiveness (Garfield 1998). Investigators noted that therapeutic processes derived from the same theory vary and that clients with identical diagnoses often differ considerably. Others pointed out that there is considerable variation within therapy types. A related criticism concerned the task force's endorsement of treatment manuals. Therapies identified as efficacious by the task force used treatment manuals that provided detailed descriptions of the therapy employed, thus allowing for the possibility of replication in other trials. While the use of treatment manuals was acceptable to many psychologists, others warned that an overreliance on manuals might limit and narrow the scope of training in clinical psychology and other educational programs.

CLINICAL SIGNIFICANCE The task force's reluctance to include measures of clinical, as opposed to statistical, significance in the criteria for efficacy was also criticized. In the past decade, several investigators have developed procedures to assess the clinical significance of a treatment-related effect. However, achievement of a specific level of clinical significance was not included in the criteria for determining which treatments were empirically supported. Commentators noted that criteria for efficacious treatments that are based only on statistical significance may be of limited utility to therapists and practitioners, who are more interested in the actual therapeutic gains they can expect their patients to make when a given intervention is employed.

EFFICACY VERSUS EFFECTIVENESS The task force defined an *efficacious treatment* as one that was tested in RCTs or under controlled conditions. To date, little research has been conducted to assess the effectiveness of "efficacious" approaches in actual practice settings. Task force members recently called for the evaluation of efficacious treatments in diverse clinical settings to aid in the determination of effectiveness (Chambless and Hollon 1998).

SUMMARY The work of the APA Task Force has been embraced by many psychologists; however, debates about the appropriateness of the criteria used to designate selected therapies as empirically supported, the proper role of manualized therapies, and reliance on RCTs to identify efficacious treatments will likely continue.

Adequate dissemination and utilization of empirically supported treatments remain major challenges in attaining goals established by the task force. Underutilization of empirically supported therapies has been a long-standing problem in psychology. Therapists' reluctance to use empirically supported treatments may be related to inadequate dissemination of efficacious treatments.

To counter the problem of inadequate dissemination, investigators have called for systematic training of students in graduate psychology programs in the use of empirically supported treatments (Barlow, Levitt, and Bufka 1999; Persons 1995). Practice guidelines have also been identified as a promising way to disseminate information about efficacious treatments for many psychological disorders.

As noted above, variability in treatment delivery has been a persistent problem in medicine, psychiatry, and psychology. Concerns raised by anecdotal reports suggesting that patients frequently receive ineffective treatment for medical or psychological disorders heightened in the late 1980s. Congress established the AHCPR to disseminate information about efficacious treatments for specific health and mental health disorders, and the AHCPR subsequently became a leader in developing guidelines that identify effective treatments for disorders such as depression.

The APA has taken a somewhat different approach to guideline development than medicine or psychiatry has. Rather than constructing specific guidelines for mental health disorders or populations, the APA has developed a template for evaluating the utility of existing or newly developed guidelines. The template requires that guidelines be evaluated with regard to the efficacy of the intervention (Axis 1) and its applicability to different practice settings (Axis 2). Axis 1 ratings reflect the internal validity of an intervention, whereas Axis 2 ratings address questions of clinical utility. Feasibility, generalizability, and cost-effectiveness criteria are also included as indicators of clinical utility.

Research is needed to promote the development of guidelines in psychology. Several large outcome studies using empirically supported therapies and guidelines have recently been initiated in psychology. Proponents of guidelines await the findings of these investigations. At present, it is fair to conclude that guideline development in the nonmedical helping professions has occurred much more slowly than in medicine proper.

A meeting of the American Association of Applied and Preventive Psychology addressed many issues critical to the development of scientific standards for psychological practice (Hayes et al. 1995). Conferees concluded that psychologists should adopt only safe and empirically validated treatments, psychology should develop proscriptive and prescriptive standards for practitioner conduct, and clients should be fully informed about the scientific justification for any of the treatments they are offered. Participants held that psychologists are slow to adopt effective interventions because they receive little training in empirically supported treatment methods, do not read the outcome literature, find research results difficult to apply, and tend to regard all psychotherapeutic treatments as equally effective.

MEDICAL PRACTICE GUIDELINES

DESIRABLE ATTRIBUTES OF GUIDELINES

Although there was significant agreement about the general utility of guidelines by 1990, some observers argued for greater attention to the processes by which guidelines are developed and disseminated. Kaegi (1992) later contended that the important questions had changed from those relating to *who* should develop guidelines and *how* they should be developed to those concerned with the *effects* of guidelines on physicians' behaviors and patients' outcomes and the *cost-effectiveness* of competing treatments.

Desirable features of guidelines and effective methods for implementing them have been identified. Most observers agree that guidelines should be widely disseminated, based on a developmental process that is open to public scrutiny, revised regularly and in response to significant scientific advances, and based on empirical findings of the highest quality. Leape (1990) suggested that guidelines should be *comprehensive*, including all indications for an intervention; *specific*, clearly describing conditions under which an intervention is recommended; *inclusive*, incorporating all factors that should be considered before recommending a treatment or procedure; and *manageable*, easy to understand and apply in practice. The IOM (1992) suggested that guidelines should have *validity*, *clarity*, *clinical flexibility* and applicability, and *reliability*, and should be *developed by a multidisciplinary process* that includes participation of key affected groups, including patients.

Contemporary guideline development protocols have many common features:

• Extensive reviews of published and unpublished research findings are conducted.
• Scientific investigations are selected and weighted according to predetermined criteria (usually on the basis of their methodological rigor), and findings are summarized, when feasible, using quantitative methods such as meta-analysis.
• Guideline panels are constituted and convened, and guidelines are revised through an iterative feedback process that includes members of relevant professional, specialty, and patient groups.
• Scientific findings are melded with expert opinion, and consensus is achieved via explicit or informal procedures. Areas where disagreement or uncertainty remains are noted.

GUIDELINE DISSEMINATION AND EFFECTIVENESS

Guideline development efforts at the national level are frequently unsuccessful in changing physicians' practices because of their failure to adequately disseminate guidelines to practitioners (Grilli et al. 1991).

Evaluations of the NIH Consensus Development Program reached similarly discouraging conclusions (Kosecoff, Kanouse, and Brook 1990). Medical care was examined prior to and following the introduction of guidelines that addressed the surgical management of primary breast cancer, use of steroid receptors in breast cancer treatment, and appropriate indications for caesarean section and coronary artery bypass surgery. Relevant guidelines were widely published in lay and professional publications. Whereas some success was achieved in disseminating guidelines to targeted recipients, conference recommendations generally failed to change physicians' practices.

Other studies suggest that problems in guideline dissemination persist. Lomas et al. (1989) assessed the effects of distributing to Canadian obstetricians a consensus statement designed to reduce the incidence of caesarean sections among women with previous delivery by caesarean section. Questionnaires administered before, and two years following, the dissemination of the guidelines indicated that obstetricians' knowledge of the content of the guidelines was poor and that their practices had changed little.

Guidelines developed by national organizations can affect physician behavior if there are incentives promoting their use. Guidelines adopted by the American College of Cardiology in 1984, which detailed inappropriate indications for pacemaker implantation, were widely accepted by physicians. These guidelines resulted in more appropriate use of cardiac pacemakers and in significant reductions in the use of pacemakers in Medicare patients (Kelly and Swartout 1990).

Locally developed or adapted guidelines are generally more effective and better received than national guidelines disseminated to localities without consideration of their unique circumstances (Durand-Zaleski 1992).

Webb et al. (1992) examined the effects of status asthmaticus treatment guidelines on pediatric outcomes and pediatricians' behaviors within a large health maintenance organization (HMO). The recommendations of a national panel of experts were the basis for the draft guidelines. Key personnel from multiple disciplines reviewed the guidelines and aided in revising them. Guideline development activities exerted positive effects. Comparisons of patients treated before and after the guidelines were implemented showed superior results in patients treated under the new guidelines and significant changes in pediatricians' behaviors.

Several tentative conclusions can be drawn from studies evaluating the effectiveness of guidelines in changing clinicians' behaviors. Merely disseminating guidelines passively is not effective. Instead, *incentives* such as reduced malpractice insurance premiums should be offered to practitioners to encourage them to adopt guidelines. The *active participation* of physicians in the guideline development process via small-group consensus building and *local adaptation* of national guidelines are also potentially fruitful approaches. Use of *physician opinion leaders, physician profiling,* and *feedback and clinical auditing* has proven effective in some studies. In general, the more intense and multifaceted the dissemination methods and the greater the practitioner involvement, the more likely it is that clinicians will apply the guidelines in practice.

Are some methods of developing guidelines or guideline formats particularly effective in shaping practitioners' behaviors? A report (IOM 1992) noted that "as the guidelines development process evolves, more attention is being paid to who takes part in the process, when and how they participate, and what such participation should achieve" (p. 170). Different methods of creating guideline panels, selecting panel members, identifying reviewers of draft guidelines, establishing consensus, and incorporating patient preferences into guidelines should also be evaluated vis-à-vis their differential effectiveness.

Current findings pertaining to guideline efficacy are mixed. Grimshaw and Russell (1993) reviewed fifty-nine rigorous evaluations of the effects of practice guidelines on the processes and outcomes of medical care; only four studies failed to report statistically significant positive findings related to guideline implementation on the processes of care, although the effects were of widely varying magnitude. Nine of eleven studies examining the impact of guidelines on clients' outcomes reported significant positive findings. The authors concluded that "explicit guidelines do improve clinical practice" (p. 1321).

More recently, however, Worrall, Chaulk, and Freake (1997) reported that only five of thirteen randomized or quasi-experimental studies examining the effects of practice guidelines on patients' outcomes in primary care produced statistically significant findings. The authors noted that there is relatively little evidence that the use of practice guidelines improves patients' outcomes in primary care, but observed that most studies published to date have used older guidelines and methods.

POSITIVE AND NEGATIVE CONSEQUENCES OF MEDICAL GUIDELINES

Some observers argue that guidelines codify knowledge in a way that stifles innovative practice and contend that continuing investigation in a practice domain is undermined by the perception of strong agreement among guideline panelists in given practice areas. "Cookbook medicine" may contribute to a disinterest in medical careers, and the quality of physicians entering medicine may decline as the practice of medicine becomes increasingly constrained.

Legal implications of guidelines are the focus of a number of reports. Bulger (1993) considered the possible liability of guideline developers and users, the respective roles of federal and state governments in institutionalizing guidelines, the effects of guidelines on medical malpractice and decision making, and other important emerging issues.

Physicians are increasingly concerned that guidelines will constitute inculpatory evidence that will be used against them in court proceedings. Dwyer (1998) reported that Australian surgeons were evenly divided in their expectations of whether a new guideline for the management of early breast cancer would be used in suits against them or for exculpatory purposes. Debate currently centers around the question of whether guidelines should be used as the standard of care or simply as evidence of the standard of care. Some observers have also expressed concern that guidelines, once established, would become static standards of care, unresponsive to new clinical developments. The IOM supports the use of guidelines as evidence of the standard of care, in preference to their use as mandatory standards, in malpractice cases. To date, most guideline proponents have called for scheduled guideline review and revision and ad hoc guideline revision in response to important clinical advances. Another contentious issue concerns whether guidelines represent customary practice or promote exemplary care. If the latter tends to be the case, then the use of guidelines to establish the legal standard of care for a condition would be improper, given that the standard of care is what a reasonable practitioner would do in a given clinical context. At present, the courts prefer expert testimony to practice guidelines in making a determination regarding the prevailing standard of care. Some legal analysts argue that guidelines make medical expert opinion more useful to courts and reduce uncertainty vis-à-vis the definition of "reasonable" medical care.

EMERGING ISSUES

EVIDENCE-BASED MEDICINE

Medical practice has long been characterized by the adoption of treatment approaches later found to be ineffective. Reilly, Hart, and Evans (1998) noted that bleeding by leeches was the standard therapy for pneumonia only 175 years ago, until Pierre Louis demonstrated that the intervention was without merit in 1928. More recently, the routine application of Class I antiarrhythmic agents to the treatment of asymptomatic ventricular arrhythmias in the 1970s was discontinued when it was learned that use of these drugs was associated with *decreased* survival rates. Heffner (1998:173) observed that "whether recognized or not, the harsh reality of medicine is that many, if not most, daily clinical decisions are not based on valid scientific fact."

Evidence-based medicine is a practice and training philosophy that emerged in the early 1990s in an effort to improve the integration of published research with physicians' clinical experience and patients' preferences, such that patients' outcomes were improved. Sackett et al. (1997) defined *evidence-based medicine* as "the conscientious and judicious use of current best evidence from clinical care research in the management of individual patients." Heffner (1998) maintained that *conscientious* use of evidence entails consistently applying the evidence to the care of all patients for whom it is pertinent. *Judicious* use of evidence means "weighing an *individual* patient's unique clinical circumstances against a clinical practice guideline's general recommendations for patient care" (p. 176).

Physicians frequently encounter clinical situations that raise perplexing questions about appropriate diagnostic and treatment approaches. Covell, Uman, and Manning (1985) reported that physicians providing office-based care had an average of two unanswered questions for every three patients they treated. Although reliance on textbooks, associates, and other traditional sources of authority-based information is widespread, recent findings suggest that such information is frequently dated, conflicting, or at odds with scientific findings.

The practice of evidence-based medicine includes the following processes: *formulating specific questions* about patient care; *searching and retrieving scientific information* with which to answer the questions; *critically appraising* the relevance and validity of the information found and its pertinence to the case at hand; and *evaluating the process* to determine if optimal patient outcomes were achieved. This approach has been called a "new paradigm for medical practice [that] de-emphasizes intuition, unsystematic clinical experience, and pathophysiologic rationale as sufficient grounds for clinical decision-making and stresses the examination of evidence from clinical research" (Evidence-Based Medicine Working Group 1992:2420).

In 1997, the AHCPR's Center for Practice and Technology Assessment (CPTA) was formed. While the primary focus of the Office of the Forum for Quality and Effectiveness in Health Care, the predecessor to the CPTA, had been on the development of practice guidelines, the CPTA moved to establish twelve evidence-based practice centers (EBPCs). Although the AHCPR, through the forum, had produced nineteen widely praised clinical practice guidelines between 1991 and 1997, the guidelines were extremely expensive to produce, and so the AHCPR embarked upon a new path to achieve more-scientific medical practice. The new EBPCs are designed to produce systematic reviews, which will support local guideline development efforts, but they do not themselves develop guidelines.

Special series of articles fostering the development of critical appraisal skills for evaluating clinical trials, meta-analyses, and other primary and secondary sources of clinically relevant data have been published in leading medical journals. The *Journal of the American Medical Association* has published its Users' Guide to the Medical Literature series, consisting to date of nearly a score of reports that address how to critically assess articles about diagnostic tests, preventive measures, prognosis, analysis of clinical decisions, and guidelines (Churchill 1998).

A number of *online sources* have been developed for practitioners of evidence-based medicine. The *National Guideline Clearinghouse* (NGC; www.guideline.gov) was established jointly by the AHCPR, the AMA, and the American Association of Health Care Plans. The NGC offers structured summaries to guidelines, full text of guidelines, comparisons of guidelines for similar conditions, and electronic forums for guideline developers and users.

One of the most significant organizational developments vis-à-vis evidence-based medicine was the establishment of the *Cochrane Collaboration* (CC). The origins of the CC were rooted in the work of Ian Chalmers, who endeavored to summarize all clinical trials pertaining to pregnancy and childbirth. In 1992 the *Cochrane Center* was established by the British National Health Service to extend the strategy to other fields of medicine.

Sundry other developments may also serve to increase the viability of evidence-based practice. Structured abstract formats became the norm at many medical journals over the past decade, facilitating readers' efforts to assess and sort studies by their methodological rigor and findings. Several residency programs in internal medicine began to teach evidence-based medicine. Organizations such as the Preventive Services Task Force employed evidence-based methods as they conducted comprehensive reviews of the medical literature.

Currently, it is unclear to what extent modern medical practice is evidence-based. Gill et al. (1996) found that 81 percent of patients treated at one suburban general practice received treatments supported by RCTs or "convincing" nonexperimental evidence. Other studies suggest that even when computers and Internet access are made available to physicians, they conduct fewer than four searches of the medical literature monthly (Evidence-Based Medicine Working Group 1992). Many physicians also feel that they have neither the time nor the computer skills nor the requisite methodological acumen to routinely access and evaluate the medical literature.

The evidence-based practice and guideline movements share many similarities (Lohr 1998). Both emphasize the importance of RCTs as the gold standard of practice knowledge, but recognize the limitations they impose on generalizability. Hence, the calls for more "effectiveness" research in both fields. The evidence-based practice and guidelines movements also stress client outcomes as the key standard by which interventions should be evaluated. Issues that are more specific to evidence-based medicine include the questionable feasibility vis-à-vis time, preparation, and resources of evidence-based practice and the sharp distinction that some proponents of evidence-based practice draw between research evidence and clinical experience. Concerns specific to guidelines have focused on how timely they are, how expensive and time-consuming they can be to develop, how conflicting guideline recommendations can be resolved, and how national guidelines can be adapted for local implementation. In some senses, evidence-based medicine as embodied in systematic reviews of relevant scientific data is a necessary precursor to the development and dissemination of clinical practice guidelines.

ECONOMIC ISSUES

Perhaps the chief early concern with practice guidelines was the perception that they were primarily cost-saving measures rather than instruments intended to increase the quality and value of health care.

Guidelines recommending "appropriate" lengths of inpatient and outpatient treatment for various conditions and procedures have been highly controversial. Rutledge (1998) compared Millman and Robertson's recommended length-of-stay standards for twenty-five surgical procedures to comparable mean lengths of stay recommended by a sample of fellows of the American College of Surgeons and to mean lengths of stay for actual surgical practice in North Carolina. In virtually all cases, the Millman and Robertson guidelines recommended stays that were significantly shorter than those recommended by ACS fellows. Similarly, the Millman and Robertson length-of-stay standards were substantially shorter than the stays actually observed for the relevant procedures in North Carolina. Rutledge (1998) contended that widely used guidelines like those published by Millman and Robertson (a large firm involved in health care issues since 1947) may not only promote care that harms patients but also "engender physician resistance and significantly hamper the general effort to convince physicians to support the implementation of a guideline-based approach to medical care" (p. 584).

Insurance companies have been interested in guidelines since their inception, as have employers, who increasingly pay employee health claims directly through self-funded health plans. Parker (1995) noted that reimbursement policies influence which conditions are treated and what procedures are performed and suggested that "a first role for practice guidelines is helping insurance companies to establish reimbursement policies that reflect the best current opinion on which procedures are appropriate for which patients in which circumstances" (p. 57). Guideline adherence can also be used in determining whether or not selected providers will be included or excluded from provider networks. A number of insurance analysts have argued against the adoption of guidelines for cost-saving purposes because "although cost savings may occur in some areas, in others costs may increase at least temporarily. . . . Moreover, adoption of practice guidelines in insurance settings will itself require infrastructure expenditures . . . as well as human resources expenditures" (p. 60).

Recent cost-benefit analyses of guidelines have provided a number of useful insights. Methodological questions have been raised regarding the role and weight that should be accorded cost considerations in the development and evaluation of guidelines, the availability of valid and generalizable cost estimates, and the presentation of cost data to clinicians by health care economists in a manner that is most useful to them.

The IOM (1990, 1992), among other groups, has called for the inclusion of economic data in guideline discussions of the cost implications of alternative approaches to the prevention, diagnosis, and treatment of medical conditions.

Optimal means of incorporating economic data into guidelines have not yet been identified. To date, most guidelines do not address health economic issues, although there are indications that economic data can be used fruitfully in guideline development.

An important final consideration regarding the economic impact of guidelines concerns the distinction between individual- and societal-level cost-benefit assessment. Granata and Hillman (1998) demonstrated that guidelines chosen to maximize cost-effectiveness at the individual level may not maximize cost-effectiveness at the population level. They observed that we must guard against the notion that "decisions reached individually will, in fact, be the best decisions for an entire society . . . traditional cost-effectiveness research selects guidelines to maximize efficiency within individual clinical subgroups. However, it is essential to consider what is best for society as a whole."

PATIENT PREFERENCES

Patient preferences are increasingly being taken into account in medical decision making. A number of organizations have published patient/lay versions of practice guidelines in an effort to ensure that patients and their advocates understand the potential risks and benefits of the treatment options available to them. Hagen and Whlie (1998) noted that a large survey of breast cancer patients in Canada indicated that 22 percent wanted to select treatment options themselves, whereas 44 percent wanted to select treatment options in collaboration with their physicians; only 34 percent wanted to delegate treatment decisions entirely to their doctors.

The methods by which patients' views are assessed regarding the quality of life associated with various health states range from the highly informal to the highly structured. Research to date suggests that physicians often hold inaccurate views of the utilities their patients attach to different health states and outcomes and that patients with similarly severe symptoms may have very different feelings about their symptoms and the options for treating them. A number of multimedia and interactive computerized patient preference assessment software packages are currently being tested, but such assessments are not routinely incorporated into medical practice.

Guideline proponents have often recommended that patients be included on guideline development panels, but a growing call is being heard for more effective inclusion of patient preferences in clinical practice guidelines. At present, it is unclear in which settings, under what conditions, and how patients' preferences should be assessed.

ETHICAL CONSIDERATIONS

Although evidence-based guidelines can constrain practitioner and client treatment options, few analyses of the ethical consequences of guideline implementation on individual client care have been published. Some theorists have asked the questions "Who should be responsible for ensuring that clinical practice guidelines are ethical in their formulation and implementation?" and "To what extent could practice guidelines help to avoid or resolve such [ethical] conflicts or, alternatively, cause them to arise?" (Somerville 1993). Among the contexts in which guideline application could create value conflicts are "cases in which a patient wants and would benefit from a certain treatment but under the principles in the guideline will not be allocated that treatment. . . . Conflict could also arise if a physician believes that treatment is clearly indicated for an incompetent person or a child and the family adamantly refuses, relying on practice guidelines to support its case" (p. 1134).

INTERNET AND COMPUTER DEVELOPMENTS

A host of new Web sites is available to health care practitioners interested in accessing clinical guidelines. Furrow (1999) discussed the NGC (www.guideline .gov), which provides a comprehensive listing of all available guidelines on a topic, a standardized abstract of each guideline, and a systematic grading of the scientific basis and developmental process on which each guideline rests. The Ottawa Hospital General Campus Library Evidence-Based Medicine and Practice Resources (www.ogh.on.ca/library/evidence.htm) Web site offers access to individual guidelines and to sites such as the Cochrane Collaboration. McMaster University has developed a useful Web site (http://hiru .mcmaster.ca/ebm/userguid/8_cpg.htm) titled "How to Use a Clinical Practice Guideline," which teaches the user to select from available guideline-based treatment recommendations.

EVALUATING AND COMPARING GUIDELINES

Different methods for evaluating and comparing practice guidelines are currently in development. Shaneyfelt, Mayo-Smith, and Rothwangl (1999) developed a twenty-five-item instrument to assess guideline adherence with the recommended guideline development standards of twenty-five experts in the field. Evaluations of 279 guidelines published between 1985 and 1997 revealed that an average of fewer than 11 standards (43.1%) were met. Grilli et al. (2000) found that only 5 percent of the 431 practice guidelines they examined involved a multidisciplinary development process, reported study selection criteria, and provided confidence ratings for guideline recommendations based on the quality of the underlying evidence. Ward and Grieco (1996) examined Australian guidelines developed before the publication of the National Health and Medical Research Council's "guidelines for guidelines" in 1995. Few of the thirty-four guidelines examined met even a majority of the eighteen criteria across which they were assessed.

GUIDELINE DEVELOPMENT IN ALLIED HEALTH CARE FIELDS

Although guideline development activity has been greatest in medicine, other health professions, including nursing, dentistry, and pharmacy, have also developed guidelines.

HEALTH CARE AND SOCIAL WORK PRACTICE

Some readers may question how previous experience with practice guidelines in medicine can be relevant to social work guideline development. We believe that medical and social work practice share many commonalities and that social work guideline developers should become familiar with the empirical findings relating to medical practice guidelines.

Like their social work counterparts, physicians often rely on an admixture of professional experience, research results, and their detailed assessment of the individual client to formulate a course of action addressing a client's concerns. Referring to the "art of medicine," Hippocrates noted that "some practitioners are poor, others very excellent; this would not be the case if an art of medicine did not exist at all, and had not been the subject of any research and discovery, but all would be equally inexperienced and unlearned therein, and the treatment of the sick would be in all respects haphazard. But it is not so; just as in all other arts the workers vary much in skill and in knowledge, so also it is in the case of medicine" (Jones 1995:13).

Medical and social work interventions begin with a detailed assessment of the client's presenting problems (and assets) and the many contextual issues that exacerbate or mitigate these conditions. One of the leading guides to physical examination, history taking, and assessment in medicine encourages physicians to use reflection, clarification, empathic responses, and other traditional social work interviewing methods to address a broad range of historical, familial, behavioral, and environmental factors that may contribute to a client's problems (Bickley 2000). Perhaps the dominant trend in twentieth-century medicine was its recognition that social and behavioral influences critically influence the development and outcome of illness. One might argue, in fact, that social work has been remiss in failing to attend to transactions at the biological level, given their known impact on social functioning. Competent medical and social work practice requires a detailed understanding of clients' presenting problems, which are increasingly of a chronic, rather than acute, nature. As medicine has moved away from an acute care–infectious disease model of care and become increasingly concerned with the catastrophic social and health consequences of illnesses such as AIDs, diabetes, high blood pressure, alcoholism, and drug addiction, the parallels to social work practice have become even more obvious.

In the absence of a significant corpus of directive research findings, medical and social service providers have traditionally relied on practice experience—theirs and others'—to guide their interventions. Hippocrates contended that "one must attend in medical practice not primarily to plausible theories, but to experience combined with reason . . . now I approve of theorizing also if it lays its foundation in incident [experience], and deduces in accordance with phenomena" (Jones 1995:313). Of course, as long experience in medicine and the social services clearly indicates, unsystematic observation can be misleading. In this regard, both medicine and social work have benefited significantly from the widespread application of scientific methods to the testing of putatively effective interventions.

In sum, medical and social work practitioners intervene in human problems that must be understood in their full complexity if they are to be successfully treated. Initial and ongoing assessment processes must be comprehensive, and to this end many guidelines have been published to encourage appropriate evaluation and treatment planning. Interventions, too, are becoming ever more complex and effective. Social work should draw upon the substantial available literature vis-à-vis medical practice guidelines to identify the most promising methods for social work guideline development and dissemination.

The notion that guidelines could ever obviate the need for individualized decision making in client care is patently erroneous. However, practice decisions in social work and medicine have remained largely uninformed by research advances for too long. Because the human capital, research monies, and other resources devoted to medicine significantly outstrip those dedicated to social work, efforts to translate research findings into more effective practice are more advanced in medicine than in social work. Thus, social workers should critically examine this literature for what it might have to offer to our field.

———

Guideline development has proceeded at an exponentially increasing rate in medicine over the past decade. Current evidence indicates that many physicians have been involved in guideline development, and that the attitudes of surgeons and family physicians, and other medical specialists, are generally positive toward guidelines. Numerous surveys suggest, however, that physicians often perceive some negative consequences to guideline use. For example, Christakis and Rivara (1998) noted that significant minorities of pediatricians felt that practice guidelines for the treatment of otitis media and fever were "too cookbook" in nature. Thus, although current survey findings suggest that physicians' attitudes toward guidelines are more positive than they were a decade ago, it is clear that many medical practitioners view the emergence of guidelines with ambivalence.

Although guidelines have proliferated widely, much remains unknown about them. How best might they be developed? What are the standards by which they should be judged and how effective are they and under which conditions? How should patients' preferences, economic considerations, and explicit and implicit value judgments be incorporated into published guidelines? The one issue about which little is questioned is that guidelines are here to stay. Guidelines will continue to sweep the medical landscape and change the very nature of medical practice. Moreover, they portend significant changes in social as well as medical services. The answers to these questions will, of course, require further research. But it is currently unclear how future investigational efforts can keep pace with guideline development, which has been described as a "growth industry" by more than one health care pundit. Only further experience with and evaluation of guidelines will enable health care policymakers to determine if guidelines are a panacea or a problem.

Social work has much to contribute to the guideline development enterprise. Client-specific factors, such as developmental history, family functioning, ethnicity, gender, and social class are of core significance to social work practice but have rarely been addressed in practice guidelines. Significantly more research is needed in identifying factors that might moderate or mediate recommended treatment approaches to the care of specific clients in selected treatment contexts.

Evidence-based practice within social work could be fostered if (1) the Council on Social Work Education broadened the standards in its *Curriculum Policy Statement* to encourage the teaching of evidence-based practice and the use of practice guidelines; (2) the National Association of Social Workers, Society for Social Work and Research, and Institute for the Advancement of Social Work and Research became more involved in guideline development, perhaps through a consortium devoted to guideline creation, testing, and dissemination; (3) a National Center for Social Work Research was established to lead profession-wide efforts to generate intervention research and publish practitioner-friendly literature syntheses such as treatment manuals, systematic reviews, and practice guidelines; (4) social work education was upgraded such that students learned to identify practice-relevant research findings, appraise their evidentiary value, and apply the findings to practice; and (5) potential obstacles to the use of guidelines, such as practitioners' low level of awareness of guidelines were addressed.

To date, few scholars in the profession have questioned the authority-, rather than evidence-based, training characteristic of the profession. Given the historical dearth of directive empirical findings, this state of affairs is not surprising. Recent findings in social work and other areas, however, suggest that an adequate foundation now exists for guideline development in the practice areas of mental health, substance abuse, and child and adolescent problem behavior. Faculty should be encouraged to teach evidence-based practice and to employ guidelines and other literature syntheses in their instructional efforts, for the continued viability and future credibility of social work depend critically on the profession's capacity to promote scientifically tested treatment approaches. Practice guideline development within social work should commence immediately, beginning with those conditions that are commonly encountered by social workers and for which the field has special expertise. While little is known currently about how social work practitioners will react to efforts to promote evidence-based practice, recent findings suggest that practitioners and administrators are interested in learning more about such approaches.

REFERENCES

American Academy of Child and Adolescent Psychiatry. (1997). Practice parameters for the forensic evaluation of children and adolescents who may have been physically or sexually abused. *Journal of the American Academy of Child and Adolescent Psychiatry, 36*, 423–442.

American Psychiatric Association. (1995). Practice guideline for the treatment of patients with substance use disorders: Alcohol, cocaine, opioids. *American Journal of Psychiatry, 152* (supplement), 3–50.

Barlow, D. H., Levitt, J. T., and Bufka, L. F. (1999). The dissemination of empirically supported treatments: A view to the future. *Behaviour Research and Therapy, 37*, S147–S162.

Bergman, R. (1994). Getting the goods on guidelines: Practice parameters are proliferating but the question remains: Do they really work? *Hospital and Health Networks,* October 20, 70.

Bickley, L. (2000). *Bates' Guide to Physical Examination and History Taking* (7th ed.). New York: Lippincott, Williams, and Wilkins.

Bulger, R. J. (1993). Letter from the Interest Group on Health Services Research, Association of Academic Health Centers. *Journal of Quality Improvement, 19*, 303–304.

Chambless, D. L., Baker, M. J., Baucom, D. H., Beutler, L., Calhoun, K. S., Cris-Cristoph, P. Daiuto, A. DeRubeis, R., Detweiler, J., Haaga, D. A., Bennett Johnson, S., McCurry, S., Meuser, K. T., Pope, K. S., Sanderson, W. C., Shoham, V., Stickle, T., Williams, D. A., and Woody, S. R. (1998). Update on empirically validated therapies II. *The Clinical Psychologist, 51*, 3–15.

Chambless, D. L., and Hollon, S. D. (1998). Defining empirically supported therapies. *Journal of Consulting and Clinical Psychology, 66*, 7–18.

Christakis, D. A., and Rivara, F. P. (1998). Pediatricians' awareness of and attitudes about four clinical practice guidelines. *Pediatrics, 101*, 825–830.

Churchill, R. (1998). Critical appraisal and evidence-based psychiatry. *International Review of Psychiatry, 10*, 344–352.

Covell, D. G., Uman, G. C., and Manning, P. R. (1985). Information needs in office practice: Are they being met? *Annals of Internal Medicine, 103*, 596–599.

Durand-Zaleski, I. (1992). The usefulness of consensus conferences: The case of albumin. *Lancet, 230*, 1388–1390.

Dwyer, P. (1998). Legal implications of clinical practice guidelines. *Medical Journal of Australia, 169*, 292–293.

Eddy, D. M. (1990). Designing a practice policy: Standards, guidelines, and options. *Journal of the American Medical Association, 263*, 3077–3084.

Evidence-Based Medicine Working Group. (1992). Evidence-based medicine: A new approach to teaching the practice of medicine. *Journal of the American Medical Association, 268*, 2420–2425.

Field, M. J. (1993). Overview: Prospects and options for local and national guidelines in the courts. *Journal of Quality Improvement, 19*, 313–318.

Furrow, B. R. (1999). Broadcasting guidelines on the Internet: Will physicians tune in? *American Journal of Law and Medicine, 25*, 403–421.

Gambrill, E. (1999). Evidence-based practice: An alternative to authority-based practice. *Families in Society: The Journal of Contemporary Human Services, 80*, 341–350.

Garfield, S. L. (1998). Some comments on empirically supported treatments. *Journal of Consulting and Clinical Psychology, 66*, 121–125.

Gaus, C. R., and DeLeon, P. H. (1995). Thinking beyond the limitations of mental health care. *Professional Psychology, 26*, 339–340.

Gill, P., Dowell, A. C., Neal, R. D., Smith, N., Heywood, P., and Wilson, A. E. (1996). Evidence-based general practice: A retrospective study of interventions in one training practice. *British Medical Journal, 312*, 819–821.

Granata, A. V., and Hillman, A. L. (1998). Competing practice guidelines: Using cost-effectiveness analysis to make optimal decisions. *Annals of Internal Medicine, 128*, 56–63.

Grilli, R., Apolone, G., Marsoni, S. Nicolucci, A., Zola, P., and Liberati, A. (1991). The impact of patient management guidelines on the care of breast, colorectal, and ovarian cancer patients in Italy. *Medical Care, 29*, 50–63.

Grilli, R., Magrini, N., Penna, A., Mura, G., and Liberati, A. (2000). Practice guidelines developed by specialty societies: The need for critical appraisal. *Lancet, 335*, 103–106.

Grimshaw, J. M., and Hutchinson, A. (1995). Clinical practice guidelines: Do they enhance value for money in health care? *British Medical Bulletin, 51*, 927–940.

Grimshaw, J. M., and Russell, I. T. (1993). Effect of clinical guidelines on medical practice: A systematic review of rigorous evaluations. *Lancet, 242,* 1317–1322.

Hagen, N. A., and Whlie, B. (1998). Putting clinical practice guidelines into the hands of cancer patients. *Canadian Medical Association Journal, 158,* 347–348.

Hayes, S. C., Barlow, D. H., and Nelson-Gray, R. O. (1999). *The Scientist Practitioner: Research and Accountability in the Age of Managed Care* (2d ed.). Boston: Allyn and Bacon.

Hayes, S. C., Follette, V. M., Dawes, R. M., and Grady, K. E. (1995). *Scientific Standards of Psychological Practice: Issues and Recommendations.* Reno, Nev.: Context Press.

Haynes, B. R. (1990). Loose connections between peer-reviewed clinical journals and clinical practice. *Annals of Internal Medicine, 113,* 724–728.

Heffner, J. E. (1998). Does evidence-based medicine help the development of clinical practice guidelines? *Chest, 113,* 172S–178S.

Howard, M. O., and Jenson, J. M. (1999). Clinical practice guidelines: Should social work develop them? *Research on Social Work Practice, 9,* 283–301.

Howard, M. O., and Lambert, M. D. (1996). The Poverty of Social Work: Deficient Production, Dissemination, and Utilization of Practice-Relevant Scientific Information. In P. R. Raffoul and C. Aaron McNeese (Eds.), *Future Issues for Social Work Practice* (pp. 279–292). Boston: Allyn and Bacon.

Institute of Medicine. (1990). *Clinical Practice Guidelines: Directions for a New Program.* Washington, D.C.: National Academy Press.

———. (1992). *Guidelines for Clinical Practice: From Development to Use.* Washington, D.C.: National Academy Press.

Jones, W. H. S. (1995). *Hippocrates* (Vol. 1). Loeb Classical Library. Cambridge: Harvard University Press.

Kaegi, L. (1992). Foreword to *Quality Review Bulletin, 18,* 392.

Kelly, J. T., and Swartout, J. C. (1990). Development of practice parameters by physician organizations. *Quality Review Bulletin, 16,* 54–57.

Kelly, J. T., and Toepp, K. (1992). Practice parameters development by physician organizations. *Quality Review Bulletin, 18,* 1–5.

Kendall, P. C. (1998). Empirically supported psychological therapies. *Journal of Consulting and Clinical Psychology, 66,* 3–6.

Kirk, S. A. (1999). Good intentions are not enough: Practice guidelines for social work. *Research on Social Work Practice, 9,* 302–310.

Kosecoff, J., Kanouse, D. E., and Brook, R. H. (1990). Changing practice patterns in the management of primary breast cancer: Consensus development programs. *Health Services Research, 25,* 809–823.

Leape, L. (1990). Practice guidelines and standards: An overview. *Quality Review Bulletin, 16,* 42–49.

Lohr, K. N. (1998). Health policy issues and applications for evidence-based medicine and clinical practice guidelines. *Health Policy, 46,* 1–19.

Lohr, K. N., Brook, R. H., Kamberg, C. J., Goldberg, G. A., Leibowitz, A., Keesey, J., Reboussin, D., and Newhouse, J. P. (1986). Use of medical care in the RAND health insurance experiment: Diagnosis- and service-specific analyses in a randomized controlled trial. *Medical Care, 24,* S1–S87.

Lomas, J., Anderson, G. M., Domnick-Pierre, K., Vayda, E., Enkin, M. W., and Hannah, W. J. (1989). Do practice guidelines guide practice? The effect of a consensus statement on the practice of physicians. *New England Journal of Medicine, 321,* 1306–1311.

Parker, C. W. (1995). Practice guidelines and private insurers. *Journal of Law, Medicine, and Ethics, 23,* 57–61.

Persons, J. B. (1995). Why Practicing Psychologists Are Slow to Adopt Empirically Validated Treatments. In S. C. Hayes, V. M. Follette, R. W. Dawes, and K. E. Grady (Eds.), *Scientific Standards of Psychological Practice* (pp. 141–157). Reno, Nev.: Context Press.

Reilly, B., Hart, A., and Evans, A. T. (1998). Part 2. Evidence-based medicine: A passing fancy or the future of primary care? *DM, August,* 370–399.

Rosen, A., Proctor, E., Morrow-Howell, N., and Staudt, M. (1995). Rationales for practice decisions: Variations in knowledge use by decision task and social work service. *Research on Social Work Practice, 5,* 501–523.

Rutledge, R. (1998). An analysis of 25 Millman and Robertson guidelines for surgery: Data-driven versus consensus clinical practice guidelines. *Annals of Surgery, 4,* 579–585.

Sackett, D. L., Hayes, R. B., Guyatt, G. H., and Tugwell, P. (1997). *Evidence-Based Medicine: How to Practice and Teach EBM.* New York: Churchill Livingston.

Shaneyfelt, T. M., Mayo-Smith, M. F., and Rothwangl, J. (1999). Are guidelines following guidelines? The methodological quality of clinical practice guidelines in the peer-reviewed medical literature. *Journal of the American Medical Association, 281,* 1900–1905.

Somerville, M. A. (1993). Ethics and clinical practice guidelines. *Canadian Medical Association Journal, 148,* 1133–1137.

Sommer, A., Weinter, J. P., and Gamble, L. (1990). Developing specialty-wide standards of practice: The experience of ophthalmology. *Quality Review Bulletin, 16,* 65–70.

Task Force on Promotion and Dissemination of Psychological Procedures. (1995). Training in and dissemination of empirically-validated psychological treatments. *Clinical Psychologist, 48,* 3–23.

Taubes, G. (1996). Looking for evidence in medicine. *Science, 272,* 22–24.

Walker, R. D., and Howard, M. O. (1996). The American Psychiatric Association's guideline for the treatment of patients with substance use disorders: Alcohol, cocaine, opioids. Commentary. *Abstracts of Clinical Care Guidelines, Joint Commission on the Accreditation of Health Care Organizations, 8,* 1–4.

Walker, R. D., Howard, M. O., Walker, P. S., Lambert, M. D., and Suchinsky, R. T. (1995). Practice guidelines in the addictions. *Journal of Substance Abuse Treatment, 12,* 63–73.

Ward, J. E., and Grieco, V. (1996). Why we need guidelines for guidelines: A study of the quality of clinical practice guidelines in Australia. *Medical Journal of Australia, 165,* 574–576.

Webb, L. Z., Kuykendall, D. H., and Zeiger, R. S. (1992). The impact of status asthmaticus practice guidelines on patient outcome and physician behavior. *Quality Review Bulletin, 18,* 471–476.

Wennberg, J. E., Freeman, J. L., and Culp, W. J. (1987). Are hospital services rationed in New Haven or overutilised in Boston? *Lancet, 1,* 1185–1189.

White, L. J., and Ball, J. R. (1990). Integrating practice guidelines with financial incentives. *Quality Review Bulletin, 16,* 50–53.

Worrall, G., Chaulk, P., and Freake, D. (1997). The effects of clinical practice guidelines on patient outcomes in primary care: A systematic review. *Canadian Medical Association Journal, 156,* 1705–1712.

6

THE STRUCTURE AND FUNCTION OF SOCIAL WORK PRACTICE GUIDELINES

ENOLA K. PROCTOR AND AARON ROSEN

The introductory chapter to this volume presented our rationale for developing practice guidelines for social work. In this chapter we introduce our conception of practice guidelines as a blueprint for organization of empirically tested practice knowledge in a manner that facilitates its utilization by practitioners. Our working definition of *practice guidelines* is "a set of systematically compiled and organized knowledge statements designed to enable practitioners to find, select, and use appropriately the interventions that are most effective for a given task." Practice guidelines, then, help practitioners discharge their functions successfully, yet they must provide for the uncertainty and tentativeness inherent in science-based professional knowledge. We limit our focus to the subset of practice guidelines that aim to help practitioners discharge their responsibility for effective intervention. Hence, we do not address guidelines for diagnosis, assessment, or other practice functions. Although much of our discussion could apply to social work practice in a variety of contexts, we discuss practice guidelines in the context of direct, or clinical, practice.

We previously described the process of practice and its primary decision tasks (Rosen and Proctor 1978; Rosen, Proctor, and Livne 1985; Rosen 1993), and more recently we focused on the knowledge needs of practitioners for choice and implementation of interventions (Rosen, Proctor, and Staudt 1999). Here we build on that work, conceptualizing the desired structure for intervention guidelines, and conclude with a preliminary outline of an agenda for research to further guideline development, dissemination, and use, a topic pursued more fully in the concluding chapter to this volume

The preparation of this paper was supported in part by the Center for Mental Health Services Research (NIMH Grant MH50857), Washington University, and by a Faculty Research Award from the George Warren Brown School of Social Work.

(Proctor and Rosen, chapter 16). Our conception of the function of practice guidelines for intervention posits that they be structured to include, minimally, each of the following four components:

1. A taxonomy of the target outcomes toward which interventions are directed, to serve as organizing criteria for entry and use of the guidelines.
2. Arrays of possible interventions and interventive programs that are linked to the targets for pursuit.
3. Criteria for choice among alternative interventions to enhance particularization.
4. Attention to gaps in knowledge and uncertainty of application through procedures for practitioner implementation, improvisation, and evaluation.

Guidelines developed in medicine and psychiatry reflect some of these components (e.g., American Psychiatric Association 1993), but they typically encompass only a limited set of interventions for a given condition. In contrast, we conceive of guidelines as more comprehensive, encompassing a wide range of professionally sought outcomes and guiding practitioners to select and implement the most fitting interventions to pursue those outcomes. Thus, in our conception of guidelines, once developed, they have content and procedures sufficient to guide a practitioner's intervention with any client in treatment, in at least a given area of practice. Although we address the four components of guidelines sequentially here, they are interrelated and recursive in practitioners' use of the guidelines. That is, locating the relevant target outcome (first component) and selecting an interventive program from within an array of alternatives (second component) need to be informed for best fit to a particular situation (third component), and the uncertainty in applying that knowledge to an individual client is addressed through procedures for implementation, improvisation, and evaluation (fourth component).

COMPONENTS OF GUIDELINES

TARGETS OF INTERVENTION

A most fundamental question in the development of practice guidelines is, How should interventive knowledge be organized in order to be readily retrievable by and useful to practitioners? Organization of knowledge implies an index and the use of a classification or taxonomy of the targets of intervention to provide practitioners with efficient means to enter compilations of knowledge statements and connect with those that are relevant to the task at hand. The taxonomy by which practice guidelines on intervention are organized serves to focus and anchor the selection of interventions and has far-reaching implications for practice and research. First, a target taxonomy gives the practitioner a focus for assessment and planning of treatment; second, a taxonomy directs research efforts to the targets for which effective interventions must be developed; and third, the terms of the taxonomy provide a statement of where the profession targets its efforts, thereby signaling the profession's potential contribution to society. Thus the choice of a target taxonomy should not be undertaken lightly or follow uncritically the traditions of other professions.

We view all professional intervention as aimed to achieve desired outcomes (Rosen and Proctor 1978, 1981). Hence we claim that the appropriate concepts for a nosology of targets of interventions are those that describe the desired outcomes of interventions. However, as reflected in its educational curricula and textbooks on practice, social work knowledge has seldom been organized according to the outcomes of service. Instead, it has been organized according to fields of practice (e.g., child welfare, corrections, mental health), treatment modalities (e.g., group work, family treatment, individual treatment), or theoretical approaches (e.g., behavioral, psychodynamic, cognitive). But increasingly in social work, as in medicine and psychiatry, practitioners use problem- or diagnosis-based taxonomies to organize intervention knowledge (e.g., major depression, eating disorders, low back pain). Perhaps because of social work's historical view of medicine as the model for professional practice (cf. the Flexner report [Flexner 1915]), it assumed the disease model of medical practice as the way of organizing interventive knowledge.[1] Because the disease model views intervention as directed primarily toward the repair of an undesirable condition (i.e., a problem) inherent in the client or client situation, within this model problem or diagnostic taxonomies seem appropriate for guiding the choice of interventions.

Indeed, recent efforts to organize empirically tested knowledge on interventions in social work and allied professions used problem- and diagnosis-based conceptions. For example, reviewing meta-analyses of intervention studies in order to assess differential effectiveness of interventions, Reid (1997) grouped studies according to problem areas, thus implying that the interventions aimed to reverse problems rather than to achieve other or additional outcomes. A recent two-volume compilation of empirically tested interventions (Thyer and Wodarski 1998) was organized according to *DSM-IV* diagnostic classifications (volume 1) and social problem areas (volume 2). The problem-centered focus was chosen explicitly, citing precedents in clinical psychology and psychiatry: "Like these related books, our handbook takes a problem-focused approach, as we believe that this affords greater utility for social work practitioners. Clients present with problems, which they would like some assistance in resolving. Clinicians need a convenient compendium of practice guidelines that provide some clear and concise directions about how to assess and what to do" (p. vii). Characteristically, problem reversal as the goal of intervention was linked to and justified by Thyer and Wodarski (1998) in terms of extant conceptions on assessment, most of which follow the disease model—"client presents with problem (illness), practitioner reverses (cures) the problem." In clinical psychology a handbook of empirically supported treatments incorporating recommendations of Division 12 of the American Psychological Association was similarly organized according to *DSM-IV* categories (Nathan and Gorman 1998).

We believe that interventions will be most accessible for use by practitioners if they are organized according to a taxonomy of targets that summarize the outcomes that social workers pursue through their interventions (Proctor and Rosen 1998; Rosen, Proctor, and Staudt 2003). Outcome-based targets of intervention are favored over problem reversal concepts as the primary concepts for accessing practice guidelines because the latter are inappropriate and insufficient to characterize the outcomes pursued by social workers in practice. Although clients usually "present" to workers with a problem, workers seldom automatically undertake to reverse the problem. Instead, in deliberate and responsible treatments, workers decide what goals (ultimate outcomes) to pursue in relation to a client's problem, situation, and constraints on treatment. The intermediate outcomes and interventions necessary to attain the ultimate outcomes are then outlined (Rosen, Proctor, and Livne 1985). In such treatments the outcomes to be pursued are usually more numerous and involve different behaviors than the presenting problem (Rosen and Proctor 1981), and hence the appropriate interventions can be selected only in relation to the outcomes.

With some clients, moreover, reversal or correction of presenting problems may not be the appropriate outcome to pursue—problems are often not correctable, or they are too entrenched for change, or treatment resources (money, time, skill) may be inadequate. Under such circumstances—and they are many—the problem may be addressed by working toward an outcome that, while not ameliorative of the problematic condition, enhances the client's well-being. For example, when addressing spousal abuse (the problem), the worker and the client may decide that under the particular circumstances, the desired outcome is to secure placement in a shelter rather than to change the spouse's abusive behavior. As in this example, when the outcome sought is not a reversal of the problem, we may need to affect a condition or behavior that is different substantively from that of the problem. In such cases, the appropriate intervention for the desired outcome is likely to be different from that for a reversal of the problem. In a recent study of practice comparing workers' formulation of clients' problems with the ultimate outcomes that they decided to pursue, we found that fewer than one half of the ultimate outcomes pursued involved a reversal or attenuation of the problem (Proctor, Rosen, and Rhee 2002).

Our advocacy of an outcome-based rather than a problem-based focus for intervention is also consistent with increasing calls for professionals to deemphasize the negatives in the human condition in favor of focusing on the positives. In a special section of *American Psychologist* devoted to that topic, for example, Seligman and Csikszentmihalyi (2000) advocated a "perspective focused on systematically building competency, not on correcting weakness" (p. 7). Kazdin (1999) questioned the universal adequacy of problem attenuation and symptom reduction as clinically significant outcome criteria for clinical psychologists. He suggested that it is important to pursue outcomes of enhanced functioning, and that these may be independent of and comprise different constructs than does symptom reduction. He urged considering a typology of treatment goals (outcomes) as organizing foci of treatments. We think that the shift in focus advocated for clinical psychology is imperative for social work. Outcome-based target taxonomies are the concepts of choice for organizing social work knowledge on intervention and for serving as the primary index for accessing practice guidelines. Development of such classifications is a professional priority. We focused on that task in two recent studies. One derived classifications of target domains and their more specific outcome categories from clients' treatment records (Proctor, Rosen, and Rhee 2002); the other derived a taxonomy from the outcomes addressed in intervention studies published in social work journals (Rosen, Proctor, and Staudt 2003). These studies yielded a taxonomy of eight target domains and forty more-specific outcome categories.

ARRAYS OF INTERVENTIONS

The arrays of interventions that are linked to outcome categories within each target domain are the raison d'être of practice guidelines. This component places in the hands of practitioners the knowledge of what intervention is likely to be most effective for achieving a desired outcome. Figure 6.1 is a content-free depiction of the relationship between the first two components in practice guidelines.

It shows the target domains and their associated outcome categories, and the arrays of alternative interventions that are linked to each of the outcome categories. In our recent attempt to construct a substantive prototype of the

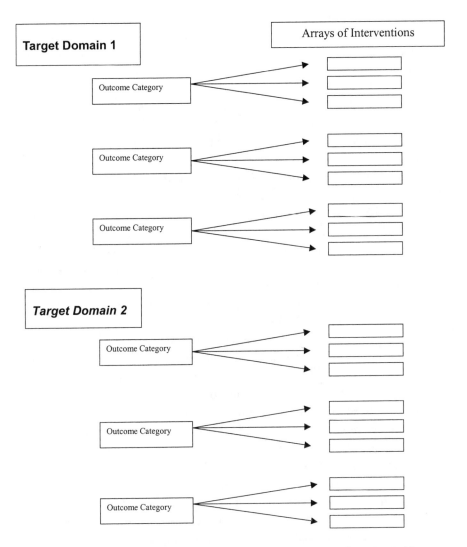

FIGURE 6.1 Schematic Illustration of the First Two Components of Practice Guidelines: Target Domains and Outcome Categories, and Arrays of Intervention

first two components of practice guidelines from published intervention research in social work, we identified eight target domains and forty outcome categories and grouped 231 different interventions into arrays in relation to the outcome categories (Rosen, Proctor, and Staudt 2003).

Attainment of an ultimate outcome, which is the goal of treatment, seldom involves merely the use of a discrete intervention. Rather, it commonly requires implementation of a treatment plan consisting of a number of sequentially ordered intermediate outcomes (steps in the treatment process) and the interventions appropriate for their attainment (Rosen, Proctor, and Livne 1985; Rosen 1993). We refer to such an inclusive treatment plan, necessary to attain a desired outcome, as an interventive program (Rosen and Proctor 1978). For example, reaching the outcome of stable community residence following hospitalization for a person with serious psychiatric disorder requires an interventive program consisting of both a number of intermediate outcomes (e.g., medication compliance, acceptance of client as tenant by a landlord) and the interventions capable of attaining these intermediate outcomes. Interventive programs, then, are distinguished from discrete interventions by their complexity and organization—the variety of components (intermediate outcomes and the interventions to achieve them), which are detailed and interrelated—that are necessary to reach a desired outcome.

Because attainment of an ultimate outcome usually requires implementation of an interventive program in contrast to a discrete intervention, it is useful to conceive of the arrays of interventions as heavily represented by interventive programs. From a practitioner's use perspective, the interventive program, encompassing a whole articulated treatment plan, has greater "guidance value" than a comparable assembly of discrete interventions—and is therefore preferable. In general, the more numerous the factors that influence or control a desired outcome are, the more complex the interventive program that will be required for its attainment. Figure 6.2 illustrates and partially details an interventive program in the target domain of social functioning.

It depicts the intermediate outcomes and their sequencing that were designated as necessary steps for attaining the ultimate outcome, as well as the interventions that were selected for achieving two of the intermediate outcomes.

Interventive programs within a given array may vary from one another in the intermediate outcomes specified, in their sequencing, and in the component interventions. Interventive programs also may differ in theoretical underpinnings, in the constructs that are involved in effecting change (e.g., cognitive, affective, or motor behaviors), and in the skills and other resources required for implementing the interventions. To facilitate the practitioner's choice of an interventive program from within an array, each program should detail the specific outcomes in relation to which it has been tested, their operational measures, and the average effect sizes obtained (with different client populations, as relevant). Also needed, of course, is detailed specification (manualization) of the component interventions to enable reliable enactment. Thus, within limits of the knowledge available at any point in time, interventive programs included in guidelines should outline detailed treatment plans as necessary and sufficient for guiding practitioners in reliable

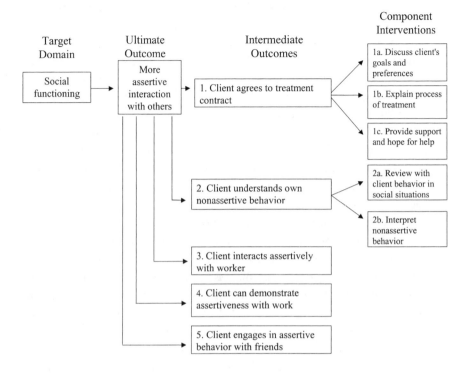

FIGURE 6.2 Excerpt from an Interventive Program

implementation. Such interventive programs are the preferred units in the arrays of interventions in practice guidelines.

The complexity of the treatment process has often been acknowledged (Garfield 1995). Yet most compilations of empirically tested guides to treatment do not address that complexity, implicitly assuming that presentation of discrete tested interventions in different problem areas is sufficient to help practitioners attain desired ultimate outcomes of treatment (Nathan and Gorman 1998; Thyer and Wodarski 1998). These compilations are usually mute regarding the difficult task of selecting and assembling a subset of discrete interventions in order to implement an effective treatment. Even critical commentaries on compilations of empirically tested interventions failed to address this issue (Garfield 1996, 1998). But the utility of developing practice guidelines for social work had been questioned for that very reason, claiming that they "will not likely delineate the specific order, combination, or amount of intervention components" (Richey and Roffman 1999:314). Our advocacy for inclusion of interventive programs as the units of intervention in practice guidelines addresses such criticism. Moreover, because interventive programs more fully respond to the demands of practice, their inclusion will likely attenuate some of practitioners' resistance to use of empirically based guidelines. Just as important, viewing interventions as interventive programs will focus research and generate the knowledge necessary for guidelines development.

To be included in practice guidelines, interventive programs should meet certain requirements. First, their component interventions must refer to behaviors that can be volitionally manipulated by practitioners—that is, behaviors that are capable of being enacted and varied at will. Such a basic requirement will avoid the problem of interventions being formulated through concepts that are difficult for practitioners to control and vary, such as affective states and their behavioral manifestations. Second, interventions must be specified in detail, so that they can be measured and enacted reliably (Rosen and Proctor 1978). Manualized interventions usually meet these two requirements, and therefore they can be applied across different practitioners and practice situations and are amenable to research evaluation (Rosen, Proctor, and Staudt 1999). A third requirement is that component interventions must all be linked causally to the intermediate outcomes that the program aims to attain (Rosen and Proctor 1978). This characteristic enables interventive programs to generate specific active predictions—predicting that the desired outcomes will result from practitioners' (or their agents') behavior (Rosen, Proctor, and Staudt 1999). Fourth, the order in which component outcomes should be pursued in the process of implementing the program must be delineated.

And last, empirical evidence must demonstrate that the interventive program and its component interventions are efficacious for attaining the designated outcomes, for the interventive program as a whole and for its component interventions. Following the recommendations of the American Psychological Association Task Force on Psychological Intervention Guidelines (1995), criteria for asserting the effectiveness of an intervention were extensively discussed. Because the term "empirically validated therapies," originally used by the Task Force, tends to overstate the actual validity status, Kendall (1998) suggested using "empirically supported therapies," also emphasizing thereby that the supporting evidence must be based on research and that other types of evidence will not suffice. Chambless and Hollon (1998) proposed minimal criteria for considering an intervention "empirically supported," designated efficacious, and meriting inclusion in guidelines. These include evidence from at least two independent randomized controlled comparisons showing that statistically significant superiority and moderate effect size favor the intervention in question, manualized interventions, and valid outcome measurements. Our proposed requirements for inclusion of interventive programs in guidelines encompass the methodological implications of evidence for efficacy suggested by Chambless and Hollon (1998), but emphasize requirements for formulation and the structure of interventions.

A consideration of inclusion of interventions in practice guidelines will have to address a number of additional issues. For example, what probability level should denote statistical significance? That is, what is the tolerated level of risk of a type I error, and how might it vary in relation to the type of outcome pursued, the client condition, and the available alternative treatments? Further, in addition to the statistical robustness of the results, what constitutes a clinically meaningful level of attainment of the desired outcome (i.e., effect size), and by what criteria should that vary? Among the considerations for interventions in general, and particularly pertinent to interventive programs, are those falling under the rubric of "dose-effect relationships." For optimal effectiveness, any given intervention may require varying "doses" of its elements when employed in relation to different outcomes and/or client characteristics. Practice guidelines should indicate the optimal dose in terms of frequency, duration, or intensity (Rosen and Proctor 1978). Dose-effect relationships have been much studied in medicine and also in pharmacotherapy for addictions and other psychological problems. But they have only recently been addressed in social-psychological interventions, primarily in relation to treatment duration and in the context of managed care services (Constantine 1999; Johnson and Shaha 1996; Salzer, Bickman, and Lambert 1999). Work on "stepped care"—fitting the components of established interventions for maximal cost-effectiveness for specific client groups—is a pertinent recent example of sensitivity to the dose-effect issue (Newman 2000).

Perhaps because of lack in conceptual and operational specificity for distinguishing among components of intervention in the first place, many approaches to intervention in our field typically pay little or no explicit attention to concerns with frequency, duration, or intensity of components (Hoagwood 2000; Howard et al. 1986). Variability in doses of intervention components may have been ignored also because components of globally formulated interventions were not distinguished but were instead lumped together with "nonspecific factors" in the proverbial black box of the treatment process. But whatever the history and reasons for neglect, dose-effect relationships for components of interventions must be investigated and incorporated into practice guidelines and implementation manuals, detailing the frequency, duration, and intensity of components in relation to the different outcomes and treatment circumstances.

Accompanying our advocacy for use of empirical evidence as criteria for inclusion in practice guidelines is awareness of the many issues that are inherent in such an approach. Because scientific evidence, by its very nature, is tentative and fraught with uncertainty, inclusion of interventions in guidelines must always be conditional, subject to reevaluation and to replacement as a result of newly developed and more appropriate alternatives. Although other criteria, such as expert opinion, consensus, and a political process, may also be factors in decisions on including interventions in guidelines, because of our advocacy for empirical criteria as necessary and primary, we do not address other criteria here. Acknowledging their inherent uncertainty, we believe that practice guidelines, if they are to be usable, need to help reduce the uncertainty of application by enabling practitioners to select interventions that are most appropriate for particular clients and situations. This function is discussed below in relation to the third and fourth components of guidelines.

PARTICULARIZING SELECTION OF INTERVENTIONS FOR CLIENTS AND SITUATIONS

To be maximally useful to practitioners, guidelines should aid in selecting the best interventive program for a particular client and a desired outcome from among an array of alternative interventions. To function in that role, guideline statements need to be qualified and modified in accordance with the relevant variables that moderate the relation between the intervention and the desired outcome (e.g., variables referring to client and population diversity, practice situation, and features of the problem). Most of the current formulations address intervention-outcome linkages as if they were universally and uniformly valid and applicable, irrespective of variability in client, problem, diagnosis, setting, or practitioner characteristics. However, variability on any one or more of these characteristics may materially affect and qualify the effectiveness of interventions. In recent years attention to these issues has been expressed by the distinction between efficacy as compared to effectiveness of interventions (Chambless and Hollon 1998; Newman and Tejeda 1996). Efficacy refers to the testing and validation of an intervention in relation to its hypothesized outcomes under relatively uniform and controlled conditions, with the primary focus on assessing its internal validity. Effectiveness refers to field-testing an intervention and assessing its validity in relation to client, setting, and practitioner factors, thus establishing its differential external validity.

The distinction between efficacy and effectiveness is related to the notion of "aptitude x treatment" interactions that can differentially affect the hypothesized relationship between an intervention and its purported outcomes

(Shoham-Solomon and Hannah 1991; Smith and Sechrest 1991). Although originally discussed primarily in terms of practitioner variables, aptitude can refer to any of the relevant dimensions (client, setting, practitioner, and so on) that characterize the variability between different treatment situations and qualify the basic hypothesized intervention-outcome relationship. Thus, for practice guidelines to function well as aids to selection and use of interventions, they must take into account the variables in the practice situation that impinge on and qualify the effectiveness of interventions. A variable would merit incorporation into practice guidelines if it moderates the effectiveness of an intervention when applied across different values of that variable.

Considering moderator variables adds complexity to the structure of guidelines but does not yet fully reflect the likely complexity of guidelines under ideal knowledge conditions. Just as the effectiveness of an intervention needs to be considered in relation to the relevant moderating conditions, one must not ignore the fact that the moderator variables themselves may interact to affect the effectiveness of the intervention. That is, if age moderated the effect of intervention A on outcome X, other dimensions (e.g., diagnostic status, ethnicity, gender, education) may also be relevant moderators of that effect. Ideally, the joint influence (interaction) of such dimensions should also be reflected in guidelines. Although one can imagine a long and unwieldy list of potential moderator variables, their number will be practically limited to those that are investigated and found to account for the largest proportion of the variance. In any event, the challenge of addressing the influence of moderator variables in a manner that enables practitioner-friendly use must be eventually confronted and provided for in guidelines. That requires also developing the requisite technology (conceptual, statistical, and electronic) for integrating and presenting both the "main effects" of interventive programs and their interactions with moderator variables.

This portrayal of the features necessary (albeit ideal) for realizing the potential of practice guidelines acknowledges the complexity of factors that influence and maintain human behavior, on the one hand, and the resultant complexity of the means for behavior change, on the other. Our advocacy for development of practice guidelines in spite of the seemingly daunting task is based in part on the assumed futility (at least near-term) of searching for "magic bullet" treatments—simple treatments whose influence will be relatively independent of relevant moderator variables and hence more universally applicable. Were such magic bullets found, practice guidelines could be appreciably simplified.

To summarize, the third component of practice guidelines should consist of a series of qualifying statements that, for each array of interventions and interventive programs in relation to an outcome category, direct the practitioner to the empirically tested interventive program most appropriate for the outcome pursued in relation to the characteristics of a particular client and practice situation. This component of practice guidelines assists the practitioner in particularizing treatment decisions for individual clients. In that sense it responds to a major source of practitioner concern and helps address constructively one of the basic dilemmas of evidence-based clinical practice—the idiographic application of empirical generalizations (Rosen 1983, 1994, 2002). But it is unlikely that all of the uncertainty regarding the fit between a pretested intervention and the needs of an individual client can be removed as a result of conclusions drawn from effectiveness research using samples of clients and situations. In order for practitioners to willingly apply empirical generalizations fraught with uncertainty to an individual client, they need a tool for implementation, an explicit and guiding algorithm that enables them to help the client maximally (Rosen 2002). This is one of the functions of the fourth component in the structure of practice guidelines.

ADDRESSING GAPS IN KNOWLEDGE AND UNCERTAINTY OF APPLICATION

Realistically, even under the best of circumstances practice guidelines are not immutable, nor can they address satisfactorily all practice situations. Indeed, use of empirically based practice guidelines is more likely to reveal the shortcomings of available knowledge to address treatment needs of a particular client than can be expected of unaided practice. Therefore, practice guidelines must also enable practitioners to deal with gaps in knowledge and with the uncertainties that are attendant in applying research-based guidelines to a particular case. We conceived this component in the structure of practice guidelines as helping practitioners deal with the limitations of knowledge and contributing to further guidelines development by feeding practice-derived hypotheses to the research enterprise. More specifically, this guidelines component should have four primary functions: (1) highlighting gaps in knowledge and limitations attendant with applying the best-fitting intervention (selected through the third component) to the particular client and outcome sought, and thereby also legitimating the notion that the best available practice knowledge may have only an imperfect fit; (2) providing an algorithm for systematic implementation of interventions, with recursive evaluation of the effects of planned interventions as well as of improvisations; (3) through the use of such an implementation algorithm, encouraging practitioners to innovate and improvise; and (4) providing the means for communicating and centrally cumulating (via a Practice Research Network [PRN]) highlights of practitioners' implementation process and conclusions, including newly derived clinical hypotheses.

Thus, whereas the first three components of practice guidelines serve practitioners as decision guides, the fourth component aims to facilitate implementation. By having procedures that guide practitioners to systematically implement and evaluate, innovate as necessary, and draw conclusions, it gives them constructive means to deal with the inevitable uncertainty associated with applying research-based knowledge rather than be daunted by it. By eliciting practitioners' evaluations and feedback (through a PRN), this component also allows practitioners to become full partners in the profession's knowledge development efforts. In our previous studies of systematic planned practice (SPP) we have used a paper-and-pencil procedure for eliciting and obtaining practitioners' reports of the information addressed in this component (Rosen 1992; Rosen et al. 1995). On the basis of these experiences we believe that such information could be assembled with the aid of a user-friendly system.

From the profession's perspective, this component of practice guidelines ensures that the research arm of the profession constantly has an "ear to the field," gathering information through systematic practitioner feedback on implementation, which in turn can suggest practice-generated clinical hypotheses and pose cutting-edge questions for further research. In that manner, with the help of effective PRNs, this component of practice guidelines facilitates an organized and systematic effort by researchers to retrieve, process, and incorporate ongoing feedback from practice into the continuously evolving practice research agenda. Our conception of the function and structure of guidelines, and particularly this component, assumes a user-friendly electronic system for both the retrieval of knowledge statements and the recording of practitioners' experience in applying the guidelines. Further, we foresee development of practitioner-friendly PRNs for central retrieval, distillation, and integration of this information (profession-wide or by sectors) with the aim of generating practice-based hypotheses for more systematic study.

DIRECTIONS FOR RESEARCH

In addition to utilizing the relevant research from allied fields, social work is largely dependent upon its own research activity to generate practice guidelines for the domains of its responsibility. Each practice guideline for intervention must be based upon a body of evidence that supports its effectiveness. We view the field's knowledge-development efforts for formulation of practice guidelines and for enhancing their use in practice within a framework of three interrelated clusters of research and other activities (Proctor and Rosen 1998). Using this framework, we provide here a brief outline of some aspects of the research agenda that social work should pursue in order to develop practice guidelines for intervention. (For a fuller discussion, see Proctor and Rosen, chapter 16, this volume.)

Figure 6.3 represents the three clusters of activity for developing practice guidelines. Each activity cluster addresses unique aspects, but activities in the three clusters are interdependent and iterative. The first cluster, A, includes the research activities needed to create the building blocks for practice guidelines—research to identify and classify outcomes, and formulation and testing of interventions. Cluster B contains the conceptual and research activities that are necessary to consolidate and assemble knowledge of the building blocks into usable guidelines. Activities in this cluster include review and synthesis of the relevant research, initial formulation of guidelines, field-testing, revising, and retesting. Some of the activities in this cluster are similar to processes of design and development highlighted by Thomas (1984) and Rothman and Thomas (1994). The third cluster, C, concerns the many and complex tasks necessary to ensure the dissemination and proper implementation of the guidelines in practice.

A. DEVELOPMENT OF BUILDING BLOCKS

RESEARCH TO IDENTIFY OUTCOMES AND DEVELOP TAXONOMIES OF TARGETS An outcome-based taxonomy of the targets of intervention should be a fundamental component of practice guidelines on intervention, organizing the knowledge statements and facilitating their retrieval. Our review of the literature (Proctor, Rosen, and Rhee 2002) revealed no profession-wide nomenclature for outcome-based targets nor any suggested classifications of outcomes. Hence, research leading to identification and taxonomy of the outcomes that social workers pursue should be of high priority on a research agenda to develop practice guidelines.

RESEARCH TO DEVELOP ARRAYS OF INTERVENTION Research to develop and test effective interventions and interventive programs for designated outcomes provides the core building blocks for practice guidelines. Our analysis of the social work literature revealed that only a small proportion of its research can contribute to compilation of tested interventions (Rosen, Proctor, and Staudt 1999). In a four-and-a-half-year sample of publications, we found that less than 14 percent of the published research related to development of effective interventions, and the majority of these studies were unarticulated and ill-defined discrete interventions or interventive programs (Rosen, Proctor, and Staudt 2003). No doubt a critical need exists to develop

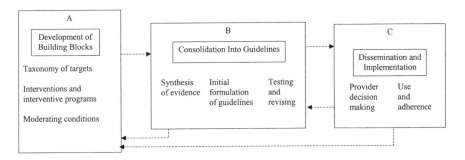

FIGURE 6.3 Activity Clusters in Guidelines Development

and test interventions and interventive programs targeted for specific outcomes and client populations.

RESEARCH TO GUIDE THE SELECTION OF INTERVENTIONS AMONG ALTERNATIVES Such research needs to be undertaken in real field conditions in order to address the gamut of moderating variables that are likely to affect the relationship between interventions and outcomes and that help to guide the differential applicability of interventive programs according to practice settings and client diversity factors. Because social work practice spans a broad range of populations, cultures, and service settings, its research must deliberately address the applicability and modification of interventions in relation to such factors.

B. CONSOLIDATION INTO GUIDELINES

The second necessary cluster of activities for developing guidelines concerns the challenges of synthesizing and consolidating building-blocks knowledge into statements that are integrated into practice guidelines. Outcome-based target domains will serve as the logical beginning foci for consolidating the building-blocks knowledge. It could then be further refined according to outcome categories within domains, as our derived guidelines prototype suggests (Rosen, Proctor, and Staudt 2003) and perhaps also organized according to problems or fields of practice (Kirk, chapter 8, this volume). These activities involve critical review of the extant research in relation to a particular outcome category. Activities within this cluster should focus on assigning priorities to the different interventive programs within an array according to the differential influence of moderator variables, which could lead to specification of conditional statements for choosing among interventions according to the relevant characteristics of a particular case. Of course, all the consolidation activities should be articulated with feedback to, and compose a recursive process with, research activities in the building-block cluster.

C. DISSEMINATION AND IMPLEMENTATION

The third cluster consists of research and other activities needed for the dissemination of practice guidelines to practitioners and for facilitation of appropriate implementation of the guidelines. Particular attention should be given to the development of a user-friendly algorithm to help practitioners in the process of implementing interventions, as specified for the fourth component of practice guidelines. Research in this cluster may need to draw heavily upon theoretical and empirical work in other disciplines concerning knowledge dissemination, clinical judgment, and decision making. Means for training and educating both new and seasoned practitioners in the use of guidelines and their application with the requisite fidelity must be addressed. Further development is needed of decision support mechanisms to facilitate practitioner selection of guideline-congruent treatments and to enhance their evidence-based clinical skills. The effect of alternative sources of authority and sanction on persuading practitioners to actually apply practice guidelines must also be addressed. A related line of investigations should test the effects of incentives in influencing guidelines-congruent practice at both the individual practitioner level and the service organization level.

As practice guidelines increasingly address the outcomes that practitioners pursue in the field, as they outline in greater detail the interventive programs to be followed, and as they become more capable of reducing uncertainty regarding their effects on client populations of interest, it should become easier to "sell" them to practitioners. At present in the field of social work, the rudimentary knowledge base on interventions and the infancy of guideline development render the dissemination and adoption of evidence-based practice especially challenging. That notwithstanding, efforts to develop dissemination procedures and means for practitioners' use of research-based intervention knowledge should commence with vigor.

——

Our view of practice guidelines is conditioned by the current state of empirically tested knowledge on intervention and the extent of its utilization in practice. As is by now common knowledge, social work research capable of guiding interventions is scant (Rosen, Proctor, and Staudt 1999), and the extent of research utilization in practice is correspondingly meager (Rosen

1994; Rosen et al. 1995). This situation led colleagues in our profession and in others to doubt the fields' readiness for practice guidelines (Kirk 1999; Garfield 1996; but see Howard and Jenson 1999). Nonetheless, we view the development of practice guidelines for intervention as but one of the necessary steps to redress this situation. Practice guidelines will surely not evolve easily or on their own—the challenge of their development must be confronted by social work, researchers, and practitioners alike.

The complexity of our conception for the function and structure of practice guidelines notwithstanding, we acknowledge the "short shrift" we have given to many difficult issues—such as the intricacy of conditional hypotheses incorporating the effects of moderating variables and the consequent challenges of applying guidelines to a specific client and situation. We also acknowledge that our depiction of guidelines is tilted toward the ideal, rational decision-making model, leaving to future technological developments the capacity to fully and elegantly integrate the variety of knowledge statements and conditions in a manner that can aid ongoing decision making and application. We take solace in the burgeoning interdisciplinary research on problem solving and decision making, for we believe it offers direction for enhancing use of guidelines by individual practitioners. Although optimal decision making in a multivariable decision space is a goal worth pursuing, we can strive in the meantime for "good enough," satisficing decisions (Gigerenzer and Goldstein 1996; Janis and Mann 1977). We trust that as better knowledge of the complex processes involved in decision making is gained, and as intervention knowledge grows, practitioners' decision making will be improved and will more closely approximate the optimal.

NOTE

1. We use the term *disease model* to refer to a general orientation that views professional practice as aiming to remove, correct, reverse, cure, or negate some inherently undesirable condition (that is, disease, illness), thereby restoring a state of "health."

REFERENCES

American Psychiatric Association. (1993). Practice guidelines for the treatment of major depressive disorder in adults. *American Journal of Psychiatry, 150* (supplement 4), 1–26.

American Psychological Association Task Force on Psychological Intervention Guidelines. (1995). *Template for Developing Guidelines: Interventions for Mental Disorders and Psychological Aspects of Physical Disorders*. Washington, D.C.: American Psychological Association.

Chambless, D. L., and Hollon, S. D. (1998). Defining empirically supported therapies. *Journal of Consulting and Clinical Psychology, 66,* 7–18.

Constantine, J. L. (1999). Mental health service delivery: The relationship between mental health financing components and consumer outcomes. Ph.D. diss., Washington University, St. Louis.

Flexner, A. (1915). *Is Social Work a Profession? In Proceedings of the National Conference of Charities and Corrections.* Chicago: National Conference of Charities and Corrections.

Garfield, S. L. (1995). *Psychotherapy: An Eclectic-Integrative Approach.* New York: Wiley.

———. (1996). Some problems associated with "validated forms of psychotherapy." *Clinical Psychology: Science and Practice, 3* (3), 218–229.

———. (1998). Some comments on empirically supported treatments. *Journal of Clinical and Consulting Psychology, 66,* 121–125.

Gigerenzer, G., and Goldstein, D. G. (1996). Reasoning the fast and frugal way: Models of bounded rationality. *Psychological Review, 103,* 650–669.

Hoagwood, K. (2000). Commentary: The dose effect in children's mental health services. *Journal of the American Academy of Child and Adolescent Psychiatry, 39,* 172–175.

Howard, K. I., Kopta, S. M., Krause, M. S., and Orlinsky, D. E. (1986). The dose-response relationship in psychotherapy. *American Psychologist, 41,* 159–164.

Howard, M. O., and Jenson, J. M. (1999). Barriers to development, utilization, and evaluation of social work practice guidelines: Toward an action plan for social work. *Research on Social Work Practice, 9,* 347–364.

Janis, I. L., and Mann, L. (1977). *Decision Making: A Psychological Analysis of Conflict, Choice, and Commitment.* New York: Free Press.

Johnson, L. D., and Shaha, S. (1996). Improving quality in psychotherapy. *Psychotherapy, 33,* 225–236.

Kazdin, A. E. (1999). The meanings and measurement of clinical significance. *Journal of Consulting and Clinical Psychology, 67,* 332–339.

Kendall, P. C. (1998). Empirically supported psychological therapies. *Journal of Consulting and Clinical Psychology, 6,* 3–6.

Kirk, S. A. (1999). Good intentions are not enough: Practice guidelines for social work. *Research on Social Work Practice, 9,* 302–310.

Nathan, P. E., and Gorman, J. M. (1998). *A Guide to Treatments That Work.* New York: Oxford University Press.

Newman, F. L., and Tejeda, M. J. (1996). The need for research that is designed to support decisions in the delivery of mental health services. *American Psychologist, 51,* 1040–1049.

Newman, M. G. (2000). Recommendations for a cost-offset model of psychotherapy allocation using generalized anxiety disorder as an example. *Journal of Consulting and Clinical Psychology, 68,* 549–555.

Proctor, E. K., and Rosen, A. (1998). "Guidelines for Direct Practice: A Research Agenda." Paper presented at the International Conference on Social Welfare, Jerusalem, Israel, July.

Proctor, E. K., Rosen, A., and Rhee, C. (2002). Outcomes in social work practice. *Social Work Research and Evaluation, 3* (2), 1–17.

Reid, W. J. (1997). Evaluating the dodo's verdict: Do all interventions have equivalent outcomes? *Social Work Research, 21,* 5–16.

Richey, C. A., and Roffman, R. A. (1999). On the sidelines of guidelines: Further thoughts on the fit between clinical guidelines and social work practice. *Research on Social Work Practice, 9,* 312–321.

Rosen, A. (1983). Barriers to utilization of research by social work practitioners. *Journal of Social Service Research, 6,* 1–15.

———. (1992). Facilitating clinical decision making and evaluation. *Families in Society, 73,* 522–532.

———. (1993). Systematic planned practice. *Social Service Review, 67,* 84–100.

———. (1994). Knowledge use in direct practice. *Social Service Review, 68,* 561–577.

———. (2002). "Evidence-Based Social Work Practice: Challenges and Promise." Invited address at the Society for Social Work and Research, January, San Diego, California.

Rosen, A., and Proctor, E. K. (1978). Specifying the treatment process: The basis for effectiveness research. *Journal of Social Service Research, 2* (1), 25–43.

———. (1981). Distinctions between treatment outcomes and their implications for treatment evaluation. *Journal of Consulting and Clinical Psychology, 49,* 418–425.

Rosen, A., Proctor, E. K., and Livne, S. (1985). Planning and direct practice. *Social Service Review, 59,* 161–177.

Rosen, A., Proctor, E. K., Morrow-Howell, N., and Staudt, M. (1995). Rationales for practice decisions: Variations in knowledge use by decision task and social work service. *Research on Social Work Practice, 5,* 501–523.

Rosen, A., Proctor, E. K., and Staudt, M. (1999). Social work research and the quest for effective practice. *Social Work Research, 23,* 4–14.

———. (2003). Targets of change and interventions in social work: An empirically based prototype for developing practice guidelines. *Research on Social Work Practice, 13,* 208–233.

Rothman, J., and Thomas, E. J. (Eds.). (1994). *Intervention Research: Design and Development for Human Service.* New York: Haworth.

Salzer, M. S., Bickman, L., and Lambert, E. W. (1999). Dose-effect relationships in children's psychotherapy services. *Journal of Consulting and Clinical Psychology, 67,* 228–238.

Seligman, M. E. P., and Csikszentmihalyi, M. (2000). Positive psychology: An introduction. *American Psychologist, 55,* 5–14.

Shoham-Salomon, V., and Hannah, M. T. (1991). Client-treatment interaction in the study of differential change processes. *Journal of Consulting and Clinical Psychology, 59,* 217–225.

Smith, B., and Sechrest, L. (1991). Treatment of aptitude: Treatment interactions. *Journal of Consulting and Clinical Psychology, 59,* 233–244.

Thomas, E. J. (1984). *Designing Interventions for the Helping Professions.* Beverly Hills, Calif.: Sage.

Thomas, E. J., and Rothman, J. (1994). An Integrative Perspective on Intervention Research. In J. Rothman and E. J. Thomas (Eds.), *Intervention Research: Design and Development for Human Service* (pp. 3–24). New York: Haworth.

Thyer, B. A., and Wodarski, J. S. (Eds.). (1998). *Handbook of Empirical Social Work Practice* (Vols. 1–2). New York: Wiley.

7

SOCIAL WORK SHOULD HELP DEVELOP INTERDISCIPLINARY EVIDENCE-BASED PRACTICE GUIDELINES, NOT DISCIPLINE-SPECIFIC ONES

BRUCE A. THYER

n Proctor and Rosen's chapter "The Structure and Function of Social Work Practice Guidelines" it is evident that the authors support the development of practice guidelines (PGs) for use by social workers, and so do I. Let me review what I see as some of the main points of their chapter, and my reactions thereto.

Proctor and Rosen spend much time discussing the importance of PGs' being based upon an appropriate organizing taxonomy. They note that virtually all PGs developed to date have been structured around a taxonomy of *disorders,* usually the conditions adumbrated in the *Diagnostic and Statistical Manual of Mental Disorders* (American Psychiatric Association 1994). There are sound reasons for this. The *DSM,* for all its faults, represents the most advanced nosological system for behavioral, emotional, and intellectual dysfunctions ever developed. Each new edition comes closer than the previous one to approximating nature's truth pertaining to the realities of human psychopathology. The *DSM* has stimulated an immense amount of empirical research on the *treatment* of the conditions enumerated therein, and the aggregated results of these studies have served as the foundation for the practice guidelines developed by psychiatry and psychology. Given that mental health has been and remains one of the most active fields of practice for social workers, it is fortunate indeed that practice guidelines have proliferated in this area.

While not explicitly repudiating the disorder-orientation of PGs, Proctor and Rosen hold out a tantalizing vision of an alternative or supplementary organizing principle, "a taxonomy of the target outcomes toward which interventions are directed." Proctor and Rosen favor using "a nosology of targets of intervention . . . that describe the desired outcomes of intervention," citing the inappropriateness of what they label the dominant "problem-reversal" approach found in many clinical situations. In making their case for developing an outcome-based taxonomy to structure practice guidelines, Proctor and Rosen present some purported shortcomings of the current approaches to practice guideline development. I believe that several of these purported shortcomings misrepresent the assumptions undergirding the development of practice guidelines, and I present my reactions to these in the next sections of this chapter.

IS PROBLEM REVERSAL THE INHERENT ORIENTATION OF A DISORDER-BASED TAXONOMY?

I am not persuaded by Proctor and Rosen's chapter that the disorder-based structure of PGs implies a "problem-reversal" approach to intervention. One may employ the *DSM* as a component of an assessment process, yet use, for example, a behavior-analytic approach to treatment, one that may well involve a careful functional analysis of the personal, interpersonal, and psychosocial factors, and environmental setting, antecedents, behaviors, and consequences. Behavior-analytic intervention, itself the original Person-in-Environment (PIE) approach to practice (Thyer 1999; Thyer and Myers 1997), may be directed toward the client him/herself, toward significant others in the client's environment, toward the environment itself, toward the provision of concrete services, or toward information and referral. Proctor and Rosen paint a picture of PGs based on disorders as automatically resulting in problem-reversal interventions. I do not believe that this is true, any more than that contemporary medicine should be characterized by the outdated label of "allopathic," e.g., treat fever with a fever-reducing agent. Sometimes allopathic treatments are needed (aspirin can be very helpful for someone with the flu), but if fever is secondary to a bacterial infection, then antibiotic therapy is needed to eliminate the causative agent. This is not symptomatic or problem-reversing treatment—it is curative.

For example, a client may meet the *DSM*-defined diagnostic criteria for "severe mental retardation." This certainly does not imply that treatment is aimed at improving the client's intelligence! Rather, we would expect a thorough assessment of her needs, abilities, strengths, and problems to generate a comprehensive treatment plan. Perhaps spectacles for poor eyesight; a behavior-management plan for self-injurious behavior; case management to help her obtain all services to which she is entitled; family psychoeducation and support; respite care; social skills training; special educational services; and yes, maybe, anticonvulsant medications to control seizures (even if the cause of the seizures remains unknown)!

To reiterate—the use of PGs structured around disorders does not imply a problem-reversal orientation toward intervention. In fact, such an allopathic approach would contravene the central premise of PGs and of evidence-based practice—namely, the selection of first-choice treatments based upon the available scientific research, regardless of the discipline or theory from which it emerged. Thus, while welcoming Proctor and Rosen's proposals to develop an alternative taxonomic scheme for use in the development of PGs, I suggest that they do not preface this effort by implying that the current system inevitably results in an obviously deficient problem-reversal approach to treatment.

MEDICAL OR DISEASE MODEL?

Proctor and Rosen engage in the common practice of equating the use of "disorder" as an organizing principle for practice guidelines with the "disease" model of medicine, viewing practice "as aiming to remove, correct, reverse, cure, or negate some inherently undesirable condition (that is, disease, illness), thereby restoring a state of 'health'" and "client presents with problem (illness), practitioner reverses (cures) the problem" (Proctor and Rosen, chapter 6, this volume, p. 111). However, the concept of disorder is not equivalent to the concept of disease. The medical model assumes that a given disease has a biological etiology, that biologically based treatments are the first-choice interventions, and that physicians have primacy in both diagnosis and treatment. By contrast, most common typologies for disorders, such as those enumerated in the *DSM*, are theoretically neutral with respect to etiology (the *DSM* itself states this, and etiological content is very rarely presented in the manual), and both etiology and appropriate treatment are viewed as issues that require adequate empirical support, neither endorsing nor excluding any approach (e.g., medical treatment versus psychosocial intervention) *a priori*.

The *DSM* itself *does not* endorse a medical or disease model of human dysfunction, although this misreading has been repeated enough times as to be accepted by many within the profession. The inaccurate use of the pejorative label "medical model" as a method of criticizing structuring practice guidelines around the concept of "disorders" does not further informed discussion of the topic. Using the term *disorder* does not imply disease, and social work intervention need not be conceptualized as bringing about a "cure" of these purported illnesses. To use evidence-based assessment methods, and to select treatments from evidence-based psychosocial interventions found in practice guidelines is not to follow a medical model. It follows what can be more accurately termed a "scientific" model, and it is indeed a very good thing. In fact, it is the best approach we have.

WE NEED CONCRETE EXAMPLES OF ALTERNATIVE TAXONOMIES

Proctor and Rosen favorably cite Kazdin's (1999) recent article in which he suggests that some alternative or additional issues apart from symptom reduction are needed to comprehensively address the determination of clinical significance of change. "Impairment," "functioning in everyday life," "quality of life," and "social significance" are some of the additional considerations mentioned by Kazdin. In my reading of his article, reducing problems is not seen as misguided or unimportant, only that there are other factors that may need to be taken into account when making a determination of whether of not a given intervention may be considered adequately evidence-based. Problem reversal may well be a necessary but not sufficient criterion to assess the meaningfulness of change. Kazdin did not, however, provide such an alternative organizing taxonomy; nor, significantly, do Proctor and Rosen. Their proposal would be considerably strengthened by one or more concrete examples of the types of alternative concepts that they envision.

Consider the efforts involved in attempting to develop an alternative or supplemental classification scheme: coming to an agreement on an initial taxonomy, refining it, demonstrating reliability (interrater, test-retest), and demonstrating validity (concurrent, predictive). Ultimately it must demonstrate its clinical utility. This would be an immense task. I wonder if there is sufficient disciplinary support to undertake such an ambitious program. The life of the Person-in-Environment (PIE) system, an approach to classifying problems of social functioning (Karls and Wandrei 1995) may be instructive in this regard. PIE, which was sponsored by the National Association of Social Workers (NASW) in the late 1980s, has not yet made an appreciable impact on professional practice or demonstrated its utility in improving the lives of social work clients. Virtually no work has been undertaken and published addressing the system's reliability or validity. If a novel classification scheme sponsored by the huge NASW, possessing as it does immense resources, has stagnated, this does not auger well for future efforts along these lines.

WHY REINVENT EVIDENTIARY STANDARDS?

Proctor and Rosen present five criteria that interventive programs must meet in order to qualify for inclusion in a practice guideline. Paraphrased, these are:

1. Interventions must consist of behaviors that can actually be carried out.
2. Interventions must be adequately proceduralized, e.g., replicable by others.
3. Interventions must be causally linked to specific delineated outcomes.
4. Interventions must specify the order in which intermediate outcomes should be pursued.
5. Interventions must possess satisfactory evidence of being able to bring about the desired client outcome.

I must confess to being a bit confused over this list, in terms of both the criteria and the intent. Criteria 1, 2, and 3 are subsumed under criterion 5, for example. Also, it may not be wise to try and replicate the efforts of others to develop inclusionary criteria for use in developing practice guidelines. For example, in the early 1990s, Section III (Society for a Science of Clinical Psychology) of Division 12 (Clinical Psychology) of the American Psychological Association (Big APA) created a "Task Force on Promotion and Dissemination of Psychological Procedures" (Task Force 1995). This group had a twofold mandate: (1) to develop scientifically defensible criteria as to what would constitute adequate "evidence" that a given treatment was genuinely helpful for clients with particular disorders, and (2) to then survey the published literature to see what interventions met these evidentiary standards. The scientific standards decided upon by the APA Task Force to designate a particular intervention as "well established" in the treatment of clients with a particular disorder were modest indeed (see table 7.1). Setting aside the question of whether requiring only two suitable randomized controlled clinical trials is a sufficiently rigorous standard, you will note that the task force did include the requirement that the interventions be available in a manualized format, which certainly addresses the first and second criteria of Proctor and Rosen. The third criterion is precisely the point of the entire set of standards—to be able to make the claim that Intervention X benefits clients with Disorder Y. Clearly, other disciplines are much further along in thinking about, refining, and indeed applying, inclusionary criteria for use in the development of practice guidelines.

Following the establishment of the evidentiary standards that appear in table 7.1 (itself a very arduous process), the APA Task Force then undertook reviews of the literature to begin determining what interventions met these criteria (somewhat less stringent standards are used to endorse a treatment as "probably efficacious"). Compilations of these findings have also appeared, organized by various disorders and those psychosocial interventions that may be considered to be well established (Chambless et al. 1998; Nathan and

TABLE 7.1 Criteria for Empirically Validated Therapies

WELL-ESTABLISHED TREATMENTS

I. At least two good between-group design experiments demonstrating efficacy in one or more of the following ways:
   A. Superior (statistically significantly so) to pill or psychological placebo or to another treatment
   B. Equivalent to an already established treatment in experiments with adequate sample sizes

OR

II. A large series of single-case-design experiments ($N > 9$) demonstrating efficacy. These experiments must have:
   A. Used good experimental designs
   B. Compared the intervention to another treatment, as in I-A above.

FURTHER CRITERIA FOR BOTH I AND II

III. Experiments must be conducted with treatment manuals
IV. Characteristics of the client samples must be clearly specified
V. Effects must be demonstrated by at least two different investigators or investigating teams

---

SOURCE: REPRODUCED FROM CHAMBLESS ET AL. 1998.

Gorman 1998). The task force has also produced bibliographies of protocol-based treatment manuals for these evidence-based therapies (e.g., Sanderson and Woody 1995). These impressive accomplishments represent very significant steps in moving the human services along in the direction of evidence-based practice.

Another set of inclusionary standards in the development of evidence-based practice guidelines in the field of mental health can be found in the editorial reviewing policies of the journal *Evidence-Based Mental Health*. In order for a published outcome study to qualify for abstracting in this journal, the report must meet the following criteria (paraphrased from Staff 2000):

1. The study used random assignment of participants to comparison groups.
2. The study must present follow-up data on at least 80 percent of those beginning the study.

3. The outcome measures must have known or probable clinical importance.
4. The data analysis must be appropriate to the research design.
5. Clients must be diagnosed according to some classification scheme with acceptable reliability (e.g., the *DSM* or the *International Classification of Diseases*) after assessment by clinically qualified interviewers, preferably with documentation of interrater reliability in diagnosis.
6. Outcome assessments must be blind to client assignment to experimental conditions.
7. Outcome data must be collected *prospectively* and involve comparison groups, with the order of preference in acceptability of conclusions descending from randomized controlled trials (the strongest form of evidence) to quasi-randomized controlled trials, non-randomized controlled trials, cohort studies with case-by-case matching or statistical adjustment to create comparable groups, or nested case control studies (the weakest form of evidence).

Now, these are stringent standards indeed! Few social work outcome studies could be found to meet all of the above criteria, but these criteria at least have the virtue of clarity and begin to provide answers to the question of what constitutes scientifically acceptable evidence. These can also provide standards toward which social work can strive. Of course, other forms of evidence can also provide valuable leads regarding the potential effectiveness of psychosocial interventions (e.g., single-system research designs, prospectively designed studies, chart reviews), but in terms of the development and potential impact of practice guidelines on practice, it can be contended that these should be based upon the *best* available evidence, evidence judged according to standards similar to those described above.

DO WE REALLY NEED *SOCIAL WORK* PRACTICE GUIDELINES?

The title of this chapter, "Social Work Should Help Develop Interdisciplinary Evidence-Based Practice Guidelines, Not Discipline-Specific Ones," makes what I believe to be an important point. Client problems, client disorders, taxonomies of targets—choose whatever label you prefer, are *not discipline specific*. In today's interdisciplinary world there are no "social work problems." All of the helping professions are involved in assisting clients with their problems—psychiatry, psychology, behavior analysis, all now share our field's historic concern with working with the most vulnerable, the most oppressed, and victims of social injustice. It simply makes no good sense for social workers to busily set about the task of developing discipline-specific practice guidelines, and in the same building in Washington, D.C. (the American Psychological Association building, which also houses the NASW headquarters) to have psychologists doing the same thing! And literally down the street to have the psychiatrists and nurses each similarly and independently creating practice guidelines for their own respective disciplinary practitioners. Shall we have Social Work Practice Guidelines for Helping Clients with Major Depression and parallel but independently developed Practice Guidelines for Psychologists, another set for psychiatrists, and yet another for nurses, each of which addresses the proper and presumably evidence-based care of depressed individuals? And shall we replicate this absurdity over dozens of disorders? Of course not.

Figure 6.1 in Proctor and Rosen's chapter presents their attempt to illustrate a prototype of practice guidelines based on current *social work* research on interventions, as reviewed in Rosen, Proctor, and Staudt (1999). Heaven help the distressed couple or family whose practitioner offers them interventions drawn exclusively from the *social work* literature! It is obvious that any effort in developing practice guidelines, whether for a disorder or a desired client outcome, must both ethically and scientifically draw upon *all* relevant, scientifically credible research, not just the limited samples of pertinent studies that appear in our often under-read and poorly cited disciplinary journals.

Do I think that our profession should work toward the development of *social work* practice guidelines? Absolutely not. It would be a grave mistake, ultimately prove unworkable, and waste an immense amount of professional resources. Simply put, our disciplinary knowledge base is far too thin to support PGs specific to our field. In fact, the whole notion of discipline-specific "social work" knowledge is untenable, but that is the subject of another paper (Thyer 2002). As Howard and Lambert (1996) summarize, we have too few doctoral-level practitioner-researchers, insufficient research training, deficient scholarly activity, an inadequate scientific journal infrastructure, and deficient dissemination and utilization of scientific information within social work to "go it alone" in the development of practice guidelines.

Here are some facts. Practice guidelines are here to stay. They will continue to be developed for additional disorders, including some of the more complex psychosocial problems alluded to by Proctor and Rosen. Practice guidelines will play an increasing role in the provision of services under managed care, and perhaps goaded by legal liability issues, in the provision of agency-based and private-practice services. Furthermore, practice guidelines will continue to be organized around the concept of *disorders,* primarily those found within the *DSM* but hopefully broadening in scope to address additional psychosocial dysfunctions. Some steps are being taken in this direction (e.g., Torrey et al. 1998).

FUTURE DIRECTIONS FOR SOCIAL WORK AND PRACTICE GUIDELINES

What shall we do? The answer is relatively simple to describe but perhaps more difficult to undertake. Rather than initiate the development of *social work* practice guidelines for particular disorders, we should act assertively to become much more involved in the *interdisciplinary* development of practice guidelines.

I would like to see the leadership of the NASW and of the Society for Social Work and Research proactively reach out to their counterparts in psychiatry and psychology and say, in effect, "Let's work together." Let's urge the abandonment of practice guidelines developed with a disciplinary focus in mind in favor of practice guidelines created by interdisciplinary teams of experts drawn from all the major helping professions, individuals committed to following the leads of the best evidence that science has to offer. It is an embarrassing commentary on our professional leadership that social work involvement has been so minimal in past efforts to develop practice guidelines. Perhaps the best-developed guidelines have been those produced by the American Psychiatric Association. At the end of each guideline is a list of those individuals and professional organizations that contributed comments. I found the NASW to have provided comments on two of these ten guidelines (those for eating disorders and for bipolar disorder). When it came to the development of PGs for clients with schizophrenia, dementia, delirium, major depression, and panic disorder, our organizational input was absent. This must change. And equivalent outreach efforts should be undertaken with the Agency for Health Care Policy and Research and with the American Psychological Association, as well as other groups involved in developing practice guidelines. Do I think that our field should collaborate with others in the development of evidence-based practice guidelines, structured around selected disorders, for use by *all* members of the helping professions? Yes, indeed. I see no other reasonable choice.

It is also important that, to the maximum extent possible, practice guidelines be based upon careful reviews of the scientific literature conducted in accordance with the principles of evidence-based practice—and *not* emerge from so-called panels of experts who develop standards based upon clinical consensus. Consensus-based practice guidelines have much lower credibility than evidence-based ones and represent not much of an advance over current practices.

What else shall we do? As educators we need to begin working to ensure that social work students are exposed to training in the use of evidence-based practice guidelines, and in the interventions contained therein. For all their limitations, the currently developed practice guidelines and compilations of empirically supported treatments represent the state of the art in human services, at least in the field of mental health. As behavioral and social scientists, we should be supporting these PGs as training tools and providing instruction in how to locate evidence-based PGs. Indeed, it would be appropriate for the Council on Social Work Education to be much more specific in its accreditation standards, endorsing the role of scientific research findings in social work training and requiring their inclusion in the M.S.W. curriculum. This change will help to ensure that our students are prepared to work in today's managed care environment; it is also consistent with evolving ethical standards that are moving in the direction of asserting that clients have a right to evidence-based interventions (Myers and Thyer 1997).

It is a sign of the maturity of the human services professions that we now see that demonstrating that an intervention reliably produces statistically significant improvements under tightly controlled experimental conditions is an insufficient justification to label that intervention as helpful to clients (although it is an *essential* early step in that process). Discussions are now common in the literature on the distinctions between efficacy and effectiveness studies (what I prefer to call research therapy versus clinic therapy) and of the importance of including additional measures of the magnitudes of change, such as effect sizes and proportions of variance potentially explained (Hudson, Thyer, and Stocks 1987), not as a replacement for conventional alpha levels in the context of null hypothesis testing but as a required supplement. Additional approaches to conceptualizing client change are being developed, including the reliable change index (RCI) (Jacobson et al. 1999) and normative comparisons (Kendall et al. 1999), as is an expansion of viewing outcomes to include factors such as social validity, quality of life, functional impairments, and consumer satisfaction. Although these are not necessarily new considerations (most have been around for one or more decades), they are a welcome expansion.

I wish Proctor and Rosen well in their parallel efforts to develop practice guidelines oriented toward what they are calling "outcome-based targets of change." It is a potentially monumental undertaking, if done well. And for it to be done well, we need to involve qualified members of other human services disciplines. Social work cannot and should not attempt to develop such guidelines from a purely disciplinary perspective.

REFERENCES

American Psychiatric Association. (1994). *Diagnostic and Statistical Manual of Mental Disorders* (4th ed.). Washington, D.C.: APA.

Chambless, D. L., Baker, M. J., Baucom, D. H., Beutler, L. E., Calhoun, K. S., Crits-Christoph, P. Daiuto, DeRubeis, R., Detweiler, J., Haaga, D., Bennett Johnson, S., McCurry, S., Meuser, K., Pope, K., Sanderson, W., Sholam, V., Stickle, T., Williams, D., and Woody, S. (1998). Update on empirically validated therapies II. *Clinical Psychologist, 51* (1), 3–16.

Howard, M. O., and Lambert, M. D. (1996). The Poverty of Social Work: Deficient Production, Dissemination, and Utilization of Practice-Relevant Scientific Information. In P. R. Raffoul and C. Aaron McNeece (Eds.), *Future Issues for Social Work Practice* (pp. 279–292). Boston: Allyn and Bacon.

Hudson, W., Thyer, B. A., and Stocks, J. T. (1985). Assessing the importance of experimental outcomes. *Journal of Social Service Research, 8,* 87–98.

Jacobson, N. S., Roberts, L. J., Berns, S. A., and McGlinchey, J. B. (1999). Methods for defining and determining the clinical significance of treatment effects: Description, application, and alternatives. *Journal of Consulting and Clinical Psychology, 67,* 300–307.

Karls, J. M., and Wandrei, K. E. (1995). Person-in-Environment. In R. L. Edwards (Ed.), *Encyclopedia of Social Work* (19th ed.) (pp. 1818–1827). Washington, D.C.: NASW Press.

Kazdin, A. E. (1999). The meanings and measurement of clinical significance. *Journal of Consulting and Clinical Psychology, 67,* 332–339.

Kendall, P. C., Marrs-Garcia, A., Nath, S. R., and Sheldrick, R. C. (1999). Normative comparisons for the evaluation of clinical significance. *Journal of Consulting and Clinical Psychology, 67,* 285–299.

Myers, L. L., and Thyer, B. A. (1997). Should social work clients have the right to effective treatment? *Social Work, 42,* 288–298.

Nathan, P. E., and Gorman, J. M. (Eds.). (1998). *A Guide to Treatments That Work.* New York: Oxford University Press.

Sanderson, W. C., and Woody, S. (1995). Manuals for empirically validated treatments: A project of the Task Force on Psychological Interventions. *Clinical Psychologist, 48* (4), 7–11.

Staff. (2000). Purpose and procedure. *Evidence-Based Mental Health, 3,* 66–67.

Task Force on Promotion and Dissemination of Psychological Procedures. (1995). Training in and dissemination of empirically-validated psychological treatments. Report and recommendations. *Clinical Psychologist, 48* (1), 3–23.

Thyer, B. A. (1991). Guidelines for evaluating outcome studies on social work practice. *Research on Social Work Practice, 1,* 76–91.

———. (1999). Clinical behavior analysis and clinical social work: A mutually reinforcing relationship. *Behavior Analyst, 22,* 17–29.

————. (2002). "Developing Discipline-Specific Knowledge for Social Work: Is It Possible?" *Journal of Social Work Education, 38,* 101–113.

Thyer, B. A., and Myers, L. L. (1997). Social learning theory: An empirically-based approach to understanding human behavior in the social environment. *Journal of Human Behavior in the Social Environment, 1,* 33–52.

Torrey, W. C., Bebout, R., Kline, J., Becker, D. R., Alverson, M., and Drake, R. E. (1998). Practice guidelines for clinicians working in programs providing integrated vocational and clinical services for persons with severe mental disorders. *Psychiatric Rehabilitation Journal, 21,* 388–393.

8

THE ROLE OF DIAGNOSTIC AND PROBLEM CLASSIFICATION IN FORMULATING TARGET-BASED PRACTICE GUIDELINES

STUART A. KIRK

The opportunity to consider the role of problem classification in formulating practice guidelines enabled me to link an old topic (the development and uses of diagnostic classification) to a new one (target-based practice guidelines). This chapter is neither for nor against problem classification or practice guidelines. It is intended to stimulate discussion about practice guidelines. First I will describe my understanding of target-based guidelines. Then I will very briefly describe how problem diagnosis and classification have been discussed traditionally in social work and how recent formal problem classification systems (namely, *DSM* and PIE) depart from that tradition. Finally, I will address the challenges of organizing intervention knowledge on the basis of intervention targets.

THE IDEA OF TARGET-BASED PRACTICE GUIDELINES

My task is to think about the role of diagnosis and problem classifications in developing target-based practice guidelines. Proctor and Rosen (chapter 6, this volume) suggest a novel way of organizing intervention knowledge and practice guidelines. Currently, practice guidelines in medicine and psychiatry are organized by diagnosis or problem, e.g., schizophrenia, depression, and so on. Proctor and Rosen propose that we organize knowledge and guidelines on the basis of what the interventions are supposed to achieve—the targets or

An expanded version of this chapter appears in S. A. Kirk and W. J. Reid, *Science and Social Work: A Critical Appraisal* (New York: Columbia University Press, 2002). Readers of earlier drafts of this manuscript have tried to save me from my own confusions and excesses. Whether their rescue efforts have been effective is another matter. Nevertheless, for their advice I want to thank Rebecca Hawes, Tally Moses, Carrie Petrucci, Bill Reid, Poco Smith, and Karen Staller.

goals of the interventions—rather than on the basis of the client's problem. They reason that since intervention often does not attempt either to reverse or to remove the problem, it is not very useful for intervention purposes to codify knowledge in terms of types of client problems.

They suggest that intervention guidelines (and by implication, the intervention knowledge on which they are based) be organized according to what the practitioner tries to achieve, i.e., the targets or intermediate goals of the intervention. They use the following illustration:

> For example, when addressing spousal abuse (the problem), the worker and the client may decide that under the particular circumstances, the desired outcome is to secure placement in a shelter rather than to change the spouse's abusive behavior. . . . When the outcome sought is not a reversal of the problem, we may need to affect a condition or behavior that is different substantively from that of the problem. In such cases, the appropriate intervention for the desired outcome is likely to be different from that for a reversal of the problem.
>
> (CHAPTER 6, THIS VOLUME, P. 111)

On the surface at least, the proposal to organize intervention knowledge by target, rather than by client problem, has considerable appeal. It appears to provide a practical handle that social workers could grasp in deciding how to intervene most effectively. Proctor and Rosen's proposal is a recommendation to social work scholars to consider classifying empirical knowledge by the targets or goals of intervention and developing practice recommendations based on those targets. For example, a worker who needed to place a battered woman in a shelter might examine a practice guideline organized under an index term like "placing women in shelters" to find a useful summary of knowledge about what the worker needs to do to achieve this goal. Target-based guidelines would be forward-looking (how to get from here to where you want to go) rather than backward-looking (how we got here).

A few realities need to be recognized in assessing any proposed classification scheme. First, the evaluation of any classification system depends on whether its stated purpose is advanced. There is no coherent argument that can be made for or against classification systems in general. Second, classification is fundamental to the way in which humans organize information about the world and their experiences. To classify is simply to assign persons or things to a group by reason of presumed common attributes, characteristics, qualities, or traits. In biology, classification involves a system of categories distinguished by features like structure or origin. Human physical, mental, and social maladies have been labeled and grouped for centuries by features like etiology, pathological processes, or observable symptoms. Diagnosis is a form of classification in medicine in which the nature and circumstances of a diseased condition is recognized.[1] Third, classification of client problems or human behavior always produces simplification. People are multidimensional. Classification forces attention to selected characteristics as the basis for grouping, ignoring more information and more diversity than it captures. Classifying is a decision to ignore some information on the hunch that whatever characteristic is chosen as the basis for assignment to groups will fulfill some central purpose. For example, grouping by male and female highlights some physiological characteristics but ignores thousands of other human traits. Whether it is a useful classification depends on its purpose. For example, classification by gender for the purpose of identifying intellectual ability would be useless, but it would be useful if the purpose was to identify those most likely to get prostate or breast cancer. Classification in social work always has this issue of purpose as a backdrop.

ASSESSMENT AND PURPOSE IN SOCIAL WORK

Almost all of the early casework theorists viewed assessment as an attempt to understand the nature, meaning, and evolution of the client's problem and to develop a plan of action on the basis of that understanding. Mary Richmond in *Social Diagnosis* (1917) saw assessment of clients as a central task of social casework. She viewed assessment not as a decision about the placement of an individual into a diagnostic category but as a process of gathering information systematically, making careful inferences, and developing a plan of intervention (Kirk, Siporin, and Hutchins 1989; Mattaini and Kirk 1991).

One representative example of the thinking about assessment from the midcentury casework literature is Helen Perlman's 1957 book, *Social Casework: A Problem-Solving Process,* in which she recognizes the variety of problems that draw the attention of social workers:

> There is probably no problem in human living that has not been brought to social workers in social agencies. Problems of hunger for food and of hunger for love, of seeking shelter and of wanting to run away, of getting married and of staying married, of wanting a child and of wanting to get rid of a child, of needing money and of wasting money, of not wanting to live and of not wanting to die, of making enemies and of needing friends, of wanting and of not wanting medication, of loving and of being unloved, of hating and of being hated, of being unable to

get a job and of being unable to hold a job, of feeling afraid, of feeling useless—all these, and the many other problems of physical and emotional survival as a human being, come to the door of the social agency.

(PERLMAN 1957:27)

In this passage Perlman is not proposing a problem classification system (although in my modest opinion her listing might serve as well as most); she is emphasizing the diversity of clients and their struggles and misfortunes. In fact, in her chapters "The Problem" and "Diagnosis: The Thinking in Problem-Solving," Perlman barely mentions classification, although she has much to say about client problems. For example, she makes it clear that there is almost never simply one client problem, but an interrelated multitude. First, she says, there is the problem that the client wants help with, the one that serves as the impetus to seek help. Second, there is the problem identified by the caseworker, based on professional knowledge and judgment. The caseworker's identified problem, however, is not one but a multilayered series of problems. She uses a case example (pp. 31–32) of an overwhelmed mother whose baby was hospitalized in a diabetic coma to describe how the caseworker might identify the "basic problem" (possibly the mother's neurotic character disorder), the "causal problem" (the mother's parental relationships), the "precipitating problem" (the baby's illness), the "pressing problem" (the baby's imminent release from the hospital) and the "problem-to-be-solved" (the mother's insecurity about caring for the sick child). And, finally, there is the purpose(s) of the social agency, which directs the attention of the caseworker employed there. Perlman concludes her chapter on problems by saying: "The problem brought by the person to the agency, then, is likely to be complex, ramified, and changing even as it is held to analysis" (p. 39).

She describes diagnosis as a process of organizing "intuitions, hunches, insights, and half-formed ideas," putting them "together into some pattern that seems to make sense . . . in explaining the nature of what we are dealing with and relating it to what should and can be done" (p. 166). The "diagnostic process," in her view, involves the caseworker marshaling the facts of person, problem, and place; analyzing and organizing them; reflecting upon them and making judgments of their meaning for what to do and how to do it. "Diagnosis," she states, "if it is to be anything more than an intellectual exercise, must result in a 'design for action'" (p. 164). This is the central point also emphasized in other early texts: social work assessment strives for an understanding of the client's problem as a guide for treatment, and classification per se is not particularly important (Hamilton 1951; Hollis 1964). Nevertheless, in recent years, two classification schemes for client problems that have received considerable attention have departed from these traditions. These are the successful effort in psychiatry that produced various revisions of the *DSM* and the sustained effort in social work that has created PIE.

THE DSM

Nowhere in the general purview of social work is there a more developed and institutionalized system of problem classification than the American Psychiatric Association's *Diagnostic and Statistical Manual of Mental Disorders* (*DSM*). The *DSM*, of course, is a classification of more than three hundred mental disorders that has appeared in its modern versions in 1980, 1987, and 1994 (APA 1980, 1987, 1994).[2] The recent editions of the *DSM* were explicitly designed to be "descriptive" and "atheoretical." These editions list the observable signs and symptoms (i.e., diagnostic criteria) that a clinician should find in order to determine whether a client has a particular mental disorder, without making assumptions about etiology. In making the *DSM* atheoretical with respect to etiology, the developers also wanted to make the system neutral in regard to recommended treatment. Thus, the *DSM* explicitly rejected the casework premise that diagnosis itself was a nascent form of treatment planning.

The *DSM*'s success is attributable to its usefulness for different purposes. Among clinicians, it is primarily a codebook that is used to qualify for reimbursement for treatment (Kutchins and Kirk 1988; Kirk and Kutchins 1988). For managed care companies, the widespread acceptance of the *DSM* facilitates their decision making and administrative work. Among researchers, the *DSM* is a handy (and now required) screening tool for selecting people to participate in studies of etiology and treatment effectiveness. Among educators, the *DSM* provides a rubric for teaching students by organizing information and knowledge about different kinds of personal difficulties. And, finally, for all mental health professions, the *DSM* provides the aura of rigor and scientific respectability to psychiatric diagnosis, which had for decades been the whipping boy of critics. For our purposes, it is worth noting that the *DSM*'s singular focus on defining internal psychopathology is radically different from social work's general historical concern with family, kinship, culture, and institutional context in assessment and treatment (Kirk, Siporin, and Kutchins 1989).

PERSON-IN-ENVIRONMENT (PIE)

The quest for scientific and professional respectability was the key factor in the development of a problem classification system by social workers in the mid-1980s, with some support from the National Association of Social

Workers. Unlike *DSM-III*, PIE was not a revision or replacement of an earlier system; it was a new endeavor. James Karls and Karin Wandrei (1994) worked for many years to develop and promote the Person-in-Environment (PIE) system of classification. Promoting the social work profession was at the center of their efforts. They introduced the system by asserting that it was an "important step in the development of the profession" and that it would lead to "a universal classification system for our profession" (p. xvii). They admitted that they were "unabashedly ambitious" for social work and wanted everyone to

> recognize social work as *the* profession that can best help with the social functioning problems that befall us all. We are convinced that, for this to happen, social work must acquire and use its own language to communicate the work it does and the role it plays in eliminating or alleviating problems in the human condition. We are advocating that PIE be that language [emphasis in original].   (P. XVII)

The incredible success of the *DSM* had stimulated Karl and Wandrei's search for a "new language," a language that would capture social functioning rather than internal psychopathology. PIE was an ambitious reaction to the *DSM*. But in that ambition were confusions about what the PIE system was attempting to accomplish and how it would be accomplished by borrowing disparate concepts from social work and the social sciences, such as social functioning, social role, client strengths and coping ability, and community environment.

Like the *DSM*, the PIE system has many categories arrayed around distinct "axes," and also like the *DSM* there are types and subtypes, and ratings of severity and code numbers for all of this. Even in terms of its own purpose of attempting to provide a more clear language for communication among practitioners or to devise a shorthand for problem description, PIE appears to fail. Like the *DSM*, PIE gets bludgeoned by its own parameters, pushing practitioners into thinking that placing clients in complicated categories was the clinical objective, or assigning obscure code numbers was the scientific goal, or filling out multi-axial administrative forms constituted stepping-stones to professional status.

ORGANIZING KNOWLEDGE FOR INTERVENTION

As classification systems—and guides to organizing knowledge—both the *DSM* and PIE have distanced themselves from links to etiology, meaning, and intervention. Thus the proposal for practice guidelines to be organized around intervention targets is, in part, an attempt to redress this more recent neglect of a "design for action," an attempt to shift the focus from diagnosis to treatment.

As Perlman indicated, clients arrive at social agencies with problems of many kinds. The social worker attempts to understand the nature of the problem and then develops with the client some treatment goal (i.e., objective, target) and selects some method (i.e., intervention) to achieve it. As Rosen and Proctor recognize, social workers have many options in selecting treatment goals. The treatment target may be to alter the contributing causes, to alter directly the client's presenting problem, or to alter some secondary undesirable effect of the client's problem (see figure 8.1). For example, interventions may attempt to remove, modify, or ameliorate one of the contributing causes of the client's presenting problem. In the case of a child who is being maltreated, the worker may help the parents improve their parenting skills so that they will not neglect or abuse the child (Target 1). Or the worker could focus efforts on removing, modifying, or ameliorating the presenting problem itself without attempting to remove a contributing cause. For example, the abused child could be removed from the home (Target 2). Or the worker might move first to arrange medical and psychiatric care for the traumatized abused child (Target 3).[3]

Would it be better to organize social work intervention knowledge around goals to be achieved rather than around problems that have already occurred?[4] Proctor and Rosen recognize that problem analysis can't be totally abandoned: "We are aware that diagnosis and problems do play a legitimate role in treatment considerations. The question is, what role should they play" (personal communication, December 2, 1999). They argue, however, that since practitioners often choose interventions on the basis of the goals they want to achieve rather than according to the problem classification, guidelines should be organized around the clinical targets. Their proposal suggests that practitioners (and perhaps scholars) view the nature of clients' problems, at least when it comes to choosing interventions, as only one of a series of relevant variables that moderate the relationship of intervention to outcome.[5]

How important is problem assessment in selecting targets or interventions? For the sake of discussion, we will assume that intervention knowledge could be organized around intervention objectives, that practice guidelines could be formulated on the basis of this knowledge, and that practitioners would be motivated and able to access these guidelines. Under those assumptions, what would be the role of diagnosis or problem classification for practitioners?

Although Proctor and Rosen (chapter 6, this volume) do not propose this, one way of clarifying the role of diagnosis is to ask if problem analysis

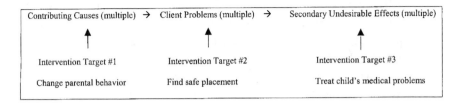

FIGURE 8.1. Intervention Targets

is expendable. It is possible that goals can be achieved (e.g., parents given parenting skills training, children placed in safe environments, and youth provided with medical attention), without great effort expended to understand or identify a focal problem. Let us consider this possibility, using the extreme case of trying to select targets and interventions without any problem identification. Could practitioners dispense with diagnosis, problem classification, and assessment altogether? Could they select targets and interventions without identifying problems?

SELECTING TARGETS WITHOUT IDENTIFYING PROBLEMS

Let's take the example of the battered woman being placed in a shelter, in which the target (the placement) does not involve altering the spouse's abusive behavior (the immediate cause of the woman's problem). How was shelter placement selected as the target? In this brief example, of course, we really don't know, but the outcome selected is not the only or the obvious target when a woman has been abused. A practitioner would usually want to explore the extent and dynamics of the abusive situation. On the basis of that exploration and understanding, other immediate intervention objectives might be chosen, such as to have the husband arrested, to refer the husband to a treatment group for batterers, to return the woman to her home, to arrange alcohol or substance abuse treatment for the husband, to arrange marital therapy, to refer the woman to a hospital for a physical examination, and so on. A shelter placement may be the appropriate intervention in this case, but how could a practitioner possibly determine what is the most appropriate target without considerable understanding of the nature, dynamics, and history of this woman's experiences in her marital relationship? (e.g., see Mills 1998, 1999).

Individual client characteristics must also be considered when selecting targets. For example, the practitioner who is studying guidelines for the target "finding shelter" would expect different instructions if the client was a homeless man, a thirteen-year-old female runaway, an elderly person with Alzheimer's, or a battered woman. Similarly, under "finding employment" the practice guidelines might need to address different approaches depending on whether the client was a high school dropout, a single mother, an AIDS survivor, an alcoholic former executive, or a parolee.

As the early casework scholars demonstrated, a careful formulation of the problem does not require formal problem classification, but it seems unlikely that practitioners can select targets without first identifying and understanding the nature of the problem and its meaning in the life of a particular client. Even when problem reversal is not the goal, even when no attempt will be made to reverse causal mechanisms, problem formulation is the unavoidable first step in treatment. Undoubtedly there are clinical examples in which appropriate targets might be chosen without problem analysis, but I can't imagine that these would be more than rare instances.

SELECTING INTERVENTIONS WITHOUT IDENTIFYING PROBLEMS

Similarly, it is difficult for me to find examples of effective intervention without problem identification. I thought I had found one in a front-page article in the *Washington Post* (Brown 1999, "Medicine's Growth Curve: Healthy Patients"). The article opened with the sentence "What's most noticeable about the steady stream of patients into Charles F. Hoesch's medical office in the Baltimore suburb of Perry Hall is how few are actually sick" (p. A-1). The article described the rise of the use of medical intervention, particularly pharmacology, in the absence of physical disorders.[6] It features a patient, a sixty-year-old engineer, whose slight elevation in blood pressure would never have provoked notice a generation ago. The patient didn't have heart disease, kidney problems, or any of the other complications of high blood pressure. Nevertheless, he was under medical care. The article's main theme was that the definition of disease has so expanded that it includes people who may be "at risk," a definition so broad that it now touches just about everybody at any age, even if he or she is currently "healthy." One can be "at risk" even when the probability of getting the disease is slight and when the vast majority of those at risk will never get the disease, with or without treatment.

Although this may appear to be a case of treatment without an identified disease, the case is murky because it resembles many familiar public health preventive efforts to inoculate healthy populations against specific contagious diseases (e.g., polio and influenza). Thus, even treating healthy people rests on some assumptions about preventing possible future diseases.

Social welfare examples of intervention without identified problems are hard to come by, although some social policies and social programs at times appear to be stimulated by vague concerns and promote nonspecific interventions in order to achieve nonspecific goals. (I would be tempted to use community mental health as an example here.) We could consider these as interventions intended to achieve some general salutary social effects, disconnected from any careful problem analysis. In popular culture, one could view some New Age, feel-good-about-yourself efforts as interventions in the absence of specific identified problems. For example, various promotions to eat right, exercise, cultivate friends, and pursue your dreams may be attempts to promote healthy development and raise one's general quality of life. I can imagine the development of Quality-of-Life Clinics in which clients are helped to develop general life skills and are advised about how to make their life better and more fulfilling, all without any attempt to diagnose or identify a particular client problem.

Although it may be possible to contrive interventions without problems, for the most part, social work intervention assumes that a client has a problematic condition that is to be altered, prevented, or ameliorated. Most interventions imply some undesirable state that will be changed in some way. How that problematic or undesirable state is understood by the practitioner is usually relevant to the selection of the intervention and its objectives.

TARGET-BASED CLASSIFICATION

Let's now consider the scholar's task of organizing knowledge for use by practitioners. Currently, we have some knowledge organized by general intervention technique (e.g., skills training, cognitive-behavioral therapy, casework), some knowledge organized by problem (e.g., child abuse, substance abuse, schizophrenia), and not much at all organized by intervention target. Even if we possessed a valid etiologically based diagnostic system, one could still argue that organizing intervention knowledge by targets would be more useful and more appropriate for practice guidelines, particularly in social work, where distant causes of human anguish are not readily manipulatable by practitioners who are nonetheless compelled to offer assistance. For example, the inability to walk can be caused by birth defects, traumatic injuries, or disease, but a social worker can often ignore the etiology and focus instead on acquiring a wheelchair, transportation services, design modifications in the home and office, and so forth. Having guidelines organized under the goal of "increasing physical mobility" could be an advance for the profession, which currently has wavering schema for its intervention knowledge, spread across

TABLE 8.1 Practice Guidelines by Problem, Target, and Client Demographics

	TARGETS/OBJECTIVE		
PROBLEMS	**1.** **PARENTING** **SKILLS**	**2.** **SAFE** **ENVIRONMENT**	**3.** **TREATMENT** **OF INJURIES**
	Client Demo A–Z	*Client Demo A–Z*	*Client Demo A–Z*
A. Child sexual abuse	Guidelines A1	Guidelines A2	Guidelines A3
B. Child malnutrition	Guidelines B1	Guidelines B2	Guidelines B3
C. Child neglect	Guidelines C1	Guidelines C2	Guidelines C3

dimensions of problem, setting, field of practice, and a variety of personal variables, such as gender, ethnicity, age, and so on. Organizing intervention knowledge around targets might be an advance that is useful in practice. What are the requirements and potential difficulties for such a taxonomy?

The proposal for a target-based taxonomy is an argument about making intervention objectives the primary dimension for organizing knowledge and practice guidelines. According to this proposal, the practitioner should first decide what is to be accomplished (i.e., select intervention targets) and then seek knowledge about which type of intervention is most likely to achieve that objective. But, as I have suggested, selecting a target is insufficient for the practitioner; targets and interventions almost always presuppose some prior identification and understanding of the client's problems.

In addition to the nature of the problem, the practitioner also has to consider client characteristics (Proctor and Rosen, chapter 6, this volume; Videka, chapter 10, this volume) in choosing an intervention strategy. What this suggests to me is a knowledge taxonomy that has practice guidelines nested in a multidimensional matrix framed by client problems, intervention targets, and client characteristics. The menu of recommended interventions or guidelines would be listed in each cell (see table 8.1).

Currently, if one uses the American Psychiatric Association's guidelines as models, knowledge is organized first by disorder (e.g., schizophrenia, cocaine-related disorders) and second within each disorder by intervention technique (e.g., pharmacologic treatments, psychosocial treatments); little is said about targets. So the suggestion of Proctor and Rosen to use targets as a major dimension for guidelines is radically different, although both schemes require problem classification of some kind. With a problem by target by client characteristics matrix (as in table 8.1), a practitioner would be directed to the same cluster of guidelines whether he or she begins by selecting a target or a client problem.

CHALLENGES FOR TARGET-BASED GUIDELINES

The challenge of an appropriate taxonomy does not end with the labeling of target categories. Organizing intervention knowledge by targets must meet the same requirements as any other aspiring classification system. The target categories need to be meaningful (valid), and the system must be used consistently (reliably). Since it is only the general idea for such an organization that I am addressing, rather than a specific proposal that can be closely examined, I can only speculate about what challenges might be encountered.

VALIDITY

In terms of validity, there will undoubtedly be much work to be done in defining the meaning of target terms. Let's examine the earlier example of the shelter for an abused spouse. How did the practitioner define the intervention objective in that case? Was it separation from the abuser, placement in a safe environment, the provision of food and a place to sleep, acquisition of transitional housing, or help in terminating an intimate relationship? With each type of definition, a slightly different body of knowledge would be accessed and a different set of guidelines might be found. For example, if the goal was to end a relationship, the guidelines might be anchored in knowledge of separation and divorce. On the other hand, if the goal was transitional housing, the worker would look at some index term for temporary housing to find guidelines about best placement practices. In order to organize knowledge regarding placements of this type, there would need to be considerable research to clarify how that "target" is different from the guidelines that might be developed for other out-of-home transitional placements for adults, including adult foster care, board-and-care homes for those with serious mental illness or Alzheimer's, nursing homes, halfway houses for parolees, residential treatment facilities for substance abusers, and so on. Some of these placements would undoubtedly share practice guidelines, but determining which ones are similar in consequential ways would take considerable research effort.[7] The definitions of all the common intervention targets would have to be scrutinized in this way, and the overlaps and conceptual connections and distinctions would have to hammered out. This difficult, labor-intensive scholarship will occupy a platoon of practice researchers.

PRACTICAL USE AND RELIABILITY

The developers of the *DSM* and PIE know firsthand the enormous challenge in getting committees of experts to agree on the meaning of categories and to use them consistently. Even after the experts finally achieve agreement on the definition of targets, there is always the challenge of assessing whether practitioners facing the same client or picking the same general target would use the matrix and the guidelines reliably. As the architects of the *DSM* and PIE know, it is one thing to develop a tidy classification system on paper and quite another to have actual practitioners use it consistently in the way it was intended. This problem of the difference between the laboratory and the field has spawned a small field of clinical study about the differences between "efficacy" in a controlled research setting and "effectiveness" in the real world where clinical discretion, self-selection, organizational pressure, bias, and misuse occur (Seligman 1995). The reliable use of guidelines, whether organized by problems or targets, will be an enormous challenge.

OTHER ISSUES

There are other potential problems, so familiar in social work, such as the multi-problem client, or in this case, the multi-target client. The abused spouse may need more than a safe environment for a few days. She may need permanent alternative housing, a job, child care, and skills to manage the abusive partner, each target directing the practitioner to a different practice guideline. Will there be a hierarchy of targets or will they be treated equally? In addition, a frequently made mistake is the practitioner's attempt to fashion a solution from a list of targets without taking into account the broader context of the client's life. This is a fundamental flaw in the *DSM*'s descriptive classification, where the symptoms of mental disorder could be indicators of adaptive functioning rather than of pathology, if the social context were permitted inside the diagnostic tent (Kirk et al. 1999). Goals and interventions must be sensitive to the contour of the client's life and history, and they can fall short when there is insufficient understanding of what the client needs. These are not new problems created by the proposal for target-based intervention; on the contrary, they are nettlesome issues as old as social work.

Finally, target-based classification cannot supplant problem classification in one specific arena: the search for explanatory knowledge about the causes of problems. (I am not assuming that this is what is being proposed.) Assessment of the value of any classification system has to be in terms of its purposes. In the search for etiology, whether of AIDS, child maltreatment,

Alzheimer's, or violent behavior, enormous scientific efficiencies are to be gained by systematically defining the problematic condition. Doing so permits replication by the same researcher and by others at different sites, so that findings are comparable and accumulative regarding correlates and possible contributing causes. This search may not lead immediately to effective interventions, but it does lead to the accumulation of basic knowledge. Moreover, without an established method of identifying problem conditions, it would be difficult, if not impossible, to replicate intervention research, or to know the limits of a treatment's generalizability. In this general search for knowledge through research, problem classification is indispensable. Organizing knowledge for intervention has a different purpose than organizing it for understanding. We need not disparage or dismiss one purpose in order to pursue the other.

———

Social workers have long been concerned about the iatrogenic effects of labeling, the stigma that can be associated with being categorized as the unworthy poor, delinquent, or insane, and the obstacles that labels can create for rehabilitation. Yet categorization is a fundamental part of our cognitive ability to organize our experiences and perceptions and to study our world. The suggestion that we organize practice guidelines in terms of target-based outcomes is more than a reaction to negative labeling. It is also a reaction to the professional penchant for peering into a client's biographical past for tentative and at times dubious explanations for personal problems at the expense of preparing a plan for effective intervention. Although early casework theorists emphasized diagnosis as a basis for developing a plan of action, there was always the danger that the search for the "true" diagnosis would become an obsessive end in itself and that the plan of action would receive less attention. Thus, the proposal for shifting the organizing rubric for intervention knowledge for practitioners from client problems to targets is intriguing. The proposal has the advantage of being action-oriented, tied directly to the practitioner's immediate decisions, and prescriptive of how the current empirical literature might be reorganized.

Organizing intervention knowledge by targets, however, will not obviate the need for problem analysis by practitioners. Practitioners will always need to attend to a client's discomfort, dig into its origins, map its contours, and tentatively formulate some understanding of its nature *before* selecting a target of intervention. And researchers will still need to struggle with the subtle details of problem categorization in the search for contributing causes and common dynamics that may eventually lead to effective treatment or prevention. But practitioners and researchers do not necessarily need the same level of problem diagnosis or classification to do their respective work. Their work serves different purposes, and to assume that one formal classification system will be good for both, as the promoters of the *DSM* did, may lead to a confused system that serves neither well.

It is perfectly sensible for practitioners to formulate a tentative understanding of the client's problem first, before deciding what they want to achieve and how to do it. Nevertheless, while problem assessment is primary, it does not require a formal classification system of problems, sprinkled with awkward category labels, filled with constantly changing criteria, and encrusted with meaningless administrative code numbers. It may be fine merely to distinguish, in the words of Helen Perlman, among problems "of wanting a child and of wanting to get rid of a child, of needing money and of wasting money, of not wanting to live and of not wanting to die." Any reorganization of social work knowledge should acknowledge our need to understand clients' problems as we develop plans to help them.

NOTES

1. *Diagnosis* can have other meanings, including the process of determining the nature of a condition, the description that classifies a phenomenon, the identification of a cause or nature of a problem, and the answer or solution to a problem (*Random House Unabridged Dictionary* [2d ed.]).
2. I will resist the temptation to criticize its scientific shortcomings or its political purposes. (This can be found elsewhere in numbing detail [Kirk and Kutchins 1992; Kutchins and Kirk 1997; special section of the *Journal of Abnormal Behavior,* August 1999]).
3. It should be noted that in all these cases, the intervention is preceded by some assessment of the problem, regardless of which aspects of that assessment guide the choice of treatment objective.
4. We need to be mindful of an important distinction between the tasks of the practitioner who is deciding how to intervene with a particular client and those of the scholar who is attempting to organize knowledge. The role of problem classification in their respective tasks needs to be addressed separately.
5. Proctor and Rosen's deliberate emphasis on intervention and their critique of guidelines based on problem diagnosis can leave the misleading impression that problems are relevant only as a moderating variable in choosing interventions and play no role in selecting the targets of intervention. This is not their position, and my analysis that follows suggests why problems must be considered before choosing intervention goals.
6. In our culture's medicalization mania, even the healthy are now sick and treatable, and since drug therapy is the frequent treatment, it is a bonanza for pharmaceutical companies.

7. Similarly, client characteristics (such as gender, age, and ethnicity) may interact with these best practices and require further refinement.

REFERENCES

American Psychiatric Association (1980, 1987, 1994). *The Diagnostic and Statistical Manual of Mental Disorders*. Washington, D.C.: APA Press.

Brown, D. (1999). "Medicine's Growth Curve: Healthy Patients," *Washington Post*, October 22, p. A-1.

Hamilton, G. (1951). *Theory and Practice of Social Case Work* (2d ed.). New York: Columbia University Press.

Hollis, F. (1964). *Casework: A Psychosocial Therapy*. New York: McGraw-Hill.

Journal of Abnormal Psychology (1999). The Concept of Disorder: Evolutionary Analysis and Critique), 108 (Special Section), 371–472.

Karls, J., and Wandrei, K. (1994). *Person-in-Environment System: The PIE Classification System for Social Functioning Problems*. Washington, D.C.: NASW Press.

Kirk, S., and H. Kutchins. (1988). Deliberate misdiagnosis in mental health practice. *Social Service Review, 62* (2), 225–237.

———. (1992). *The Selling of DSM: The Rhetoric of Science in Psychiatry*. Hawthorne, N.Y.: Aldine de Gruyter.

Kirk, S., M. Siporin, and H. Kutchins. (1989). The prognosis for social work diagnosis. *Social Casework, 70* (5), 295–304.

Kirk, S. A., Wakefield, J., Hsieh, D., and Pottick, K. (1999). Social context and social workers' judgments of mental disorder. *Social Service Review, 73*, 82–104.

Kutchins, H., and Kirk, S. A. (1988). The business of diagnosis: DSM-III and clinical social work. *Social Work, 33* (3), 215–220.

———. (1997). *Making Us Crazy: DSM: The Psychiatric Bible and the Creation of Mental Disorders*. New York: Free Press.

Mattaini, M., and Kirk, S. (1991). Assessing assessment in social work. *Social Work, 36* (3), 260–266.

Mills, L. (1998). *The Heart of Intimate Abuse*. New York: Springer.

———. (1999). Killing her softly: Intimate abuse and the violence of state intervention. *Harvard Law Review, 113*, 550–613.

Perlman, H. (1957). *Social Casework: A Problem-Solving Process*. Chicago: University of Chicago Press.

Richmond, M. (1965). *Social Diagnosis*. New York: Free Press (Original work published 1917).

Seligman, M. (1995). The effectiveness of psychotherapy: The Consumer Reports study. *American Psychologist, 50*, 965–974.

9

CONSTRUCTING PRACTICE: DIAGNOSES, PROBLEMS, TARGETS, OR TRANSACTIONS?

MARK A. MATTAINI

R ed Jacket, a respected Seneca orator, politely rejected an invitation to convert to Christianity on behalf of his people, indicating that "Kitchi-Manitou [The Great Mystery] has given us a different understanding" (Johnston 1992:vii). I find myself in a similar position here. Kirk (chapter 8), as well as several other contributors to this volume, raises critical questions, questions that social work clearly must address. In many cases, however, I find myself understanding the questions differently, which may profoundly shift the possible answers.

Kirk is concerned about the intensity of research that would be required to identify which interventive strategies are needed for which target, given specifics of problem, client characteristics, and contextual factors. This level of effort is, however, exactly what is needed to guide practice, guidelines or no guidelines. There is no real alternative to that process, which incidentally is why single-system research is more important than is often acknowledged. On the other hand, a "formal classification system" including awkward category labels, meaningless administrative code numbers, and the other attributes that Kirk elaborates surely does risk complexity without utility. Categorical systems that seek to encompass all of social work tend to oversimplify the phenomena of interest, reducing dimensional and transactional phenomena to nominal levels of measurement, while, ironically, complicating practice through the requirement for large numbers of subcategories (Mattaini and Kirk 1991).

PROBLEMS AND TARGETS

Can social workers practice without in some way identifying problems? The "Working Statement on the Purpose of Social Work" developed at a consensus conference of leaders of the profession at O'Hare airport in May 1979

(Working Statement, 1981) tried to avoid a problem focus, indicating that "the purpose of social work is to promote or restore a mutually beneficial interaction between individuals and society in order to improve the quality of life for everyone" (p. 6). While laudatory, this statement is often inconsistent with everyday practice. People come to social workers because someone (be it client, parent, or society) is experiencing an aversive condition; someone has a problem. A problem, therefore, is a ticket into service. Even prevention requires a problem that programming is designed to prevent. What is less clear, however, is the extent of problem exploration and analysis required. The target-based alternative is, as Kirk notes, intriguing.

With their focus on targets, I believe, Proctor and Rosen (chapter 6, this volume) are contributing something meaningful that could advance the field. The term *target* may be unnecessarily aggressive, unidirectional, and perhaps patronizing; alternatives are considered later in this chapter. The central concept, however, is much more important than may be immediately obvious. It is also not entirely novel. Israel Goldiamond, in the early 1970s, described a "constructional" approach to social problems (1974), and he and Arthur Schwartz (1975) wrote an elegant and frankly groundbreaking book elaborating a constructional model of social work practice. The core notion was that the social worker and the client define the outcomes to be achieved by their work and analyze the factors needed to construct those outcomes. Only limited attention is paid to "problems" in this approach.

Such a stance offers two major advantages. First, those involved know where they are going, rather than just where they are not going. If one is in St. Louis and wishes to get to Albuquerque, it is of some use to know that St. Louis is not where one wants to be; it is slightly better to know that one should not take Interstate 70 to the east. It is much more useful, however, to know where one wants to go and that one should take Interstate 44 to Interstate 40, a relatively direct route to Albuquerque. Knowing where one wants to go and how to get there provides real direction for action. Targets are the "where," and guidelines could be the "how to get there."

A second advantage of a target-based or constructional approach is grounded in what we know about how behavior changes. The primary technologies for reducing problem behaviors (whether of the client or of other system actors) are punishment, threat, and extinction, all of which produce serious side effects (Sidman 2001); if they result in behavior change, the kind of change produced is commonly unpredictable. One alternative is what is technically called differential reinforcement of other behavior (DRO), in which anything other than the problem behavior is reinforced. Again, this provides little direction for action. The principal remaining technology for reducing a problem behavior is the construction of an alternative, which takes us back to target-based, constructional practice. Think about battering as an example. If the problem is battering, which on the face of it makes sense, so long as the objective is to reduce battering, we are stuck with behavior deceleration technologies, primarily punishment and threat. It is no accident, however, that in most programs involving batterers, the primary task is constructing new behaviors (cognitive and relational). Note that this issue does not arise when the problem is originally not defined as a behavior—for example, if the problem is defined as unemployment. But even then, no one tries to cure a condition called "unemployment"; rather, practitioners and clients usually move immediately to the constructional alternative, employment. Once that shift is made, however, someone needs to act, so the issue does become behavioral.

A constructional approach focuses on collaboratively building an improved reality as envisioned with the client, through a process of shared power. That process relies on recognition of strengths and gifts, and mutual contribution toward the goal. This is far more direct, and far more respectful, than problem-focused practice. For this reason, the ecobehavioral practice process (Mattaini 1997, 1999), developed as an elaboration of Goldiamond's work, regards envisioning the improved case configuration to be constructed as a central practice function, which ordinarily precedes assessment and intervention, although of course the process is really iterative. This perspective also explains, for example, the importance in supervision of asking questions like "What does the client want?" (Harkness and Hensley 1991) or "What are the family's goals for treatment?" (Henggeler et al. 1998), which the research suggests contribute to improved outcomes.

Constructional, or target-based, guidelines may be more useful than those that are problem-based, because they move attention away from pathology and toward a more respectful stance. Constructional guidelines are more likely to rely on enriching clients' lives, rather than relying on aversives to control their—or others'—behavior. The discussion so far still leaves two issues unaddressed: (1) the kinds of targets that are consistent with the purpose and realities of social work practice and (2) the utility of a classification of targets. I consider each of these issues here in turn.

TARGETS AND TRANSACTIONS

The function of social work is to intervene in social reality. Social reality, at its core, involves networks of transactions. Changing the individual, the organism, in relative isolation is the essence of medical practice, for example, but not of social work. Social work by definition is not organocentric; changing the person as organism is not the core of our work.

Social work certainly involves behavior, and behavior is by definition transactional. In the most adequate definition, operant *behavior* is understood as "the things a person gets done . . . instances of the person's impact on the world" (Lee 1999:68). In other words, behavior is defined not topographically (by how an observer sees someone's body move) but functionally, as an equifinal class defined by its results. For example, "going to work" means action that results in arriving at a specific location, whether on a particular day the person chooses to walk, drive, or take the bus. A parent can "recognize positive child behavior" verbally or nonverbally in many different ways; what is common is the transactional exchange. "Recognizing positive child behavior" is defined by the child's initial behavior and the parent's subsequent behavior in the context of the child's attentive presence. If these events and conditions are not present, the parent may be doing something, but what is being done is not "recognizing the child's behavior." Behavior does not happen at the person, *it is the transaction.*

So far, so good, although this already complicates classification. In social work practice, however, this is still not enough. To paraphrase Lee (1988:114), our interest lies in the interpenetration of the organism with interlocking patterns of environmental events and conditions, which are often maintained by the cultures (family, organizational, community) within which the person is embedded. In the case of my own clinical and community practice, the most effective work has nearly always focused on "targets" that consisted of changes in networks of transactions, not a change "in the person" or a change in a single transactional behavior.

We know, for example, that excellent parent training consistently changes parenting behavior under certain social and economic conditions and consistently fails to do so under differing conditions (Dumas and Wahler 1983). Attention to ecobehavioral networks is often required. Those transactional webs often constitute or are sustained by autopoietic systems (Capra 1996). (Such systems are the subject of considerable current research in biology, significantly deepening the insights of early systems theories that have often been used in social work. *Autopoiesis* is the process by which living systems construct, organize, and maintain themselves in a dynamic state that is in transaction with, but separate from, environmental events [Maturana and Varela 1980]. Human beings, as well as social and cultural networks, are among the systems to which this research is being applied.) The processes involved in maintaining such systems, therefore, often need to be the targets of intervention. Adapting a statement by Harry Specht (1990), we must have a vision of social work that enables us to direct our energies toward constructing and supporting healthy transactional networks in and among families, organizations, and communities. "That is how we make healthy people" (Specht 1990:356).

From this view, *target* may be too narrow a term. Kanfer and Schefft (1988) use the term *goal-state,* and terminology like this may begin to capture what we are really addressing here. At its core, the function of social work is to contribute to a process that moves from a current case configuration (think of a dynamic, transactional ecomap capturing the case at present) toward an envisioned new configuration, the goal-state (think of an ecomap of the case situation if the work of client and social worker were successful). Proctor and Rosen (personal communication, November 1, 2000) indicate that they see the term *target* as potentially encompassing transactions or multidimensional sets of conditions or transactions. Certainly, one is free to define terms as one wishes; the term *target* to my eye, however, connotes something quite narrowly focused, as well as something that is aggressively and unidirectionally attacked, as, for example, a bull's-eye at which an arrow is shot. The first definitions of *target* in the dictionary are "an object . . . aimed or fired at" and "an object of criticism or attack." Contemporary language is "pervaded by aggression" (Nagler 2001:228), and the negative cultural effects are serious. This terminology may not, therefore, be ideal for purposes of social work practice.

TARGET-BASED GUIDELINES

Given this framework, can target-based (or goal-state-based) constructional practice guidelines help structure such practice? Further, can such guidelines be structured around a complete and exhaustive classification system? These are empirical questions, of course. The answer to the first may well be yes. The second involves much more serious challenges, given what we know of the problems of classification systems (Mattaini and Kirk 1991). Current and envisioned case configurations are potentially infinitely complex, and if social work has learned anything in the past one hundred years, it is that social phenomena are deeply and transactionally interconnected with their social, cultural, and physical environments (Kemp, Whittaker, and Tracy 1997). The Holy Grail of a classification system that captures these variables adequately and exhaustively is likely to elude us. What might be achieved is a classification that would narrow and deform social work practice, with professionally tragic results.

Consider Henggeler's demonstrably effective multisystemic treatment for antisocial behavior among children and youth (Henggeler et al. 1998). The approach relies on a handful of core principles, is largely constructional, and is clearly grounded in an analysis of the ecobehavioral context of the case. It includes relatively nuanced techniques for achieving commonly important targets like improved peer relations and academic competence, with recommendations that vary depending on analysis of contextual contingencies. Is an effort to develop a much more specific multidimensional matrix of target by problem by client demographics by contextual conditions justified? Perhaps, although the likelihood of nonlinear interactions among variables may make this even more challenging than it already seems. An individualizing assessment is likely to be much more helpful than a standardized classification system. Note that Henggeler's approach moves very quickly away from problem (the ticket to service) and toward what is to be constructed. Not surprisingly, then, an emphasis on supporting and extending strengths and a marshaling of resources in a collaborative process then becomes the core of the work.

Consider an example at larger system levels. (Social work practice is not just—and in fact is not primarily—practice with individuals; the division between clinical practice and "everything else" is clearly artificial and probably quite damaging.) Effective youth violence prevention strategies rely on certain basic principles, including targeting multiple systems (organization, community, family, for example) and taking the dynamics of settings into account (Astor et al. 1999; U.S. Department of Health and Human Services 2001). We also can identify the central practices supporting prevention that need to be constructed within the networks in which young people live out their lives (Mattaini, with the Peace Power Working Group, 2001). Such programs need to be flexible enough to be adapted to local values and sustainable with available resources (Fawcett 1991), factors that vary enormously and currently require extensive analysis of local conditions. Would it be helpful to know prescriptively, based on a very detailed classification system, what variations will work best under what conditions? Certainly. Is this realistic? So far, there is no evidence that it is, and in fact it appears unlikely.

If social work sticks to simple issues, classification may be adequate, but if we are committed to messy realities, I am deeply skeptical of the utility of such classifications. What may be much more realistic, however, are inductively constructed sets of guidelines in particular areas of practice, directed toward particular clusters of goal-states. Perhaps someday these might be combined into a single system, but particularized guidelines may be possible—and extremely useful—now, so long as no one expects that they will be exhaustive. Guidelines that identify useful practice principles, gradually refined through research and experience, and that incorporate variations that may be useful given particular configurations of person and antecedent/consequent/contextual situation, could provide substantial guidance in some areas of practice now and could already be more useful than problem-based guidelines. Collections of such guidelines for particular areas of practice or clusters of goal-states could easily be assembled once adequate numbers of such specific guidelines were constructed.

TOWARD CONSTRUCTIONAL GUIDELINES: AN EXAMPLE

An example of what constructing such guidelines could look like might be helpful. It is common in many social work settings for a "concerned other" (CO), often a spouse or partner, to approach a practitioner because of concerns about substance abuse by someone else (often a spouse or partner, but sometimes a child, or a parent). The CO's concerns are the problem. Traditional practice would suggest one of two approaches: referral to an Alanon or similar group to teach loving detachment, or treatment of the CO for codependence (a supposed "condition" with no established empirical basis [Anderson 1994]). (Perhaps just as often, social workers may advise the CO to leave the person using substances, on the basis of what the worker considers "common sense.") Moving immediately to one of these approaches, with only limited assessment and limited data, is common, though clearly unjustified.

Deciding with the client (who at least at this point is the CO, not the person with the substance abuse problem) what she wants to see happen, what goal-state she envisions, is the crucial first step in an alternative, constructional approach. Several possible configurations might be targeted (reviewed in detail in Mattaini 1999):

1. Her vision may involve leaving the relationship, in which case guidelines for leaving safely and with as many resources as possible may be useful. Note that such guidelines, with some adjustment, may be useful in other cases in which the target is leaving the relationship, for example, in many cases of battering.

2. Her vision may involve removing herself emotionally from the situation, without disrupting the rest of her life too much. In this case, a referral to Alanon may in fact be among the recommendations outlined in the guidelines. (As it happens, such referral may also, according to the research, produce change in the behavior of the person who is abusing substances [Dittrich

and Trapold 1984, cited in Meyers, Dominguez, and Smith 1996].) While such referrals have not been extensively researched, it is likely that when such investigation is undertaken, some principles may emerge that can be widely applicable to other clinical goals involving reducing emotional involvement (as, for example, in some cases of emotionally overinvolved family members of persons with severe mental illness).

3. The goal-state envisioned by the CO may involve active efforts to have an impact on the behavior of her substance-abusing loved one. One approach that is familiar to many social workers for such situations is the "intervention" (Johnson 1986). Unfortunately, the outcomes of interventions appear to be disappointing (Liepman, Nirenberg, and Begin 1989). There are, however, at least three better-supported approaches that might be incorporated into practice guidelines. One, *pressures to change* (Barber and Gilbertson 1996, 1997), involves a graduated series of steps, with the CO exerting a greater degree of pressure at each step. Given the somewhat coercive underpinnings of the approach, which may be inconsistent with the ethic of shared power that characterizes contemporary social work, practice guidelines would need to be somewhat cautious about recommending widespread application, but might recommend the approach under certain contextual conditions.

Unilateral family therapy (UFT) (Thomas and Yoshioka 1989) is a second approach with some support, although final project data have not been published. In cases where the CO is clear that she wishes to be involved in a discrete "intervention," and in which certain exclusionary criteria are not present (e.g., battering or substance abuse on the part of the CO), practice guidelines might well suggest UFT as an option. Unilateral therapy is likely to be more effective than traditional "intervention" given the preliminary empirical support for the approach and UFT's consistency with very well-established behavioral principles.

The third option, *community reinforcement training* (Sisson and Azrin 1986; Meyers, Dominguez, and Smith 1996) would probably be presented in practice guidelines as a favored option because of its empirical support, consistency with shared power, focus on not only initiating but also promoting treatment, and applicability to cases that one or both of the other approaches might exclude because of potential violence or other contextual factors common in social work cases. Another advantage of the approach is that it has been thoroughly manualized and could therefore easily be incorporated into practice guidelines.

In other words, although the "problem" is the same, entirely distinct strategies would be required depending on whether the goal-state envisioned is ending the relationship, detachment, or active participation in efforts to encourage the loved one to engage in treatment. Separate sets of guidelines are likely to be helpful for each of these outcomes. Comparable variations in goal-state are likely in many other areas of social work practice. For example, work in child maltreatment might benefit from guidelines for foster care placement, improving parenting, and other areas. Depending on the specific goal-state envisioned (for example, family reunification, establishing and maintaining long-term kinship care, or successful emancipation), as well as on case specifics and contextual factors, approaches to best practice even in, say, foster care, would vary dramatically. Tested and well-documented guidelines for, for instance, successful kinship care placement that incorporated variations and elaborations depending on contextual factors could be enormously valuable—so long as the critical importance of individualizing each case is never discounted. By comparison, knowing or classifying the problem does not take us very far.

—

The examples given involve constructing and stabilizing new sets of interlocking practices within autopoietic networks (families, schools, communities). They are not organocentric, nor do they emphasize changing single behaviors amputated from context. Social work has struggled over its entire history, not always successfully, to avoid those dangers. This leads to an additional question: Will practice guidelines, even if constructional, inform or further deform social work practice? The function of social work is to intervene in social reality, to intervene in transactional networks, and to do so in ways consistent with social and economic justice. Healthy transactional networks imply attention to justice and human rights. Practice guidelines that privilege both science and justice may contribute to achieving the mission of the profession.

But serious questions remain. Will guidelines, constructional or otherwise, be developed and applied in settings in which the common range of social workers partners with the common range of clients, working toward healthy and just transactional outcomes? Whose voices will be honored in deciding which outcomes are included in sets of guidelines, which outcomes are valued enough to pay for, and which interventions are acceptable means for achieving those outcomes? Practice guidelines that fail to take these questions seriously may contribute primarily to positive outcomes for those who are already advantaged, while further disempowering those who are not (Wambach, Haynes, and White 1999), by assuring funding only for oversimplified procedures that address the simplest of issues, without addressing the uniqueness of individuals, the complexity of many practice situations, or the hopes and aspirations of clients.

As social work tries to escape from the periphery of science, which I believe is possible, will the critical transactional networks that shape lives and social collectives be privileged? Or, for the sake of cognitive simplicity, protection of privilege, and economic advantage, will we slip back yet again into "targeting"—in the dictionary sense—those who are least insulated from the impact? Constructional guidelines have the potential to improve practice, but they, like all powerful tools, also carry genuine risks. What assurances can we give that those risks will be honestly addressed?

REFERENCES

Anderson, S. C. (1994). A critical analysis of the concept of codependency. *Social Work, 39,* 677–685.

Astor, R. A., Vargas, L. A., Pitner, R. O'N., and Meyer, H. A. (1999). School Violence: Research, Theory, and Practice. In J. M. Jenson and M. O. Howard (Eds.), *Youth Violence: Current Research and Recent Practice Innovations* (pp. 139–171). Washington, D.C.: NASW Press.

Barber, J. G., and Gilbertson, R. (1996). An experimental investigation of a brief unilateral intervention for the partners of heavy drinkers. *Research on Social Work Practice, 6,* 325–336.

———. (1997). Unilateral interventions for women living with heavy drinking. *Social Work, 42,* 69–78.

Capra, F. (1996). *The Web of Life.* New York: Anchor Books.

Dumas, J., and Wahler, R. G. (1983). Predictors of treatment outcome in parent training: Mother insularity and socioeconomic disadvantage. *Behavioral Assessment, 5,* 301–313.

Fawcett, S. B. (1991). Some values guiding community research and action. *Journal of Applied Behavior Analysis, 24,* 621–636.

Goldiamond, I. (1974). Toward a constructional approach to social problems. *Behaviorism, 2,* 1–84.

Harkness, D., and Hensley, H. (1991). Changing the focus of social work supervision: Effects on client satisfaction and generalized contentment. *Social Work, 36,* 506–512.

Henggeler, S. W., Schoenwald, S. K., Borduin, C. M., Rowland, M. D., and Cunningham, P. B. (1998). *Multisystemic Treatment of Antisocial Behavior in Children and Adolescents.* New York: Guilford.

Johnson, V. E. (1986). *Intervention: How to Help Those Who Don't Want Help.* Minneapolis: Johnson Institute.

Johnston, B. H. (1992). Foreword to R. Ross, *Dancing with a Ghost* (pp. vii–xvi). Toronto: Reed Books Canada.

Kanfer, F. H., and Schefft, B. K. (1988). *Guiding the Process of Therapeutic Change.* Champaign, Ill.: Research Press.

Kemp. S. P., Whittaker, J. K., and Tracy, E. M. (1997). *Person-Environment Practice*. New York: Aldine de Gruyter.

Lee, V. L. (1988). *Beyond Behaviorism*. Hillsdale, N.J.: Lawrence Erlbaum Associates.

———. (1999). "Behavior" does not mean "behavior of the organism": Why conceptual revision is needed in behavior analysis. *Behavior and Social Issues, 9*, 67–80.

Liepman, M. R., Nirenberg, T. D., and Begin, A. M. (1989). Evaluation of a program designed to help family and significant others to motivate resistant alcoholics into recovery. *American Journal of Drug and Alcohol Abuse, 15*, 209–221.

Mattaini, M. A. (1997). *Clinical Practice with Individuals*. Washington, D.C.: NASW Press.

———. (1999). *Clinical Intervention with Families*. Washington, D.C.: NASW Press.

Mattaini, M. A., and Kirk, S. A. (1991). Assessing assessment in social work. *Social Work, 36*, 260–266.

Mattaini, M. A., with the Peace Power Working Group. (2001). *Peace Power for Adolescents: Strategies for a Culture of Nonviolence*. Washington, D.C.: NASW Press.

Maturana, H., and Varela, F. (1980). *Autopoiesis and Cognition*. Dordrecht, Holland: D. Reidel.

Meyers, R. J., Dominguez, T. P., and Smith, J. E. (1996). Community Reinforcement Training with Concerned Others. In V. B. Van Hasselt and M. Hersen (Eds.), *Sourcebook of Psychological Treatment Manuals for Adult Disorders* (pp. 257–294). New York: Plenum.

Nagler, M. N. (2001). *Is There No Other Way? The Search for a Nonviolent Future*. Berkeley, Calif.: Berkeley Hills Books.

Schwartz, A., and Goldiamond, I. (1975). *Social Casework: A Behavioral Approach*. New York: Columbia University Press.

Sidman, M. (2001). *Coercion and Its Fallout* (2d ed.). Boston: Authors Cooperative.

Sisson, R. W., and Azrin, N. H. (1986). Family member involvement to initiate and promote treatment of problem drinkers. *Journal of Behavior Therapy and Experimental Psychiatry, 17*, 15–21.

Specht, H. (1990). Social work and the popular psychotherapies. *Social Service Review, 64*, 345–357.

Thomas, E. J., and Yoshioka, M. R. (1989). Spouse interventive confrontations in unilateral family therapy for alcohol abuse. *Social Casework, 70*, 340–347.

Wambach, K. G., Haynes, D. T., and White, B. W. (1999). Practice guidelines: Rapprochement or estrangement between social work practitioners and researchers. *Research on Social Work Practice, 9*, 322–330.

PART III

RESPONSIVENESS OF PRACTICE GUIDELINES
TO DIVERSITY IN CLIENT POPULATIONS
AND PRACTICE SETTINGS: THE IDIOGRAPHIC
APPLICATION OF NORMATIVE GENERALIZATIONS

ACCOUNTING FOR VARIABILITY IN CLIENT, POPULATION, AND SETTING CHARACTERISTICS: MODERATORS OF INTERVENTION EFFECTIVENESS

LYNN VIDEKA

E
fforts to promote the use of scientifically based knowledge to guide health and human services interventions are among the most promising products of research advances in recent years. Although to date the social work profession has created neither practice guidelines nor related consensus statements regarding scientifically based intervention protocols, several social work scholars have been interested in practice guidelines (Howard and Jenson 1999; Williams and Lanigan 1999; Thyer and Wodarski 1998; Rothman 1992). Empirically based social work practice is a concept whose time has come.

From the point of view of clinical practice, evidence-based practice should be founded on high-quality scientific studies that are relevant to the knowledge needs of practitioners and on knowledge synthesis that uses the best scientific review methodology available. Evidence-based guidelines for practice should be posited on defined *practice-relevant questions, treatment decision alternatives* (e.g., group or individual intervention, or medication or no-medication approaches), and evidence about the effects of the intervention on *outcomes* (e.g., problem alleviation, cost, benefits, harms). Evidence-based practice guidelines should rest on a review and summary of scientific studies with relevance to clinical decision making in mind. And they should identify decision points for practitioners, points at which the high-quality research-based evidence should be integrated with other clinical factors such as comorbid conditions and patient risk and protective factors (Fields 2000).

Some scholars have argued that social work has neither a sufficient scientific knowledge base nor sufficiently specified treatments upon which to base consensus statements or practice guidelines (Thyer 1996; Witkin 1996). These authors have assessed that social work's practice domain is broad, that social work interventions are usually not described specifically, that research studies often do not ask practice-relevant questions, and that the number of well-controlled scientific studies relative to practice is limited. But recent social work research reviews have been conducted on practice with the elderly (Grenier and Gorey 1998), in substance abuse prevention (Tobler 1992), and in psychosocial intervention with adult cancer patients (Cwikel, Behar, and Rabson 2000). Similarly, many reviews in related fields are directly relevant for social work practice. For example, reviews on intervention for depression are pertinent for social workers who practice in mental health settings and provide treatment to persons with depression. These reviews indicate that social work's scientific base is increasing in some fields of practice.

In medicine and psychology, professions that have developed practice guidelines, there has been more rather than less debate about effective practice and the role of guidelines. The post-guideline debate has centered on the utility of practice guidelines for clinical practice and on the challenge of changing practitioners' behavior so that they use practice guidelines in their work. For practitioners who are faced with the task of implementing interventions to achieve desired results for clients, the lack of attention paid by most practice guidelines to individual variation in terms of the people being served, who is providing service, the service setting, and the client's social environment creates a huge challenge for the relevance of scientific knowledge for clinical practice.

Social work researchers often describe social work practitioners as resistant to research and as preferring non-research-based information (Grasso and Epstein 1992; Rubin and Rosenblatt 1979; Witkin 1996). Social work practice is often viewed by researchers as less rigorous and more ad hoc than the practice of other professions. Social workers often feel alone or different from other, presumably more scientifically based, professions in this regard. A review of evidence-based practice in psychology and in medicine, however, shows that these professions also struggle with many dilemmas as they translate science into practice. For a review of the development of practice guidelines in medicine, see Howard and Jenson (chapter 5, this volume). For a more extensive review of practice guidelines in psychology, see Hayes et al. (1995).

This chapter will consider the role of individual human variation, of variability in client and practitioner factors, in social work service settings, and in client environments in the future development of evidence-based practice models for social work. The clinical (idiographic, which tunes in to individual nuances and variations) perspective will be contrasted to the research (nomothetic, which aims to produce generalizable knowledge) perspective, and the resulting challenge for clinicians who try to use research-based knowledge will be identified. The chapter then goes on to summarize the extent to which current practice guidelines include attention to individual variation in providing evidence-based interventions. It includes a model for understanding the range of factors that influence the effects of social work intervention in working with a specific case.

I suggest three strategies to improve knowledge of client, practitioner, and environmental variation on social work intervention effectiveness. The first involves producing a new generation of research that better informs practitioners about the effects of individual and environmental variations on clinical outcomes. The second involves using critical-thinking methods to create tools that will help practitioners to implement evidence-based practice in the typical clinical situation—one that goes beyond available scientific evidence in the particular constellation of client, practitioner, and environmental variations. The third requires a new kind of reciprocal dialogue between researchers and practitioners so that research is informed by practice as well as informing it. The chapter concludes with research and knowledge–building directions for the future of developing evidence-based knowledge in social work. Linking the growing empirical research tradition with the demands of real-world practice in social work is one of the most important challenges facing the field today.

THE LIMITED USE OF EXISTING PRACTICE GUIDELINES IN CLINICAL PRACTICE

A growing body of evidence in medicine shows that even when practice guidelines are developed, are disseminated, and are made widely available, there is great variability in whether practitioners use them. Howard and Jenson, in chapter 5, note that the develpment of practice guidelines has been far from uniform and smooth. Factors that enhance the use of practice guidelines include planned dissemination campaigns, introduction of the concept to medical students, and specialty training for physicians in the area covered by the practice guideline (Edep, Shah, and Tateo 1997).

Medical practitioners have been highly critical of practice guidelines, rating them as having limited to moderate utility and as having a minimal influence on their practice (Christakis and Rivara 1998). Among their criticisms of the guidelines are "leave no room for personal experience and judgment" and "not well accepted by patients" (pp. 825–826). These findings suggest that from the clinician's perspective, there will always be factors that are likely to moderate or mediate the application of research findings to a particular clinical situation.

Similar studies in psychology and social work show that practitioners' use of empirically derived knowledge is limited. Persons (1995) reviews many studies of the use of scientifically based knowledge among practicing psychologists. One conclusion drawn from her review is that research findings are difficult for clinicians to use because research samples are typically unrepresentative of clinical populations and because comorbid conditions and many aspects of client diversity (age, gender, and co-occurring conditions, to name a few) are excluded from most controlled clinical trials. Furthermore, clinical practice emphasizes the use of individualized treatment plans instead of standardized protocols that are the product of most manualized, empirically validated treatments.

Studies in social work have shown that clinicians do not regularly read the outcomes research literature (Rubin and Rosenblatt 1979; Grasso and Epstein 1992). Historically, social work education has not prioritized teaching scientifically based knowledge. However, the Council on Social Work Education's Educational Policy and Accreditation Standards (2001) is groundbreaking in that it is the first social work curriculum policy and accreditation standards statement to emphasize the importance of scientific knowledge as the basis for practice (http://www.cswe.org/). If this aspect of accreditation standards is implemented systematically, it will support evidence-based social work practice.

THE PRACTITIONER'S CHALLENGE

The fundamental challenge for the practitioner who tries to use scientific evidence in clinical work is the charge to adapt probabilistic evidence to a particular individual, by a particular practitioner, in a particular culture and location, and in a particular service setting. Is there any way for scientific knowledge to be relevant to this clinical task?

Clinical practice is an inherently individual enterprise. Debate over the decades has contrasted the essentially individualized point of view, the "idiographic" clinical perspective, with the "nomothetic," probabilistic nature of science that aims to predict population rather than individual effects of an intervention. Allport (1937) launched the debate on these contrasting perspectives in his pioneering work on personality. In social work, the charity organization society's emphasis on scientific charity (Richmond 1917) actually emphasized the idiographic over the nomothetic perspective for social work, albeit with a positive nod toward practice based in science. As Beutler and Davison (1995) conclude, three decades of intervention research have not answered the question first posed by Gordon Paul (1967): "What treatment, by whom, is most effective for this individual with that specific problem under which set of circumstances?" (Beutler and Davison 1995:27). This question is as relevant for social work today as it is for psychology.

It is appropriate to begin with an empirical question concerning the amount of individual variation that is explained in outcome studies of efficacious treatments. A review of effect sizes in six meta-analyses of social work interventions shows that median effect sizes for effective interventions range from .21 to .39 (Videka-Sherman 1988a, 1988b; Tobler 1992; Grenier and Gorey 1998; Gorey, Thyer, and Pawluck 1998; Cwikel, Behar, and Rabson 2000). These are small to moderate effects, indicating that the majority of individual variation in studied outcomes is unexplained by the treatments rendered. Therefore, even the best empirically supported interventions are, from a clinical point of view, severely limited in guiding the client-oriented practitioner to make effective, efficient choices to maximize intervention effects for a particular case.

THE CURRENT STATUS OF INDIVIDUAL DIFFERENCES IN TREATMENT GUIDELINES

A review of the Agency for Healthcare Research and Quality (AHRQ) practice guidelines on treatment of depression and treatment of schizophrenia indicates that evidence-based differential treatment (based on individual client differences) is speculative at best. Guidelines and consensus statements consistently emphasize that much more research should be focused on studying individual variation in treatment response (National Guideline Clearinghouse 2000; Workgroup on Schizophrenia 1997; Diagnosis and Treatment of Attention Deficit Hyperactivity Disorder 2000; Diagnosis and Treatment of Depression in Late Life 2000; American Academy of Child and Adolescent Psychiatry 1997).

While many guidelines mention variation on the basis of such factors as cultural background of the client, age, and developmental considerations in the treatment of children, family considerations, and personality style of the client, guidelines typically do not advise specific treatment modifications or variations on the basis of these factors. Though such factors are mentioned as clinically important, they are not differentially addressed by the available research. This statement is true even for psychopharmacologic treatments, which have the strongest evidence base in treating mental health disorders and in most areas of health care (Mood Disorders: Pharmacological Prevention of Recurrences 1984; Workgroup on Bipolar Disorder 1994).

In the NIH consensus statement on late-life depression (Diagnosis and Treatment of Depression in Late Life 1991 [2000]) seven of twelve recommendations for future research have to do with studies of individual differences and their effects on treatment outcomes. Included in this list of research priorities are "Clarify the cause and effect relationship between depression and medical illness" and "Conduct clinical trials and observational studies of treatment in the very old, on the elderly in minority and underserved communities and in institutional settings, and on the elderly with medical illness." The consensus statement goes on to recommend development of "demonstration projects focused on innovative models of care delivery, particularly those that emphasize coordinated services and outreach efforts to depressed elderly people." These statements identify some of the patient and setting characteristics that are thought to affect clinical intervention for depression in late life. From a clinician's point of view, it is frustrating to read guidelines that acknowledge the importance of client and treatment service system variations but that are so limited in providing guidance for how to address these and other important moderating factors in the delivery of services to individual persons or families.

A review of practice guidelines indicates that some have been developed with respect to specific client subpopulations. For example, the treatment of depression is distinguished for children, adults, and elders. However, most existing guidelines give little or no consideration of the effects of practitioner, setting, or contextual factors on treatment outcome. Similarly, most guidelines give virtually no attention to cultural relevance of intervention approaches, although there is a growing body of evidence that the gender and cultural relevance is essential in delivering meaningful and effective interventions (Davis and Proctor 1995; Lum 1999). Integration of client factors into existing guidelines, when it occurs, is typically heuristic. Guidelines must go beyond the scientific evidence to mention them. Integration of differences in practitioner, treatment setting, or cultural context is virtually nonexistent.

There are three strategies that could enhance the practice utility of scientific evidence. The first is to improve the quality of the scientific evidence about practice through use of research methods that capture and describe rather than suppress or control the effects of human variation on social work outcomes. The second is to attend to the factors influencing the implementation of scientific findings in practice, including developing critical-thinking tools that practitioners can use to make rational choices in implementing interventions that have scientific evidence but not necessarily for the particular type of client or delivered in the kind of agency setting in which the social worker is employed. The third approach is to create avenues for dialogue between practitioners and researchers in order to forge mutual planning for scientific knowledge development.

IMPROVING THE QUALITY OF SCIENTIFIC EVIDENCE: TWO DISTINCT RESEARCH TRADITIONS

A review of the literature on almost any social problem reveals two distinct literatures and two distinct research traditions that seldom come together in research on clinical practice. These traditions are that of *epidemiological research,* or the study of the etiology and origins of human problems, and that of *efficacy research* on interventions to prevent, reduce, or ameliorate the effects of the problems.

Epidemiology is defined as the study of health and illness in human populations (Kleinbaum, Kupper, and Morgenstern 1982). Epidemiological research involves the study of risk factors, protective factors, and processes that lead to the development of health and illness conditions such as depression or substance abuse or problems such as juvenile delinquency. Although originally designed for health research, the epidemiological model of thinking is now widely used in the study of social and mental health problems (Kosterman et al. 2000; Stern, Smith, and Joon-Jang 1999).

Epidemiological research is conducted on populations in natural settings and environments rather than through experimental manipulation in a laboratory-like environment. According to Kleinbaum, Kupper, and Morgenstern (1982), epidemiological research has four goals: The first is to describe the health status of populations by identifying the occurrence of illness and health in populations and subpopulations. The second is to explain the etiology of health and illnesses by determining risk factors or protective factors and their modes of transmission. The third is to predict the occurrence and distribution of an illness within a population. And the fourth is to control the onset of diseases through prevention efforts in a population.

Epidemiological methods are designed to study natural variation in human environments, but they do not posit strict or complete determinism of human and health problems. Epidemiological research is oriented toward accommodating the *multifactorial etiology* of most disorders or human problems, including individual human characteristics such as gender, race, culture, and human social environment characteristics such as family system interaction styles and the presence or absence of socially supportive relationships. Epidemiology also allows the study of the *multiplicity of effects,* that is, the multiple consequences of certain behaviors such as smoking or substance abuse or a personal history of child maltreatment (Kleinbaum, Kupper, and

Morgenstern 1982:29). Epidemiological research acknowledges *limited knowledge of causative factors* in the development of disorders. It reflects the reality of social work research and practice, that we cannot fully explain the development of problems or disorders.

Epidemiological methods allow researchers to study population variations that influence risk for disorders and problems. Although epidemiological research is nomothetic (focused on populations) rather than idiographic (focused on individuals), many of the risk and protective factors that it studies are the client characteristics that clinicians work with in developing an individualized treatment approach. As an example, the well-developed epidemiology of depression has produced a list of risk factors, including female gender, youthful age, residing in a nursing home or other institutional setting, comorbid health conditions, and poverty (American Psychiatric Association 1993; Diagnosis and Treatment of Depression in Late Life 2000; American Academy of Child and Adolescent Psychiatry 1997; Mood Disorders: Pharmocologic Prevention of Recurrences 1984).

What implications are offered by the growing body of evidence of the epidemiology of disorders and social conditions that social workers encounter? First, social work needs to do a better job of integrating the latest epidemiological knowledge about human problems into knowledge that is relevant to intervention. Epidemiological evidence, typically taught in human behavior courses, should be integrated into the development of social work practice guidelines on assessment and treatment of social problems, with analysis of implications for social work intervention. Second, studies of risk and variation in individual human response to the course of illness or to problems should be incorporated in studies of intervention outcomes. Epidemiological and experimental research should be better integrated. Third, social work is in an ideal position to fulfill the prevention intervention potential of the epidemiological research approach. Prevention to avoid the onset of social problems or to minimize their debilitating effects is consistent with the mission and values of the social work profession.

THE EFFICACY APPROACH

The experimental method, the sine qua non of intervention efficacy research, stands in contrast to the epidemiological method. Table 10.1 gives a summary of this comparison. The gold standard to determine intervention effectiveness is the randomized clinical trial, the experimental design. This type of study primarily aims to answer a deductive hypothesis about the relative effectiveness of the tested intervention on a restricted study population, under controlled, ideal

TABLE 10.1 A Comparison of Epidemiological and Experimental Research Traditions

METHODOLOGICAL CHARACTERISTIC	EPIDEMIOLOGICAL APPROACH	CLINICAL TRIALS APPROACH
Scientific aim	Explanation of the problem	Testing hypotheses about the effects of an intervention
Study environment	Integral	Not a focus; effort to control
Sampling	Population-based, diverse, and heterogeneous; random sampling methods	Selective, often convenience or restricted on key characteristics
Approach to managing individual variation	Identification of as many potent factors as possible to predict the development of a disorder or problem	Elimination of sources of variation through restricting study to homogeneous samples
Role of social environment	Integral to studying the etiology of problems	Effects assumed to be equivalent across experimental groups
Role of clinical setting	Often omitted; emphasis is on preclinical problem origin	Restricted; assumed to be homogeneous
Study of processes	Currently emphasized in epidemiological study of social problems	Typically omitted except in change-process research

conditions. The logic of this methodological approach requires restricting as many sources of variability as possible, except the intervention condition. The study environment approximates a laboratory, and the approach is to control rather than to study natural variations in environmental factors. Sampling is usually restricted. At most, one or two client factors such as gender or severity of condition are treated as covariates in the classic experimental study design.

In a controlled clinical trial, individual variation is controlled or delimited as much as possible. Neither is the social environment an object of study. The logic of random assignment is to create control and experimental groups that are equivalent on all unmeasured variables. The clinical setting is typically restricted and highly supported. One explanation of why the results of a small controlled trial are so difficult to replicate in larger effectiveness studies that are conducted in the scientifically messy world of service and practice is that clinical trial settings select certain (and similar) clients for the intervention and are much better supported than practice in the typical clinical setting. Some reviewers have called the experimental sites "hot houses" in comparison to the "typical plots" of the multi-site field trial (Tobler 1992; Lehman 2000). Finally, the study of treatment processes or variations in client application is seldom examined, other than to verify the "fidelity" of application of the original treatment model, which is highly specified and "manualized." Thus, the controlled clinical trial is actually designed to remove or at least to minimize the effects of client, practitioner, and environmental variation.

A RAPPROCHEMENT OF THE TWO RESEARCH TRADITIONS: BLENDING EFFICACY AND EPIDEMIOLOGICAL RESEARCH TRADITIONS

The epidemiological researcher studies population variations and environmental conditions in the development of or resistance to health or social problems. In essence, this is the study of the problem inputs and throughputs, the risk and protective factors for the development of a disorder or social problem. Efficacy, or controlled clinical trials, conditions study outputs of interventions that are designed to moderate or change the course of illnesses or disease conditions. In order to enhance the relevance of empirical knowledge based on efficacy studies for individual clinicians treating individual clients in individual settings, a combination of the two research traditions is needed (figure 10.1). The blended model embodies the "effectiveness" research paradigm for which many federal panels are calling.

The typical epidemiological study focuses on the left side of the model in figure 10.1. The typical clinical trial focuses on the right side of the model (minus the practitioner and intervention-setting characteristics oval). Blending the two research traditions, plus adding careful study of intervention implementation and client, practitioner, and intervention-setting characteristics, would promote the study of these moderating effects on treatment outcomes. This explanation-oriented research approach will result in the findings from clinical trials being more informative to the idiographic assessment-treatment approach, since it incorporates the study of individual and environmental characteristics with the study of service outcomes.

The model in figure 10.1 is consistent with the recommendations for "effectiveness" research to complement "efficacy" studies made in *Bridging Science and Service* (National Mental Health Advisory Council Clinical Treatment and

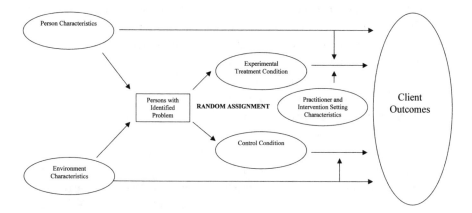

FIGURE 10.1. Explanation-Based Model for Understanding Clinical Effectiveness

Services Research Workgroup 1999). This document stresses the need for "more emphasis . . . devoted to translating the yield of basic and clinical research into effective treatments for patients encountered in non-research settings" (p. v). The model depicted in figure 10.1 is consistent with the effectiveness research model—defined in the document as research conducted in real-world settings, including client populations more diverse than those of clinical trials or efficacy studies, practitioners who may not receive specialized training and supervision in the specific intervention protocol, and quality-of-life and cost-effectiveness outcomes. Effectiveness research may or may not be experimental.

EXAMPLES OF EFFECTIVENESS RESEARCH Current research that uses the effectiveness research paradigm to explain variations in treatment outcomes in field settings with typical clients is represented by several studies. One is Robert Drake's team's research on the implementation of Assertive Community Treatment (ACT) teams for persons with severe mental disorders (Tyrrell et al. 1999; McHugo et al. 1999). These studies focused on practitioner and treatment-setting characteristics as well as treatment fidelity in garden-variety mental health service settings. The research group found that the effectiveness of ACT teams was enhanced when a site demonstrated fidelity in implementing the ACT model (McHugo et al. 1999). Tyrrell and her colleagues (1999) found that when personal styles of the case manager and the client were similar, better ACT treatment outcomes were achieved. Specifically, clients and case managers who were similar in their attitudes about the importance of attachment in treatment relationships fared better than client–case manager pairs who were dissimilar on this dimension. When *both* client and case manager believed that attachment is central to effective mental health treatment, *or* both minimized the importance of attachment, treatment effects were greater than when there was a mismatch between client and case manager on the importance of attachment (client high and practitioner low or client low and practitioner high).

In a series of studies explaining variation in outcomes for families who receive family preservation services, Littell and Tajima (2000) use hierarchical linear modeling (HLM) to examine the effects of client, worker, program characteristics, client participation in treatment, and case-level service delivery variables on client outcomes. Although the earlier analysis of this experiment (Schuerman, Rzepnicki, and Littell 1994) found no family preservation treatment effect, Littell and Tajima showed that several client and environmental factors, as well as workers' perceptions of their and their clients' working conditions, predicted variation in treatment outcomes.

In a study of the effects of service coordination teams on clinical outcomes for children placed in state custody, Glisson (1994) showed that service coordination teams (an agency organizational variation) resulted in less-restrictive placements and in better outcomes for children after six months and one year in care. Together these studies illustrate how explanatory research can complement efficacy research, and they also show that clinical outcomes can vary dramatically depending on the mix of client, practitioner, agency, and environmental factors.

Is it feasible to find support to conduct research based on the blended "explanatory" model of intervention effectiveness? Two recent National Institute of Mental Health (NIMH) requests for applications call for such complex, multifactorial research. In PA-99-068, Dissemination Research in Mental Health, NIMH calls for studies "on the array of influences and their interaction, that beneficially or adversely affect the adoption of valid mental health research findings into clinical practice" (p. 1). Among the priorities in this announcement are studies that "identify factors that influence the delivery of mental health treatments and that contribute to their adherence by consumers and providers" (p. 2). Another announcement calls for research on the etiology and prevention of comorbidity in mental health care (NIMH PA-99-071). This announcement calls for research on "the impact of treatment for a secondary physical disorder on a primary or co-occurring mental disorder" and on "the development of models of co-occurring mental disorders, substance abuse and other medical conditions that specify the mediators and moderators responsible for translating risk into co-morbidity over time, or for protecting from risk over time," and "the role of subclinical symptoms on the development and modulation of co-morbid disorders" (p. 3). The findings of studies to be funded under these announcements will be useful for the practitioner because they focus on some of the complex person–environment–clinical setting interactions to which clinicians must respond on a daily basis. These types of announcements are promising in terms of yielding a new generation of research that addresses some of the complexities of mental health practice today.

It is challenging to mount an explanation-oriented study. Large sample sizes are needed for the statistical power to detect complex, multivariate relationships among interventions, client, practitioner, and intervention-setting characteristics. It is doubtful that single-site studies can produce sufficient numbers and sufficient variations in clinical settings and client populations to answer questions about complex interacts among variables. Multi-site trials, now common in drug studies, must be used in studies of social interventions as well. On the resource side, new analytic methods such as random effects regression (Bryk and Raudenbush 1992) and latent growth curve analysis (Fearn 1977; Rao 1965; Guo and Hussey 1999) make analysis of complex interaction processes based on field data possible. The growing body of risk- and protective-factor studies about the etiology and processes leading to the development of social problems, including juvenile delinquency and substance abuse (Kosterman et al. 2000) and child abuse and neglect (Belsky 1993), is a resource for developing the sound conceptual frameworks that are needed to support the type of complex, blended-type studies called for in figure 10.1. A great deal of science has already been conducted on the left and right sides of the model. What is needed now is a new generation of studies that examine the moderating effects of epidemiological risk and protective factors on processes with the outcomes of interventions. Researching the person and environment factors that influence outcomes in interventions that already have a scientific basis should be a top priority for the profession of social work.

Explanation-oriented methods should also be employed in meta-analyses and in other literature reviews used to synthesize research findings for practice. Meta-analysis is a set of commonly used quantitative tools for research synthesis. The methods for conducting explanation-oriented literature syntheses call for the reviewer to specifically address individual and environmental variation in explaining intervention effects. The techniques for explanation-oriented meta-analyses and literature reviews are well explicated (Cook, Cooper, and Cordray 1994). Although individual studies will seldom include all relevant client, environment, practitioner, agency, and setting variables, a selected array of studies may include variations that collectively point to how these factors explain variation in treatment outcomes.

A TYPOLOGY OF MODERATING AND MEDIATING INFLUENCES ON CLINICAL OUTCOMES Figure 10.2 shows a model of factors that clinicians take into account when delivering and making decisions about how to adjust interventions to meet the individualized needs of a particular client. This same model can be used to illustrate the complexity of implementing evidence-based interventions. Two implications are evident. One is that practitioners inevitably must apply research findings in complex contexts that go beyond available research evidence. The second is that practitioners could provide a valuable source of ideas for intervention refinement on the basis of their actual implementation of evidence-based models under environmental conditions with clients who were never part of a scientific environment in which the intervention was developed. To reach this potential, researchers and practitioners must strengthen communication pathways.

In addition to factors embedded in the different person-environment system levels, social interaction occurs among systems at various levels. Therapeutic alliance and treatment adherence are italicized in figure 10.2 to show that they are interaction variables rather than variables that reside in any given single system in the client-service social framework.

Figure 10.2 shows a framework and a partial list of moderating and mediating variables that can be studied in evidence-based practice research. The growing and rich epidemiological knowledge base on a variety of social problems can serve to identify a specific empirically validated typology for any given problem or condition. For example, there is a rich epidemiology of depression. These findings become the basis for a beginning typology of factors that are germane to the onset and severity of the depression and that may moderate intervention effects.

Several strategies to improve the quality of research evidence for practice and to improve the responsiveness of the research agenda to the needs and realities of practice must be pursued simultaneously. First, social work needs to continually improve its own scientific knowledge base and to review and use, as appropriate, the scientific knowledge base of other disciplines, including psychology and psychiatry. Providing intervention for human problems is ever more interdisciplinary. No single profession controls knowledge on particular human problems or human interventions. Every social worker and every social work education program should use the increasing amount of information about the etiology, risk, and protective factors and mechanisms for illness and social problems.

Given that the current science, even in the best-researched fields of human intervention, is an incomplete basis upon which to make idiographic clinical decisions, how can social work optimize the utility and relevance of

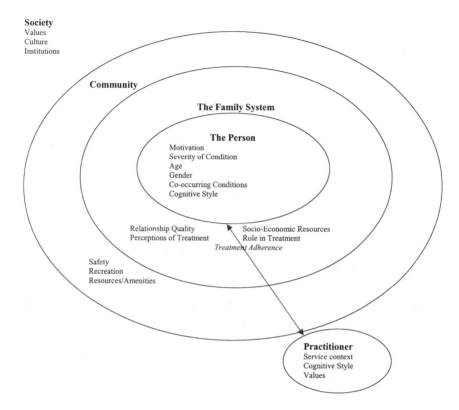

FIGURE 10.2 A Person-in-Environment Typology Framework

empirical knowledge for the practitioner? The strategy previously discussed in this chapter—the integration of clinical trials and epidemiological research approaches in effectiveness research—will improve the ability to articulate key variables that account for treatment variation and to use these articulated factors for clinical decision making. Social work, as a profession, has the opportunity to make a special contribution by conducting the new generation of effectiveness studies that focus on the implementation (often by social workers) in naturalistic clinical settings of interventions shown to be efficacious in optimal-condition experiments. Epidemiological and experimental approaches can be combined in field effectiveness trials. The expanding scientific knowledge base of risk and protective processes for various disorders provides an opportunity for the conceptual design of multifactorial, naturalsetting clinical studies that focus on explanation of variations of treatment outcomes.

Social work should take the lead in studying agency-level factors in the implementation of evidenced-based practice models. In mental health practice, experience with psychiatric rehabilitation and with the PORT project on developing practice guidelines for schizophrenia show that even when evidenced-based models exist and are well articulated, the uptake and implementation of them in everyday clinical practice settings fall far short of what is hoped for. Lehman (2000) found that fewer than 25 percent of persons with schizophrenia receive treatments that are consistent with the guidelines developed in the PORT study. He found substantial gaps in the delivery of interventions that are particularly suited to social work, including the family psychoeducation models and coping and "disease self-management" by disabled individuals themselves. Fewer than 10 percent of families of persons with schizophrenia were enrolled in these kinds of services.

Corrigan and McCracken (1995) found that without an explicit organizational development plan for implementing evidence-based psychiatric rehabilitation, few milieu settings modified their practice protocols to adopt this approach. The effects of practitioner characteristics and service system structures and processes on clinical intervention outcomes is a virgin area of study. Most services research studies focus on macro aspects of service systems, but there is a great need to focus on the effects of service systems on the delivery of clinical services. This knowledge promises to be instructive in optimizing the effectiveness of clinical services.

PROCESS AS WELL AS CONTENT STANDARDS: USING CRITICAL-THINKING-DERIVED METHODS IN IMPLEMENTING EVIDENCE-BASED PRACTICE MODELS

Even if the will and the resources were available to mount explanation-oriented research, would this approach completely link individual variation with treatment outcomes so that clinicians were aided in using research findings in their idiographic work with clinical cases? The answer is no. The limits of applying nomothetic research findings to the idiographic practice situation call for an approach that is dialectical rather than deductive. It must also be multimodal; no single strategy for linking research evidence with clinical practice will be sufficient. What, then, are some of the additional strategies that should be pursued?

One approach to understanding more about client, practitioner, and environmental effects on intervention outcomes is to develop what Hayes (1995) calls "process standards" for clinical practice. Process standards contrast with content standards, the substantive directives of clinical practice guidelines.

An example of a content standard is the PORT study's recommendation that psychoeducational family interventions be a part of treatment for all individuals with schizophrenia (Lehman et al. 1998a). This content standard instructs the clinicians about the substance of the intervention that has been shown to be empirically effective. An example of a process standard would be a family psychoeducation implementation guide that includes tools to monitor family response to psychoeducation, with guidelines for decision making when the family does not respond positively to the intervention.

Process standards include strategies for applying critical-thinking procedures (Gambrill 1990) or single-case design empirical tools (Bloom, Fischer, and Orme 1995) to clinical practice. Process standards include tools and systematic procedures designed to minimize bias as the practitioner makes idiographic clinical decisions in everyday practice. Another example of a process standard is the systematic monitoring of specified client outcomes in treatment decision making. The clinician identifies a focus for work with a client, selects an indicator or measure of the target goal, monitors the target before and during application of the intervention, and then uses the target goal status as a basis for clinical decision making with the case. With process standards, the clinician can systematically assess the effects of individual client or environment or setting variables within the context of the effectiveness of his or her own practice. With the broad exposure in B.S.W. and M.S.W. programs to single-case design and times-series methods of monitoring outcomes, most social work clinicians learn how to use basic tools for rational clinical decision making. Although substantial debate exists about the use and practicality of single-case methods in social work research (Thyer 1996; Witkin 1996; Meyer 1996; Epstein 1996), these methods hold promise as a base for "process standards" in social work practice. Instead of relying on single-subject and time-series methodologies as basic tools for generating *new* knowledge (the arena in which they have had disappointing impact), practitioners could use the methods as *clinical process tools* for making decisions about applying nomothetic scientific evidence to the particulars of the idiographic case. Gambrill develops this idea further (chapter 3, this volume).

SUPERVISION AS A TOOL TO SUPPORT EVIDENCE-BASED PRACTICE
Supervision can also play a role in assuring adherence by practitioners to evidence-based treatment approaches, while at the same time responding to individual variation in specific clinical situations, if the supervisor is facile with the use of critical-thinking methods in supervision. Supervisory methods that guide deviations from the best available evidence-based practice only through use of explicit critical-thinking and observational criteria will require

a change in mind-set and approach in social work supervision. Clinical supervisors must be knowledgeable about evidence-based practice for the relevant client group, and supervision must focus on desired client outcomes and on influencing clinical decision making to maximize those outcomes.

CONTINUOUS QUALITY IMPROVEMENT METHODS

Another "process standard" method for checks and balances in clinical decision making is Continuous Quality Improvement (CQI), a method used in many health care settings. Under CQI, the practitioner who deviates substantially from evidence-based clinical standards for practice in a particular setting with a particular case should be prepared to justify his or her intervention with the client. It requires that the clinician's justification be sensible (meet critical-thinking standards) to a peer or a supervisory-level clinician. This approach is compatible with the traditional investment that our profession has made in supervision for clinical practice. CQI can incorporate evidence-based elements both in how quality is defined and in practice standards that are identified for quality treatment (Lehman 2000). Under CQI it is also possible to use an evidence standard—of patient outcomes or progress toward goals, for example—as a tool with which to measure deviations in clinical practice from accepted quality (and hopefully evidence-based) approaches.

METHODS FOR EVOLVING EVIDENCE-BASED PRACTICE METHODS THAT ARE SENSITIVE TO INDIVIDUAL VARIATION

In order for the evidence-based practice revolution to change our profession, what methods should we adopt? Consensus panels hold great promise for creating relevant, usable evidence-based models in social work. Social work should adopt the consensus method of creating evidence-based standards of practice. The consensus method involves critical review and discussion of research evidence from diverse perspectives, including those of researchers, ethicists, practitioners, other disciplines, and clients themselves. Diverse stakeholder participation in creating consensus statements and evidence-based practice guidelines on problems of concern to social work provides a key strategy for creating usable practice guidelines that are sensitive to diverse points of view and to our values-based profession. Stakeholders should be identified and involved in the creation of evidence-based practice statements. Consumerism in medical and social care should be seen as a positive direction by social workers who are interested in empowerment and consumer self-determination.

IMPLICATIONS FOR EDUCATION OF PRACTITIONERS

Educators should take the lead in incorporating the results of evidence-based practice and critical-thinking methods in social work education programs. Studies in psychology and medicine show that social workers are not alone in finding a substantial gap between what is taught in graduate education intervention courses and what is known as evidence-based practice. Persons (1995) found that approximately one quarter of clinical psychology programs teach *none* of the evidence-based models of clinical practice. The social work profession's newest educational accreditation standards support the need to teach evidence-based social work practice courses. Studies in medicine show that specialized training leads to greater use of practice guidelines. Exposure to evidence-based practice during their professional education is likely to enhance the use of practice guidelines by social work practitioners.

THE LIMITS OF EMPIRICAL EVIDENCE FOR PRACTICE

Scientists should adopt a dialectical view of the relationship between clinical practice and science. It is not realistic or desirable to think that scientific knowledge is likely to ever be used in a mechanistic manner in clinical practice. The nomothetic, scientific approach is incomplete in its ability to inform the specific idiographic decisions that the clinical practitioner must make. A recent book on cardiology practice in medicine refers to the "art" of clinical practice (Bing 1999). In a more empirical, behavioral framework, Davison and Lazarus (1995) refer to subtle interpersonal skills and sensitivities evidenced by master psychological clinicians that are below the screen of most psychological measures.

It is unlikely that empirically based evidence will ever produce lock-step "cookbooks" for clinical practice. Clinical practice does not have to be "either-or." It is possible to use empirical knowledge and to complement it with clinical judgment based on critical thinking for application to a particular client. In this kind of adapted application the practitioner will use his or her judgment about the specific client, practitioner, service system, and environmental variables that make this particular client different from the typical client for whom the treatment has been shown to be effective.

The "either-or" philosophy about science and clinical practice should be jettisoned, and, instead, dialectical methods should be developed to bring together clinical action with the scientific evidence. How is this dialectic integration to be achieved? It will be achieved through inclusive dialogue, through consensus panels, and through ongoing discussion and debate about research findings and their application to clinical practice. In order for evidence-based practice to be responsive to individual variation in clinical work, clinicians as well as researchers must be involved in their creation.

CONCLUSION

Evidence-based practice holds the promise of consistent, high-quality practice. It is unlikely that the development of practice guidelines will eliminate the needs for clinical judgment and decision making, particularly when it comes to integrating specific client, practitioner, and environmental characteristics that affect the course of treatment. Evidence-based practice raises the question of the utility of investing so much education and emphasis on generic or generalist practice in social work practice unless the generalist approach is held to the same scientific standards that are used to adopt other practice approaches.

The process of developing evidence-based practice should not be reductionistic or linear. Research must reflect more of the complexity of the practice situation. There must be a balance between the perspectives of research and practice. The process of developing evidence-based practice models should be more dialectical than deductive. The analysis of scientific findings is strongly affected by culture, perspective, and values. Ethical standards must be integrated with scientific evidence. Dialogue, debate, and discussion that include practitioners and researchers will be indispensable in ongoing refinement of evidence-based models for clinical practice.

REFERENCES

Allport, G. W. (1937). *Personality: A Psychological Interpretation.* New York: Holt, Rinehart, and Winston.

American Academy of Child and Adolescent Psychiatry. (1997). Practice parameters for the assessment and treatment of children and adolescents with bipolar disorder. *Journal of the American Academy of Child and Adolescent Psychiatry, 36* (10, supplement), 157S–177S.

American Psychiatric Association. (1993). Practice guidelines for major depressive disorder in adults. *American Journal of Psychiatry, 150* (supplement), 1–26.

Basky, G. (1999). Doctors resist adopting clinical guidelines. *British Medical Journal, 318* (7195), 1370–1374.

Beaulieu, M. D., Hudon, E., Roberge, D., Pineault, R., Forte, D., and Legare, J. Practice guidelines for clinical prevention: Do patients, physicians, and experts share common ground? *Canadian Medical Association Journal, 161* (5), 519–524.

Belsky, J. (1993). Etiology of child maltreatment: A developmental-ecological model. *Psychological Bulletin, 114* (3/4), 413–434.

Beutler, L. E., and Davison, E. H. (1995). What Standards Should We Use? In Hayes, S. C., Follette, V. M., Dawes, R. M., and Grady, K. E. (Eds.), *Scientific Standards of Psychological Practice: Issues and Recommendations* (pp. 11–24). Reno, Nev.: Context Press.

Bing, R. J. (1999). *Cardiology: The Evolution of the Science and the Art.* (2d ed.). New Brunswick, N.J.: Rutgers University Press.

Bloom, M., Fischer, J., and Orme, J. G. (1995). *Evaluating Practice: Guidelines for the Accountable Professional.* (2d ed.). Needham Heights, Mass.: Allyn and Bacon.

Bryk, A. S., and Raudenbush, S. W. (1992). *Hierarchical Linear Models: Applications and Data Analysis Methods.* Newbury Park, Calif.: Sage.

Christakis, D. A., and Rivara, F. P. (1998). Pediatricians' awareness and attitudes about four clinical practice guidelines. *Pediatrics, 101* (5), 825–831.

Cook, T. H., Cooper, H., and Cordray, D. S. (1994). *Meta-analysis for Explanation: A Casebook.* Newbury Park, Calif.: Sage.

Corcoran, J. (2000). *Evidence-Based Social Work Practice with Families: A Lifespan Approach.* New York: Springer.

Corrigan, O. W., and McCracken, S. G. (1995). *Refocusing the training of psychiatric rehabilitation staff. Psychiatric Services, 46* (11), 1172–1177.

Council on Social Work Education (2001). *Educational Policy and Accreditation Standards.* Alexandria, Va.: Council on Social Work Education.

Cwikel, J., Behar, L., and Rabson, H. J. (2000). A comparison of vote-count and a meta-analysis review of intervention research with adult cancer patients. *Research on Social Work Practice, 10* (1), 139–158.

Davis, L. E., and Proctor, E. (1995). *Race, Gender, and Class: Guidelines for Practice with Individuals, Families, and Groups.* Needham Heights, Mass.: Allyn and Bacon.

Davison, G. C., and Lazarus, A. A. (1995). The Dialectics of Science and Practice. In S. C. Hayes, V. M. Follette, R. M. Dawes, and K. E. Grady (Eds.), *Scientific Standards of Psychological Practice: Issues and Recommendations.* Reno, Nev.: Context Press, 95–120.

Diagnosis and Treatment of Attention Deficit Hyperactivity Disorder. (2000). *NIH Consensus Statement* 1998, November 16–18; 16 (2), 1–37.

Diagnosis and Treatment of Depression in Late Life. (2000). *NIH Consensus Statement Online* 1991, November 4–6: [cited 3/15/00]; 9 (3), 1–27.

Edep, M. E., Shah, N. B., and Tateo, I. M. (1997). Differences between primary care physicians and cardiologists in the management of congestive heart failure: Relation to practice guidelines. *Journal of the American College of Cardiology, 30* (3), 618–626.

Epstein, I. (1996). In quest of a research based model for clinical practice: Or, why can't a social worker be . . . *Social Work Research, 20* (2), 97–101.

Fearn, T. (1977). A two-stage model for growth curves which leads to Rao's covariance-adjusted estimates. *Biometrika, 64,* 141–143.

Fields, S. D. (2000). Clinical practice guidelines. *Geriatrics, 55* (1), 59–68.

Gambrill, E. (1990). *Critical Thinking in Clinical Practice.* San Francisco: Jossey-Bass.

Glisson, C. (1994). The effects of service coordination teams on outcomes for children in state custody, *Administration in Social Work, 18* (4), 1–24.

Gorey, K. M., Thyer, B. A., and Pawluck, D. E. (1998). Differential effectiveness of prevalent social work practice models: A meta-analysis. *Social Work, 43* (3), 269–278.

Grasso, T., and Epstein, I. (1992). *Research Utilization in the Social Services.* New York: Haworth.

Grenier, A. M., and Gorey, K. M. (1998). The effectiveness of social work practice with older people and their families: A meta-analysis of conference proceedings. *Social Work Research, 22* (1), 60–64.

Grilli, R., Magrini, N., Penna, A., Mura, G., and Liberati, A. (2000). Practice guidelines developed by speciality societies: The need for a critical appraisal. *Lancet, 355* (9198), 103–106.

Grol, R., Mokkink, H., Dalhuijsen, J., Thomas, S., in't Veld, C., and Rutten, G. (1998). Attributes of clinical guidelines that influence the use of guidelines in general practice: An observational study. *British Medical Journal, 317* (7162), 858–861.

Guo, S., and Hussey, D. (1999). "Analyzing Longitudinal Rating Data: A Three-Level Hierarchical Linear Model." Paper presented at the Society for Social Work and Research Conference, Austin, Texas.

Hayes, S. C. (1995). What Do We Want from Scientific Standards of Practice? In Hayes, S. C., Follette, V. M., Dawes, R. M., and Grady, K. E. (Eds.), *Scientific Standards of Psychological Practice: Issues and Recommendations* (pp. 49–66). Reno, Nev.: Context Press.

Hayes, S. C., Follette, V. M., Dawes, R. M., and Grady, K. E. (Eds.). 1995. *Scientific Standards of Psychological Practice: Issues and Recommendations.* Reno, Nev.: Context Press.

Howard, M. O., and Jenson, J. M. (1999). Clinical practice guidelines: Should social work develop them? *Research on Social Work Practice, 9* (3), 283–301.

Kleinbaum, D. G., Kupper, L. L., and Morgenstern, H. (1982). *Epidemiologic Research: Principles and Quantitative Methods.* New York: Van Nostrand Reinhold.

Kosterman, R., Hawkins, J. D., Guoi, J., Catalano, R. F., and Abbott, R. D. (2000). The dynamics of alcohol and marijuana initiation: Patterns and predictors of first use in adolescence. *American Journal of Public Health, 90,* 360–366.

Lehman, A. (2000). "Evidence-based practice in schizophrenia." Seminar presentation, School of Social Welfare, State University of New York at Albany, Albany, N.Y., March 15, 2000.

Lehman, A., Steinwachs, D. M., Dixon, L. B., Goldman, H. H., Osher, F., Postrado, L., Scott, J. E., Thompson, J. W., Fahey, M., Fischer, P., Kasper, J. A., Skinner, E. A., Buchanan, R., Carpenter, W. T., Levine, J., McGlynn, E. A., Rosenheck, R., and Zito, J. (1998a). At issue: Translating research into practice: The schizophrenia patient outcomes research team (PORT) treatment recommendations. *Schizophrenia Bulletin, 24* (1), 1–10.

———. (1998b). Patterns of usual care for schizophrenia: Initial results from the schizophrenia patient outcomes research team (PORT) client survey. *Schizophrenia Bulletin, 24* (1), 11–20.

Lescoe-Long, M., and Long, M. J. (1999). Defining the utility of clinically acceptable variations in evidence-based practice guidelines for evaluation of quality improvement activities. *Evaluation and the Health Professions, 22* (3), 298–324.

Littell, J. H., and Tajima, E. A. (2000). A multilevel model of client participation in intensive family preservation services. *Social Service Review, 74* (3), 356–369.

Lum, D. (1999). *Culturally Competent Practice: A Framework for Growth and Action.* Pacific Grove, Calif.: Brooks-Cole.

Manderscheind, R. W. (1998). Managed mental health care. *Journal of Behavioral Health Services and Research, 25* (2), 233–237.

McHugo, G. L., Drake, R. E., Teague, G. B., and Xie, Haiyi. (1999). Fidelity to assertive community treatment and client outcomes in the New Hampshire dual disorders study. *Psychiatric Services, 50* (6), 818–824.

Meyer, C. (1996). My son the scientist. *Social Work Research, 20* (2), 101–105.

Mood disorders: Pharmacologic prevention of recurrences. (1984). *NIH Consensus Statement Online,* April 4–26, 1984 [cited 2000, March 13].

Moore, J. D., Jr. (1999). AHCPR posts clinical practice guidelines. *Modern Healthcare, 29* (2), 24–26.

National Guidelines Clearinghouse. (2000). http://www.guideline.gov/index.

National Institute of Mental Health. (1999, March 11). Research on co-morbidity: Etiology and prevention. Retrieved Jan. 28, 2003 from http://www.nimh.nih.gov/grants/archives/PA-99-071.cfm.

National Mental Health Advisory Council Clinical Treatment and Services Research Workgroup. (1999). *Bridging Science and Service.* Washington, D.C.: National Institute of Mental Health, National Institutes of Health.

Paul, G. L. (1967). Strategy of outcome research in psychotherapy. *Journal of Consulting Psychology, 31* (1), 109–118.

Persons, J. B. (1995). Why practicing psychologists are slow to adopt empirically validated treatments. In S. C. Hayes, V. M. Follette, R. M. Dawes, and K. E. Grady (Eds.), *Scientific Standards of Psychological Practice: Issues and Recommendations.* Reno, Nev.: Context Press, 141–157.

Preston, M. G., and Mudd, E. H. (1956). Research and service in social work: Conditions for a stable union. *Social Work, 1* (1), 34–40.

Rao, C. R. (1965). The theory of least-squares when the parameters are stochastic and its application to the analysis of growth curves. *Biometrika, 52,* 447–458.

Richmond, M. (1917). *Social Diagnosis.* New York: Russell Sage Foundation.

Rothman, J. (1992). *Guidelines for Case Management: Putting Research to Professional Use.* Itaska, Ill.: Peacock.

Rubin, A., and Rosenblatt, A. (1979). *Sourcebook on Research Utilization.* New York: Council on Social Work Education.

Schuerman, J., Rzepnicki, T., and Littell, J. (1994). *Putting Families First: An Experiment in Family Preservation.* Hawthorne, N.Y.: Aldine de Gruyter.

Stern, S., Smith, C., and Joon-Jang, S. (1999). Urban families and adolescent mental health. *Social Work Research, 23* (1), 15–27.

Tobler, N. (1992). *Meta-analysis of Adolescent Drug Prevention Programs.* Final report to the National Institute of Drug Abuse. Rockville, Md.: National Institute of Drug Abuse.

Thyer, B. A. (1996). Forty years of progress toward empirical clinical practice? *Social Work Research, 20* (2), 77–82.

Thyer, B. A., and Wodarski, J. S. (Eds.) (1998). *Handbook of Empirical Social Work Practice.* New York: Wiley.

Tyrrell, C. L., Dozier, M., Teague, G. B., and Fallot, R. D. (1999). Effective treatment relationships for persons with serious psychiatric disorders: The importance of attachment states of mind. *Journal of Consulting and Clinical Psychology, 67* (5), 725–733.

Videka-Sherman, L. (1988a). A meta-analysis of social work practice effectiveness. I. Outpatient mental health. *Social Work, 33* (4), 325–330.

————. (1988b). A meta-analysis of social work practice effectiveness. II. The chronically mentally ill. *Social Work, 33* (4), 330–338.

Williams, J. B. W., and Lanigan, J. L. (1999). Practice guidelines in social work: A reply, or "Our glass is half full." *Research on Social Work Practice, 9* (3), 338–342.

Witkin, S. L. (1996). If empirical practice is the answer, then what is the question? *Social Work Research, 20* (2), 69–76.

Workgroup on Bipolar Disorder. (1994). Practice guideline for treatment of patients with bipolar disorder. *American Journal of Psychiatry, 151* (12, supplement), 1–36.

Workgroup on Schizophrenia. (1997). Practice guidelines for the treatment of patients with schizophrenia. *American Journal of Psychiatry, 154* (4, supplement), 1–63.

11

SERVICE-DELIVERY FACTORS IN THE DEVELOPMENT OF PRACTICE GUIDELINES

LUIS H. ZAYAS

As our profession moves toward the development of evidence-based practice guidelines, it faces myriad issues, many of which are addressed in this volume and in a recent issue of *Research in Social Work Practice* (1999). Within this lively debate, this chapter weighs in with a discussion of client, provider, and service-setting characteristics that are necessary for developing practice guidelines.

Practice guidelines typically focus first on diagnoses, disorders, or problems brought by clients to clinicians. Then they consider specific developmental groups (e.g., infants, children, adolescents, adults, seniors) or preferred treatment modalities (e.g., family, group, individual). This static approach fails to account for the most dynamic and varied elements of practice: the persons who receive interventions, the persons who provide interventions, and the persons who collectively create service contexts within which interventions are delivered. The professional culture of the service setting, the professional and ethnic culture of the providers, and the ethnicities, languages, and cultures of clients are seldom given the attention they deserve in practice guidelines. Absent inclusion of these fluid, changing, and confounding characteristics, the ecological validity of treatment guidelines is suspect (Bernal, Bonilla, and Bellido 1995).

My discussion of these essential aspects of practice guidelines is organized around treatment services to ethnic and racial minority clients. In tracing misunderstandings about service utilization by ethnic and racial minority clients, I argue that the treatment-adherence literature has commonly failed to account for group differences in premature termination or "dropping out" by clients. Instead, studies have more typically used client characteristics to

Work on this chapter was supported, in part, by grants R24MH60002 and R24MH57936.

assign blame or responsibility for treatment failure, when a focus on provider practice and service settings factors would have been more appropriate. In fact, the literature on treatment adherence—whether we are referring to dropping out, premature termination, or inconsistent compliance by clients—has been one-sided at best. Most notable is that it operates from the (flawed) assumption that factors associated with client characteristics (whether intrapsychic or extrapsychic) lead to premature termination and that service provisions are adequate. Much of this literature fails to recognize that providers and their service context make a powerful contribution to premature termination and underutilization of services among the population of interest in this chapter. Without considering clients' social and psychocultural factors, practice with guidelines may be no more effective in improving outcomes than practice without guidelines.

CLIENT CHARACTERISTICS

Since the 1970s, the behavioral and social sciences have given attention—even if slowly and erratically—to individual and group differences associated with race, culture, and ethnicity. In a now classic paper, Graham (1992) persuasively demonstrated the marginalization of African Americans in psychological research, a situation that mirrors the status of other racial and ethnic minorities in research. It became evident during the development of the *Diagnostic and Statistical Manual of Mental Disorders, Fourth Edition (DSM-IV;* American Psychiatric Association 1994) that culture and ethnicity had also been excluded from the diagnostic process. In response, *DSM-IV* included a glossary of culture-bound syndromes and cultural formulations— that is, narrative descriptions that provide "a systematic review of the individual's cultural background, the role of cultural context in the expression and evaluation of symptoms and dysfunctions, and the effect that cultural difference may have on the relationship between the individual and the clinician" (APA 1994:843). Such developments in our knowledge of the impact that psychocultural and racial factors have on human functioning are intended to advance our capacity to assess and treat clients effectively and sensitively.

To further *DSM-IV*'s cultural formulations and strengthen the knowledge base that clinicians can turn to, the editors of *Culture, Medicine, and Psychiatry* created the Clinical Cases Section, which puts culture at the center of clinical evaluation and treatment in mental health. The editors' rationale is that case-based analyses reveal the contextual embeddedness of mental illness and its behavioral, interpersonal manifestations. Case analysis can establish the impact of cultural factors on clinical phenomenology by revealing the poor fit between existing nosologies and many non-Western presentations of psychopathology. As the editors of *Culture, Medicine, and Psychiatry* point out (Roberto Lewis-Fernandez, M.D., written communication, August 2000), the use of case materials and their accumulation can advance *DSM-IV* by rendering visible the socially constructed context that mediates key features of a patient's presentation and subsequent course in treatment.

While we may be making some progress toward understanding and including culture and ethnicity in our diagnoses, the literature on clients' adherence to treatment has not kept pace with our attempts to reveal the impact of social and cultural factors on clients. The classical psychotherapy literature, a favorite of practice professors and clinicians, has looked at clients' resistance or their serious personal pathology to explain treatment nonadherence. In that literature, the client's intrapsychic deficits (e.g., acting-out, defensiveness, poor insight, lack of psychological-mindedness) are identified as correlates or predictors of premature treatment termination. Only in the privacy of clinical supervision are therapist factors taken into account (i.e., countertransference, poor contracting, inappropriate or ineffective interpretations, queries, or explanations). But in this context, therapist cultural "blindness" is seldom considered. Precious little is said about social, economic, legal, cultural, and historic realities of minority clients. Worse still, many providers hold skewed views about why clients from minority groups are likely to discontinue service use. In an interesting review paper, Schnitzer (1996) describes stories told by clinicians about minority families who drop out of treatment as raising questions about the families' reliability and responsibility ("they don't come in"), cognitive capacities ("they're so disorganized"), and moral sensibilities ("they don't care").

Substantial evidence exists that service utilization and premature treatment termination continue to be serious problems among ethnic and racial minority groups, although regardless of ethnicity or race, between 30 percent and 60 percent of patients end treatment prematurely (Armbruster and Kazdin 1994; Baekeland and Lundwall 1975; Garfield 1986; Wierzbicki and Pekarik 1993). What is known about service utilization and discontinuation by ethnic and racial minority clients is that they vary by ethnic or racial group, such as that Asians and Hispanics underutilize services while blacks and Native Americans overutilize services (Sue 1977). Other patterns show that ethnic minority clients drop out of treatment more quickly; for example, African Americans have higher proportions of dropouts (attending less than one session) in comparison to Asians and Hispanics, who might stay in treatment longer but who have higher dropout rates than non-Hispanic Whites (Sue 1977; Sue et al. 1991). Overall, we find in the treatment-adherence research literature—whether focused on adults or children and families—that those who drop out are typically poor, relatively uneducated members of ethnic and racial minority groups (Baekeland and Lundwall 1975; Garfield 1986; Kazdin, Stolar, and Marciano 1995; Sue et al. 1991; Wierzbicki and Pekarik 1993). Children and families who leave treatment early often have more severe symptoms, are from one-parent ethnic and racial minority families with mothers who reported greater stress, and are more socioeconomically disadvantaged than those who remain in treatment (Armbruster and Fallon 1994; Kazdin 1990). In short, most of the treatment-nonadherence literature details client characteristics that predict premature termination.

Despite this serious problem of service underutilization, ethnic and racial minority families consistently demonstrate that they *want and seek* services. Service-use research shows that ethnic minority groups seek treatment in proportions equal to or greater than their proportion in the population (e.g., Sue et al. 1991). Barker and Adelman (1994) found that at least 50 percent of minority clients indicate a need for help for personal, emotional, or behavior problems. These findings are borne out by the documented increase in outpatient mental health treatment use between the early 1980s and the early 1990s reported in the National Comorbidity Survey (Kessler et al. 1999). Data on adult outpatient mental health services utilization in New York City show that 27 percent were Hispanic, 25 percent non-Hispanic black, and 43 percent non-Hispanic. Service-utilization rates, however, show that Hispanics use services at a rate of 90.7 per 10,000 population and non-Hispanic blacks at a rate of 79.0, both exceeding the rate of 66.4 for non-Hispanic Whites (Department of Mental Health, Mental Retardation, and Alcoholism Services 1995).

Two issues emerge as paramount during the development of practice guidelines that will enhance treatment outcomes with minority clients: one is the establishment of productive treatment relationships, and the other is the selection of treatment approaches that have demonstrated success with ethnic and racial minority clients.

TREATMENT RELATIONSHIPS

In building therapeutic relationships, the values, beliefs, and behavioral norms of minority clients need to be observed. Culturally competent practice is built on the awareness of and sensitivity to client differences. Clinical practice wisdom from accumulated knowledge of clients' cultures and practice techniques informed by this knowledge has advanced our understanding and skills.

Incorporating this knowledge into practice guidelines moves us closer to improving our responsiveness to minority clients. Take, for instance, child-socialization behaviors of parents from different ethnic groups. Culture influences how parents behave with their children (Rothbaum et al. 2000; Harkness and Super 1996; Zayas and Solari 1994). To engage parents from minority or immigrant groups as clients, awareness of differences between clinician and clients in, say, the cultural importance of independence versus dependence for each is imperative. Privileging one cultural system over another in the treatment relationship may not only lead to client alienation and premature termination but, worse, do harm to clients. From practice experience, supervisors can teach clinicians how best to engage clients and minimize attrition. However, little of the kind of practice wisdom that comes with the accumulation of experiences that have "worked" has been subjected to qualitative or quantitative empirical scrutiny. We are, therefore, left with appealing, intuitive treatment ideas that remain untested.

Developing practice guidelines is not simply a matter of matching a specific treatment to specific problems presented by persons of a specific age. Competent practice guidelines must also consider client characteristics—such as culture, race, ethnicity, immigration status, and history, to name a few—that will ensure retention in treatment and successful outcomes. Practice guidelines that include suggestions for developing and sustaining therapeutic relationships with Hispanic clients, for example, would lead practitioners to think about and interact effectively in many areas, guiding them to take a more interpersonal rather than impersonal stance in relating to clients from this group. The practitioner would reflect on the need for some self-disclosure to enhance interaction based on the *personalismo* of Hispanic culture (i.e., preference for informal and personal exchanges with service providers). Exploration of immigration and migration history, including reasons for immigration, extended-family reactions to the clients' immigration, separation of children from parents for long periods and their reunification, and possible trauma in the course of immigration, as well as religious beliefs and affiliations, would be among the elements incorporated in practice guidelines with Hispanics. More important, practice guidelines would warn practitioners against presuming that all Hispanic groups are alike. Gender roles, child-to-adult and adult-to-adult interaction, and differences in definitions about the individual and the collective would also be included in practice guidelines to enhance the treatment relationship. Much like the clinical case studies in *Culture, Medicine, and Psychiatry,* practice guidelines would amass knowledge on issues that foster strong client-worker relationships and stem premature treatment termination.

TREATMENT APPROACHES

Practice guidelines must also lead practitioners to recognize that therapies have been created or adapted to meet the specific characteristics and needs of ethnic minority clients, though the literature in this area is not yet very extensive. There are, however, several valuable examples of child and adolescent treatments that have been tested with minority populations with good effect and that can serve as models for future treatment development and practice guidelines. These treatments can also be further modified to match the cultural, ethnic, and contextual features of different groups and then linked to practice guidelines.

One example of creating a therapy comes from the work of Costantino, Malgady, and Rogler (1986), who developed *cuento* therapy (storytelling therapy) to meet the unique needs of Hispanic children coming to an inner-city community mental health service. The researchers set about developing a treatment that would be responsive to the characteristics of the group they were most familiar with, the one most in need: Puerto Rican children from young, single-parent, mother-headed, father-absent households who had been referred for behavioral and emotional problems. Drawing from folk-healing practices of Puerto Rico and the function of folktales as enduring repositories of cultural heritage and modes of transmission of values, *cuento* therapy was intended to promote adaptive personality development in the children. *Cuentos,* or folktales, from Puerto Rican culture were adapted to reflect the environment of Puerto Rican children in an urban setting on the United States mainland, retaining the flavor of the Puerto Rican culture through the characters, their names, and the plots but reflecting the children's ecological reality. In a randomized clinical trial with children and adolescents, *cuento* therapy improved children's socially adaptive behaviors, reduced anxiety and aggression, and increased their social judgment in comparison to a traditional treatment approach or no treatment. With the evidence that *cuento* therapy is an effective treatment for children, practice guidelines would offer clinicians this method of treatment for preadolescent Puerto Rican children in similar contexts. What's more, practice guidelines would also provide clinicians with suggestions for adapting this model for use with other Hispanic and cultural minority children.

As do other treatments that practice guidelines might suggest, *cuento* therapy has its limitations. Costantino, Malgady, and Rogler (1986) tested *cuento* therapy with Puerto Rican adolescents within the same ecology and found that it was less effective; in fact, adolescents perceived *cuentos* as juvenile and less interesting, and they were more resistant to therapeutic change. In response to this finding, Costantino, Malgady, and Rogler (1988) drew on the importance of cultural heroes to adolescents and developed a treatment modality called "hero/heroine" therapy. Heroic figures in Puerto Rican history who had faced and overcome severe adversity were identified and their biographies elaborated. Heroes and heroines had to embody important ego psychology features: sense of reality, interpersonal strength, social judgment, self-identity, and autonomous functioning. Using a small-group approach to deliver the intervention, the researchers found that adolescents exposed to the hero therapy significantly improved in their ethnic identity and self-concepts and showed lower anxiety levels than adolescents in traditional psychotherapy. Since hero worship is a common phenomenon among adolescents, practice guidelines might point clinicians in the direction of incorporating principles and approaches from hero/heroine therapy for adaptation to adolescents from other cultural and ethnic groups.

Creating a therapy model is not always necessary when working with minority youth. In most instances, all that may be needed is the modification and adaptation of an extant model. In an example of this approach, Rosselló and Bernal (1996, 1999) demonstrated how both interpersonal psychotherapy (IPT) and cognitive-behavioral therapy (CBT) for the treatment of depression in adolescents can be effective with a minority group. To test the efficacy of CBT against that of IPT for the treatment of depression among Puerto Rican adolescents living on the island, Rosselló and Bernal adapted both treatment approaches for their specific population. Using a conceptually based approach, they first determined that to gain ecological validity for the treatments, they would have to consider: (1) language and idiomatic adaptations, (2) persons giving and receiving the treatment, (3) metaphors and their meaning to the target population, (4) content of the treatment to reflect cultural values and preferences of the target group, (5) goals of the treatment, (6) methods and how they meshed with the population, and (7) the sociocultural, economic, and political context (Rosselló and Bernal 1996).

Rosselló and Bernal (1999) found that the culturally adapted forms of CBT and IPT proved equally effective in reducing depression and improving self-esteem (over a wait-list group). The advantage of IPT was that it provided "added value" by not only enhancing mood and self-esteem but also improving adolescents' self-concept and social adaptation. Also, IPT, according to Rosselló and Bernal (1999), appeared to be more compatible with Puerto Rican cultural norms of social interaction (e.g., personalismo and familism) than CBT. Practice guidelines might also promote the same theoretically based approach to adapting and evaluating treatments for different cultural and ethnic groups. These examples of therapies that were created and adapted show that treatment adherence and effectiveness among minority clients can be significantly improved when practice guidelines are adapted to the idiographic characteristics of the clients served.

SERVICE-SETTING CHARACTERISTICS

In the treatment-adherence literature, the structures and organization of mental health services and their service-delivery procedures are seldom explored as reasons for premature termination. Ethnic and racial minority populations may consistently underuse services (by not seeking them or by discontinuing prematurely) because of constraints imposed by the ways in which services are designed and offered. Cumbersome agency procedures may affect utilization of services. Intake and evaluation procedures in child and adolescent mental health services are a good example of this problem. Although these procedures are now more expedited because of managed care requirements, there are still some steps that must take place.

Intake usually begins with a referral call placed by parents at the urging of a family member, teacher, minister, or health professional. After basic information is exchanged, an initial appointment is made—sometimes weeks, if not months, later because of the large service demands on agencies. The evaluation process may then take from one to three sessions, if it is to be thorough. (In one study [Armbruster and Fallon 1994], the intake required that parents complete a packet of diagnostic instruments followed by an evaluation of up to eight sessions before assignment to therapy.) Then, assuming a relatively uncomplicated clinical picture, the "case" was assigned to a therapist, possibly a person that the family had not met previously, during the intake process. Weeks may have elapsed between intake and the "first session." In more complicated clinical situations, the case may require additional visits, such as an evaluation by a child psychiatrist (adding one or two more appointments) and psychological testing (adding one to three additional interviews). When these are completed, the case is assigned to a therapist. When parents need or request treatment for themselves (separate from the child's treatment), they may be assigned their own therapist(s), adding other actors to the cast.

Although such a complex arrangement does not occur in all clinics, this illustration shows that entry into treatment can be elaborate in child and adolescent mental health services. Unlike the typical pediatric encounter, with its sense of immediacy for treating an illness, the mental health evaluation process can seem long, slow, arduous, and arcane, particularly for linguistically and culturally distant persons and for those with few resources or little understanding of the system. Such a process highlights structural factors that lead to premature termination, especially among minority clients.

Kazdin, Holland, and Crowley (1997) recognized that structural barriers to participation in treatment contributed significantly to the dropout rates for therapy and that, conversely, the perception of few barriers attenuated dropout rates, even among high-risk families. Perceived barriers were not explained by family, parent, and child characteristics (although these same characteristics predicted dropping out). Rather, parents' perceptions of the difficulties in participating in treatment (such as stressors and obstacles associated with treatment, perceiving the treatment as irrelevant, and poor parent-therapist relationship) influenced who dropped out (Kazdin, Holland, and Crowley 1997). Henggeler et al. (1996) found that home-based treatment resulted in a 90 percent treatment-completion rate among substance-abusing and conduct-disordered adolescents in a multisystemic intervention. Seventy-eight percent of those in a standard outpatient condition failed to receive treatment in the months following referral. I argue here, as do Henggeler et al. (1996), that high dropout rates can be attenuated by increasing service accessibility and placing greater responsibility for engagement on service providers.

The relevance of this discussion to practice guidelines is quite apparent: It is not enough to promote practice guidelines if our service-delivery system does not change accordingly. Thus, a key principle for practice guideline development is consideration for the structure and process of the service-delivery context. If we are to implement practice guidelines, we must do so with attention to agency or institutional features that inhibit treatment adherence by clients.

PROVIDER CHARACTERISTICS

Many provider characteristics can lead to premature termination by clients, and practice guidelines must take this into account. Interpersonal factors that might result in treatment dropout include lack of congruence between clients' and therapists' views of problems, what can be done about them, and expectations of potential treatment interventions (Black and Krishnakumar 1998; Clinton 1996); disagreement between the referral source or mental health providers and clients (Pottick, Lerman, and Micchelli 1992; Singh, Janes, and Schectman 1982); therapeutic relationship or alliance between worker and client (Kazdin, Holland, and Crowley 1997; Tyrell et al. 1999); and dissatisfaction with the specific advice offered during the diagnostic evaluation (Singh, Janes, and Schectman 1982).

Rosen (1972) has characterized these differences and clinicians' capacity to engage and retain clients in treatment as "stimulus-response congruence" (i.e., the extent to which clinicians' responses indicate to clients that they have been understood) and "content relevance" (i.e., the extent to which clients perceive that clinicians are responsive to the problems they present). Insufficient congruence and content relevance may reduce the perceived value of treatment. A study supporting Rosen's formulation is that of Mejía-Maya and Zayas (1995), which found that Hispanic adults with HIV or AIDS who had dropped out of psychotherapy reported doing so because of stimulus-response incongruities between themselves and their therapists on perceptions and expectations of therapy. In focus groups, these clients indicated that therapists' stance of neutrality and nondirectiveness, along with a perceived lack of therapist sensitivity to their emotional struggles, were primary reasons for discontinuing services. Some clients complained that therapists and their service settings did not address very real needs. Structural reasons given by women participants, for example, included the lack of assistance with child care and transportation by service agencies, and the lack of therapist action or advocacy on such matters. Both male and female participants perceived their therapists as not sufficiently willing to engage with them in anticipatory planning for custody of their children as their disease progressed or to meet with family members and friends who would assist in planning for the children. Content relevance was often shrunk by therapists' concerns with psychodynamic issues that, at that moment, were not germane to the clients' presenting concerns.

Although the incongruity between the cultural and linguistic worlds of clients and that of service systems delivery may account for some reduction in service use or increase in treatment discontinuity (Padilla, Ruiz, and Alvarez 1975), some findings indicate that therapist-patient matching on ethnicity, race, or gender does not play an appreciable role in reducing premature treatment termination (Gottheil et al. 1994; Sue et al. 1991). Instead, structural elements and the interpersonal processes in psychological evaluation and treatment may play a more pronounced role. Garland and Zigler (1994) have suggested that more research is needed on perceptions about mental health services, particularly on their accessibility and attractiveness. A few writers (Areán and Gallagher-Thompson 1996; Miranda et al. 1996; Thompson et al. 1996) have discussed ways of engaging minority clients in clinical research, and similar approaches can be integrated in practice guidelines. Perhaps changing the manner in which we conduct our evaluations and treatment can enhance the communication between clinic personnel and clients, and facilitate treatment adherence (Singh, Janes, and Schectman 1982).

Practice guidelines must, therefore, attend to questions of culture-specific factors that govern interpersonal relationships in order to arrive at what Sue and Zane (1987) call "achieved credibility," a strengthening point in the treatment relationship. Using the examples of the child and adolescent treatments developed by Costantino, Malgady, and Rogler (1986, 1988) and the adaptations made by Rosselló and Bernal (1996, 1999) to interpersonal psychotherapy, we can see how the ethnic minority client's culture can be considered in enhancing the treatment relationship. Costantino, Malgady, and Rogler emphasized the importance of folktales and metaphors in Puerto Rican culture and included attention to the therapists' interaction with children in the treatment. Likewise, Rosselló and Bernal (1996) selected interpersonal therapy for its emphasis on the culture's accent on *personalismo* and familism. Therapists in both treatment approaches are encouraged to operate within these frameworks to enhance the therapeutic relationship. Practice guidelines would help clinicians by including this accumulated knowledge and wisdom in establishing interpersonal relationships that have meaning and familiarity to ethnic minority clients.

———

Any attempt to develop and adopt practice guidelines must avoid the past errors of practice and research, namely, neglecting the importance of ethnicity, culture, and race of client groups. Moreover, practice guidelines do not simply apply to providers and their selection of culturally sensitive treatments for clients; they apply equally to the service agency and the structure of service programs. The relationships among client, provider, and service-setting characteristics are vital to the development and implementation of guidelines for interventions.

Essentially, practitioners and program developers and administrators must adjust evidence-based practice to the characteristics of client populations. Evidence-based practice guidelines are certainly needed if psychosocial providers are to show that what they do actually works. It is our responsibility to adapt our professional education, research, practice, and service-delivery systems to make empirically based intervention approaches accessible to clinicians and their clients.

REFERENCES

American Psychiatric Association. (1994). *Diagnostic and Statistical Manual of Mental Disorders* (4th ed.). Washington, D.C.: APA.

Areán, P. A., and Gallagher-Thompson, D. (1996). Issues and recommendations for the recruitment and retention of older ethnic minority adults into clinical research. *Journal of Consulting and Clinical Psychology, 64,* 875–880.

Armbruster, P., and Fallon, T. (1994). Clinical, sociodemographic, and systems risk factors for attrition in a children's mental health clinic. *American Journal of Orthopsychiatry, 64,* 577–585.

Armbruster, P., and Kazdin, A. E. (1994). Attrition in Child Psychotherapy. In T. H. Ollendick and R. J. Prinz (Eds.), *Advances in Clinical Child Psychology* (16:81–108). New York: Plenum.

Baekeland, F., and Lundwall, L. (1975). Dropping out of treatment: A critical review. *Psychological Bulletin, 82,* 738–783.

Barker, L. A., and Adelman, H. S. (1994). Mental health and help-seeking among ethnic minority adolescents. *Journal of Adolescence, 17,* 251–263.

Bernal, G., Bonilla, J., and Bellido, C. (1995). Ecological validity and cultural sensitivity for outcome research: Issues for the cultural adaptation and development of psychosocial treatments with Hispanics. *Journal of Abnormal Child Psychology, 23,* 67–87.

Black, M. M., and Krishnakumar, A. (1998). Children in low-income, urban settings: Interventions to promote mental health and well-being. *American Psychologist, 53,* 635–646.

Clinton, D. N. (1996). Why do eating disorder patients drop out? *Psychotherapy and Psychosomatics, 65,* 29–35.

Costantino, G., Malgady, R. G., and Rogler, L. H. (1986). Cuento therapy: A culturally sensitive modality for Puerto Rican children. *Journal of Consulting and Clinical Psychology, 54,* 639–645.

———. (1988). Folk hero modeling therapy for Puerto Rican adolescents. *Journal of Adolescence, 11,* 155–165.

Department of Mental Health, Mental Retardation, and Alcoholism Services. (1995). *Local Government Plan for Adult Mental Health Services.* New York: City of New York.

Garfield, S. L. (1986). Research on Client Variables Psychotherapy. In S. L. Garfield and A. E. Bergin (Eds.), *Handbook of Psychotherapy and Behavior Change* (3d ed.) (pp. 213–256). New York: Wiley.

Garland, A. F., and Zigler, E. F. (1994). Psychological correlates of help-seeking attitudes among children and adolescents. *American Journal of Orthopsychiatry, 64,* 586–593.

Gottheil, E., Sterling, R. C., Weinstein, S. P., and Kurtz, J. W. (1994). Therapist/patient matching and early treatment dropout. *Journal of Addictive Diseases, 13,* 169–176.

Graham, S. (1992). "Most of the subjects were white and middle class": Trends in published research on African Americans in selected APA journals 1970–1989. *American Psychologist, 47,* 629–639.

Harkness, S., and Super, C. M. (Eds.). (1996). *Parents' Cultural Belief Systems: Their Origins, Expressions, and Consequences.* New York: Guilford.

Henggeler, S. W., Pickrel, S. G., Brondino, M. J., and Crouch, J. L. (1996). Eliminating (almost) treatment dropout of substance abusing or dependent delinquents through home-based multisystemic therapy. *American Journal of Psychiatry, 153,* 427–428.

Kazdin, A. E. (1990). Premature termination from treatment among children referred for antisocial behavior. *Journal of Child Psychology and Psychiatry and Allied Disciplines, 31,* 415–425.

Kazdin, A. E., Holland, L., and Crowley, M. (1997). Family experiences of barriers to treatment and premature termination from child therapy. *Journal of Consulting and Clinical Psychology, 65,* 453–463.

Kazdin, A. E., Stolar, M. J., and Marciano, P. L. (1995). Risk factors for dropping out of treatment among White and Black families. *Journal of Family Psychology, 9,* 402–417.

Kessler, R. C., Zhao, S., Katz, S. J., Kouzis, A. C., Frank, R. G., Edlund, M., and Leaf, P. (1999). Past-year use of outpatient services for psychiatric problems in the National Comorbidity Survey. *American Journal of Psychiatry, 156,* 115–123.

Mejía-Maya, L. J., and Zayas, L. H. (1995). "Premature Treatment Termination by Hispanic Persons with HIV/AIDS: A Focus Group Study." Unpublished manuscript, Fordham University.

Miranda, J., Azocar, F., Organista, K. C., Muñoz, R. F., and Lieberman, E. (1996). Recruiting and retaining low-income Latinos in psychotherapy research. *Journal of Consulting and Clinical Psychology, 64,* 868–874.

Padilla, A., Ruiz, R., and Alvarez, R. (1975). Community mental health services for the Spanish-speaking surnamed population. *American Psychologist, 30,* 892–904.

Pottick, K. J., Lerman, P., and Micchelli, M. (1992). Problems and perspectives: Predicting the use of mental health services by parents of urban youth. *Children and Youth Services Review, 14,* 363–378.

Research in Social Work Practice. (1999). Special issue. *Practice Guidelines and Clinical Social Work.* Vol. 9, no. 3.

Rosen, A. (1972). The treatment relationship: A conceptualization. *Journal of Consulting and Clinical Psychology, 38,* 329–337.

Rosselló, J., and Bernal, G. (1996). Adapting Cognitive-Behavioral and Interpersonal Treatments for Depressed Puerto Rican Adolescents. In E. D. Hibbs and P. S. Jensen (Eds.), *Psychosocial Treatments for Child and Adolescent Disorders: Empirically Based Strategies for Clinical Practice* (pp. 157–185). Washington, D.C.: American Psychological Association.

———. (1999). The efficacy of cognitive-behavioral and interpersonal treatments for depression in Puerto Rican adolescents. *Journal of Consulting and Clinical Psychology, 67,* 734–745.

Rothbaum, F., Weisz, J., Pott, M., Miyake, K., and Morelli, G. (2000). Attachment and culture: Security in the United States and Japan. *American Psychologist, 55,* 1093–1104.

Schnitzer, P. K. (1996). "They don't come in!": Stories told, lessons taught about poor families in therapy. *American Journal of Orthopsychiatry, 66,* 572–582.

Singh, H., Janes, C. L., and Schectman, J. M. (1982). Problems in children's treatment attrition and parents' perception of the diagnostic evaluation. *Journal of Psychiatric Treatment and Evaluation, 4,* 257–263.

Sue, S. (1977). Community mental health services to minority groups: Some optimism, some pessimism. *American Psychologist, 32,* 616–624.

Sue, S., Fujino, D. C., Hu, L., and Takeuchi, D. T. (1991). Community mental health services for ethnic minority groups: A test of the cultural responsiveness hypothesis. *Journal of Consulting and Clinical Psychology, 59,* 533–540.

Sue, S., and Zane, N. (1987). The role of culture and cultural techniques in psychotherapy: A critique and reformulation. *American Psychologist, 42,* 37–45.

Thompson, E. E., Neighbors, H. W., Munday, C., and Jackson, J. S. (1996). Recruitment and retention of African American patients for clinical research: An exploration of response rates in an urban psychiatric hospital. *Journal of Consulting and Clinical Psychology, 64,* 861–867.

Tyrrell, C. L., Dozier, M., Teague, G. B., and Fallot, R. D. (1999). Effective treatment relationships for persons with serious psychiatric disorders: The importance of attachment states of mind. *Journal of Consulting and Clinical Psychology, 67,* 725–733.

Wierzbicki, M., and Pekarik, G. (1993). A meta-analysis of psychotherapy dropout. *Professional Psychology: Research and Practice, 24,* 190–195.

Zayas, L. H., and Solari, F. (1994). Early childhood socialization in Hispanic families: Culture, context, and practice implications. *Professional Psychology: Research and Practice, 25* (3), 200–206.

12

PERFORMANCE STANDARDS AND QUALITY CONTROL: APPLICATION OF PRACTICE GUIDELINES TO SERVICE DELIVERY

WILMA PEEBLES-WILKINS AND MARYANN AMODEO

T he need to place more emphasis on scientific evidence in social work practice has been well established (Howard and Jenson 1999a, 1999b; Kirk 1999; Mullen 1978, 1988; Richey and Roffman 1999; Videka-Sherman and Reid 1990). Certainly, with its heritage of scientific charity, social work is grounded in such a tradition. One method for addressing this need is the promulgation of practice guidelines founded on research evidence and clinical consensus. We favor this approach for several reasons, among them the importance of such guidelines for practice in a managed care environment. However, several caveats should guide the development and implementation of guidelines. In this chapter we will (1) discuss the relationship between practice guidelines and evidence-based practice, using managed care as an example, (2) highlight sources of support for guideline development, and (3) suggest a process for guideline development that includes addressing current difficulties with standards and terminology, choosing a single practice area for initial efforts, and disseminating practice guidelines through a three-tiered training plan.

EVIDENCE-BASED PRACTICE AND THE MANAGED CARE PERSPECTIVE

IMPROVING QUALITY OF CARE AND COST-EFFECTIVENESS

Among the many reasons the social work profession would benefit from comprehensive and evidence-based practice guidelines is the increased use of such guidelines in managed care decision making. Guidelines could provide valuable tools for social workers in responding to the managed care environment. In fact, the managed care environment is a potent force driving the development of practice guidelines for all health-related professions. A central benefit of such guidelines, demonstrated when other professions have developed and implemented them, is that they promote uniformity and improve the quality of care. They can also assist the profession in better responding to cost-effectiveness initiatives that reduce the number of client visits. Guidelines for short-term or brief treatment are an example. In the technical paper "Research Needs in Managed Behavioral Health Care in Massachusetts," developed at the request of representatives from the National Institute of Mental Health, Peebles-Wilkins collaborated with Boston-area social work colleagues to examine the competing goals of access, quality of care, and cost-effectiveness, all of which are prevalent aspects of the managed care perspective. While it is the quality-of-care goal that requires the research necessary for practice guideline development, access and cost-effectiveness warrant attention here as well, since both have implications for social work interventions.

ACCESS AND COST-EFFECTIVENESS

Increasingly, some social work practitioners are doing fee-for-service work reimbursed under managed care. The managed care or behavioral health care industry has promoted the development of uniform practice guidelines, which are viewed as promoting more efficient and cost-effective service delivery. The behavioral health care or managed care perspective also has the goal of creating greater access for previously underserved populations such as minorities and the poor. This perspective assumes that services are more universally accessible under systems that apply uniform standards to control health and mental health interventions (Feldman and Goldman 1997; Pigott and Broskowski 1995; Rodriquez 1994; Schreter, Sharfstein, and Schreter 1994). Guidelines resemble diagnostic-related groups (DRG), which have for some time been a part of medical review systems but such guidelines could be seen as a more extensive version of the DRG concept. Professions such as medicine, psychiatry, and nursing are way ahead of social work in developing uniform standards that respond to the mandates from a managed care system, thus their services are more reimbursable than many of the services provided by social workers. For health and behavioral health care interventions in managed care systems, practice guidelines have become essential requirements to ensure quality control and cost containment.

Closely allied to quality of care, cost containment, and access is the task of "defining good outcomes for mental health interventions" (Veeder and Peebles-Wilkins 1998). The development of evidence-based uniform guidelines for social workers would greatly inform the process of defining good outcomes. Further, the profession needs to choose a clear direction in developing uniform practice guidelines grounded in outcomes research. Research based on quality-of-care measures is needed to shape the development of uniform practice guidelines for social work interventions.

QUALITY CARE AND MEASUREMENT OF OUTCOMES

Theoreticians and researchers have placed different emphases on measures of quality of care. Donabedian's (1988) work in this area of study in the late 1980s is helpful for any discussion of practice guidelines in social work. He suggested that the quality-of-care concept has three components: structure, process, and outcome. *Structure* refers to the physical setting in which the intervention is delivered (e.g., the social work agency), *process* refers to the method by which the service is provided (e.g., psychosocial treatments, brief therapy), and of course, *outcome* refers to whether there were measurable changes in a desired effect as a result of the intervention. Bachman (personal communication 2000), a managed care researcher at the Boston University School of Social Work, believes that attention to all three components is necessary when thinking about quality of care and that the process of delivering care is as important as the outcome in ensuring quality. One aspect of the process in the context of evidence-based practice is fidelity to a model. How well do practitioners adhere to the main aspects of the intervention? Are there clear principles that social workers can integrate into their ongoing practice? Does the agency provide training in evidence-based practice guidelines? Outcome measures should relate directly to whatever change one is hoping to accomplish—for example, improved functional status for the client, fewer missed days of work, or greater life satisfaction. The social work profession can enhance the quality of care through monitoring the fidelity of guideline implementation and through agency training.

IMPROVING CULTURAL COMPETENCE AND ACCESS

Unfortunately, the literature seems either to damn practice guidelines for not distinguishing the needs of different clients or client groups or to praise them for providing equal treatment for all. What is missed in this dichotomy is the simultaneous benefits of reducing disparity in services and enhancing uniform implementation of services. Practice guidelines can play a critical role in this process.

Cultural minorities and the poor have a long history of being excluded under traditional systems of care. Some of the exclusion has been associated with traditional diagnoses. In other circumstances, the poor and cultural minorities have not had as great a degree of choice as have other groups. Managed health care systems have improved access to primary care and controlled the selective interventions that transpired under the more traditional systems. In the context of managed care, the social work profession, with its emphasis on social and economic justice and services to the disadvantaged, can be in the forefront of improving cultural competence and providing even greater access to previously underserved groups. Though the profession has not done enough in this regard, the training of bilingual social workers by some schools of social work is a positive step. Social workers could generate research-based guidelines that include more culturally effective practices. Misdiagnosis of African Americans by the mental health system is an example of one area in which a greater focus on cultural competence is needed. Thus, in addition to increasing quality of care and cost-effectiveness, practice guidelines have the potential to enhance cultural competence and serve as a guide to greater access for people of color (Davis 1997, 1998). Practice guidelines can also help to standardize health and behavioral health treatments provided to underserved groups or ethnic or racial groups such as African Americans, who historically have been offered less-expensive treatment (for example, for heart disease). It is the promotion of uniformity that can help to equalize health and mental health care in disadvantaged and minority communities and to curtail the variability that results from the whims and biases of service providers and organizations. Consequently, minority clients will receive services that are on a par with those provided to nonminority clients, and those services will presumably be of higher quality.

In contrast to this point, but not contradictory to it, different minority and cultural groups have specific needs that require different and specifically tailored services. Therefore, practice guidelines that are developed for and take into consideration the needs of specific minority groups can enhance the quality of care for these groups (e.g., African American clients might need to receive treatments that are different from those received by Hispanic clients or Anglo clients). Uniform application of these culturally focused practice guidelines would work to improve service outcomes within specific groups.

To summarize these points: (1) practice guidelines that are *applicable to all* would operate to enhance the quality of care for minority group clients by *reducing disparity in services,* while (2) practice guidelines that are *culturally specific* would operate to improve the quality of service for the targeted groups and would *enhance uniform application of services* whether for more traditional populations or special populations.

SOCIAL WORK ADMINISTRATOR SUPPORT FOR OUTCOME MEASUREMENT AND PRACTICE GUIDELINES

Supervisors and consultants are the best conduits for assisting social work practitioners with evidence-based practice because practitioners rely heavily on these professionals. There is evidence that supervisors and administrators may be receptive to such a role. In *Social Work Administration* (1997), Rick Koepke, executive director of the Society for Social Work Administration, reported the results of a survey of chapter members, chapter presidents, and a member random sample associated with developing the 1998–1999 two-year strategic plan for program emphasis. The development of social work outcome data (outcomes measurement) was at the top of the list of topics in importance to all three survey constituent groups in the society, and practice guidelines, while ranked lower on the list, still received significant support. And, of course, outcomes measurement is directly related to development of practice guidelines. Almost 84 percent of the chapter presidents, 78.7 percent of chapter members, and 61.1 percent of the member random sample ranked "providing information about outcome measurement" as most important. Among the chapter presidents or those in leadership roles, 61.3 percent thought it important to provide practice guidelines; 32.8 percent of chapter member respondents and 46.3 percent of the random sample of members concurred. The substantial interest of these constituencies in having more knowledge about practice guidelines suggests that they would be helpful in promulgating such quality control methods.

DESIGNING A PROCESS FOR PRACTICE GUIDELINE DEVELOPMENT

Given that support for development of social work practice guidelines does exist, the profession should move ahead on this agenda. Designing a rational and inclusive process, however, may prove to be challenging. The process for developing such guidelines in a managed care environment should entail the following: (1) clarifying confusing terminology; (2) examining models of closely allied health professions, such as nursing; (3) selecting a social problem, such as substance abuse, for initial guideline development; (4) recognizing the increased focus on brief treatment or limited client visits; and (5) developing a strategy for professional leadership. The authors believe that these are prerequisites to the social work response to managed care requirements that will culminate in a set of guidelines unique to the profession.

DIFFICULTIES WITH THE PROFESSION'S STANDARDS: CONFUSING TERMINOLOGY AND CONCEPTS

A recent survey of agency practitioners (Mullen and Bacon 2001) suggests that social workers (1) are poorly informed about practice guidelines, (2) seldom use them, and (3) read the professional literature less often than psychiatrists and psychologists. Before the profession embarks upon a lengthy and costly effort to rectify this situation, however, we would encourage the consideration of an alternative hypothesis: that social workers actually do use practice guidelines but do not recognize them by this name. For example, social workers may be guided by policy statements, best practices, levels of care, or other information that provides help in professional decision making. Perhaps the survey introduction, referred to by Mullen and Bacon, was detailed and explicit enough to rule out this possibility. (Since the survey introduction was not described in the article, we could not be certain.) If the survey introduction proves to be fairly perfunctory, however, we recommend that additional research be undertaken to rule out this hypothesis.

In the health and mental health profession, standards of care are often articulated under the leadership of the primary professional organization, such as the American Psychiatric Association, the American Nurses Association, or the National Association of Social Workers (NASW). Clinical practice language associated with standards of care includes competencies, practice guidelines, best practices, and, to some extent, professional policy statements that inform practice. In the profession of social work, many forms of guidance are available to assist practitioners with quality care. In addition to the previously listed terms, the NASW, assisted by specialty task forces composed of members, has developed setting-specific clinical indicators and population-specific standards to "guide practice."

The development and dissemination of practice guidelines is essential, but a necessary first step is to help practitioners understand what is meant by the term so they can differentiate practice guidelines from other similar tools that they may know or may be using to accomplish similar goals.

BEST PRACTICES, CRITICAL PATHWAYS, PRACTICE GUIDELINES VERSUS POLICY STATEMENTS, COMPETENCIES, AND STANDARDS

Most social work educators are very familiar with the NASW policy statements generated at the delegate assembly, and social work specialty groups are aware of the competencies generated by NASW practice specialty committees.

Policy statements contain broad recommendations for practice (for example, "programs should pay special attention to the needs of the disenfranchised such as clients living in poverty, with HIV/AIDS, or victimized by racism and oppression"). *Competencies* are knowledge, attitude, and skills statements that serve as prerequisites for practice and should be seen as a first step in the progression to practice guidelines or best practices (for example, "the student will be able to describe five characteristics of the ecological model"). *Practice guidelines,* on the other hand, "prescribe how clinicians should assess and treat clients" (Mullen and Bacon 2001) and are based on research, professional consensus, or some combination of the two (an example is a guideline spelling out the clients who could most benefit from abstinence contrasted with moderation management as a substance abuse treatment goal and recommendations about the appropriateness of each for various types of clients [APA 1995]). *Best practices,* a term used often in the nursing profession, refers to practices that are developed from deliberate research and result in best practice protocols. *Protocols* are developed from practice and the literature, may include any available research, and are detailed from assessment to intervention and evaluation. According to McGuire and Harwood (1996), *critical pathways* are interdisciplinary plans that serve as tools for managing patients and that are empirically grounded in practice experiences and patient outcomes. These plans incorporate mechanisms for documenting care and tracking and analyzing outcome data (p. 187). In many respects, critical pathways are similar to decision trees except that they outline not only the next step but also sites for care. For example, a given substance abuse diagnosis would point not only to the recommended long-term treatment but also to extended care in a hospital facility.

Unlike other professions, in social work the primary professional organization, the NASW, has focused primarily on the development of (1) policy statements rather than protocols and treatment standards; (2) competencies or knowledge, attitude, and skill statements rather than best practices or preferred treatment with a given diagnosis; and (3) service delivery systems rather than factors affecting choice of treatment setting. Although the NASW has broadly encouraged ongoing research as part of policy statements on social problems, it needs to turn its attention to practice guidelines.

EXAMINING MODELS OF ALLIED HEALTH PROFESSIONS: NURSING AS AN EXAMPLE

The nursing profession can serve as a useful model here; in fact, social work has used nursing as a model in the past, in developing government-funded social work research development initiatives, for example. The Association of Women's Health, Obstetric, and Neonatal Nurses (AWHONN) used the task force approach to integrate performance standards from the American Nurses Association into the 1998 version of the group's *Standards and Guidelines for Professional Nursing Practice in the Care of Women and Newborns.* These practice guidelines incorporate both research and clinical practice.

The document includes a Standards of Care statement, covering standards for (1) assessment, (2) diagnosis, and (3) outcome identification, and a Guideline for the Care of the Healthy Newborn with (1) a statement of purpose that dictates the role of the nurse with this type of patient, (2) definition of key terms, and (3) methodology that identifies eight nursing tasks related to observation, intervention, and documentation. Accompanying these documents is a statement summarizing the meaning and use of the standards and guidelines.

As noted earlier, for interdisciplinary approaches to care, nurses, in conjunction with other health care professionals, have developed critical pathways as a tool for holistic care of patients and families in case management–related interdisciplinary work. In addition to standards and practice guidelines, the nursing profession has developed competencies for the nurse practitioner associated with domains of practice. Such efforts by the American Nurses Association can serve as models to assist the NASW in moving forward with an evidence-based practice orientation, since social workers, like nurses, tend to be involved in more holistic levels of patient care, which extend beyond the individual clinical intervention.

SELECTING A PRACTICE AREA OR SOCIAL PROBLEM FOR INITIAL PRACTICE GUIDELINE DEVELOPMENT

For initial development of practice guidelines, one practice area or social problem should be chosen and the process evaluated for effectiveness. The lessons learned from this exercise can guide development of future practice guidelines. For several reasons, substance abuse is an ideal problem area for the development of social work practice guidelines: (1) it is a pervasive problem that most social workers encounter in their practice; (2) there is a lack of consensus about key issues (e.g., *etiology*—disease versus learned behavior, *assessment*—standardized questionnaires versus psychosocial history, *goals*—abstinence versus harm reduction, *type of treatment*—professional versus self-help or Twelve-Step, *counseling approaches*—confrontational versus motivational, *length of treatment*—brief versus longer term); and (3) there is no dearth of outcome research on which to base such guidelines. Substance abuse practice guidelines have been developed by other professional organizations—for example, the American Psychiatric Association—but these guidelines have limitations for social workers since their roles and functions are different from those of other health care and human services professionals. Further, existing guidelines are not likely to address the entire scope of the issues encountered by the social work profession, e.g., population-specific interventions, family-centered practice, the ecological context, or discrimination in the allocation of services.

In the interests of cost containment, managed care systems have focused on shorter inpatient stays as well as briefer outpatient treatments. In some instances, therapeutic visits in behavioral health care have been limited to six encounters. Because of the lack of objective measures of quality in the delivery of mental health and substance abuse services, these brief treatment models have dominated the field. Many social work practitioners do not support such models, but the models continue to exist nevertheless, thanks to managed and behavioral health care dictates. Without evidence and research-based practice guidelines that the profession can use to challenge such models, they will continue to represent acceptable or optimal practice in substance abuse.

Although the NASW developed the Policy Statement on Alcoholism and Other Substance Abuse–Related Problems in 1975 and has revised it over the years as knowledge in this area has increased, the association has not embarked on the development of practice guidelines focused on substance abuse or brief treatment. (To serve a different purpose, the NASW recently disseminated "substance abuse competencies," but these are for specialists who wish to receive credentials as alcohol and drug abuse counselors; thus they address a different need from the one discussed here.)

Research on the use of brief interventions in substance abuse has been well documented by the fields of medicine and psychology. "Brief treatment has one of the largest literature bases and currently the most positive" (Miller et al. 1995:23). Miller and his associates conducted a study on the efficacy of treatment modalities based on the alcohol treatment outcomes literature and published their results between 1977 and 1992. They found that brief treatment had the highest cumulative evidence score of thirty treatment approaches to patients with alcohol-related problems. (It is not clear, however, how these interventions affect triage, or referral, activities in interdisciplinary or case management situations.) Thus, the topic of social work brief interventions with substance use disorders is one possibility for uniform guideline development unique to social work intervention, once a methodology for developing practice guidelines has been selected.

In 1995 the American Psychiatric Association published "Practice Guidelines for the Treatment of Patients with Substance Use Disorders: Alcohol, Cocaine, Opioids" as a supplement to the *American Journal of Psychiatry* (1995:5–59). These psychiatric practice guidelines do include brief interventions as one of the psychosocial treatments "found to be effective for *selected* patients with alcohol use disorders" (p. 8). Here, then, is an opportunity for social work to develop a similar set of substance abuse guidelines, based on scientific research but perhaps offering a broader view than that provided by psychiatry. Social work's guidelines could include treatments found to be effective for those social work clients who are not responsive to brief interventions.

CHOOSING FROM EXISTING MODELS OR DESIGNING NEW ONES

Mullen and Bacon (2001) have suggested a careful and comprehensive methodology for developing and disseminating practice guidelines for social workers. The methodology for this Personal Practice Model Development (PPMD) is careful and comprehensive in that it (1) provides a context for individual practice guidelines by grounding them to their research or clinical routes, (2) recommends quality control methods prior to dissemination, (3) discusses methods for systematic monitoring by key practitioner, agency, and managed care constituencies, (4) operates on the premise of inclusiveness so that broad participation from professional groups is encouraged. This methodology has definite strengths but should be viewed as one model among several. If it is to be adopted, it needs to be subjected to more rigorous examination and tested in a range of client situations that involve mental disorders.

Social workers are employed in a variety of organizational settings with a range of special populations, creating a diverse perspective and barriers to uniformity. Thus, the profession may need to select a type of setting, problem area, or population for initial guideline development. One example might be the previously proposed practice guideline development for intervening with substance use disorders.

In practice guideline development, the profession must design a process that (1) relies heavily on research related to outcomes, (2) results in consensus, and (3) ensures uniform implementation of the guidelines. Once guidelines have been developed, the method of dissemination is key, and social work education has a major role to play.

USING A THREE-TIERED TRAINING MODEL FOR IMPLEMENTATION: IMPLICATIONS FOR SOCIAL WORK EDUCATION

Social work education should be viewed in the broadest sense when considering dissemination of practice guidelines. It refers to knowledge transmission and training in three professional categories: (1) the trainer (the college professors, the staff development specialists), (2) the existing workforce (*various practitioners*), and (3) the trainee (*social work students*) (Feldman and Goldman 1997).

This three-tiered training model aimed at three audiences of learners can be useful in the development and dissemination of practice guidelines for social work. First, since *agency supervisors* would be the conduit for disseminating information about practice guidelines to the existing workforce, continuing education programs would be structured to accomplish this task. Second, faculty development programs would be directed toward helping social work *faculty* retool to become knowledgeable about practice guidelines and to conduct the research that would result in practice guidelines. Finally, mechanisms would be developed for encouraging faculty to teach practice guidelines to *students* in schools of social work or, at a minimum, introduce the terminology. It goes without saying that these same students need to be socialized for continued professional development, taking the responsibility to be more autonomous and keep abreast of rapid changes in knowledge. (It would also be helpful for the profession to revisit its supervisory structures, which perhaps encourage greater dependency than those of some other helping professions.) Since supervisory and consultation mechanisms are being dismantled in many social service agencies as a consequence of managed care, practice guidelines are all the more needed—that is, workers will need to practice more independently, and this means having documents, as well as experts, accessible for consultation.

DEVELOPING A STRATEGY FOR PROFESSIONAL LEADERSHIP: ROLE OF PROFESSIONAL ORGANIZATIONS

The tasks ahead include making the decision to develop uniform guidelines for specified populations in relation to intervention settings, identifying populations for whom practice guidelines should be developed, and implementing and disseminating the guidelines once they have been developed.

As Steketee (1999) noted in her response to Howard and Jenson's article in *Research on Social Work Practice,* on the development of practice guidelines by social workers, "Organizations that might take a lead in this process include not only the National Association of Social Workers but also the Council on Social Work Education and the Society for Social Work Research. CSWE would need to address aspects of disseminating guidelines to students in training" (p. 345).

In addition to a collaborative process between agencies and practitioners, social workers need the assistance of the NASW to provide a common understanding about empirically based practice guidelines. It is our understanding from the Office of Professional Development and Advocacy that the NASW has a process under way to develop a proposed set of "core" practice standards that can be applied across a broad range of practice settings; the next step is to begin the process of developing practice guidelines. The contemporary practice environment has pushed the NASW in this direction, but the challenge is to provide practice guidelines that are relevant to social workers and linked to current knowledge development within the profession.

These tasks are complicated by professional semantics. Therefore, as noted earlier, it is imperative that we clarify existing language before moving forward to include academicians, researchers, and practitioners. A unified approach to developing practice principles is essential, and that approach should consider not just outcome but structure and process as well.

REFERENCES

American Psychiatric Association. (1995). Practice guideline for the treatment of patients with substance use disorders: Alcohol, cocaine, opioids. *American Journal of Psychiatry, 152* (11, Supplement), 5–59.

Association of Women's Health, Obstetric, and Neonatal Nurses (AWHONN). (1998). *Standards and Guidelines for Professional Nursing Practice in the Care of Women and Newborns* (5th ed.). Washington, D.C.: AWHONN.

Davis, K. (1997). *Exploring the Intersection Between Cultural Competency and Managed Behavioral Health Care Policy.* Alexandria, Va.: National Technical Assistance Center for State Mental Health Planning.

———. (1998). Managed Care, Mental Illness, and African Americans: A Prospective Analysis of Managed Care Policy in the United States. In G. Schamess and A. Lightburn (Eds.), *Humane Managed Care?* (pp. 51–64). Washington, D.C.: NASW Press.

Donabedian, A. (1988). The quality of care: How can it be assessed? *Journal of the American Medical Association, 26,* 1743–1748.

Feldman, S., and Goldman, W. (Eds.). (1997). Managed behavioral health and academia: Is there a "fit" between services and training? Papers from a national colloquium. *Administration and Policy in Mental Health, 25* (1, Special issue).

Heather, N. (1995). Brief Interventions. In R. K. Hester and W. R. Miller (Eds.), *Handbook of Alcoholism Treatment Approaches: Effective Alternatives* (2d ed.). (pp. 105–122). Boston: Allyn and Bacon.

Howard, M. O., and Jenson, J. M. (1999a). Barriers to development, utilization, and evaluation of social work practice guidelines: Toward an action plan for social work. *Research on Social Work Practice, 9,* 347–364.

———. (1999b). Clinical practice guidelines: Should social work develop them? *Research on Social Work Practice, 9,* 283–301.

Kirk, S. A. (1999). Good intentions are not enough: Practice guidelines for social work. *Research on Social Work Practice, 9,* 302–303.

McGuire, D. B., and Harwood, K. V. 1996. Research Interpretation, Utilization, and Conduct. In A. Hamric, J. Spross, and C. Hanson (Eds.), *Advanced Practice Nursing: An Integrative Approach.* (pp. 184–212). Philadelphia: WB Saunders.

Miller, W. R., Brown, J. M., Simpson, T. L., Handmaker, N. S., Bien, T. H., Luckie, L. F., Montgomery, H. A., Hester, R. K., and Tonigan, J. S. (1995). What Works: A Methodological Analysis of the Alcohol Treatment Outcome Literature. In R. K. Hester and W. R. Miller (Eds.), *Handbook of Alcoholism Treatment Approaches: Effective Alternatives* (2d ed.). (pp. 12–49). Boston: Allyn and Bacon.

Mullen, E. J. (1978). Construction of personal models for effective practice: A method for utilizing research findings to guide social interventions. *Journal of Social Service Research, 2,* 45–63.

———. (1988). Using Research and Theory in Social Work Practice. In R. M. Grinnell, Jr. (Ed.), *Social Work Research and Evaluation* (3d ed.). Itasca, Ill.: F. E. Peacock Publishers.

Mullen, E. J., and Bacon, W. F. (2001). Practitioner adoption and implementation of evidence-based effective treatments and issues of quality control. London: National Institute for Social Work. http://www. nisw.org.uk/.

National Association of Social Workers. (1994). Alcoholism and Other Substance Abuse—Related Problems. In *NASW Policy Statements: Social Work Speaks* (3d ed.). (pp. 35–39). Washington, D.C.: NASW Press.

Peebles-Wilkins, W., and Veeder, N. W. (1996). "Research Needs in Managed Behavioral Health Care in Massachusetts." NIMH unpublished technical paper, Boston.

Pigott, H. E., and Broskowski, A. (1995). Outcomes analysis: Guiding beacon or bogus science? *Behavioral Health Management, 15* (5), 22–24.

Richey, C. A., and Roffman, R. A. (1999). On the sidelines of guidelines: Further thoughts on the fit between clinical guidelines and social work practice. *Research on Social Work Practice, 9,* 311–321.

Rodriquez, A. R. (1994). Quality-of-Care Guidelines: The Managed Care View. In R. K. Schreter, S. S. Sharfstein, and C. A. Schreter (Eds.), *Allies and Adversaries: The Impact of Managed Care on Mental Health Services.* (pp. 169–185). Washington, D.C.: American Psychiatric Press.

Schreter, R. K., Sharfstein, S. S., and Schreter, C. A. (Eds.). (1994). *Allies and Adversaries: The Impact of Managed Care on Mental Health Services.* Washington, D.C.: American Psychiatric Press.

Society for Social Work Administrators in Health Care. (1997, August). SSWAHC Strategic Planning Survey. *Social Work Administration,* p. 9.

Steketee, G. (1999). Yes, but cautiously. *Research on Social Work Practice, 9,* 343–346.

Veeder, N. W., and Peebles-Wilkins, W. (1998). Research Needs in Managed Behavioral Health Care. In G. Schamess and A. Lightburn (Eds.), *Humane Managed Care.* (pp. 483–504). Washington, D.C.: NASW Press.

Videka-Sherman, L., and Reid, W. J. (1990). *Advances in Clinical Social Work Research.* Silver Spring, Md.: NASW Press.

PART IV

PRACTITIONER, ORGANIZATIONAL, AND
INSTITUTIONAL FACTORS IN THE UTILIZATION
OF PRACTICE GUIDELINES

13

PRACTITIONER ADOPTION AND IMPLEMENTATION OF PRACTICE GUIDELINES AND ISSUES OF QUALITY CONTROL

EDWARD J. MULLEN AND WILLIAM F. BACON

PROLOGUE

We once overheard a clinician complaining that New York State had announced a practice guideline for the treatment of autism.[1] The clinician was unhappy because the guideline proposed an approach to treatment that she did not favor. Her assessment was that the guideline had been endorsed because the method it proposed had research support, whereas her favored approach had not been empirically evaluated. She believed that she would be forced to use the guideline, since her social agency would require practitioner conformity. She believed the agency would not be reimbursed by the state unless the proposed treatment method was used. After hearing her voice such strong negative feelings toward the guideline, we wondered how likely it was that she would implement the new guideline even if it was adopted by the agency.

This example raises a number of issues pertaining to practitioner use of practice guidelines. First, any practitioner's approach has been molded by a complex combination of personal attitudes, preferences, beliefs, training, and experience. The simple publication of a new practice guideline is not likely to affect such a practitioner's work with his or her clients.

Second, assuming that a practitioner is open to using a new guideline, he or she will need additional knowledge and skill to use it effectively. How will such knowledge and skill be provided, especially in social agencies with limited resources, where time for anything beyond essential services is in short supply?

Third, how can practitioners draw conclusions about the relative merits of alternative interventions when some have been empirically evaluated and

Gretchen Borges and David Barnet provided valuable assistance with the research reported in this paper. We wish to acknowledge their important contributions.

others have not? While interventions that have been put to a rigorous empirical test and have failed that test provide reason to abandon a favored approach, in the majority of cases negative evidence is absent. Practitioners may wonder why they should abandon an approach that has not been shown to be ineffective simply because another approach has some degree of research support.

Fourth, the very notion of guidelines for the treatment of particular *disorders* may not sit well with some social work practitioners. While Thyer (chapter 7, this volume) is no doubt correct in his contention that disorder-based categorizations do not necessarily assume a medical, biologically oriented model of causation, such categorizations certainly do encourage a view of treatment as symptom reduction. Social workers may be inclined to think of their clients more broadly, perhaps in terms of general outcomes to be achieved, as suggested by Proctor and Rosen (chapter 6, this volume). The outcomes selected as targets of change may have rather little dependence on diagnostic category.

Finally, in complex social agencies how can guidelines best be disseminated, critically assessed, and sustained among a diverse group of practitioners with varying perspectives who are often from different professional groups?

INTRODUCTION

Central to implementation of evidence-based effective treatments is the use of practice guidelines. This chapter addresses the use of practice guidelines by social work practitioners. Clinical practice guidelines have been described by the Institute of Medicine as "systematically developed statements to assist practitioner and patient decisions about appropriate health care for specific clinical circumstances" (Field and Lohr 1990). For at least a decade professional organizations and government agencies have formulated practice guidelines for various clinical conditions such as depression and schizophrenia (American Academy of Child and Adolescent Psychiatry 1994; American Psychiatric Association 1993, 1994, 1997; United States Preventive Services Task Force 1994). These guidelines prescribe how clinicians should assess and treat clients. Sometimes the guidelines are based on research findings. Sometimes the available research is inconclusive, and therefore the guidelines are based at least partly on professional consensus. While the past decade has witnessed a marked growth in the production and dissemination of practice guidelines in medicine, psychiatry, and psychology, until recently little attention has been given to practice guideline development and use in the field of social work. Many questions arise upon consideration of this issue. How relevant are these guidelines to the functions of social work practitioners and social agencies? Are additional guidelines needed that would be of specific relevance to social work practitioners? How might social work practitioners react to and use externally as well as internally developed guidelines? What technologies are needed to assist practitioners in identification and responsible use of practice guidelines? Furthermore, since most currently available guidelines are general statements intended to guide practice, how can social work practitioners apply such broad guidelines in individual situations?

How will the move toward practice guidelines affect professional boundaries and shape the functions of social work practitioners and social agencies? In organizations where practitioners from different mental health professions work together, will practice guidelines developed by one professional group dominate the work of allied professional groups? Which professional groups will be knowledgeable about and disposed to use practice guidelines and which ones will not? What effect might these varying attitudes have on practice? What do we know about how social agencies and social work practitioners are responding to the move toward practice guidelines?

Although practice guidelines have been promoted for several decades in medicine and psychology (see Howard and Jenson, chapter 5, this volume), little has been written on the topic in the social work literature. The May 1999 issue of *Research on Social Work Practice*, which has a special section on practice guidelines and clinical social work, is a notable exception (Howard and Jenson 1999a, 1999b; Jackson 1999; Kirk 1999; Richey and Roffman 1999; Steketee 1999; Wambach, Haynes, and White 1999; Williams and Lanigan 1999). The articles in this section address many important aspects of practice guidelines, but the authors are relatively silent on the question of how agencies and practitioners view this development. A review of the literature beyond social work journals indicates that little has been written about the practitioners' views. Little is known about the use of guidelines in social work practice and how social work practitioners view the use of guidelines.

AGENCY PRACTITIONER SURVEY

Because of this lack of information about the practitioners' views we conducted a practitioner survey regarding practice guidelines. The survey respondents were from a large urban voluntary mental health/social service agency noted for the high quality of its services and training programs. This agency offers a continuum of mental health and social services, both residential and community-based. Master's-level social workers are the primary providers of service, although the staff is multidisciplinary and includes psychologists, psychiatrists, and other mental health professionals. This agency employs approximately five hundred direct-service professionals.

The survey examined practitioner awareness of practice guidelines, specification of guidelines known about and used by individual practitioners, practitioner attitudes toward the use of guidelines, and their preferences for guidelines based on expert consensus and/or empirical research findings. Because we assumed that some practitioners would be unfamiliar with what we meant by the term *practice guidelines,* the survey included the following explanatory text: "Recently professional organizations and government agencies have promulgated practice guidelines for various clinical conditions such as depression and schizophrenia. These guidelines prescribe how clinicians should assess and treat patients. Guidelines are now being promulgated in other areas of the human services such as child and family services. Sometimes the guidelines are based on research findings. Often research is not available and, therefore, the guidelines are based on professional consensus. We are interested in your views regarding this development."

Additional research pertaining to these questions is being conducted on the basis of this survey's findings, with a national sample of social work mental health practitioners who are members of the NASW (N = 150, drawn from a random sample provided by the NASW of 1,000 practitioners). These surveys and their findings are presented in Mullen and Bacon (2001) and Engstrom et al. (in preparation).

Examination of the data from the survey, which reported how practitioners working in organizations such as the one in this study view practice guidelines and other aspects of evidence-based practice yielded a number of conclusions.

The three mental health professions represented in the Mullen and Bacon survey were strikingly different in their knowledge of practice guidelines. Psychiatrists appeared to be relatively well informed about relevant practice guidelines, whereas social workers were poorly informed, typically not even aware of the meaning of the term *practice guidelines.* Psychologists were somewhere in between.

Once social workers were told what practice guidelines are, they generally reported an openness to using them. When practitioners were asked whether they would prefer guidelines that represented research evidence or those that represented professional consensus, however, the social workers stated a preference for guidelines based on professional consensus. This response contrasts with the views of the other practitioners, who more strongly valued guidelines based on research evidence.

The social workers' apparent devaluing of research evidence as a basis for practice guidelines was consistent with their reported attitudes toward research in general. As in previous research, the social workers surveyed by

Mullen and Bacon reported low levels of using research findings or research methods in their practices. Psychiatrists and, to a lesser extent, psychologists reported regularly using research-based findings and methods of assessment. Many social workers did not read the research literature or even other professional literature. Psychiatrists read this literature frequently.

So where do social workers turn for guidance on practice issues? Mullen and Bacon found that social workers depended heavily on consultation, much more so than the other professionals, who functioned more autonomously. Social workers reported frequently seeking guidance and direction from supervisors and other consultants, who were viewed as repositories of knowledge because of their experience and their roles as spokespersons for organizational policy.

Given the low use of research and infrequent reading of professional literature among social work practitioners, it is not likely that they will be influenced significantly through these avenues. Rather, supervisors and consultants seem to be the most promising source for knowledge regarding practice guidelines and other forms of evidence-based practice for social workers.

A subgroup of the surveyed social work practitioners deviated from this norm, appearing to function more autonomously through behaviors more like those of the psychiatrists in the sample. These social workers expressed preference for evidence-based guidelines, and they reported higher frequencies of reading research articles and professional publications. It is likely that they used supervisors and consultants differently as well. This subgroup of research-oriented social workers may be important resources for dissemination of evidence-based practice knowledge within social work organizations. It is likely that their training has provided them with research skills that are relevant to practice.

These findings have implications for technologies needed to assist practitioners in identification and use of evidence-based practice guidelines, for quality control and accountability, and for education.

A TECHNOLOGY FOR ADAPTING PRACTICE GUIDELINES TO SOCIAL WORK PRACTICE

Mullen's earlier work on Personal Practice Model Development (PPMD) proposed a process for individual practitioners to use so that broad summary generalizations and practice guidelines could be applied to their own personal practice situations (Mullen 1978, 1981, 1983, 1988). The approach evolved from work at the University of Chicago. Because outcome studies had raised questions about the effectiveness of conventional social work interventions, we looked to the interdisciplinary literature to find evidence of interventions that had been found to be effective. Together with graduate students, we sifted through the literature, attempted to form summary generalizations about what had been found to be effective, and drew out prescriptive implications in the form of practice guidelines. However, since our purpose was not only to codify the results of research but also to move the findings into practice, the process was further developed to integrate this codification of research with other aspects of the practitioner's intervention processes. Accordingly, information derived from research findings, theory, professional and personal experience, values and ethics, and view of professional mission and function was integrated into working models, which were designed to guide each practitioner's work with clients. The PPMD approach contextualizes individual practice guidelines. Guidelines were integrated into an understanding of professional function and mission, professional and personal values and ethics, theory, and experience. This process produced a set of working practice guidelines, which were explicitly linked to an integrated practice model. The grounding for each guideline was specified as to its source (e.g., empirical research, theory, experience, values, ethics, professional mission and function). Also, for empirical guidelines the level of evidence supporting each guideline was explicated.

Together with our students, we analyzed the process we had gone through to arrive at PPMs. Then we taught the process to first-year students at the University of Chicago, who implemented it in class and in the field. The PPMD process was further refined and elaborated on the basis of this experience.[2] In the 1970s, when the PPMD approach was developed, practitioners faced a scarcity of information regarding effective interventions. To locate such information, the practitioner had to sift through extensive library references, and to keep a model current, this needed to be an ongoing process. Today the situation is quite different. Information technology has simplified these tasks, meta-analyses have proliferated, outcomes research has come of age, and summary generalizations and practice guidelines are ever present. While the task of finding information has been simplified, however, the task of adapting that information to individual social work practice situations has become more complex.

What can be learned from the PPMD approach relevant to practitioners' use of practice guidelines today? Perhaps most important, the PPMD approach suggests that practice guidelines, whether developed on the basis of consensus or from empirical research, cannot be applied without appropriate context. Individual guidelines must be considered in relation to intervention models that address other relevant dimensions of social work practice (e.g., professional mission and function, professional and personal values and ethics, theoretical understanding, experience).

In addition, general practice guidelines cannot be applied to individual situations without considerable adaptation. Proctor and Rosen's (chapter 6, this volume) suggestion that moderator variables be explicitly incorporated into practice guidelines surely represents an important step toward creating guidelines that actually give guidance in a wide variety of circumstances. However, no guideline can anticipate all the variables operating in a complex clinical situation. Moving from practice guidelines to individual case situations will always require professional judgment and skill, drawing from accumulated clinical experience.

Moreover, as guidelines proliferate, it is increasingly clear that available guidelines are not always consistent with one another. Thus, individual practitioners must have the resources to identify and to resolve inconsistencies. The PPMD approach suggests some other sources of information that may be available and useful in such efforts.

The PPMD approach also makes explicit the need for constant refinement of any practice model. Implementation of interventions based on specific guidelines needs to be monitored and evaluated, with revisions incorporated as necessary. This critical step is represented in the fourth of Proctor and Rosen's proposed components of practice guidelines, relating to the explication of gaps in knowledge (chapter 6, this volume).

Finally, accountable use of guidelines requires a well-developed dissemination and implementation process. Social work practitioners need to be educated for accountable use of practice guidelines, and social agencies need to provide systems that are supportive of accountable use. As demonstrated by the survey findings (Mullen and Bacon 2001), while some practitioners may be capable of developing models based on reading and critical review of the research literature, this ability is beyond most social workers as they are currently educated. For the majority of practitioners, then, evidence-based guidelines will need to be communicated through supervision, consultation, and in-service training. Those few social workers who are oriented toward and skilled in the use of evidence-based practice may need to become resources for other practitioners within agencies. Social agencies will need to be the conduits for evidence-based practice, including guidelines. Since practitioners want to be effective, agencies will need to emphasize the utility of evidence-based practice, including guidelines for effective practice.

Because good guidelines can be misused, or not used at all, mechanisms to ensure quality control and accountability will be necessary to be certain that guidelines have the best possible impact on practice.

QUALITY CONTROL AND ACCOUNTABILITY

Issues of quality control and accountability can be addressed in at least three ways:

- Standards should be developed and applied for assessing the quality of practice guidelines prior to their dissemination.
- Clinicians and clients should be provided with frameworks for assessing the quality, relevance, and consequences of the application of specific guidelines.
- Those responsible for monitoring the quality of practice implementation should use systematic monitoring procedures that include collaboration with social agencies and practitioners.

STANDARDS SHOULD BE DEVELOPED AND APPLIED FOR ASSESSING THE QUALITY OF PRACTICE GUIDELINES PRIOR TO THEIR DISSEMINATION

In their review of practice guidelines published in the peer-reviewed medical literature between 1985 and 1997, Shaneyfelt and colleagues concluded that many guidelines "do not adhere well to established methodological standards. While all areas of guideline development need improvement, greatest improvement is needed in the identification, evaluation, and synthesis of the scientific evidence" (Shaneyfelt, Mayo-Smith, and Rothwangl 1999). Their list of methodological standards is useful and directly applicable to social work. Twenty-five standards are grouped into three areas:

- guideline development and format (e.g., guideline purpose is specified, specification of external review method)[3]
- evidence identification and summary (e.g., method of identifying scientific evidence is specified, benefits and harms for specific health practices are specified)[4]
- formulation of recommendations (e.g., role of value judgments by developers is specified, role of patient preferences is specified).[5]

In their editorial comment, Cook and Giacomini wonder whether these quality criteria are necessary or equally appropriate for all guideline areas (Cook and Giacomini 1999). The point is that while standards may be of general use, it is important to apply them flexibly. Both the editorial and the original article stress the need for greater "transparency" of guideline reporting, as well as more rigorous peer review prior to guideline publication.

Quality could be improved before guideline dissemination through such measures as the development of guideline standards for social work and the use of these standards by those who produce and disseminate guidelines (e.g., journal reviewers and editors, professional organizations). Proctor and Rosen (chapter 6, this volume) offer a minimal set of standards, but, as they point out, their proposed standards are quite similar to those proposed by the psychiatric profession. As Mullen and Bacon's previously described practitioner survey makes clear, however, social workers do not consume research in the same ways that other mental health professionals do, nor are they likely to use or react to practice guidelines in the same ways. In order to be effective for social work practice, then, guidelines must be held to standards that reflect the reality of the way social workers acquire and develop practice knowledge. Presentation and dissemination must be carefully considered and may be decisive in determining whether a guideline is actually used, which is a necessary (though not sufficient) condition for its effectiveness.

CLINICIANS AND CLIENTS SHOULD BE PROVIDED WITH FRAMEWORKS FOR ASSESSING THE QUALITY RELEVANCE, AND CONSEQUENCES OF THE APPLICATION OF SPECIFIC GUIDELINES

The previously described PPMD approach addresses quality control and accountability at the practitioner level by providing a framework whereby practitioners are expected to make explicit the practice guidelines that they use. These guidelines are to be developed from systematic and critical assessment of research findings, practice-derived knowledge, theory, values, and function. This framework requires practitioners to monitor and assess implementation of their practice guidelines, making revisions based on experience. The methodology comprises five interrelated steps: (a) identification of substantive findings concerning intervention variables and their effects on clients; (b) evaluation of the quality of the evidence; (c) development of summary generalizations specifying the substantive findings, the limiting conditions, and the quality of evidence; (d) deduction of practice guidelines; and (e) specification of an evaluation plan for assessing the effects of practitioner interventions based on the practice guidelines. In the PPMD approach, practitioners develop explicit frameworks that can be critically examined not only by the practitioners themselves but also by clients, supervisors, and others to whom practitioners are accountable. Because it is explicit, the model also permits revision based on feedback and new information. This approach is consistent with views recently expressed by Guyatt and colleagues.

Guyatt, Sinclair, Cook, and Glasziou (1999), writing for the Evidence-Based Medicine Working Group and the Cochrane Applicability Methods Working Group, note that "clinical decisions are likely to improve if clinicians are aware of the underlying determinants of their actions and are able to be more critical about the recommendations offered to them" (Guyatt et al. 1999:1842). They note that practice management decisions are a function of evidence and preference, including both practitioner and client values. Accordingly, quality control and accountability must provide for client and practitioner judgments and discretion. They suggest that rather than practitioners' being presented with rigid guidelines, which they are then held accountable for implementing, they may need information that is relevant to practice decision areas, with specification of implications for action under differing value scenarios. Guyatt and colleagues note that practice decisions involve "framing a question, identifying management options and outcomes, collecting and summarizing evidence, and applying value judgments or preferences to arrive at an optimal course of action" (Guyatt et al. 1999:1836). Therefore, practitioners need frameworks for assessing available information and recommendations. Guyatt et al. provide a framework for use by individual practitioners designed to support systematic review so as to avoid bias and stressing the application of "scientific principles to the collection, selection, and summarization of evidence, and the valuing of outcomes" (Guyatt et al. 1999:1837). Making such frameworks available to practitioners can support quality control and accountability at the practitioner level.

Clients should also be provided with frameworks for monitoring and assessing practice guidelines. The publication of reports of practice guidelines for consumers should facilitate quality control and accountability. Furthermore, once social agencies and practitioners make explicit their preferred intervention methods by way of guidelines and models, including their evidentiary base, clients will be better informed and, consequently, better positioned to make judgments about which agencies and practitioners to use.

THOSE RESPONSIBLE FOR MONITORING THE QUALITY OF PRACTICE IMPLEMENTATION SHOULD USE SYSTEMATIC MONITORING PROCEDURES THAT INCLUDE COLLABORATION WITH SOCIAL AGENCIES AND PRACTITIONERS

In an era of managed care, it goes without saying that standard-setting, accreditation, and funding organizations play significant oversight roles. Increasingly, these groups can be expected to monitor social work practice with an eye toward fostering implementation of best practices, use of favored practice guidelines, and engagement in outcomes measurement (Mullen and Magnabasco 1997). It is important, however, that such monitoring be done collaboratively and that it involve social agencies and practitioners in the process, thus increasing the probability that agencies and practitioners will use the resulting feedback in subsequent quality improvement efforts (Hess and Mullen 1995).

Development and dissemination of practice guidelines do not ensure accountable implementation. Studies are needed to investigate how practice in social work agencies conforms to practice guidelines and other evidence-based methods. Our survey findings suggest that at present guidelines are not explicitly used in social work practice. It is likely that this situation will change as guidelines are developed specifically for the social work profession. Little is known, however, about how practitioners will react to dissemination of guidelines, or how faithfully they will implement guidelines. Most important, the effectiveness of guideline-based practice and other forms of evidence-based practice needs to be assessed through collaborative evaluation and monitoring procedures.

IMPLICATIONS FOR SOCIAL WORK EDUCATION

We conclude with observations about changes needed in the education of social work practitioners. The survey findings reported here further underscore the fact that social work education is not preparing its students for autonomous practice. Social workers need to be prepared to take responsibility for frequent and critical reading of the professional literature, including reports of practice research. Knowledge is changing too rapidly for social workers to rely primarily on what was taught during their few years of professional education. Furthermore, social workers need to be prepared to use systematic assessment instruments and designs so that they are capable of gathering reliable and valid data regarding their clients. And information gathered through frequent reading and systematic assessment will be useless unless practitioners have developed critical thinking skills that will lead to responsible use of that information. Our survey findings indicate that many social workers are unusually dependent on supervisory guidance, in comparison to other professionals studied. Currently, social work education and agency practice reinforce this dependence. If social work practitioners are to move forward toward evidence-based practice, significant changes will be required in how social workers are educated as well as in how social agencies view their practitioners' autonomy.

NOTES

1. The guideline is described in Childs (1999).
2. The PPMD approach was developed through funding of the Ittleson Foundation of New York.
3. Other standards include the following: rationale and importance of the guideline are explained; participants in the guideline development process and their areas of expertise are specified; targeted health problem or technology is clearly defined; intended audience or users for the guideline are specified; the principal preventive, diagnostic, or therapeutic options available to clinicians and patients are specified; the health outcomes are specified; an expiration date or date of scheduled review is specified.
4. Other standards include the following: time period from which evidence is reviewed is specified; evidence used is identified by citation and references; method of data extraction is specified; method for grading or classifying the scientific evidence is specified; formal methods of combining evidence or expert opinion are used and described; benefits and harms are quantified; effect on health care costs from specific health practices is specified; costs are quantified.
5. Other standards include the following: recommendations are specific and apply to the stated goals of the guideline; recommendations are graded according to the strength of the evidence; flexibility in the recommendations is specified.

REFERENCES

American Academy of Child and Adolescent Psychiatry. (1994). Practice parameters for the assessment and treatment of children and adolescents with schizophrenia. *Journal of the American Academy of Child and Adolescent Psychiatry, 33,* 616–635.

American Psychiatric Association. (1993). Practice guideline for major depressive disorder in adults. *American Journal of Psychiatry, 150* (4, supplement), 1–29.

———. (1994). Practice guideline for treatment of patients with bipolar disorder. *American Journal of Psychiatry, 151* (12), 1–36.

———. (1997). Practice guideline for the treatment of patients with schizophrenia. *American Journal of Psychiatry, 154* (12), 1–63.

Childs, N. D. (1999). New York endorses intervention program for autism. *Clinical Psychiatry News, 27,* 8.

Cook, D., and Giacomini, M. (1999). The trials and tribulations of clinical practice guidelines. *Journal of the American Medical Association, 281,* 1950–1951.

Engstrom, M., Fletcher, T., Gangwisch, J., Mullen, E. J., and Bacon, W. (In preparation). Practice guidelines and research; Use and dissemination among social workers.

Field, M. J., and Lohr, K. N. (Eds.). (1990). *Clinical Practice Guidelines: Directions of a New Program.* Washington, D.C.: National Academy Press.

Guyatt, G. H., Sinclair, J., Cook, D. J., and Glasziou, P. (1999). Users' guides to the medical literature. XVI. How to use a treatment recommendation. Evidence-Based Medicine Working Group and the Cochrane Applicability Methods Working Group. *Journal of the American Medical Association, 281,* 1836–1843.

Hess, M., and Mullen, E. J. (Eds.). (1995). *Practitioner-Research Partnerships: Building Knowledge from, in, and for Practice.* Washington, D.C.: NASW Press.

Howard, M. O., and Jenson, J. M. (1999a). Barriers to development, utilization, and evaluation of social work practice guidelines: Toward an action plan for social work. *Research on Social Work Practice, 9,* 347–364.

———. (1999b). Clinical practice guidelines: Should social work develop them? *Research on Social Work Practice, 9,* 283–301.

Jackson, V. H. (1999). Clinical practice guidelines: Should social work develop them? *Research on Social Work Practice, 9,* 331–337.

Kirk, S. A. (1999). Good intentions are not enough: Practice guidelines for social work. *Research on Social Work Practice, 9,* 302–303.

Mullen, E. J. (1978). Construction of personal models for effective practice: A method for utilizing research findings to guide social interventions. *Journal of Social Service Research, 2,* 45–63.

———. (1981). Development of Personal Intervention Models. In R. M. Grinnell, Jr. (Ed.), *Social Work Research and Evaluation* (1st ed.). (pp. 606–632). Itasca, Ill.: F. E. Peacock.

———. (1983). Personal Personal Practice Models in Clinical Social Work. In A. Rosenblatt and D. Waldfogel (Eds.), *Handbook of Clinical Social Work.* San Francisco: Jossey-Bass.

———. (1988). Constructing Personal Practice Models. In R. M. Grinnell, Jr. (Ed.), *Social Work Research and Evaluation* (3d ed.). (pp. 503–533). Itasca, Ill.: F. E. Peacock.

Mullen, E. J., and Bacon, W. F. (2001). A survey of practitioner adoption and implementation of practice guidelines and evidence-based practice. Unpublished paper.

Mullen, E. J., and Magnabasco, J. (Eds.) (1997). *Outcomes Measurement in the Human Services.* Washington, D.C.: NASW Press.

Richey, C. A., and Roffman, R. A. (1999). On the sidelines of guidelines: Further thoughts on the fit between clinical guidelines and social work practice. *Research on Social Work Practice, 9,* 311–321.

Shaneyfelt, T. M., Mayo-Smith, M. F., and Rothwangl, J. (1999). Are guidelines following guidelines? The methodological quality of clinical practice guidelines in the peer-reviewed medical literature. *Journal of the American Medical Association, 281,* 1900–1905.

Steketee, G. (1999). Yes, but cautiously. *Research on Social Work Practice, 9,* 343–346.

United States Preventive Services Task Force (1994). Screening for Depression. In *Guide to Clinical Preventive Services* (2d ed.). (pp. 541–546). Baltimore, Md.: Williams and Wilkins.

Wambach, K. G., Haynes, D. T., and White, W. W. (1999). Practice guidelines: Rapprochement or estrangement between social work practitioners and researchers. *Research on Social Work Practice, 9,* 322–330.

Williams, J. B. W., and Lanigan, J. (1999). Practice guidelines in social work: A reply, or "our glass is half full." *Research on Social Work Practice, 9* (3), 338–342.

14

ORGANIZATIONAL AND INSTITUTIONAL FACTORS IN THE DEVELOPMENT OF PRACTICE KNOWLEDGE AND PRACTICE GUIDELINES IN SOCIAL WORK

JEANNE C. MARSH

For the last twenty-five years, social work researchers have spent considerable energy addressing the question, What is the impact of social work intervention on achieving outcomes of benefit to clients? Evidence relevant to this question is building. The research enterprise has moved from a preoccupation with outcomes to a concern with documenting and specifying the active ingredients of interventions. Increasingly, research efforts are moving to the development of practice guidelines. The interest in practice guidelines has itself led to other questions: What constitutes a practice guideline? Are guidelines organized by diagnostic category, problem area, population group, method of intervention, or practice setting? What evidence is necessary to serve as a basis for practice guidelines? Who should develop guidelines? Who should approve guidelines? Who should use guidelines and why? This chapter will address one aspect of these questions: What factors contribute to the legitimation of guidelines and social workers' adherence to them? Relevant theory and recent experience in the development of practice guidelines will be employed to identify issues related to legitimation.

Proctor and Rosen (chapter 6, this volume) define practice guidelines as knowledge statements designed to enable practitioners to find, select, and use effective interventions. Their definition highlights the role of guidelines in contributing to knowledge organization and utilization. By focusing on the structure and function of guidelines in the development of knowledge and in the social work profession more generally, Proctor and Rosen incorporate consideration of significant issues that have been ignored in other discussions of practice guidelines. They move beyond simple prescriptions for practice when they state that the raison d'être of practice guidelines is to put into the hands of practitioners knowledge about and directions for implementing effective interventions. Their interest in guidelines is appropriately lodged in their broader interest in the process of practice and its knowledge base (Rosen and Proctor 1978; Rosen, Proctor, and Livne 1985; Rosen 1993; Rosen, Proctor, and Staudt 1999).

This chapter builds on this broad definition by examining the legitimation of practice guidelines in social work in the context of social work practice and its developing knowledge base. Specifically, this paper will (1) briefly review theories of professions and professional knowledge development, focusing on the role of knowledge as the "currency of competition" for professions (Abbott 1988:9); (2) describe the processes and institutions involved in legitimating the knowledge and work of professions; (3) discuss how these processes and institutions may influence the development and use of practice guidelines in social work. Thus, practice guidelines will be examined within the context of the social work knowledge base more generally and the role it plays within the definition and development of the social work profession.

THEORIES OF PROFESSIONS AND PROFESSIONAL KNOWLEDGE DEVELOPMENT

Like all professions, social work makes claims about its knowledge base:

> Professional social workers possess the specialized knowledge necessary for an effective social services delivery system. Social work education provides a unique combination of knowledge, values, skills and professional ethics which cannot be obtained through other degree programs or by on-the-job training. Further, social work education adequately equips its individuals with skills to help clients solve problems that bring them to social services departments and human service agencies.
>
> (POLICIES APPROVED BY NASW BOARD OF DIRECTORS,
> JANUARY 1999, *NASW NEWS*, P. 14)

Thus, social work claims to have a unique knowledge and skill base (i.e., one that is not shared with other professions) that is uniquely conveyed by social work education (and not available through any other form or program of education or training). Whether there is adequate evidence to support these claims has been questioned by some (Gambrill 1999) and disputed by others who actively seek access to tasks and resources controlled by the profession of social work. When trying to understand how claims about professional knowledge are made and defended and the functions they serve in the definition and development of a profession, however, it is useful to reflect on what we know about professions and their respective knowledge bases more generally. Thus, we briefly review theories of professions as summaries of extant knowledge and understanding.

The discussion of social work as a profession has been dominated by stage theories of professions, theories that identify professions as occupational groups that have specific elements that develop in a predictable sequence over time (Marsh 2000). Flexner was operating within a stage theoretical framework in his influential 1915 paper concluding that social work was not yet a fully developed profession. He identified a set of elements distinguishing professions and suggested that social work had not achieved the status of a full profession because it lacked the element of definite and specific ends or, in his words, "[Social work] appears not so much as a definite field as an aspect of work in many fields" (Flexner 1915:585). Wilensky also used a stage theoretical perspective when he wrote his classic paper "The Professionalization of Everyone?" in 1964. In this paper he examined the history of eighteen occupations in the United States and described the typical sequence through which they moved. He suggested that a profession develops according to a sequence in which it (1) becomes a full-time occupation, (2) establishes a training school, (3) establishes a university school, (4) establishes a professional association, (5) establishes a state licensing law, and (6) establishes a formal code of ethics. He concluded that his analysis confirmed both the salience of the elements and their typical sequence of development in the emergence of professions in the United States. And, on the basis of his analysis, he defined social work as a profession in process.

More recently, institutional or systems theories have been used to understand and explain the development of professions (Abbott 1988; Freidson 1994; Scott 1995). Institutional or systems theories provide a valuable framework for examining the role of knowledge in the development of professions generally and social work more specifically (Abbott 1988; Austin 1983; Freidson 1994; Marsh 2000). From this perspective, the knowledge base of the profession plays a pivotal role in linking the profession to central cultural values, especially values of rationality and efficiency. A profession's claim to expertise based on scientifically developed knowledge in specific domains is the means by which it defines its activities in society and its boundaries vis-à-vis other professions. From this perspective there is a role for a variety of professional institutions (in social work, professional associations such as NASW and CSWE, ethics boards, licensing and standards-setting groups) and external institutions (public and private financing entities, court decisions, special-purpose legislation, special-interest groups). These professional institutions are influential in determining the character of professional practice. It is the purpose of this chapter to examine how these institutions operate in the legitimation and use of practice guidelines.

A central tenet of institutional theory is that professions are defined primarily by the specific tasks they accomplish (Abbott 1988). The fundamental task of all professions is to solve problems: problems of learning, problems of social adjustment, problems of justice, problems of health, problems of building design. The extent to which any given society defines an activity as a problem and relies on professional expertise to solve it varies across social group, time in history, and problem. Nonetheless, although professions take different forms, they are occupations requiring specialized knowledge applied in a nonroutine manner and they emerge across all societies (Abbott 1988).

Professions are defined not only by the tasks they perform but also by the related knowledge and skills associated with those tasks. Each profession identifies and uses some body of abstract knowledge. The practical skills and techniques exercised by professionals develop in part from this abstract knowledge. From the Milford Conference in 1929 to the present time, social work has concerned itself with the development of its characteristic knowledge, skills, and values. (See Breiland [1977] for a history of efforts to define social work practice.) From its inception, the profession of social work has been actively involved in the development of its knowledge base. This effort has included borrowing knowledge from related fields and disciplines as well as generating its own knowledge (Marsh 1983). In some cases, the actual application of knowledge may be delegated to workers outside the profession, but the abstract knowledge from which the technique derives is the defining characteristic of the profession. For example, social workers in residential treatment centers often delegate day-to-day interaction with children to child care workers, but the basic principles of milieu therapy that are used are part of the abstract knowledge base of social work (Redl and Wineman 1951).

A second tenet of institutions or systems theory is that professions emerge and develop in relation to other professions in an organizational field. The organizational field is the place or location where each profession makes ongoing claims over the content of the other professions. This claiming process can be played out in public opinion, in legal disputes as well as in the workplace (Abbott 1988). Austin (1983) describes the process as follows: "Legitimation of an occupation as a profession is not granted at a particular moment in time through a process of impartial review and judgment. A profession is deemed a profession when the public accepts the definition of a specialized knowledge and competency advanced by a particular occupation, regardless of internal characteristics of the occupation" (p. 366). Typically, a jurisdictional claim is made in terms of the exclusive right to control the definition and performance of a particular kind of work, i.e., to perform the work according to a professionally defined standard. Such a claim involves dominating public definition of tasks as well as excluding other workers who engage in the task. Professions communicate to the public how they define and solve particular problems through newspapers, magazines, movies, and television. Lawyers, doctors, and police officers have been particularly successful in deploying television to convey a sympathetic view of their educational domain (e.g., with series like *ER, L.A. Law,* and *Law and Order*). In addition to public media, legislatures and courts have been frequent venues for claims related to professional jurisdiction. Social workers have used legislation very effectively in many states to protect the title of "social worker," to create eligibility for third-party payments, and to prevent other professionals from engaging in certain tasks (e.g., supervision in child welfare).

Jurisdictional claims, as discussed by Abbott, are the basis for the emergence, development, and, in some cases, disappearance of professions. The strengths of claims generally rest on the effectiveness with which the profession's knowledge base solves problems and the efficacy with which the problem solving is accomplished. For example, social workers lost a dominant position in the juvenile and criminal justice system when graduates of criminal justice programs claimed more-specialized knowledge and expertise. Similarly, in hospital settings, social workers lost out to nurses when the latter claimed superior knowledge of the health care system and assumed primary responsibility for discharge planning, which had once been the exclusive domain of social workers. Abbott identifies several rhetorical strategies used to claim a more effective and efficient knowledge base. Among these strategies are *reduction* and *metaphor*. Reduction refers to the definition of a task in terms of a restricted set of activities fitting into a specific professional jurisdiction. When discharge planning is defined as one aspect of patient care, the task can be reduced to the purview of nursing. Similarly, the rhetorical strategy of metaphor is the extension of one profession's model of thinking or problem solving into the domain of another. When criminal justice programs assume primary control of probation services, they do so by emphasizing the salience of a legal as opposed to a rehabilitative approach to the treatment of offenders. And when *DSM-IV* is used to diagnose child misbehavior as attention deficit and hyperactivity disorder, the medical model is the model of inference being used, and pharmacological approaches are the most likely course of treatment.

Jurisdictional claims result from several different factors, both external and internal to a given profession. Typically, external factors influence the development of professions by either opening new task areas or destroying old ones. Most new task areas are created by new technologies or new organizational developments. For example, the aging of the population and the development of new approaches for working with the elderly in society have led to increased demand for social workers to work in gerontology with new technologies like bereavement counseling and bereavement support groups. The expansion of the profit and nonprofit sectors also has created a demand for expertise to enable employees to adjust to large, impersonal, and often stressful work environments. Large numbers of social workers have moved to meet this demand by working in human resource departments or creating employee assistance programs (EAPs) for banks, manufacturing firms, universities, and police departments. Abbott (1988) notes that most professional work is, in fact, new work, since numerous technical and organizational developments of the last century have opened entirely new domains requiring expert intervention.

Internal factors also influence the system of professions. They influence the development of professions by strengthening or weakening certain aspects that can ultimately result in shifts in jurisdiction. Internal shifts often result from the development of the professional knowledge base or increases in organizational efficiency. For example, in social work the development and application of empirically based practice methods have provided a means for greater accountability and for more effective contributions to the development of practice knowledge. Similarly, as the provision of social services has increasingly moved to community-based organizations, the development of specific community-based approaches to service provision (e.g., assertive community treatment for the chronically mentally ill and home-based services for children) has enabled social workers to work more effectively with clients in the community. Social workers have used this and other new knowledge to assert that their profession works more effectively in the community than do office-bound professions such as psychiatry and psychology. They have also used their relatively lower salaries to make claims of efficiency (Abbott 1988). These claims, along with the increasing numbers of bachelor's- and master's-level social workers trained since about 1950, have contributed to the fact that social workers provide more mental health services in the community than any other professionals (Ginsberg 1995; Lin 1995).

KNOWLEDGE AND LEGITIMATION OF PROFESSIONS

As indicated by this discussion of factors that influence the development of professions, knowledge is the currency of competition (Abbott 1988:9), serving to define professions, to strengthen interprofessional claims, and ultimately to legitimate professional work.

DEFINING PROFESSIONS

Professions are defined and differentiated both by the nature of the work and by the knowledge system that guides them. Professional tasks have both objective and subjective foundations, and knowledge is one of the objective foundations. Specifically, Abbott identifies the objective foundations of tasks as (1) the concrete focus of the work (e.g., statutes for lawyers, weather for meteorologists, people seeking services for social workers); (2) the knowledge and technology available to execute the work; and (3) the organizations where the work is performed (e.g., schools for teachers, social service organizations for social workers). All of these factors shape the work that is done. At the same time, professional work has subjective elements that derive from the ways problems are identified and interpreted by the profession. All problems have subjective components as well. Social workers have been especially sensitive to the subjective aspects of problem definition and have given significant attention to the social construction of problems. Indeed, there is substantial literature that argues that social problems are created exclusively to serve the interests of social workers, e.g., to keep their jobs, to control unattractive populations (Handler 1973; Illich et al. 1977).

DEFENDING INTERPROFESSIONAL CLAIMS

Knowledge provides an important basis on which professions stake and strengthen their claims against other professions (Abbott 1988). Professions use their knowledge base to move into new areas (i.e., the community, the corporation) and to make claims of effectiveness and efficiency. All professions develop a formal, abstract system of knowledge. It is, indeed, the development of an abstract knowledge system that sets professions apart from other occupational groups. Achieving an appropriate level of abstraction is an issue for all professions. Too much abstraction creates difficulties in connecting professional knowledge to cultural values; too little abstraction reduces claims to professionalization altogether.

Professional knowledge can be ordered by level of abstraction into academic and working or practical knowledge. Abbott posits that academic knowledge exists in logically consistent but disaggregated pieces not directly applicable to practice. The disaggregated character of academic knowledge is functional for accomplishing several professional tasks. It can be used to develop new approaches to problems and interventions; it can be used to make connections that are obscured by the pressing demands of practice; and it offers the possibility of identifying underlying patterns and regularities that can give shape to practical knowledge. Further, academic knowledge carries prestige value, Abbott conjectures, based on the illusion that there is a strong and direct link between academic and practical knowledge.

Practical knowledge is obviously less abstract than academic knowledge. It is more directly linked to professional tasks of diagnosis, inference, and evaluation. A classic paper by Rein and White (1981) argues for an organization focused on a broadly defined set of purposes and tasks. When we discuss the development of practice guidelines, we are discussing a form of practice knowledge that is directly related to the tasks of diagnosis and inference and the development and implementation of interventions. It is expected that as academic knowledge is applied to different practice problems, it will be organized in different ways. For example, currently in social work education, knowledge is organized into curricular areas such as human behavior and development, social intervention, and social policy and research, as well as into fields of practice such as mental health, health, and child and family services. In this volume, Thyer argues for organizing practice knowledge into a taxonomy of disorders identified in the *Diagnostic and Statistical Manual of Mental Disorders (DSM-IV)* (American Psychiatric Association 1994). Videka (chapter 10, this volume) points to the necessity to take client characteristics into account. Reid and Fortune (chapter 4, this volume) organize a group of empirical studies by type of intervention. Proctor and Rosen (chapter 6, this volume) argue for organizing knowledge into targets for intervention or change: behaviors, emotions, interpersonal relationships (Beutler and Clarkin 1990; Kazdin 1999). Proctor and Rosen and Thyer (chapters 6 and 7, this volume) debate the merits of organizing knowledge according to a targets-of-intervention versus a problem-reduction framework. What is revealed by these discussions and debates is that there are multiple potential approaches to organizing knowledge relevant to practice guidelines. As practice-relevant knowledge increases and as practice guidelines are developed and refined, it likely that they will be multidimensional, i.e., that they will be organized to account for client characteristics (including diagnosis and level of functioning or problem severity), type of intervention, and targets of change.

Given the centrality of knowledge to the definition and development of professions, it follows that universities are one of the key external institutions affecting professions (Abbott 1988; Pelikan 1992; Veysey 1965). In the United States, universities house research and knowledge development, professional education, and the work of legitimating the profession through the communication of important cultural values of rationality and efficiency. The modern U.S. university is founded on the German model of the research university, with the earliest examples in the United States being Johns Hopkins University (founded in 1876) and the University of Chicago (founded in 1892). The American version of the research university incorporated liberal education, i.e., broad exposure to knowledge deemed essential to a democratic society. Typically in the United States liberal education is positioned primarily at the undergraduate level and professional education is positioned at the graduate level. American universities (as compared with colleges) are defined, in fact, by their commitment to advancement of knowledge through research and the presence of graduate and professional schools.

LEGITIMATING THE WORK OF PROFESSIONS

The work of legitimation for professions is essentially the work of connecting professional tasks and related knowledge to cultural values (Abbott 1988). Abbott points out that professions must legitimate not only what they do but *how* they do it. Some professions legitimate *what* they do by connecting it with *individual* values such as happiness or salvation (e.g., psychology, medicine, and ministry). Others, such as law and social work, connect their work to *social* values such as justice or orderly adjustment. Still others, such as public administration and some forms of engineering, identify with political values such as democracy or planning. Regardless of whether values are individual, social, or political—or some combination—one of the functions of professions is to establish that the work they perform produces culturally valued results.

Professions must also establish that the work they do is conducted in a culturally approved manner—that is, they must legitimate how they do their work. As Abbott (1988) notes, "In the last century, science, with the broader, related phenomenon of formal rationality, has become the fundamental ground for the legitimacy of professional techniques. In the value scheme on which modern professions draw, science stands for logic and rigor in diagnosis, as well as a certain caution and conservatism in professional therapeutics. It implies extensive academic research based on the highest standards of rationality" (p. 189).

The social structures of professions have been designed to "guarantee that practitioners possessed the scientifically or rationally legitimated modes of practice and . . . that they carried them out properly" (Abbott 1988:193). The social structures playing central roles in legitimation are those structures that have traditionally been used to define professions: associations, accreditation, and ethics codes (Wilesky 1964). Thus these internal structures are the mechanisms that define a profession, connect it to central cultural values, and are used to defend its jurisdiction.

System and institutional theorists point out that tasks, related knowledge systems, and internal structures are not enough to define and sustain professions. Professions are also influenced by external institutions. Social and political structures come into being to enable them to defend jurisdictional claims. In highly centralized governments such as France, professions are nearly completely defined and controlled by state agencies. Social workers in France, for example, belong to one of several highly specialized groups (e.g., Assistants Sociaux, Educateurs Justice, Educateurs de Jeunes Enfants) whose work is completely authorized and funded by government agencies. In less centralized governments like that of the United States, the institutions that influence professions are more numerous and diverse. Professions use courts, legislatures, and administrative agencies to define, defend, and legitimate professional domains—for example, to seek title protection, claims for third-party payments, and monopoly of certain activities or certain work settings. A study of the structure of public education in the United States, reported in Scott (1995), describes a "classic" U.S. pattern involving professional standards, court decisions, special-purpose legislation, interest groups, political institutions, and civic discourse that influences the structure of professions.

As we attempt to understand how social work knowledge is legitimated in the United States, we can identify several internal structures and external institutions that are actively involved in shaping the social work knowledge base: professional associations, accrediting organizations, regulators, insurers, and academic institutions. It is instructive to examine the role of these groups.

Professional associations, ethics codes, and accreditation organizations are the defining organizational structures of professions (Wilensky 1964). Each of these organizational forms plays a role in legitimating the social work knowledge base. The major professional organization is the National Association of Social Work (NASW), which regulates important aspects of professional life: certification of members, support for members, definition and protection of professional jurisdiction, relations with other professions, quality control through disciplinary committees. The NASW has been the primary organization involved in protecting professional turf by promoting licensure and third-party payment claims for social workers. It also actively promotes and legitimates the knowledge base of the profession in specific ways. Through NASW Press, with its publication of major professional books and journals, the NASW plays a role in defining what knowledge and what types of knowledge will guide professional discourse and work. Further, the NASW has been actively involved in the development of the NASW Code of Ethics. The current code specifically addresses the type of knowledge that is considered to be *ethical*. For example, one provision of the NASW Code states: "A social worker should critically examine and keep current with emerging knowledge relevant to social work and fully use evaluation and research evidence in their professional practice" (5.02.c).

The Council on Social Work Education (CSWE) holds as one of its responsibilities the accreditation of social work education programs. The materials produced by the CSWE, specifically the *Educational Policy and Standards* statement, define the knowledge base of the profession by describing the content that must be conveyed in educational programs. In the United States, the primary means by which a professional is defined or certified is by graduation from an accredited school of social work. Further certification takes place on the basis of experience in the profession and passage of state licensure exams. Graduation from an accredited school and passage of a licensure exam are both entry requirements that are based on demonstrated mastery of particular knowledge. Thus, through the processes of providing educational programs, accrediting them, and developing licensure exams, universities, accrediting groups, and licensure groups work together to define and legitimate the professional knowledge base.

As noted above, professions also use external institutions such as insurers, administrative agencies, and the courts to define, defend, and legitimate professional claims. Further, when professional jurisdictions are challenged, they are often challenged in terms of the work they carry out and the knowledge base that supports that work (Abbott 1988). In social work, we observe that insurers—both public and private—have traditionally used professional degrees and licensure exams as indicators of capacity to provide relevant, quality service—i.e., reimbursable service. As a result, we find social workers lobbying state legislatures on issues of licensure and title protection. We see social workers on Capitol Hill lobbying for Medicaid reimbursement qualification for their work in nursing homes. Claims made in these lobbying efforts are based on the work that social workers do and the knowledge base that they have to do the work.

WHAT DO WE KNOW ABOUT THE DEVELOPMENT AND USE OF PRACTICE GUIDELINES?

Efforts to develop practice guidelines have been reviewed elsewhere (Nathan 1998; Howard and Jenson 1999, chapter 5, this volume) and will not be repeated here. These analyses of efforts to date in psychology, psychiatry, and social work identify both opportunities and challenges for social work. On the opportunity side, practice guidelines are seen as promoting the adoption of best current practices and facilitating accountability. On the challenges side, practice guidelines are criticized for diverse and questionable standards of proof and for constraining clinical decision making. Nathan (1998) summarizes the situation as follows: "Although practice guidelines are not yet ideal, they have the potential to enhance both the effectiveness and the accountability of interventions. Achievement of the potential depends on the continuing maturation of the research base that underlies practice guidelines, so as to provide solutions to the formidable problems that prevent their widespread acceptance" (p. 298).

DEVELOPMENT OF PRACTICE GUIDELINES

When we analyze the development of practice guidelines, we anticipate the involvement of certain specific organizational forms, which we have reviewed in our theoretical conceptualization. The development of practice guidelines in social work is in the early stages. Nonetheless, given the institutional framework we are using, we observe the beginning and potential contributions of the following institutions, both internal and external to the profession.

1. Social work *professional associations,* especially the National Association of Social Work, have a role to play in promoting the development of practice guidelines, as well as in using them to defend professional turf. Already the publication arm of the NASW, NASW Press, is moving in the direction of developing practice guidelines through the inauguration of a new book series designed to publish empirically based practice strategies in specific areas of practice. Our theoretical framework tells us that professional associations function to protect professional turf as well as to promote the development of a professional knowledge base. In this function, the development of practice guidelines within social work offers tools by which the professional association can define competent, ethical practice. These tools will no doubt prove useful in the certification and regulation of social work professionals.

2. Professional *codes of ethics* identify particular types of knowledge as relevant to ethical practice. As practice guidelines become more fully developed, reference to them in codes of ethics will be one way to promote their legitimacy and use. Many codes of ethics exist within social work. For example, the National Association of Social Workers has developed an ethics code, and so have other groups such as the National Association of Black Social Workers and the National Federation of Societies for Clinical Social Work. As noted above, the NASW code refers to the use of evaluation and research evidence as consistent with ethical practice. This is a common, but not uniform, provision in other codes.

3. The professional association responsible for *accreditation* of professional programs and schools for social work—the Council on Social Work Education (CSWE)— also has a role to play in legitimating practice guidelines, which will be enhanced to the extent that they are acknowledged as part of the knowledge base conveyed in professional education. Educational programs, accreditation entities, and licensing groups all influence the definition of the professional knowledge base. As social work practice guidelines develop, their incorporation in the requirements and standards of these groups is one means by which they will gain legitimacy.

4. *Universities and other research institutions* are often viewed as important sources of information about effective treatments, interventions, and procedures. Governmental and nongovernmental agencies often provide funding to schools of social work to develop and test particular treatment approaches. Universities and research institutions are both repositories for and developers of academic and practical knowledge. Professional schools in universities play an active role in legitimating academic knowledge as well as in legitimating and developing practical knowledge.

5. *Public and private insurers,* i.e., purchasers of services, represent external groups that can play an important role in legitimating—indeed requiring—the use of practice guidelines. To date in social work, insurers have relied on professional degrees and licenses as proxies for service quality, i.e., to determine the services that they will reimburse. In some areas of health care, use of specific protocols of demonstrated effectiveness (e.g., knee replacement surgery) is the basis for reimbursement.

Insurers have created clinician networks specifically to review evidence and generate guidelines to assist the insurers in making reimbursement decisions (Milbank Memorial Fund 2000). In the United States, directors or clinicians affiliated with health plans have been organized to sort through clinical effectiveness data. In the United Kingdom, the National Health Service Research and Development Program has funded the Cochrane Collaboration, designed to review randomized clinical trials and other studies of the efficacy of different treatments. Completed reviews are placed in an electronic database accessible through the Internet. Purchasers of health care who are interested in effective, high-quality services have developed these networks or associations of professionals. A clinician participating in one network described the rationale thus: "It doesn't make sense to keep arguing about what we should cover when we don't know what the state of the art is. Providers know best what that is, so (we're designing) processes for facilitating their coming together and developing new ways to compile this information and get it out there. If we can get this community to agree on the single best approaches to these kinds of issues, we can dramatically improve quality" (quoted in Milbank Memorial Fund 2000:17). A health care purchaser who helped organize one such network stated: "Treatments and interventions for this condition [can be] driven by best practices that stem from the data rather than from what plans think is best or want to offer" (quoted in Milbank Memorial Fund 2000:18).

6. Other groups external to the profession that could influence the legitimacy of practice guidelines include a number of governmental and private *consumer protection* agencies that could be involved in the development and promotion of practice guidelines. The Agency for Health Care Policy and Research and the Consumers Union have already been involved in guidelines for psychosocial treatment.

USE OF PRACTICE GUIDELINES

As discussed above, practice guidelines are one form of knowledge for practice. Factors that affect knowledge utilization in general are the same factors that will affect the use of practice guidelines in social work (Marsh 2002). Many social work researchers have bemoaned the limited use of empirical research findings by practitioners (Rosen 1994). We expect practitioners to make more use of abstract, conceptual knowledge than of instrumental knowledge such as practice guidelines (Marsh 1983; Cohen, Sargeant, and Sechrest 1986). We also expect that practitioners will be more likely to use knowledge they trust, that is, knowledge that is relevant and credible. The relevance and credibility of a particular piece of knowledge derives from both (1) its source (the most reliable source being their own experience or that of colleagues) and (2) its relevance to a particular practice decision (Berlin and Marsh 1983). Essentially, the most recent work on knowledge utilization specifies the necessity of bidirectional communication between researchers and practitioners through collaboration (Lamb, Greenlick, and McCarty 1998).

IMPLICATIONS OF THEORY AND EXPERIENCE FOR THE LEGITIMATION OF PRACTICE GUIDELINES

As we try to predict and perhaps shape the future development of practice guidelines, a number of implications can be drawn from theory and experience to date. First, a review of the legitimation of professional knowledge generally, and practice guidelines specifically, reveals that legitimation is a process that is neither linear nor unidirectional. Numerous institutions and organizations, both internal and external to the profession, are involved. And rather than operating in a predictable, logical sequence, these institutions operate simultaneously and often independently. In the decentralized health and social welfare system in the United States, no one group appears to have controlling interest in determining and directing the process of professional development. Professions use these institutions to define themselves, to make claims about specific tasks and related knowledge that articulate boundaries, and to legitimate their work and their specific knowledge base to the larger society.

Given that the knowledge base plays such a central role in the definition and legitimation of a profession, it is in the interest of any profession to make explicit and distinct its knowledge base. Historically, in these efforts, a defining feature of social work has been the simultaneous commitment to problem reduction on an individual level and to service provision and social change on a societal level. This characteristic is also a source of great tension and debate in the literature—indeed, even in this volume. Theory would suggest that social work has much to gain from engaging the tension, claiming a broad domain of activities, and moving beyond a focus primarily on problem reduction. Theory would support an approach to organizing knowledge that is not limited to diagnostic categories, that incorporates a broadly defined set of organizing principles.

Finally, institutional theory helps us recognize the dynamic character of knowledge development in professions. Professions are more clearly defined and a profession's knowledge base gains legitimacy every time the knowledge is used—whether in the classroom, the agency, the program accreditation, or the purchase-of-service contract. Professions that restrict or limit the development and use of knowledge are less competitive than those that actively expand their task and knowledge boundaries and use a variety of social institutions to do so.

In sum, the understanding that scientifically developed knowledge in specific domains is the basis on which professions claim expertise and defend interprofessional boundaries serves to highlight the significance of the topic of practice guidelines for social work. Further, it provides an important justification for placing the discussion of practice guidelines within a larger context of understanding social work practice and its knowledge base. Articulating the institutions, both internal and external to the profession, that are involved in defining, defending, and legitimating our professional knowledge base provides valuable direction for our work in the development of practice guidelines.

REFERENCES

Abbott, A. (1988). *The System of Professions: An Essay on the Division of Expert Labor.* Chicago: University of Chicago Press.

Austin, D. M. (1983). The Flexner myth and the history of social work. *Social Service Review, 57* (3), 357–377.

Berlin, S. B., and Marsh, J. C. (1993). *Informing Practice Decisions.* New York: Macmillan.

Beutler, L. E., and Clarkin, J. F. (1990). *Systematic Treatment Selection.* New York: Brunner/Mazel.

Breiland, D. (1977). Historical overview. Special issue on conceptual frameworks. *Social Work, 22* (5), 341–346.

Cohen, L. H., Sargeant, M. M., and Sechrest, L. B. 1986. Use of psychotherapy research by practicing psychologists. *American Psychologist, 41* (2), 198–206.

Flexner, A. (1915). Is Social Work a Profession? In *Proceedings of the National Conference of Charities and Correction* (pp. 576–590). Chicago: Hindmann Printing Company.

Freidson, E. (1994). *Professionalism Reborn: Theory, Prophecy, and Policy.* Chicago: University of Chicago Press.

Gambrill, E. (1999). Evidenced-based practice: An alternative to authority-based practice. *Families in Society: The Journal of Contemporary Human Services, 80* (4), 341–350.

Ginsberg, L. (1995). *Social Work Almanac* (2d ed.). Washington, D.C.: NASW Press.

Handler, J. (1973). *The Coercive Social Worker.* Chicago: Rand McNally.

Howard, M. O., and Jenson, J. M. (1999). Clinical practice guidelines: Should social work develop them? *Research on Social Work Practice, 9* (3), 283–301.

Illich, I., Zola, I. K., McKnight, J., Caplan, J., and Shaiken, H. (1977). *Disabling Professions.* Salem, N.H.: M. Boyars.

Lamb, S. I., Greenlick, M. R., and McCarty, D. (1998). *Bridging the Gap Between Practice and Research.* Washington, D.C.: National Academy Press.

Lin, A. M. P. (1995). Mental Health Overview. In R. L. Edwards and J. Hopps (Eds.), *Encyclopedia of Social Work.* Washington, D.C.: NASW Press.

Kazdin, A. E. (1999). The meanings and measurement of clinical significance. *Journal of Consulting and Clinical Psychology, 67* (3), 332–339.

Marsh, J. C. (1983). Research and innovation in social work practice: Avoiding the headless machine. *Social Service Review, 57* (4), 582–598.

Marsh, J. C. (2000). Theories of Professions: Implications for Social Work. In S. Muller, Suenker, H., Olk, T., and Bollert, K., eds. *Soziale Arbeit. Gesellschaftliche Bedingungen und professionelle Perspektiven [Social Work: Social Conditions and Professional Perspectives]* (Neuwied: Luchterhand, 2000).

Marsh, J. C. (2002). Using knowledge about knowledge utilization. Editorial. *Social Work, 47* (2), 101–104.

Milbank Memorial Fund. (2000). *Better Information, Better Outcomes? The Use of Health Technology Assessment and Clinical Effectiveness Data in Health Care Purchasing Decisions in the UK and US.* New York: Milbank Memorial Fund.

Nathan, P. E. (1998). Practice guidelines. *American Psychologist, 53* (3), 290–299.

Pelikan, J. (1992). *The Idea of the University: A Reexamination.* New Haven: Yale.

Redl, F., and Wineman, D. (1951). *Children Who Hate: The Disorganization and Breakdown of Behavior Controls.* New York: Free Press.

Rein, M., and White, S. H. (1981). Knowledge for practice. *Social Service Review, 55* (1), 1–41.

Rosen, A. (1993). Systematic planned practice. *Social Service Review, 67,* 84–100.

———. (1994). Knowledge use in direct practice. *Social Service Review, 68* (4), 561–577.

Rosen, A., Proctor, E. K., and Livne, S. (1985). Planning and direct practice. *Social Service Review, 59,* 161–177.

Rosen, A., Proctor, E. K., and Staudt, M. (1999). Social work research and the quest for effective practice. *Social Work Research, 23,* 4–14.

Scott, W. R. (1995). *Institutions and Organizations.* Thousand Oaks, Calif.: Sage.

Teare, R. J., and Shaefor, B. W. (1995). *Practice-Sensitive Social Work Education: An Empirical Analysis of Social Work Practice and Practitioners.* Alexandria, Va.: CSWE.

Veysey, L. (1965). *The Emergence of the American University.* Chicago: University of Chicago Press.

Wilensky, H. L. (1964). The professionalization of everyone? *American Journal of Sociology, 70,* 137–158.

15

SOCIAL WORK PRACTICE GUIDELINES IN AN INTERPROFESSIONAL WORLD: HONORING NEW TIES THAT BIND

NINA L. ARONOFF AND DARLYNE BAILEY

Social work functions within the larger context of human service professions whose mandate it is to intervene effectively in the complex social issues challenging those we serve—individuals, families, organizations, and communities. At the same time, we are painfully aware that many of our best intentions fail to make enough of a difference in quality-of-life outcomes. In response to this awareness, social work is strengthening some of its existing methods and focusing on some new areas, including engagement in a dialogue about how research can support practice that is more outcomes-oriented and evidence-based. This dialogue builds on a body of knowledge in practice-based research that focuses on the value and utility of evidence-based practice and the development of practice guidelines (Fortune and Reid 1999).

This focus in practice research is critical to our ability to function credibly in today's professional world. Professional legitimation depends, more and more, on a paradigm in which scientific evidence constitutes a substantial claim to a profession's essential knowledge base and practice venue. While other helping professions, such as medicine (Howard and Jenson, chapter 5, this volume), have also grappled with the subject, social work has its own issues to consider in developing, implementing, and disseminating practice guidelines. The challenge is how best to integrate the scientific methods of research into a very human-centered, applied profession.

Essentially, the purpose of practice research is not only to become better able to establish more-replicable avenues for effecting reliable outcomes or simply to keep up with professional fashion. It is also a response to the reality that too often the results of our existing interventions are simply not good enough. The use of practice research to develop guidelines for social work that are both reliable and flexible (Proctor and Rosen, chapter 1, this volume) is critical to the actualization of our purpose and commitments as a profession—

to find increasingly better ways to facilitate the well-being of people, organizations, and communities.

To this end, we look to a significant wave cresting in the human service professions—the evolution from intradisciplinary efforts to inter/multidisciplinary ones, and now to *interprofessional* collaborations in practice, research, and education. We are in a unique historical moment in which our consciousness of human connection and challenges around the world is greater than ever. Awareness of people and events globally is more immediate, relationships are affected on many levels at once, and individual and community access to resources (e.g., technology) is significant in new ways, whether we look to education, health care, business, technology, or politics. Even the term *global,* which used to signify a type of economic structure and practice, has become generalized to include many aspects of life. Our definition of the social group is changing, and we are consequently embracing changing definitions and even a changing scope of what constitutes a social problem. Therefore, we are exploring what outcomes to target and what resources to marshal in service to our professional goals. The trend toward professional specialization and a concomitant tendency to isolation within professions can help to develop expertise, but it also sometimes distracts vital energies from the demands of today's more complex social realities.

This new environment calls for a heightened awareness of the issues at stake in the social environment and signals a new range of choices and responsibility for social work. For those of us in the human service professions, today's social climate invites—and even demands—intersystemic collaboration and a commitment to creative dialogue about how to address the complexities of a globally influenced environment. This is really a matter of both scientific *and* social validity.

As social work assesses its existing knowledge base and methodologies for utility and validity in an increasingly intricate network of human, professional, and technological systems, we must consider the essential criteria of relevance, efficiency, and effectiveness. New questions surface, among them, What frameworks and skills need yet to be generated? Which issues and which outcomes do we target, and how do we develop effective and reliable practice guidelines to achieve those outcomes? How do we evaluate our evolving efforts in order to be relevant, effective, and efficient in today's intersystemic context? How might we better partner with others at all levels of inquiry, practice, and evaluation to build an even stronger, more relevant knowledge base? And, ultimately, how can social work thrive and also provide leadership in the emerging environment of interprofessionally collaborative practice, research, and education?

HUMAN SERVICE ISSUES AND TRENDS: SOCIAL WORK IN CONTEXT

Since professions exist and evolve in context—the sociocultural environment of their times—professional definition and mandate are socially and historically situated, determining how problems and solutions are identified, described, and assigned value (Marsh, chapter 14, this volume). Professions are also legitimated in context (Abbott 1988; Marsh). As time and context change, then, a natural tension develops between the *mission* of a profession and its *evolving and responsive* nature—how its mission remains consistent in the midst of natural sociocultural flux, when the way in which that mission manifests may change. For example, it is the mission of social work to intervene in the human condition, wherever and however possible, in order to alleviate suffering, empower the disenfranchised, and work for social and economic justice in ways that are client-centered and ecologically framed. As those ecological contexts shift, so do some of the interventions of the profession—though its mission remains constant.

Similarly, evolving social issues drive human service trends. One current trend is specialization, which benefits consumers when it represents a focused and articulate response to their needs. But the systems in which it thrives also often isolate the very people they are trying to help. Specialized knowledge and services are often part of a human services culture that is based on the partialization and, often, decontextualization of human issues, an approach that undermines the philosophy of social work.

A second current trend is outcomes-focused intervention, which, unlike specialization, can open up a range of possibility in responding to the variability of human need. In this approach, situation-specific outcomes, not necessarily diagnosis or what services are available, can drive intervention. The purpose behind the approach is that individuals, families, organizations, and communities vary, as do their needs and the changes they seek. The values of social work reflect an orientation of response to that diversity of need (Roberts, Rule, and Innocenti 1998); and it often motivates other systems to join in working together (perhaps in multidisciplinary teams) toward positive outcomes. Beyond just considering problems in context, this approach involves identifying the contextually based solution(s) being sought and the environmental factors (internal and external) necessary to achieve them. It involves asking not just what creates problem(s) but also what range of factors, resources, and relationships is involved in transforming them into desired outcomes.

A third trend is seen in practice models that go beyond the multidisciplinary team into broader, intentional service partnerships—for example, in work with families and communities (Hooper-Briar and Lawson 1996a) or among organizations (Bailey and Koney 2000). The goal is better outcomes through intersystemic partnering at every level of practice and evaluation. These models weave together some of the best aspects of both professional consistency and the need to evolve through creative dialogue, a process in which professions work together, *with* client systems, to achieve desired positive outcomes. The overarching philosophy here is, again, to apply the needed skills and relationships in an integrated approach to the issues of complex environments, particularly where clients have experienced disenfranchisement, disempowerment, or oppression.

Ultimately, the current sociocultural environment exhorts *all* professions to consider human services from a more contextual, or ecological, point of view. It is becoming almost impossible, if not simply impractical, not to do so. The search for more-positive outcomes must draw on every possible resource for change. This goal raises new questions for all the professions as to relevant task domains and the focal points for knowledge development. Now the capacity of social work to remain valid and legitimate as a profession depends on our awareness of and responsiveness to the dynamics of social change in this more interconnected, global context. How effectively are we working to advance the well-being of individuals, families, organizations, and communities by demonstrating a consistency of mission *through* an openness to innovative solutions? And how effectively are we doing this in partnership, with one another and with the people we serve?

AIMING FOR BETTER OUTCOMES: INTERPROFESSIONALISM

The strength of an intentional, collaborative approach, as in the third trend noted above, is not just an additive measure of practice perspectives and techniques. While that has obvious benefits, the real advantage of collaboration is evident in its synergistic effects. Interprofessionalism is grounded in a recognition that clients are best served by a *range* of professionals, working together and in conjunction with clients in collaborative relationships. It is based on acknowledgment of a common stake, which is the health and well-being of those we serve. It is an acceptance of the richness inherent in the values of social work as a profession and in the practice of creative partnerships, including an ethic of client-centered practice. It is a paradigm in which innovative partnerships are "a necessity and an obligation of professional leadership" (Corrigan and Bishop 1997).

Definition of terms in the context of this conversation needs to be clear. The term *interdisciplinary* or *multidisciplinary* can be defined as "persons trained in different disciplines who work together on a common problem" (Zlotnik et al. 1999:3). The capacity to engage in this type of process implies that each profession has its own information and claims to share, based on the concentration of intellectual and other resources that develops and sustains a knowledge base, a key aspect of the current paradigm of professional legitimation (Abbott 1988; Marsh, chapter 14, this volume). The term *boundary spanning* is another way to describe the interdisciplinary process—representatives from one or more systems, each with his or her own orientation, have functioning roles in other systems. This intentional exchange of claims, moreover, allows disciplines to remain separate and bounded while benefiting from each one's focused approach.

Changing contexts, however, may call for changing professional boundaries, remembering that as they are socially created they can also be socially uncreated (Wallerstein 1995). The definition of *interprofessional,* as used here, goes beyond interdisciplinary. Drawing from some of the recent work in this area (Corrigan and Bishop 1997; Hogan 1996; Hooper-Briar and Lawson 1996a; Zlotnik et al. 1999), we can say that interprofessional practice involves persons of a range of affiliations, together serving common goals of service planning, delivery, and evaluation. It implies a flexibility of professional boundaries that allows for a highly interactive process of knowledge, skill, and role exchange. This engages a participatory process that involves all stakeholders, including client systems. Interprofessionalism, then, is a *beyond-boundary-spanning* or a *boundary-synergizing* paradigm, in which a new dynamic is generated among formerly separate entities, bringing about new ways of conceptualizing and new results. Ultimately, the parts can be seen in the sum, and also the experience of the whole is greater than the sum of its parts.

Interprofessionalism incorporates collaborative models and strategic alliance building at all levels of practice, research, and education—in epistemology, methodology, and application. In the interprofessional framework, each profession *aims* to discover the gaps in its own approaches and to respond by trying to fill them through active engagement of professional and client systems in service to mutually desired outcomes. Without rejecting profession-specific values and skills, interprofessionalism invites new values, practice skills, and guidelines, along with the research methods and education models to support them. In developing guidelines for best practice, interprofessionalism offers an alternative to either/or frameworks—*either* unidisciplinary *or* multidisciplinary. This, in turn, leads to new focal points for knowledge development (e.g., an evolution in practice guidelines), as well as potentially expanded relationships with the institutions and processes of professional legitimation. The proposal made here is a call for a new sense of professional accountability that is mutually enhancing and in greater service to the needs of people, organizations, and communities. As Graham and Barter (1999) point out, interprofessionalism is not an end in itself but rather a critical tool needed to achieve the change to which we are committed.

LOCATING SOCIAL WORK IN INTERPROFESSIONALISM

If social work is to integrate interprofessionalism in practice and research, particularly in the interests of practice guidelines, it must assess what to keep, what to eliminate, and what to add. First, it means *sustaining* some fundamentals in social work's knowledge base—(1) the systemic/ecological paradigm particular to social work; (2) the integration of knowledge "borrowed" from other disciplines; and (3) the skills and values we bring to multidisciplinary work. Second, it means *going beyond* these fundamentals into a new territory of strategic, collaborative relationships. Therefore, we need to continue social work–specific guideline development (Proctor and Rosen, chapter 6, this volume) but we must not stop there (Jackson 1999). We also need to continue to resist the isolation and inefficiency of working in a unidisciplinary mode and look to other disciplines for practice guideline "wheels" that are already invented (Mayden 1996; Thyer, chapter 7, this volume); and neither can we afford to stop there. Beyond these approaches, what interprofessionalism adds to social work's development of practice guidelines is a more intentional, collaborative process, resulting in new conceptualizations applicable to practice, research, and education. Through this process, we can hope to see familiar issues (and solutions) in new ways, as well as to discover formerly "invisible" issues and solutions.

In fact, examples of social work's engagement in the interprofessional paradigm already exist and have been evolving over the past thirty years. The emerging literature on interprofessionalism documents a range of initiatives and models for practice (Corrigan and Bishop 1997; Dryfoos 1998; Graham and Barter 1999; Hooper-Briar and Lawson 1996a; Roberts, Rule, and Innocenti 1998; Zlotnik et al. 1999). Many of these are school-linked initiatives, and in their comprehensive review, Briar-Lawson et al. (1997:143) note that there are already two generations of expanded partnerships to evaluate. The first generation represents a collaborative approach among major service-delivery systems, resulting in, for example, the co-location of social services in school settings. The second generation of initiatives raises the level of engagement of relevant parties to include family and community members as empowered stakeholders and partners in developing and delivering services.

Some schools of social work have already committed to an integration of interprofessional concepts and opportunities for their students. Wheelock

College in Boston, for example, is pioneering a model that partners early childhood education, social work, and child development disciplines in a professional education and service paradigm that is family centered and community based (Bakken 1996; Hogan 1996). Others, like Bryn Mawr in Pennsylvania (Mayden 1996), offer students the opportunity to include in their training integrative seminars and mentorships that are specifically interprofessional in nature, recognizing that these, along with interdisciplinary professional education, strengthen their ability to provide more-effective, client-based services.

As social work assesses where it will continue to be situated in the growing movement of interprofessional collaborations, including how to formulate and evaluate practice and practice research, both familiar and new questions emerge. What new frameworks and skills need to be generated to suit desired outcomes in today's world? Which issues and outcomes do we target, how are they defined, and how do we develop effective and reliable practice guidelines to achieve those outcomes? How can we better partner with others, drawing on a history of participatory methods and strengthening them in practice and research? In making this work most relevant to our client systems, how shall we participate with them collaboratively in all dimensions? The answers to even these initial questions present social work with an opportunity both to strengthen professional resources and also to share key knowledge and skills. This process necessarily questions the procedures by which we are to be sustained and legitimated as a profession. Therefore, the key question of the effects of interprofessionalism upon social work needs to be addressed with regard to each of social work's primary arenas—research, practice, and education. For the purposes of this chapter, the focus will be primarily on practice and research, in particular as related to the development of practice guidelines.

THE IMPLICATIONS OF INTERPROFESSIONALISM: KNOWLEDGE, EVIDENCE, AND GUIDELINES

As noted, the guiding knowledge base of any profession, and its assumptions, are essential to how it is defined, differentiated, and, ultimately, legitimated as a profession (Abbott 1988; Marsh, chapter 14, this volume). This includes common values, skills, and knowledge, the priority given to certain lines and methods of inquiry, and the primacy of certain types of evidence. As Marsh notes, "The professional knowledge base serves to legitimize professional work by clarifying the foundations of the work and tracing it to the major cultural values of rationality, logic and science." Still, making claims about what a profession "knows" implies a consciousness about the limits to "seeing" or "knowing" all; the gaps in our knowledge base need always to be central in our commitment to inquiry. Interprofessionalism raises the level of this need. It acknowledges the importance of critical thinking and of developing integrated frameworks for thinking, within and across professional boundaries. This has particular relevance to the interface of practice and research that occurs in the development of practice guidelines. It also has relevance in terms of critically assessing current assumptions about that interface, including those that exist in adopting a particular paradigm, or culture, of science, of which we highlight three.

The first critical question is whether there is any *unitary* culture of "rationality, logic and science," particularly in the social sciences, where we deal on a regular basis with the manifest idiosyncrasies and stresses of life. Second, we must recognize that there is a *range* of cultural values to which professions adhere, of which rationality and logic are only two, although they are key. Professions also define and legitimate themselves by other values central to their paradigms, which are essential to understanding not only each profession's claims but also the tasks and domains to which it holds itself accountable. Key values in social work include a commitment to *serving society's most vulnerable,* to *empowerment,* to *social and economic justice,* and to practice that is *client-driven*—any or all of which may challenge a unitary concept of science.

The third point is that, while it is important to "speak the language" of rationality and science, we must also encourage a kind of "multilingualism," or "multiculturalism," *within* the culture of science and resist being either wholly assimilated or subsumed under values that are not ours, while also being open to the benefits that other approaches might bring to the actualization of our goals. As Mayden (1996) has stated: "Sometimes we allow ourselves to become trapped by the tenets of our disciplines rather than allowing those tenets to create new questions and areas of inquiry" (p. 141). If we need to loosen the constraints of a paradigm of science that is too narrow, it is the essential values of the profession that will be our guide.

Sustained legitimacy depends on continuous evaluation of our concurrence with both the internal culture(s) of social work and the external environment in which we are situated. This brings us to a critical assessment of our methodologies, which is especially salient in the discussion of practice guidelines. How much is social work research truly in accordance with our professional values? How well do our methodologies address the internal diversity of our own profession and the diversity of our client systems? How might elevating the place of dialogue with other professionals and with consumers improve the processes of inquiry? Are we client-driven enough, and would our clients agree with our assessment on this point?

The interprofessional context we are centralizing here invites these and other questions (and choices) about how to establish relevant practice guidelines, along with the practice, research, and education models that support their evolution. This requires more than defining new focal points for knowledge development; also necessary is a review of our definition of "relevance" (a guideline of the National Association of Social Workers [NASW] Code of Ethics) and revisiting and clarifying the very definition of evidence. The ways in which each of these is qualified may need to change.

Development of practice guidelines in an interprofessional context asks that we stay committed to emergent arenas/outcomes and avoid adherence to outmoded guidelines. Instead, we can take the opportunity to broaden our frameworks for inquiry, seeking out new types of partnership, new practices, new evaluation methods and the support of successful outcomes through relevant and effective practice guidelines, as well as educational models that match this exploration, through interprofessional experiences in the field, in the classroom, and in lifelong learning contexts.

DIRECTIONS FOR IMPLEMENTATION: PRACTICE AND RESEARCH

Theorizing and application are not the same. To begin to answer the many questions that this discussion generates, we must look to key areas of practice and research and propose some formulations for bringing interprofessionalism into social work and assessing its impact on evidence-based practice and guideline development.

In *practice*, interprofessionalism means designing and implementing a contextually based, comprehensive, and collaborative approach to assessment, intervention, and evaluation. Interprofessional practice requires, as Schorr proposes (in Zlotnik et al. 1999), "a 'new practitioner' who works more collaboratively and more respectfully with clients, patients, children, youth, and families, and who pushes the boundaries of her or his job description and sees children in the context of families and families in the context of communities" (p. 1). We would add to that the need to include organizations, state agencies, the academy, funding bodies, and supportive technologies in this collaborative approach.

Practice research agendas need to stem from this perspective. Time and other resources need to be allocated to the creation and development of interprofessional practice models and programs that include all stakeholders and that are evaluated from start to finish. This approach necessitates an active, collaborative framework to incorporate an iterative process of input and feedback from practitioners, client systems, educators, researchers, and funders. It would establish the ground on which practice research would be based and from which new practice guidelines could be developed.

In *research* and evaluation in general, interprofessionalism suggests the exploration and development of empirical models that enhance, and are enhanced by, a new definition of results-based accountability, supported by utilization of known methods as well as the development of new methods. It also includes the sharing of relevant technologies among professions and with client systems, building upon them in proactive ways to develop practice guidelines, with mutually defined outcomes as the basis of what constitutes best practice.

The goal here is to address and integrate three priorities for practice and practice research—relevance, effectiveness, and efficiency. Methodological ground is constantly being transformed and an interprofessional agenda can stand at the center of it. As noted, we need to assess and expand our notions of not only how to gather evidence but also how evidence is defined and qualified. An interprofessional paradigm necessitates the use of collaborative approaches to research methods and design in order to best capture relevant data. This includes a process of "design[ing] client-centered outcomes that provide fair measures of impact, by determining evaluation criteria from the perspective of relevant audiences, especially clients" (Zlotnik et al. 1999:15). And here we emphasize our agreement with Gambrill (chapter 3, this volume) and others that it is imperative that we integrate consumers into every arena, as informed, and informing, participants. This suggests adding the proposal of a third-generation initiative to the idea of first- and second-generation partnerships (Briar-Lawson et al. 1997), that is, an overarching research agenda, in which we are mutually partnered in every respect with other professions/disciplines and client systems.

Methodologies that fit this approach to inquiry are necessarily participatory and include client systems throughout—defining the relevant issues and what outcomes constitute a valid change, how these outcomes might best be achieved and how the practices and processes used to get those results might be validated. It is about "beginning where the client is" methodologically. This has meaning for clients and practitioners far beyond the empowerment of individual client systems; it speaks to the full range of social work values and the profession's investment in social change.

Broadly, some of the methodologies that fit this approach are grounded theory development, concept mapping, innovative use of focus groups, and other participatory and liberatory models. For example, the theories of change framework (Weiss 1995) is a participatory model that evaluates mezzo and macro practice by bringing to the surface, in individual and group process, the active assumptions operating among all the parties involved in change initiatives. Another methodology that applies across a variety of contexts and levels of analysis is participatory action research (PAR). PAR builds on the work of Kurt Lewin, Paulo Freire, William Foote Whyte, and others (Bailey and Koney 2000:167) and is based on principles of co-inquiry, which "not only increases the usefulness of the process, but . . . also fosters internal ownership of both the process and its outcomes" (p. 169). Brydon-Miller (1997) notes, "PAR and other transformative practices . . . might allow us to address issues of social justice and knowledge generation in a more democratic and direct manner" (p. 658). This approach incorporates the notion that research in and of itself can serve to empower, to generate broad community and social change, and to affect the common good through creative partnerships in inquiry (p. 663). As Hooper-Briar and Lawson (1996a) state, "Democratized relationships and decision-making structures, which are requirements for successful partnerships, make 'action researchers' of vulnerable citizens and frontline professionals alike. They become the generators of knowledge about needs and outcomes—knowledge that informs strategies and decision making" (p. 175). In the long *and* the short run, these approaches are likely to be our most reliable and valid route to achieving social work's criteria of relevance, effectiveness, and efficiency.

INSTITUTIONAL SUPPORT: OPPORTUNITIES AND THREATS

In order to help develop and integrate interprofessionalism into the field of social work, making these value-added gains as opposed to lost opportunities, we need to garner more support from the legitimating bodies of the profession—those that authorize, credential, and fund organizations, institutions, educators, practitioners, and researchers. Therefore, the dynamics of legitimation need to continue to evolve. For example, the Council on Social Work Education (CSWE) has in recent years taken the initiative in supporting scholarly exploration of interprofessional collaboration (Hooper-Briar and Lawson 1996) and how it bears upon professional social work education and accreditation (Zlotnik et al. 1999). Perhaps in the future, the CSWE could play an ongoing role in encouraging and supporting interprofessional education and training models, particularly so that accreditation is tied to innovation *across* disciplinary boundaries as well as *within* social work, rather than potentially inhibiting it through silence. If necessary, new legitimating standards and institutions could be developed. The NASW could support continuing education for interprofessional training, and it could promote and support interprofessionalism through additions to the Code of Ethics. State licensing boards could begin trial periods for adding an interprofessional licensure status or even new licensure standards. Insurance groups could sanction interprofessional provider teams. Funders could support exploration of new practice models and research endeavors. Investing in opportunities such as these would also necessitate other kinds of support for interprofessional collaboration, such as integration into academic institutions through educational practices or consideration in tenure review.

In sum, social work that is effectively outcomes-oriented and seeking to develop the practice guidelines to support that needs to and can situate itself in relationship to and with interprofessionalism in practice, research, and education. It needs to and can be integrated into some part of *all* aspects of the profession in order to develop *interprofessional competence.*

The interprofessional paradigm, thus construed, is an optimal vehicle for the development of practice guidelines *informed by (and informing)* social work, to the extent that they are based on creative, intentional partnerships in practice, research, and education and stem from our strengths in the coordination of these cornerstones in ways that are client system centered. Opportunities abound; social work could contribute significantly to the development of evidence-based practice guidelines in an interprofessional context. It is perhaps ideally situated to do so—by value, skill, and knowledge base—as no other profession is at this time. We have a professional charge; interprofessionalism is, in essence, already a part of our mission as well as a call to leadership.

QUESTIONS: RAISED AND REMAINING

A laundry list of potential barriers and challenges also inevitably arises, particularly as the profession engages change and raises challenges to "business as usual," specifically with regard to practice guidelines and professional legitimation. Once again, we choose to phrase this as a series of questions for ongoing discussion, as the responses will necessarily evolve in context. For example, how do we work through resistance to change, which may be experienced by some of our colleagues? How do we deal with resistance and doubt in our legitimating organizations? How do we reconcile some of the different disciplinary values and systems for external reward? How would accountability for the process of developing practice guidelines be allocated, monitored, and evaluated? How would we determine disciplinary/intellectual ownership?

What would be likely resources for funding and how would funds be allocated? How might new technologies be creatively utilized to generate knowledge development and dissemination? And, finally, how do we ensure that our processes and priorities are truly focused on doing more good than harm (Gambrill 1997)? These questions are answerable, but only after an active and honest discourse, and in a climate of mutual commitment to better outcomes for the people, organizations, and communities we serve and in which we are embedded.

———

In an applied field, good research serves practice, helping us better understand and respond to social issues through evolution of best practices and a relevant knowledge base. Effective practice is served by research when we rigorously avoid simply *confirming* what we think we already know by collecting evidence to support answers, rather than *discovering* the evidence through a process of true inquiry. Evidence-based practice and practice guidelines can function on either agenda. The choice is one of accountability to what makes any profession truly legitimate in the context of sociocultural change. For social work, this is the defining context of social and economic justice, in which it is our responsibility to partner with any and all resources to foster desired change.

Today, the professions need to focus less on staking claims to the boundaries that identify them *against* other professions and more on exploring how implementation of disciplinary practices and boundaries needs to change to create better outcomes for client systems through more-inclusive, integrated partnerships. In an environment that is increasingly both globally and locally interconnected, new pathways need to be forged, with new values to which *all* professions can be mutually accountable in order to stay relevant, effective, and, therefore, legitimate.

If, in this search, we also assume a common purpose of discovery, manifested in positive outcomes to social problems through effective, empirically supported best practices and practice guidelines, then let us stay creative, open-minded, and smart about how we achieve those goals. Reproducing narrow models can result in the reproduction of narrow results and thereby undermine the discovery of authentic, innovative knowledge and ways of knowing. Let us instead find ways to link, and even redefine, disciplinary boundaries in intentional alliances with others, embracing discovery *along with* our sustainable claims for existing knowledge and a commitment to accountability.

We coexist in community with a number of professions charged with an ethic of service to others in a broad variety of contexts; and we coexist with those whom we are charged to serve. It is our common purpose that allies us—the alleviation of human suffering, improvement in the quality of life for individuals, families, organizations, and communities, and the advancement of social and economic justice. For this vision, we can all stand in service to change that supports better outcomes, and we can do it in partnership, if we remain wise and ethical in our search to balance consistency and innovation. The profession of social work, including the people and environments we serve, is ideally situated to embrace the creativity, mystery, and leadership that this future invites. The choice belongs to all of us.

REFERENCES

Abbott, A. (1988). *The Systems of Professions: An Essay on the Division of Expert Labor.* Chicago: University of Chicago Press.

Bailey, D., and Koney, K. M. (2000). *Strategic Alliances Among Health and Human Services Organizations: From Affiliations to Consolidations.* Thousand Oaks, Calif.: Sage.

Bakken, M. (1996). Building Responsive Universities and Helping Disciplines to Better Serve Children and Families. In K. Hooper-Briar and H. A. Lawson (Eds.), *Expanding Partnerships for Vulnerable Children, Youth, and Families* (pp. 166–173). Alexandria, Va.: Council on Social Work Education.

Briar-Lawson, K., Lawson, H. A., Collier, C., and Joseph, A. (1997). School-linked comprehensive services: Promising beginnings, lessons learned, and future challenges. *Social Work in Education, 19* (3), 136–148.

Brydon-Miller, M. (1997). Participatory action research: Psychology and social change. *Journal of Social Issues, 53* (4), 657–666.

Corrigan, D., and Bishop, K. K. (1997). Creating family-centered integrated service systems and interprofessional educational programs to implement them. *Social Work in Education, 19* (3), 149–163.

Dryfoos, J. G. (1998). *Safe Passage: Making It Through Adolescence in a Risky Society.* New York: Oxford University Press.

Fortune, A. E., and Reid, W. J. (1999). *Research in Social Work* (3d ed.). New York: Columbia University Press.

Gambrill, E. (1997). *Social Work Practice: A Critical Thinker's Guide.* New York: Oxford University Press.

Graham, J. R., and Barter, K. (1999). Collaboration: A social work practice model. *Families in Society, 80* (1), 6–13.

Hogan, P. (1996). Transforming Professional Education. In K. Hooper-Briar and H. A. Lawson (Eds.), *Expanding Partnerships for Vulnerable Children, Youth, and Families* (pp. 222–230). Alexandria, Va.: Council on Social Work Education.

Hooper-Briar, K., and Lawson, H. A. (Eds.) (1996a). *Expanding Partnerships for Vulnerable Children, Youth, and Families.* Alexandria, Va.: Council on Social Work Education.

———. (1996b). Facilitating Responsiveness in Colleges and Universities. In K. Hooper-Briar and H. A. Lawson (Eds.), *Expanding Partnerships for Vulnerable Children, Youth, and Families* (pp. 174–175). Alexandria, Va.: Council on Social Work Education.

Jackson, V. H. (1999). Clinical practice guidelines: Should social work develop them? *Research on Social Work Practice, 9* (3), 331–337.

Mayden, R. (1996). An Interdisciplinary Approach to Child Welfare Education. In K. Hooper-Briar and H. A. Lawson (Eds.), *Expanding Partnerships for Vulnerable Children, Youth, and Families* (pp. 141–144). Alexandria, Va.: Council on Social Work Education.

Roberts, R. N., Rule, S. and Innocenti, M. S. (1998). *Strengthening the Family-Professional Partnerships in Services for Young Children.* Baltimore: Paul H. Brookes.

Wallerstein, E. (1995). What are we bounding, and whom, when we bound social research. *Social Research, 62,* 839–856.

Weiss, C. H. (1995). Nothing as Practical as Good Theory: Exploring Theory-Based Evaluation for Comprehensive Community Initiatives for Children and Families. In J. P. Connell, A. C. Kubisch, L. B. Schorr, and C. H. Weiss (Eds.), *New Approaches to Evaluating Community Initiatives: Concepts, Methods, and Contexts* (pp. 65–92). Queenstown, Md.: Aspen Institute Roundtable on Comprehensive Community Initiatives for Children and Families.

Zlotnik, J. L., McCroskey, J., Gardner, S., Gil de Gibaja, M., Taylor, H. P., George, J., Lind, J., Jordan-Marsh, M., Costa, V. B., and Taylor-Dinwiddle, S. (Project Collaborators). (1999). *Myths and Opportunities: An Examination of the Impact of Discipline-Specific Accreditation on Interprofessional Education.* Alexandria, Va.: Council on Social Work Education.

PART V

CONCLUSION

16

ADVANCING THE DEVELOPMENT OF SOCIAL WORK PRACTICE GUIDELINES: DIRECTIONS FOR RESEARCH

ENOLA K. PROCTOR AND AARON ROSEN

D ebate about practice guidelines for social work has focused not only on their desirability (Thyer, chapter 7, this volume) but also on the profession's readiness to develop them. Indeed, serious questions surround social work's current capacity to generate the research needed for formulating guidelines. As Kirk succinctly stated: "Practice guidelines are only as good as the knowledge base" that underlies them (Kirk 1999:309). Because practice guidelines need to be based upon a relatively strong body of tested evidence, the profession's progress toward developing them will depend largely upon the extent and quality of its research activity. The conduct of more and better intervention research is imperative in order to meet the knowledge needs of practice.

With knowledge for practice our overriding concern, this chapter outlines some of the primary elements of an agenda for research that we propose should guide the development, testing, refinement, and implementation of guidelines for social work intervention. Of course, it is implausible that social work, or any other field, will find its knowledge needs fully satisfied by existing research at any point in time. Rather, consistent with our view of the process of guideline development and refinement as iterative (Proctor and Rosen, chapter 6, this volume), we believe that the articulation and use of practice guidelines serves to reveal additional needs for and gaps in knowledge, which in turn point to directions for further research.

As noted in preceding chapters (Howard and Jenson, chapter 5, and Thyer, chapter 7, this volume), allied professional groups have made considerable progress in the research for and formulation of guidelines, many of

The preparation of this paper was supported in part by the Center for Mental Health Services Research (NIMH Grant MH50857), Washington University, and by a Faculty Research Award from the George Warren Brown School of Social Work.

which are also relevant to social work practice (e.g., depression, eating disorders). Therefore, the undertaking of research and guidelines development by and for social work was viewed as redundant and ill advised (Thyer, chapter 7, this volume). Although we strongly advocate social workers' use of research knowledge developed by other professions, as appropriate, such knowledge is often not sufficient for the needs of social work practice. For in addition to dealing with issues in common, social workers strive also to attain outcomes that either are not or are less likely to be addressed by allied professions—for example, outcomes that focus on enhanced social functioning, improved interpersonal relationships, and securing services and resources.

Kirk also noted that existing guidelines typically have gaps and do not sufficiently inform the decision-making needs of social work practitioners in areas of high relevancy to social work (Kirk 1999). Even in mental health, where guidelines developed by allied professions proliferate, considerable further guidelines development is needed to address the concerns of social work. While such work is clearly social work's "turf" and responsibility, this does not exclude active collaboration with allied fields in intervention research and in guidelines development in areas of common interest (Rosen and Proctor, chapter 1, this volume).

A RESEARCH AGENDA FOR GUIDELINES DEVELOPMENT

The development of practice guidelines with the function and structure that we envisioned (Proctor and Rosen, chapter 6, this volume) requires that social work research be rationalized and organized in a manner that best supports such an undertaking. Developing such guidelines necessitates the formulation of a clearly articulated, comprehensive, substantially differentiated, and long-range research agenda to counter the currently prevailing piecemeal approach to intervention research by social workers (Rosen, Proctor, and Staudt 1999, 2003). Such an agenda will serve to stimulate and guide sustained research initiatives, as well as provide a framework for interrelating and integrating findings from discrete ongoing studies in social work and related fields. This chapter outlines an agenda for research that, in our view, is necessary if social work is to efficiently progress in the development, dissemination, implementation, and continual revision of practice guidelines. We identify and organize our proposed agenda in terms of three distinct, yet interrelated domains of research and other activities, with an emphasis on identifying issues for research, but in doing so we may occasionally address methodological issues as well.

DOMAINS OF ACTIVITIES FOR DEVELOPMENT OF PRACTICE GUIDELINES

In chapter 6 we outlined our conception of the research and related activities that should be undertaken as part of the profession's effort to develop practice guidelines. We suggested a model encompassing three interrelated and interacting domains of activity clusters—the building-blocks cluster, the consolidation cluster, and the dissemination and utilization cluster. Here, that model serves as a point of departure for further explication of the suggested agenda for research, and is presented as figure 16.1.

Each of the activity clusters in the model has unique products and functions, yet all three clusters are interdependent and iterative.

BUILDING-BLOCKS RESEARCH

The first cluster of developmental activities for practice guidelines consists primarily of research devoted to formulating and testing the basic knowledge components that are necessary for assembling preliminary guidelines. Hence we characterize this cluster of activities as "development of building blocks." Although we'll discuss research in the building-blocks cluster first, and in a certain logical order, research activities within and between clusters are likely to be concurrent, and all research should be informed by the relevant activities in any of the clusters.

We propose three types of "building blocks" research products as necessary for preliminary formulation of practice guidelines: (1) delineation of the target outcomes for social work intervention and of their priorities for research; (2) empirically tested and supported interventions that are efficacious for attaining their targeted outcomes; and (3) testing and adaptation of interventions for maximal effectiveness in relation to diversity in client characteristics and variability in practice situations.

TARGETS OF SOCIAL WORK INTERVENTION

Each practice guideline is constructed in an effort to organize for practitioners the best existing knowledge for addressing some target, usually referred to as a condition, a problem, or (preferably, in our view) a desired outcome (Proctor, Rosen, and Rhee 2002). Accordingly, social work must identify the outcomes it pursues in order to develop effective interventions for their attainment. Specific outcomes need to be further classified and organized in terms of

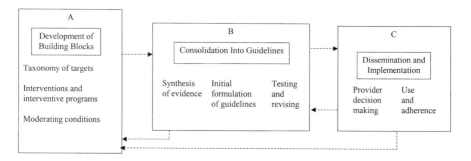

FIGURE 16.1   Activity Clusters in Guidelines Development

more general outcome categories and target domains (Proctor, Rosen, and Rhee 2002; Rosen, Proctor, and Staudt 2003). Hence, the building-block research related to targets of intervention should lead to delineation of the outcomes pursued in social work practice, classification of outcomes, and deciding on an order of priorities among the outcomes for the development of appropriate interventions.

Delineating social work outcomes may be approached from two perspectives—each with its attendant research implications (Proctor and Rosen 2001). The first perspective is that of current practice, assessing the nature and the prevalence of outcomes actually pursued by practitioners, for different client populations and in various practice settings. Such research may use practice research networks (PRNs) of practitioners who systematically provide data on their practice and clients (Williams and Lanigan 1999) or other methodologies. The other perspective would seek to identify salient outcomes for social work to pursue whether or not the outcomes are reflected in current practice. Salient social work outcomes can be identified through need surveys of various population segments. Consistent with our view of ultimate outcomes as the goals for treatment (Rosen and Proctor 1981), Foster and Mash (1999) recently advocated that the "social validity" of the target outcomes of treatment be determined—that is, the acceptability and importance of treatment outcomes to various client populations.

Outcomes pursued with individual clients are typically formulated in client- and situation-specific terms. Such outcome terms are likely to be too numerous and too specific for a profession-wide taxonomy of the targets of intervention. The specific outcomes need to be summarized into higher-order and more-inclusive classifications in order to organize interventive knowledge appropriately and efficiently. Our previous studies of outcomes and their classification suggested two levels of generality beyond the specific outcomes—outcome categories and target domains, the most general (Proctor, Rosen, and Rhee 2002; Rosen, Proctor, and Staudt 2003). In these studies we derived empirically forty outcome categories that were included in eight target domains. Classification of specific outcomes can also be informed by values, policy, mandates of service agencies, and conceptual considerations. Because the salient outcomes and their classifications may vary in relation to varying population groups and practice settings, developing population and/or setting specific target classifications should be considered, as also implied by Kirk (chapter 8, this volume).

Clearly, social work cannot attend concurrently and with dispatch to all of its many and varied practice research needs, including development of practice guidelines for intervention. Research efforts therefore must be focused and resources allocated selectively, according to a rationalized order of priorities. Because we recommend that practice guidelines be organized according to the targeted outcomes, establishing priorities for intervention research among the targets should be a pressing concern. It is important to assess the volume and adequacy of existing intervention research; to consider, by both professional and general social values criteria the saliency and social costs of related needs and problems; to take into account the prevalence of outcomes pursued in practice; and to weigh the benefits that accrue when outcomes are attained. And, of course, professional values must also influence the setting of priorities.

RESEARCH ON INTERVENTION EFFECTIVENESS

Testing the effectiveness of interventions to achieve specified outcomes is perhaps the most obvious research activity for producing the building blocks of practice guidelines, as the core of practice guidelines should be arrays of interventions whose effectiveness has been demonstrated (Proctor and Rosen, chapter 6, this volume). Although social work has made some progress toward a body of building-blocks research (Reid and Fortune, chapter 4, this volume), we found that, overall, intervention studies were the focus of only a fraction of social work research. A review of research published in thirteen social work journals over a five-year period revealed that only 14 percent of the total research published was related to effectiveness of interventions (Rosen, Proctor, and Staudt 1999).

The production of knowledge that can inform interventions and guide efforts to attain client-related outcomes is a critical foundation for practice guidelines and a central responsibility of human service professions. Expressing a similar view, the Task Force on Social Work Research (1991) observed,

"There is a substantial body of social, behavioral, and biological research on many of the underlying causes of the human problems social workers address. But there are many gaps in our knowledge about 'what works'—that is, about the most effective . . . means of helping" (p. 4). Similarly advocating more intense efforts to develop and test effective interventions were McMahon, Reisch, and Patti (1991), Schilling (1997), and Ell (1996). So that the implications of such commitment would not be underestimated, a respected researcher in clinical psychology estimated that more than six thousand clinical trial studies are needed to derive one "empirically validated treatment" for a particular disorder (Parloff 1982, cited in Goldfried and Wolfe 1996).

To yield knowledge that is useful to practitioners and appropriate for inclusion in practice guidelines, interventions need to be tested in relation to important ultimate outcomes, consistent with their priority (as discussed above). Historically, social work research has not differentiated between outcomes in terms of their role in treatment, ultimate or intermediate, and has focused disproportionately on evaluating interventions in relation to attaining intermediate outcomes (Proctor 1982). In addition to a more discriminating focus on ultimate outcomes, studies also need to address the frequently targeted intermediate outcomes and test specific interventions to attain them (Proctor and Rosen, chapter 6, this volume).

Once the targeted outcomes are identified, attention must focus on formulating the interventions most likely to effectively attain them. In other words, clinical hypotheses that causally link interventions to outcomes must be formulated and investigated. A number of sources of knowledge may be used (often in tandem) for formulating clinical hypotheses about effective interventions. Theoretical propositions regarding human behavior and the process of behavior change have traditionally been utilized as a source for formulating and testing clinical hypotheses (intervention-outcome links). Another source is the so-called practice wisdom (Scott 1990). Our view and past research indicate that all practitioners' behaviors that are directed toward outcome attainment are guided by clinical hypotheses supported in large part by practice wisdom. That practice wisdom is often implicit, unscrutinizable, and based on varied and often unknown sources (Reid and Fortune 1992; Rosen 1994; Rosen et al. 1995). As Zeira and Rosen (2000) have recently shown, the clinical hypotheses embedded in workers' practice wisdom can be explicated, yielding practice-relevant and practitioner-credible hypotheses to guide research on intervention.

Another source of clinical hypotheses for systematic testing is the direct feedback that could be obtained from workers in the process of implementing practice guidelines as we have conceived them (Proctor and Rosen, chapter 6, this volume). In the implementation component (fourth) of the guidelines, workers continuously evaluate outcome attainment and are encouraged to improvise on and modify the preformulated intervention as needed in order to maximally attain the desired outcome. Systematic collection of such information will yield not only evidence on the "in the field" effectiveness of already formulated interventions but also practice-based new clinical hypotheses. All of that information should be utilized for further research and guidelines development by being centrally accumulated through a practice research network (PRN) (Rosen 2002). Of course, a not-to-be-neglected source of practice hypotheses for adaptation and testing is those that were tested and supported by allied professions for outcomes and/or in contexts that somewhat diverge from the concerns of social work.

All intervention concepts contained in clinical hypotheses must be clearly specified in terms of their behavioral components in order to be amenable to empirical testing and replication, and to reliable implementation in practice (Proctor and Rosen, chapter 6, this volume; Rosen and Proctor 1978). Our review of published intervention research indicated that fewer than half of the studies (42%) defined the interventions sufficiently clearly to enable replication (Rosen, Proctor, and Staudt 1999). If building-blocks research is to cumulatively contribute to the development of intervention knowledge, it must concentrate on better specification and measurement of the components of interventions.

In order to attain the targeted ultimate outcome, most treatments are more complex than using one discrete intervention in relation to a single outcome. Treatments typically consist of interventive programs that contain a number of intermediate outcomes and the interventions necessary to attain them that must be employed, as a package, in order to reach the desired outcome (Rosen and Proctor 1978). Consequently, building-blocks research is needed to formulate and then to test the effectiveness of not only discrete interventions but also complex interventive programs. Research and development methodologies (Thomas 1984; Rothman 1980; Rothman and Thomas 1994) may be particularly suitable for generating and testing interventive programs.

Formulation and testing of interventions must also address issues of optimal dosage, timing, and ordering of the specific intervention components. Dose-effect relationships, as these issues are called, have been much studied in medicine, but only recently addressed in relation to social-psychological interventions, perhaps because this kind of intervention so often lacks operational specificity (Proctor and Rosen, chapter 6, this volume; Rosen, Proctor, and Staudt 2003). Particularly for interventive programs, practice guidelines should indicate the temporal ordering of component outcomes and interventions; and for all interventions, the optimal weights of components in terms of frequency, duration, or intensity need to be specified (Rosen and Proctor 1978). Hypotheses regarding dose-effect relationships need to be explicated, tested, and incorporated into practice guidelines.

In summary, the following steps are involved in research to develop efficacious interventive programs:

- explication of the treatment plans, delineating and ordering the intermediate outcomes that are necessary for attaining targeted ultimate outcomes (see Rosen and Proctor 1978)
- detailing and testing the interventions for attaining the intermediate outcomes
- determining the optimal dose-effect relationships for the component interventions and evaluating the efficacy of the interventive program, as constructed, for attaining the ultimate outcome

ADAPTING INTERVENTIONS TO CLIENT AND PRACTICE DIVERSITY

Research must address the effectiveness of interventions for the diverse client populations and service conditions that characterize social work practice. Although interventions can have common applicability across a variety of client populations and situations, for maximal effectiveness they should also be tested and adapted to client and situation variability on treatment-relevant dimensions (Rosen and Proctor, chapter 1, this volume). Intervention efficacy studies must be followed by rigorous field testing of the generalizability and the effectiveness of these hypotheses for the diverse conditions and population of social work practice. Studies of effectiveness will often involve altering the doses and order of components to adapt purportedly efficacious interventions for best fit with the needs of different client groupings (Newman 2000).

Part III of the book addressed the need for practice guidelines to be responsive to such factors as client culture, gender, age, personality, capacity, and race from a variety of perspectives (Peebles-Wilkins and Amodeo, chapter 12; Videka, chapter 10; Zayas, chapter 11). There is also no doubt that if practitioners are to choose to use practice guidelines, the guidelines must enable them to maximally particularize and address the individual needs of their clients. Thus, research to refine and adapt general guidelines to the needs of identifiable client groupings will render guidelines more useful to practitioners and will also support social work's commitment of service to diverse clienteles.

CONSOLIDATION AND SYNTHESIS

We characterize the second cluster of activities in development of practice guidelines as one of consolidation and synthesis—in which evidence regarding effective interventions is assembled, synthesized, and formulated into practice guidelines for practitioners. Two general approaches to consolidation of research findings may be distinguished—critical reviews and consensus panels. Critical reviews range in structure from systematic literature reviews to formal meta-analyses that statistically analyze the results of samples of studies in given areas. In consolidating research results for the purpose of formulating practice guidelines, the primary aim is to review systematically and assess critically the evidentiary base of various interventions. The products of such reviews should be statements on the state of evidence about best practices and acknowledgment of the limits of the evidence (Drake et al. 2001; Ioannidis and Lau 2000), thus highlighting gaps in knowledge and stimulating further research. Critical reviews follow systematic and explicit criteria for assessing individual studies (Balas and Boren 1999), as well as a methodology for the conduct of the review, as that recently proposed by the Campbell Collaboration, for example (Campbell Collaboration Steering Committee 2001).

Locating studies and determining criteria for their inclusion in the body of evidence to be assessed are the essential first steps. The operative inclusion and exclusion criteria are consequential. For example, conclusions about effective treatments will assume greater credibility in reviews that include only studies of randomized clinical trials (RCT) as compared with reviews that also include case studies with less rigorous designs. Certainly, decisions on the criteria for inclusion of studies in critical reviews will be influenced by the nature of the body of evidence available for review (Schulberg and Rush 1994). In a recent symposium devoted to critical reviews of research in five areas of social work practice, the criteria used for inclusion varied considerably in relation to the volume and quality of research in a given area (Rosen, Proctor, and Howard 2002).

Although consensus panels may be viewed as another approach to consolidation, they often complement and go beyond critical reviews of research by using their findings for formulating specific practice guidelines for particular topics. Unlike systematic reviews, which have as their primary function presenting the state of evidence in an area, the aim of consensus panels is often to recommend "best practices," which may entail going beyond the evidence. Hence, the goals of consensus panels are not only to formulate "best practices" but also potentially to influence their use. When panel members are acknowledged experts and also opinion leaders in realms relevant to practice, the influence over guidelines' use can be enhanced (Rogers 1995).

Our position is that in formulating guidelines, panels should first and foremost rely on persuasive research evidence regarding the effectiveness of interventions in relation to outcomes. Only then, and only with agreed-upon explicit criteria, should they critically evaluate the strength of, discuss, and rate the available evidence. Such criteria may involve demonstrated effect sizes of an intervention, the range and results of replication studies, and the demonstrated durability of effects over time. But consensus panels often use considerations other than those based on research—such as drawing upon theory, case studies, and clinical experience. Other considerations may include the cost and feasibility of interventions and the likelihood of acceptance by clients and practitioners. Panel members' biases and those prevailing in a particular field are more likely to be involved in nonresearch considerations (Drake et al. 2001). Obviously, the process of arriving at consensus among panel members with varying orientations and preferences is also political and likely requires compromises. The synthesizing process and formulation of practice guidelines therefore should be pursued with caution, especially in view of consensus panels' important gatekeeping function in influencing practice.

Consistent with processes of R and D and developmental research (Rothman 1980; Rothman and Thomas 1994), guidelines, interventive programs, and their components must be subjected to testing and further adaptation (repeatedly if necessary) as an integrated operating system in the field. The process should also involve effectiveness studies with varying populations and service settings. We think that a recursive development and testing process can be materially enhanced by obtaining ongoing feedback from practitioners on implementation, adaptation, and evaluation in practice, coupled with central accumulation of these experiences via PRNs (Proctor and Rosen, chapter 6, this volume).

In summary, guidelines development requires a systematic, progressive, and continual process of consolidating, synthesizing, and formulating the results of discrete studies of intervention into practice guidelines containing interventive programs and reflecting the evidentiary support for their effectiveness under different circumstances. Whereas focused activity by researchers can generate building-blocks knowledge, consolidation and synthesis of those products into practice guidelines will also require organized and systematic efforts in partnerships with high-expertise practice opinion leaders.

DISSEMINATION AND UTILIZATION

The third cluster of activities in the process of guidelines development concerns a gamut of issues relating to practitioners' use and appropriate implementation in practice of empirically based guidelines. As previously noted, "utilization of research findings has been a persistent concern for science-based professions in general, and more recently, and perhaps with greater saliency, to the human helping professions" (Rosen 1983:1). The history of guidelines use in other fields, particularly medicine, demonstrates that no profession can assume that evidence-based practices or guidelines, once developed, will be easily disseminated to providers, adopted, and applied consistently. Rather, the dissemination and adoption of innovative practice guidelines constitute a considerable challenge and pose important research questions (Hoagwood et al. 2001). We address here research efforts to enhance utilization of research-based knowledge in practice from four different, yet broad and interrelated, foci of inquiry: dissemination and transmission of guidelines to practitioners; practitioner acceptance of research-based guides to practice; the actual use and the fidelity of guideline implementation; and inquiry into the auspices and the processes through which the use of evidence-based guides to practice can be legitimated for practitioners.

DISSEMINATION AND TRANSMISSION

Although transmission is often subsumed under dissemination, we distinguish between the two concepts because we believe that they involve different processes. Whereas "dissemination" concerns the source (auspices), form, and means through which knowledge is "sent out" from producers or compilers, "transmission" involves the intended consumers, focusing on whether that knowledge actually reaches them. But dissemination and transmission need to be studied in tandem, addressing the relation of variability in the former to the latter. Hence, inquiry into guidelines' dissemination source (e.g., NASW, government agency, third-party insurer), form (e.g., guidelines including supporting rationales as compared with summary statements only), and means (e.g., via newsletters, Web sites, journals) should be in relation to the efficacy of transmission to the intended consumers.

Indeed, two recent surveys on attitudes toward evidence-based guides (practice guidelines and treatment manuals) highlight the importance of transmission as a separate concept. Mullen and Bacon (2001) found that about 57 percent of the social workers and 19 percent of the clinical psychologists that they surveyed had not heard of practice guidelines. In a national survey of clinical psychologists' attitudes toward treatment manuals, Addis and Krasnow (2000) found that 23 percent have not heard of them. These findings underscore the fact that published and disseminated materials alone are insufficient for transmission—making practitioners aware of their existence.

Research needs to address and compare the relative effectiveness of different auspices, forms, and means of practice guidelines' dissemination to the actual transmission of that information.

PRACTITIONER ACCEPTANCE OF GUIDELINES

Effective dissemination and transmission to practitioners is a necessary, yet insufficient, component in the process that leads from guideline production to implementation. A major challenge in that process is increasing practitioners' acceptance of the appropriateness and legitimacy of evidence-based guidelines for making treatment decisions. Clinical psychologists were divided on whether treatment manuals made a positive or negative contribution to treatment (Addis and Krasnow 2000). The social workers surveyed by Mullen and Bacon were positive toward consensus-based practice guidelines, but they generally devaluated empirically based guidelines (Mullen and Bacon, chapter 13, this volume). A number of avenues for enhancing acceptance by practitioners of evidence-based guides merit consideration and systematic evaluation.

As suggested elsewhere, practitioner acceptance of research-based evidence (in contrast to intuitive, personally validated knowledge) as the preferred foundation for clinical decisions is particularly tenuous in a profession like social work, where the problems that practitioners address in their professional roles are very similar to those that they face in daily life as laypersons, often quite successfully. This similarity is conducive to practitioners' reliance on modes of lay functioning in professional contexts (Rosen 1996). Consequently, it is important to clearly distinguish between lay and professional modes of functioning, and to shift away from use of tacit knowledge acquired uncritically (the lay mode, cf. Reber 1993) to the use of evidence-based, rational decision making. Therefore, a major challenge for social work research is to investigate how to instill in practitioners attitudes and habits of thought that will lead them to accept and prefer evidence-based and explicit decision making in professional contexts.

In the quest for practitioner acceptance of evidence-based guidelines it is also important to investigate means of enhancing the influence of relevant practice opinion leaders on practitioners' acceptance of guidelines. For example, the role of agency supervisors in influencing acceptance of guidelines needs to be further studied, as suggested by findings of Mullen and Bacon (chapter 13, this volume). Studies in Great Britain of the process of promoting transfer of research evidence to medical practice highlight the variety of opinion leaders and roles, and the complexity of affecting clinicians' practice (Locock et al.

2001). Researchers in the field of medical decision making have developed methodologies for assessing stakeholders' preferences, or "utilities," and advocate their incorporation into guideline-related initiatives to enhance guideline acceptance (Miyamoto 2000). Social work researchers may likewise explore means for enhancing practitioners' perceived utilities attendant to the use of evidence-based guidelines. For example, the perceived personal utility to practitioners of using guidelines may increase if using them is included in the criteria for job advancement; and a clearer explication of the linkage between the use of guidelines and the attainment of client outcomes may contribute to their perceived professional utility.

Social work can also investigate the applicability of strategies for practitioner acceptance of guidelines by studying this factor in related fields. "Passive" dissemination, such as mailing information directly to providers, was somewhat effective in increasing awareness of desired behaviors but was generally ineffective in changing provider behavior, whereas programs of educational outreach, provider reminders, and multifaceted interventions were thought to be more promising (Grimshaw et al. 2001). And "academic detailing"—the active engagement of an information disseminator with the provider—was found in pharmaceutical research to be an effective means of enhancing reliance on practice guidelines (Soumerai and Avorn 1990).

THE USE OF GUIDELINES AND FIDELITY OF IMPLEMENTATION

Practitioners' acceptance of evidence-based guidelines as professionally legitimate and desirable is only a necessary first step. They still face complex challenges in the appropriate use of guidelines in practice. Some of the primary issues are engaging in a rational, systematic, and critical clinical decision-making process; selecting the appropriate guidelines for implementation; implementing interventions and interventive programs with the requisite consistency and fidelity; and satisfactory resolution of the uncertainty that accompanies "idiographic application of normative generalizations." We mentioned these challenges in our introductory chapter (Rosen and Proctor, chapter 1, this volume) and addressed them conceptually through our proposed structure for practice guidelines (Proctor and Rosen, chapter 6, this volume), but for progress to be made, they must be addressed by focused and cumulative programs of inquiry.

Reliable and valid application of research findings is at the core of using evidence-based practice guidelines critically. Because clinical judgment and rational decision making are vulnerable to many systematic and random errors, we cannot assume that practitioners engage critically in clinical application of evidence-based standardized interventions without assistance (Kuhn, Amsel, and O'Loughlin 1988; Wilson and Brekke 1994). Accordingly, social work needs to recognize the importance of, and invest in development of, decision-support tools to aid practitioners to engage critically in ongoing practice decisions. A number of decision-support procedures have been tried, and more need to be developed. For example, Systematic Planned Practice (SPP) was formulated and used as a decision aid to enhance explicit, reasoned, and critical planning, implementation, and evaluation of treatment (Rosen 1992, 1993; Rosen et al. 1993). In general, structured records (paper or electronic) can prompt practitioners to make explicit and reasoned decisions and, as in practice guidelines, may help them to choose among arrays of alternative treatments. Tools that guide practitioners through detailed steps of the decision-making process are widely viewed as reducing error variance, ensuring greater accountability, and bolstering practitioner authority when treatment decisions are scrutinized by peer review or by payers (Gottlieb 1989; Talbott 1990).

There can be no doubt that a critical area for research is the development of tools that promote consistency and fidelity (integrity) in the implementation of evidence-based guidelines (Waltz et al. 1993). In a review of social work research Rosen, Proctor, and Staudt (1999) found that most studies did not specify or detail interventions sufficiently to allow for research replication or reliable implementation in practice. Fraser addresses these issues and reflects on the importance of detailed treatment manuals that contain implementation protocols and guides for session content as necessary supports to evidence-based practice in general and to the use of practice guidelines in particular (Fraser, chapter 2, this volume).

A formidable challenge both to the acceptance of research-based guidelines and to their use, we believe, is the uncertainty that accompanies probabilistic scientific knowledge in general and its tenuous applicability to the individual client in particular. The last component in our proposed four-component practice guidelines for intervention is aimed at helping practitioners to address this challenge constructively (Proctor and Rosen, chapter 6, this volume). This component is conceived to guide practitioners through an algorithm for systematic and critical implementation of the best-fitting intervention available in the guidelines for a given client. It acknowledges that uncertainty remains, and it encourages adaptations and improvisations on the intervention, drawing upon the practitioner's experience and "practice wisdom." Practitioners are also guided in this implementation process through ongoing and recursive evaluations of the outcomes, combining elements from systematic planned practice (SPP) and single-system designs (Rosen 2002). Research must focus on further development and testing of support tools to help practitioners cope with the challenges that are inherent in application of evidence-based practice guidelines and other standardized interventions to individual clients.

PROFESSIONAL LEGITIMATION AND SANCTION

In preceding chapters Jeanne Marsh, and Nina Aronoff and Darlyne Bailey (chapter 14 and 15, respectively) underscore the professional and interprofessional contexts that can influence both the development of practice guidelines and their use in practice. There is little doubt that research must focus on the role and likely influence of professional and service organizations, and of other relevant sources of authority or persuasion, on the acceptance and use of practice guidelines. How does endorsement or encouragement by professional organizations, agencies, and educational institutions affect practitioners' adoption of guidelines? For guideliness to be maximally utilized, under whose auspices and in what circumstances should they be developed, disseminated, and endorsed? Is endorsement sufficient, or should the use of practice guidelines be mandated, and if so, by whom? What is the influence on adoption of advocacy by consumer groups (e.g., the National Alliance for the Mentally Ill), and under what circumstances should such be sought? These are some of the issues that need to be addressed by research in the quest for furthering the use of guidelines through the support and endorsement by the variety of auspices that make up the context of social work practice.

————

This chapter outlined a relatively comprehensive and long-term agenda for the research required for development, testing, dissemination, and adoption of practice guidelines for intervention. Practice guidelines do not represent the "end state" of knowledge development. Rather, by capitalizing on and formulating what is known, guidelines also underscore what is not known. The use of guidelines by practitioners will undoubtedly reveal knowledge gaps, generate new uncertainty, and lead to more research questions. Indeed, as suggested throughout this chapter, guidelines development requires a sustained program of research to test, refine, update, revise, and reformulate existing guidelines and to develop new ones. Hence, because guidelines have inherent limitations and are subject to obsolescence as new knowledge is gained, all guidelines and their components should be viewed only as provisional, ever subject to reexamination, revision, and replacement. The research arm of the profession, together with professional organizations, should assume the responsibility of institutionalizing processes for review, updating, and sanctioning of guidelines.

Although the scope and implications of the proposed agenda for research to develop practice guidelines may seem daunting, we think that the social work profession is ready for practice guidelines and its researchers are capable of engaging in the process of their development. Pursuing an explicit and overarching research agenda for guidelines development will enable researchers to be more focused on and responsive to the needs of practice, and more attuned to and informed by relevant research in related professions. We presented our outline for a research agenda not to discourage but to stimulate, direct, and energize social work research toward what we believe to be critical knowledge needs of the field.

REFERENCES

Addis, M. E., and Krasnow, A. D. (2000). A national survey of practicing psychologists' attitudes toward psychotherapy treatment manuals. *Journal of Consulting and Clinical Psychology, 68,* 331–339.

Balas, E. A., and Boren, S. A. (1999). Clinical Trials of Information Interventions. In E. S. Berner (Ed.), *Clinical Decision Support Systems: Theory and Practice* (pp. 199–216). New York: Springer.

Campbell Collaboration Steering Committee. (2001). Guidelines for the Preparation of Review Protocols. (1.0 ed.) [Brochure]. Philadelphia, Pa.: University of Pennsylvania.

Drake, R. E., Goldman, H. H., Leff, H. S., Lehman, A. F., Dixon, L., Mueser, K. T., and Torrey, W. C. (2001). Implementing evidence-based practices in routine mental health service settings. *Psychiatric Services, 52* (2), 179–182.

Ell, K. (1996). Social work and health care practice and policy: A psychosocial research agenda. *Social Work, 41* (6), 583–592.

Foster, S. L., and Mash, E. J. (1999). Assessing social validity in clinical treatment research: Issues and procedures. *Journal of Consulting and Clinical Psychology, 67,* 308–319.

Goldfried, M. R., and Wolfe, B. E. (1996). Psychotherapy practice and research: Repairing a strained relationship. *American Psychologist, 51,* 1007–1016.

Gottlieb, G. L. (1989). Diversity, Uncertainty, and Variations in Practice: The Behaviors and Clinical Decision Making of Mental Health Care Providers. In C. A. Taube, D. E. Mechanic, and A. A. Hohmann (Eds.), *The Future of Mental Health Services* (pp. 225–251). Washington, D.C.: U.S. Government Printing Office.

Grimshaw, J. M., Shirran, L., Thomas, R., Mowatt, G., Fraser, C., Bero, L., Grilli, R., Harvey, E., Oxman, A., and O'Brien, M. A. (2001). Changing provider behavior: An overview of systematic reviews of interventions. *Medical Care, 39* (8), 112–145.

Hoagwood, K., Burns, B. J., Kiser, L., Ringeisen, H., and Schoenwald, S. K. (2001). Evidence-based practice in child and adolescent mental health services. *Psychiatric Services, 52* (9), 1179–1189.

Ioannidis, J. P. A., and Lau, J. (2000). Evidence-Based Medicine: A Quantitative Approach to Decision Making. In G. B. Chapman and F. A. Sonnenberg (Eds.), *Decision Making in Health Care* (pp. 110–144). Cambridge: Cambridge University Press.

Kirk, S. A. (1999). Good intentions are not enough: Practice guidelines for social work. *Research on Social Work Practice, 9,* 302–310.

Kuhn, D., Amsel, E., and O'Loughlin, M. (1988). *The Development of Scientific Thinking Skills.* San Diego: Academic Press.

Locock, L., Dopson, S., Chambers, D., and Gabbay, J. (2001). Understanding the role of opinion leaders in improving clinical effectiveness. *Social Science and Medicine, 53,* 745–757.

McMahon, M. O., Reisch, M., and Patti, R. J. (Eds.). (1991). *Scholarship in Social Work: Integration of Research, Teaching, and Service.* Washington, D.C.: National Association of Deans and Directors of Schools of Social Work.

Miyamoto, J. M. (2000). Utility Assessment Under Expected Utility and Rank-Dependent Utility Assumptions. In G. B. Chapman and F. A. Sonnenberg (Eds.), *Decision Making in Health Care* (pp. 65–109). Cambridge: Cambridge University Press.

Mullen, E. J., and Bacon, W. F. (2001). A survey of practitioner adoption and implementation of practice guidelines and evidence based treatments. National Institute for Social Work, London. Retrieval available from http://www.intsoceval.networkshop .htm.

Mu$oz, R. F., Hollon, S. D., McGrath, E., Rehn, L. P., and Vandenbos, G. R. (1994). On the ACHPR depression in primary care guidelines: Further considerations for practitioners. *American Psychologist, 49,* 42–61.

Newman, M. G. (2000). Recommendations for a cost-offset model of a psychotherapy allocation using generalized anxiety disorder as an example. *Journal of Consulting and Clinical Psychology, 68* (4), 549–555.

Proctor, E. K. (1982). Defining the worker-client relationship. *Social Work, 27* (5), 430–435.

———. (2001). Building and consolidating knowledge for practice. *Social Work Research, 25* (4), 195–197.

Proctor, E. K., and Rosen, A. (2001). "Formulating Target Taxonomies for Practice Guidelines: Issues and an Agenda for Research." Paper presented at the Fifth Annual Conference of the Society for Social Work and Research, January, Atlanta, Georgia.

Proctor, E. K., Rosen, A., and Rhee, C. W. (2002). Outcomes in social work practice. *Social Work Research and Evaluation, 3* (2), 1–17.

Reber, A. (1993). *Implicit Learning and Tacit Knowledge: An Essay on the Cognitive Unconscious.* New York: Oxford University Press.

Reid, W. J., and Fortune, A. E. (1992). Research Utilization in Direct Social Work Practice. In A. J. Grasso and I. Epstein (Eds.), *Research Utilization in the Social Services* (pp. 97–115). New York: Haworth.

Rogers, E. M. (1995). *The Diffusion of Innovation* (4th ed.). New York: Free Press.

Rosen, A. (1983). Barriers to utilization of research by social work practitioners. *Journal of Social Service Research, 6,* 1–15.

———. (1992). Facilitating clinical decision making and evaluation. *Families in Society: The Journal of Contemporary Human Services, 73,* 522–530.

———. (1993). Systematic planned practice. *Social Service Review, 67,* 84–100.

———. (1994). Knowledge use in direct practice. *Social Service Review, 68,* 561–577.

———. (1996). The scientific practitioner revisited: Some obstacles and requisites to fuller implementation in practice. *Social Work Research, 20,* 105–111.

———. (2002). "Evidence-Based Social Work Practice: Challenges and Promise." Paper presented at the Sixth Annual Conference of the Society for Social Work and Research, January, San Diego, California.

Rosen, A., and Proctor, E. K. (1978). Specifying the treatment process: The basis for effectiveness research. *Journal of Social Service Research, 2* (1), 25–43.

———. (1981). Distinctions between treatment outcomes and their implications for treatment evaluation. *Journal of Consulting and Clinical Psychology, 49* (3), 418–425.

Rosen, A., Proctor, E. K., and Howard, M. O. (2002). "Assessing the Building Blocks for Developing Practice Guidelines in Social Work." Paper presented at the symposium "Promoting Evidence-Based Social Work Practice" at the Sixth Annual Conference of the Society for Social Work and Research, January, San Diego, California.

Rosen, A., Proctor, E. K., Morrow-Howell, N., Auslander, W., and Staudt, M. (1993). Systematic planned practice: A tool for planning, implementation, and evaluation. [Brochure]. St. Louis: Author.

Rosen, A., Proctor, E. K., Morrow-Howell, N., and Staudt, M. (1995). Rationales for practice decisions: Variations in knowledge use by decision task and social work service. *Research on Social Work Practice, 5,* 501–523.

Rosen, A., Proctor, E. K., and Staudt, M. (1999). Social work research and the search for effective practice. *Social Work Research, 23,* 4–14.

———. (2003). Targets of change and interventions in social work: An empirically based prototype for developing practice guidelines. *Research on Social Work Practice, 13* (2), 208–233.

Rosenblatt, A., and Attkisson, C. C. (1993). Assessing outcomes for sufferers of severe mental disorder: A conceptual framework and review. *Evaluation and Program Planning, 16,* 347–363.

Rothman, J. (1980). *Social R and D: Research and Development in the Human Services.* Englewood Cliffs, N.J.: Prentice Hall.

Rothman, J., and Thomas, E. J. (Eds.). (1994). *Intervention Research: Design and Development for Human Service.* New York: Haworth.

Schilling, R. F. (1997). Developing intervention research programs in social work. *Social Work Research, 21,* 173–180.

Schulberg, H. C., and Rush, A. J. (1994). Clinical practice guidelines for managing major depression in primary care practice: Implications for psychologists. *American Psychologist, 49* (1), 34–41.

Scott, D. (1990). Practice wisdom: The neglected source of practice research. *Social Work, 35,* 564–568.

Soumerai, S. B., and Avorn, J. (1990). Principles of educational outreach ("academic detailing") to improve clinical decision making. *JAMA, 263* (4), 549–556.

Talbott, J. A. (1990). Developing practice parameters: An interview with John McIntyre. *Hospital and Community Psychiatry, 41* (10), 1103–1105.

Task Force on Social Work Research. (1991). *Building Social Work Knowledge for Effective Services and Policies: A Plan for Research Development.* Washington, D.C.: NASW.

Thomas, E. J. (1984). *Designing Interventions for the Helping Professions.* Beverly Hills: Sage.

Waltz, J., Addis, M. E., Koerner, K., and Jacobson, N. S. (1993). Testing the integrity of a psychotherapy protocol: Assessment of adherence and competence. *Journal of Consulting and Clinical Psychology, 61* (4), 620–630.

Williams, J. B. W., and Lanigan, J. (1999). Practice guidelines in social work: A reply, or "our glass is half full." *Research on Social Work Practice, 9,* 338–342.

Wilson, T. D., and Brekke, N. (1994). Mental contamination and mental correction: Unwanted influences on judgment and evaluation. *Psychological Bulletin, 116,* 117–142.

Zeira, A., and Rosen, A. (2000). Unraveling "tacit knowledge": What social workers do and why they do it. *Social Service Review, 74,* 103–123.

INDEX

Abbott, A., 240, 241, 242

Abstracts of Clinical Care Guidelines (journal), 87

abuse, 32; child, 146, 164, 181; sexual, 85; spousal, 141, 151. *See also* domestic violence

Academic Medical Center Consortium, 87

accessibility, 112, 201; and cost-effectiveness, 208–9; improving, 209–10; of mental health services, 202; of research, 1, 4, 43, 121; of technology, 254

accountability, 2–3, 88, 227, 247; and dissemination, 229, 230–33; and EBP, 241; and implementation, 229, 233, 284; and interprofessionalism, 257, 264; and legitimacy, 265; results-based, 262

accreditation, 232–33, 250, 263; organizations for, 87, 172, 245, 246, 248

activity clusters, 122, 123, 273, 274, 280

adaptation, 273, 280; of interventions, 278, 284; local, 93, 96, 97; of practice guidelines, 93, 96, 97, 227–29

Addis, M. E., 281

Adelman, H. S., 196

adolescents, 199, 203; problem behavior of, 63, 66, 69, 104, 181. *See also* children

African Americans, 194, 195, 196, 210

agencies, social-service: and accountability, 229; clients in, 202, 232; collaboration of, 230; and culture, 193, 203; and effectiveness research, 180, 181; and monitoring of practice, 232–33; multidisciplinary staff in, 225; and practice guidelines, 218, 223, 224, 225, 285; and practitioner autonomy, 233; and problem identification, 143; and quality of care, 209; supervisors in, 217, 282; survey of practitioners in, 225–27, 231; as variables, 184, 200–201

Agency for Health Care Policy and Research (AHCPR), 87, 90, 96, 136, 249

Agency for Healthcare Research and Quality (AHRQ), 87, 173

AIDS, 63, 102, 202

alcohol use, 32, 66, 102, 215, 216. *See also* substance abuse

Allport, G. W., 172

American Academy of Child and Adolescent Psychiatry (AACAP), 85

American Academy of Ophthalmology, 85

American Association of Applied and Preventive Psychology, 91

American Association of Health Care Plans, 96

American Cancer Society, 87
American College of Cardiology, 92
American College of Physicians, 87
American College of Surgeons, 98
American Journal of Psychiatry, 216
American Medical Association (AMA),
    85, 96
American Nurses Association, 212, 214
American Psychiatric Association
    (APA), 85, 136, 212, 216; practice
    guidelines of, 150, 215
American Psychological Association
    (APA), 26, 27, 111, 135, 136; Task
    Forces of, 88, 90, 116, 132–33
American Psychologist (journal), 112
Amodeo, Maryann, 11, 207–18
applicability, 232; in EBP, 44, 45, 47–48,
    52; of generalizations, 11, 283; of
    practice guidelines, 90, 91, 123
Aronoff, Nina L., 12, 253–66, 285
Asians, 195
Assertive Community Treatment
    (ACT), 179–80, 241
assessment: of clients, 6, 7, 99, 101–2,
    142–45, 161, 214; of EBM, 96; educa-
    tion in, 233; of effectiveness, 38, 39,
    83; of evidence, 20, 26–27, 39, 40–42,
    43; evidence-based, 130, 134, 176;
    experimental designs for, 69; and
    local knowledge, 23; by natural
    raters, 30–31; of outcomes, 1, 19, 86,
    88; and practice guidelines, 1, 10, 102,
    108, 231; of practice guidelines, 9, 39,
    90, 100–101, 230; in psychology, 89;
    of research, 33, 37, 42, 45–46, 53, 96;
    and targets, 110, 158; of technology,
    87, 96
assessment measures, 38, 43, 51
Association of Women's Health,
    Obstetric, and Neonatal Nurses
    (AWHONN), 214
Austin, D. M., 239
autopoietic systems, 159, 164

Bachman, 209
Bacon, William F., 12, 212, 216, 223–33,
    281, 282
Bailey, Darlyne, 12, 253–66, 285
Barker, L. A., 196
Barter, K., 258
behavior: analysis of, 134; antisocial, 161;
    and applicability challenges, 47;
    change in, 116, 119, 157–58, 276; child-
    socialization, 197; child/youth
    problem, 63, 66, 69, 104; classification
    of, 142; cognitive, 158; commonalities
    in, 5; differential reinforcement of
    other (DRO), 157; as focus of social
    work profession, 9–10; and health
    care, 101–2; hypotheses on, 276; and
    incentives, 92–93; individual, 6, 11;
    medicalization of, 53; multiplicity of
    effects of, 175; of practitioners, 92–93;
    and research, 29, 175, 277; and social
    context, 158, 159, 161, 164; and target-
    based practice, 157–58; and variability,
    3, 6, 119. *See also* cognitive-behavioral
    therapy
beliefs, 29, 47, 197. *See also* culture
Bernal, G., 199, 203
best practices, 233, 247, 249, 265, 279;
    defined, 213
between-group design, 133
Beutler, L. E., 172
Blenkner, M., 50
Boulder Conference (1949), 17, 88
boundary-spanning model, 257, 265
breast cancer, 92, 94, 99
Bridging Science and Service (National
    Mental Health Advisory Council
    Clinical Treatment and Services
    Research Workgroup), 178–79
Brydon-Miller, M., 263
Bryn Mawr College, 259

Campbell Collaboration, 4, 41, 42, 46, 51,
    279

case-based analysis, 194
case management, 66, 67
Center for Practice and Technology
    Assessment (AHCPR), 96
Centers for Disease Control and
    Prevention (CDC), 87
Chalmers, Ian, 96
Chambless, D. L, 116, 117
change: assessment of, 30, 131;
    behavioral, 116, 119, 157–58, 276; and
    interdisciplinary guidelines, 137; and
    interprofessionalism, 256, 262, 264,
    266; in knowledge, 29–30, 233;
    measurement of, 28–30, 32; models
    of clinical, 28–29; organizational,
    240–41; pressures to, 163;
    psychoeducational model of, 29, 30,
    184, 185; and research, 21, 177; social,
    250, 254, 256, 257, 262, 263, 265;
    theories of, 262–63
Chaulk, P., 94
Chekov, Anton, 83
children: abuse and neglect of, 146, 164,
    181; and effectiveness research, 180;
    problem behavior of, 63, 66, 69, 104;
    and professional jurisdiction, 240;
    socialization of, 197; treatment for,
    89, 198–99, 203, 239
Christakis, D. A., 103
classification, 140–55; and clients, 150,
    164–65; and guidelines, 160–62, 164,
    193, 236; of interventions, 150, 243; of
    knowledge, 141, 145–51, 161, 274–75;
    and negative labeling, 153; of out-
    comes, 122, 273–75; problem-based,
    140, 142–45, 154n5, 193, 236; problem
    vs. target-based, 146, 149, 156–58, 161,
    243; and research, 149, 151, 152–53;
    target-based, 140–41, 146, 149–53, 156,
    158; and transactions, 159–60
client caregivers: critical appraisal skills
    of, 43, 44–45, 47; and practice
    guidelines, 48, 60

clients: and accountability, 230;
    adaptation to, 118–20, 278; and
    applicability, 47; assessment of, 6, 7,
    99, 101–2, 142–45, 161, 214; and
    attachment, 179–80; characteristics
    of, 29, 32, 147–48, 150–51, 155n7, 156,
    194–200, 243; and classification, 150,
    164–65; collaboration with, 158, 161,
    163, 164, 180, 256, 259; critical
    appraisal skills of, 43, 44–45, 46;
    culture of, 193–200, 278; and
    development of guidelines, 93, 99;
    diversity of, 4, 6, 123, 143, 170, 172,
    179, 196, 255, 260, 273, 278; and EBP,
    19, 37, 41–42, 44, 48, 49, 50, 51, 52, 53;
    effects of guidelines on, 94;
    empowerment of, 256, 258; and
    ethics, 49–50, 100; and evidence,
    51–52, 280; individuality of, 7–8, 37,
    38, 48, 103; and interprofessionalism,
    256, 257, 261, 262, 264, 265; and
    legitimacy, 260–61; in medicine, 8,
    91, 171; minorities as, 193–200; and
    outcomes, 44, 157, 262, 274; and
    practitioners, 157, 164, 196–97, 201–3,
    231, 232; preferences of, 48, 99, 103,
    230; and problem-based model, 111;
    problems of, 101–2, 142–45, 146–47;
    vs. professions, 52–53; in psychology,
    89, 91; and research, 46, 60, 83,
    177–78, 179, 202; resistance to
    treatment of, 195–96; in social work,
    260; subpopulations of, 174; values
    of, 232; and variability, 118, 186
clinical trials. *See* randomized clinical
    trials
cluster analysis, 67, 71n2
Cochrane Applicability Methods
    Working Group, 232
Cochrane Collaboration (CC), 39, 41,
    42, 46, 51, 96–97, 248; website of, 50,
    100
codependence, 162

coercion theory, 30
cognitive-behavioral therapy (CBT), 64, 65, 67, 68, 70, 199
community, 28, 43, 241, 261; and individual, 254; and social work practice, 256, 258, 259. *See also* Assertive Community Treatment
community reinforcement training, 163
comorbidity, 180–81, 196
competencies, 214, 215; defined, 213
concept mapping, 262
concerned other (CO), 162–63. *See also* client caregivers
confirmation biases, 41
Congressional Office of Technology Assessment, 87
congruence, stimulus-response, 201–2
consensus, professional: and consolidation of evidence, 280; *vs.* EBM, 37; and PPMD, 228; in practice guidelines, 136–37, 169, 213, 224, 226, 282; *vs.* research, 226, 279
Consensus Development Program (NIH), 92
consensus statements, 173, 174, 186, 187, 207
Constantino, G., 198–99, 203
constructional model, 156–65
construct validity, 32–33
consumer protection agencies, 249, 285
consumers, 255, 260, 262, 281; and EBP, 18, 19, 186. *See also* clients
Consumers Union, 249
Continuous Quality Improvement (CQI), 186
Coohey, C., 32
Cook, D. J., 230
Corrigan, O. W., 184
cost-benefit analyses, 26, 98–99
cost-effectiveness, 90, 91, 99, 179; and accessibility, 208–9; and brief interventions, 215–16; and dose-effect relationship, 117; and quality of care, 207–8; standards of, 234n4
Council of Medical Specialty Societies, 87
Council on Social Work Education (CSWE), 17, 20, 103, 238, 263; and accreditation, 246, 248; and development of practice guidelines, 137, 218; Educational Policy and Accreditation Standards of, 172
Covell, D. G., 95
CQI. *See* Continuous Quality Improvement
credentialism, bogus, 45
criminal justice system, 240
critical appraisal skills, 43–47, 49, 51–53
Critical Appraisal Skills Program (CASP), 47
critical pathways, 85, 214; defined, 213
critical thinking, 171, 184–87, 260; education in, 187, 233; in research, 174, 184–85
Crowley, M., 201
Csikszentmihalyi, M., 112
cuento (storytelling) therapy, 198, 203
cultural competence, 196, 209–10
cultural diversity, 11–12, 32, 33, 260
culture: and alcohol use, 32; client, 193–200, 278; and client-practitioner relationship, 196–97, 202–3; and EBP, 188, 203; and gender, 27, 197; Hispanic, 32, 33, 195, 196, 197, 199, 203; and interpersonal relations, 202–3; and knowledge, 22, 23, 259; and measurement, 26, 27, 28; and practice guidelines, 193–203, 203, 210; and practitioners, 193, 194, 195; professional, 193, 238, 255; and professional legitimacy, 244, 260–61; Puerto Rican, 198–99, 203; and research, 26, 27, 32, 203; of science, 260; sensitivity to, 26, 27, 28, 203; of social work profession, 193, 260–61;

and treatment adherence, 195–96, 200; and treatment models, 198–200; and values, 232, 243; and variability, 173, 174

Culture, Medicine, and Psychiatry (journal), 194, 195, 197

Curriculum Policy Statement (CSWE), 103

databases, electronic, 41, 42, 50, 51, 60, 121, 248. *See also* internet resources

Davison, E. H., 172

Davison, G. C., 187

decision making, 169, 186, 232, 272; democratic, 263; idiographic, 182, 187; individualized, 102; intuitive, 3; lay *vs.* professional, 282; in managed care, 207; medical, 94, 283; and practice guidelines, 1, 121, 124, 125, 185, 188, 247, 283–84

dentistry, 101

depression, 182, 272; late-life, 174; practice guidelines for, 90, 173, 224; research on, 170, 174; treatments for, 88, 89, 199

Deweaver, K. L., 42

diagnosis, 6, 11, 153; classification by, 140–55; defined, 143, 154n1; as moderator variable, 119; and practice guidelines, 1, 108, 193, 224, 236; and practice knowledge, 243; role of, 146–47; and social context, 152; and social work profession, 250

Diagnostic and Statistical Manual of Mental Disorders (DSM), 152, 154; classification in, 110, 111, 140, 243; on culture and ethnicity, 194, 195; and development of practice guidelines, 128, 129, 135; and disease model, 130; and evidentiary standards, 134; *vs.* PIE, 145; and professional jurisdiction, 240

diagnostic-related groups (DRGs), 208

disease model, 110, 111, 125n, 130–31

Dishion, T. J., 31

disorders: classification by, 150; medical, 63, 92, 93, 94, 99, 102, 170; taxonomies based on, 128, 129–30, 135, 243; and use of guidelines, 224. *See also* mental disorders; problems

dissemination: and accountability, 229, 230–33; of EBP, 227, 281; and education, 124, 217; incentives for, 92–93, 124; and interprofessionalism, 265; of medical guidelines, 91–93; methods of, 216, 283; of practice guidelines, 108, 122, 123, 124, 272; and quality control, 216, 229, 230–33; of research, 46, 83, 84, 88, 90, 135, 273; and social agencies, 224; *vs.* transmission, 281–82; and utilization, 171, 231, 280–85

domestic violence, 66, 111, 147

Donabedian, A., 209

dose-effect relationship, 117, 277–78

Drake, Robert, 179

Dwyer, P., 94

eating disorders, 136, 272

EBM. *See* evidence-based medicine

EBP. *See* evidence-based practice

economic issues, 39, 40, 47, 97–99, 103. *See also* cost-benefit analyses; cost-effectiveness; funding

Eddy, J. M., 31, 40, 85

education: and accreditation, 246; authority- *vs.* evidence-based, 104; and autonomy, 227, 233; continuing, 264; in critical thinking, 187, 233; and *DSM*, 144; and EBP, 44, 51; evidence-based, 104, 172, 188; interdisciplinary, 137, 254; and interprofessionalism, 257, 258–59, 261, 262, 263–64; as intervention technique, 67; liberal, 244; as moderator variable, 119; and practice guidelines, 124, 137, 216, 217, 285; and practice knowledge, 243;

education (*continued*)
     professional, 44, 45, 237, 243, 244;
     public, 245; and quality of care, 209;
     in research, 135, 182, 217, 229, 233;
     social work, 103, 104, 110; and
     utilization, 171, 283. *See also*
     psychoeducational model; training
*Educational Policy and Accreditation
     Standards* (CSWE), 172, 246
effectiveness, 254; and adaptation, 273,
     278; and agencies, 229; assessment
     of, 21, 38, 39, 83; claims of, 49, 51, 53;
     and consolidation of evidence, 280;
     and culture/ethnicity, 200; and
     dose-effect relationship, 117; of EBP,
     18, 37, 44; and effect sizes, 173; *vs.*
     efficacy, 89–90, 118, 137, 152; and
     ethics, 49, 50; evidence of, 3, 26,
     116–17, 121, 265; and insurers, 248;
     and interdisciplinary practice
     guidelines, 137; and inter-
     professionalism, 262; of
     interventions, 4, 59, 61, 70; of
     interventive programs, 116–17; of
     medical practice guidelines, 92–94;
     and PAR, 263; and PPMD, 228; and
     practice guidelines, 1–12, 214, 231,
     233, 247; and problem-based model,
     110; and professional jurisdiction,
     240, 242; research on, 11, 20, 24, 97,
     120, 171, 178–81, 183–84, 227–28,
     275–78, 280; of transmission of
     knowledge, 282; and variability, 3,
     86, 119, 169–88. *See also* cost-
     effectiveness
efficacy: and adaptation, 278; and
     clinical significance, 89; and EBP, 37;
     vs. effectiveness, 89–90, 118, 137, 152;
     and empirically supported *vs.*
     validated treatment, 89, 116; and
     evidentiary standards, 132; of
     medical practice guidelines, 93–94;
     and practice guidelines, 248; and

professional jurisdiction, 240; in
     psychology, 88–89, 90; research on,
     4, 11, 20, 24, 175, 176–78, 278; testing
     of, 21, 27
efficiency, 3, 9, 44, 47, 254; as cultural
     value, 243; and interprofessionalism,
     262; organizational, 241; and PAR,
     263; and professional jurisdiction,
     241, 242; and professional knowl-
     edge, 238; and scarce resources, 50.
     See also cost-effectiveness
elder care, 170, 174, 241
Ell, K., 276
Emerson, Ralph Waldo, 83
employee assistance programs (EAPs),
     241
empowerment, 66, 186, 255, 258, 260,
     263; and collaboration, 256; and
     interprofessionalism, 262
Engstrom, M., 226
epidemiology: defined, 175; and
     knowledge, 20, 21, 22, 182; research
     on, 175–78, 183
ethics: and clients, 49–50, 100; codes of,
     244, 245, 261, 264; and development
     of practice guidelines, 247; and EBP,
     37, 41, 42, 43, 44, 45, 49–50, 53, 54,
     188; and effectiveness, 49, 50; and
     evidence, 246; and fraud, 51; and
     interdisciplinary practice guidelines,
     137; and interprofessionalism, 266;
     and knowledge, 245–46; in practice
     guidelines, 100, 103; professional, 9,
     237, 238, 244; in research, 246; and
     uncertainty, 49; and variability, 186
ethnicity, 193–200; and culturally-
     sensitive measurement, 27; and
     familism, 32; and interventive
     research, 26; as moderator variable,
     119; and practice guidelines, 103; and
     treatment relationships, 196–97,
     202–3; and utilization of services,
     195–96, 200

etiology: classification by, 142; and disease model, 130; in *DSM*, 144, 145; and effectiveness research, 181; knowledge of, 20–22, 24, 28–30, 33, 152–53; multifactorial, 175; and PIE, 145; research on, 175–76, 182; of substance abuse, 214; and target-based classification, 149, 152–53

Evans, A. T., 95

event history analysis, 30

evidence: assessment based on, 130, 134, 176; assessment of, 20, 26–27, 39, 40–42, 43; censorship of, 54; and clients, 51–52, 280; *vs.* clinical experience, 97; consolidation of, 279–80; definition of, 261; in EBM, 95, 96; in EBP, 7, 37, 45, 133; in education, 104, 172, 188; of effectiveness, 3, 26, 116–17, 121, 265; empirical, 7, 117, 187–88; and ethics, 246; fallibility of, 6; and insurers, 248; and interprofessionalism, 259–61, 262; interventions based on, 130, 131, 132, 171; *vs.* intuitive approach, 3; in journals, 40, 133–34; lack of, 52; nomothetic, 185; for outcomes, 132, 134, 169; and PPMD, 228; and practice guidelines, 8, 26–27, 231, 271; and RCTs, 116, 132, 134, 279; and research, 26–27, 33, 282; standards of, 131–34, 186, 230, 234n4; strong, 24–27; synthesis of, 123, 279–80; in treatment manuals, 26–27, 132, 133; and uncertainty, 118; and variability, 182

evidence-based medicine (EBM), 37, 95–97

Evidence-Based Medicine (journal), 87

Evidence-Based Medicine Working Group, 232

Evidence-Based Mental Health (journal), 87, 133–34

evidence-based practice (EBP), 10, 17–71; and accountability, 241; applicability in, 44, 45, 47–48, 52; authoritarianism of, 51; and clients, 19, 37, 41–42, 44, 48–53; contributions of, 43–51; and critical thinking, 171, 184–87, 233, 260; and culture, 188, 203; dialectical, 187, 188; dissemination of, 227, 281; and dissemination of guidelines, 124; *vs.* empirical practice, 18–20, 41–42; and ethics, 37, 41, 42, 43, 44, 45, 49–50, 53, 54, 188; evidence in, 7, 37, 45, 133; and generalization, 120; in health-related professions, 83–104; implementation of, 171, 228–29; individualization of, 48, 52; and interprofessionalism, 253, 261, 264; knowledge in, 19, 20–24, 37–54, 227; legitimacy of, 281; and local knowledge, 22–23; and managed care, 207–10; management in, 44; obstacles to, 51, 52–53; opposition to, 6, 51–52; and practice guidelines, 5, 42–43, 83–104, 136, 207, 224, 247; and practitioners, 5, 18–19, 39, 229, 233; and problem-reversal model, 130; in psychology, 88, 187; and research, 33, 182; steps in, 19; and supervisors, 185–86, 211; and uncertainty, 120; and variability, 169, 186, 187–88

evidence-based practice centers (EBPCs), 96

experience, 162, 171, 229, 249, 280; and EBP, 51, 52. *See also* practice wisdom

explanatory models, 20–22, 24, 28–30, 33, 152–53; and research, 21, 27, 32, 178–81, 184

families: empirically supported treatment for, 88, 89; and interprofessionalism, 261; interventions for, 30, 63, 163; preservation of, 61, 66–68, 180; in

families (*continued*)
   social work practice, 215, 256, 258, 259
familism, 32, 33, 199, 203
flexibility: and classification, 161; and interprofessionalism, 257; in practice guidelines, 85, 91, 109; and research, 253; in social work practice, 25; and standards, 230, 234n5
Flexner, A., 238
focus groups, 262
Food and Drug Administration (FDA), 87
Fortune, Anne, 10, 18, 24, 26, 27, 59–71, 243
Foster, S. L., 274
France, 245
Fraser, Mark W., 10, 17–33, 60, 284
Freake, D., 94
Freire, Paulo, 263
funding: and classification, 164; and interprofessionalism, 261, 262, 264, 265; and monitoring of practice, 232–33; and professional status, 238; for research, 20, 28, 46, 180–81, 213–14; and social work profession, 248
Furrow, B. R., 100

Gambrill, Eileen, 10, 18, 37–54, 185, 262
Garfield, S. L., 89
Garland, A. F., 202
gender, 21, 103, 142, 278; and client-practitioner relationship, 202–3; and culture, 27, 197; and variability, 119, 174
generalization, 5, 120, 153, 278; idiographic application of normative, 11, 283
gerontology, 241
Giacomini, M., 230
Gil, A. G., 32
Gill, P., 97
Glasziou, P., 232

Glisson, C., 180
globalization, 254, 256, 265
goal-states, 160, 161, 162–64
Goldiamond, Israel, 157
Gorey, K. M., 60
government, 87, 94, 245
Graham, J. R., 258
Graham, S., 194
Granata, A. V., 99
Grieco, V., 101
Grilli, R., 100
Grimshaw, J. M., 93
grounded theory development, 262
groups, 50, 278; diagnostic-related (DRG), 208; interventions for, 63, 65, 66, 70; and intervention structure, 67; in practice guidelines, 193, 236; in research design, 26, 31, 88, 133
group-specific commonalities, 6, 10
growth curve modeling, 30
Guyatt, G. H., 231, 232

Hagen, N. A., 99
Harrison, W. D., 6
Hart, A., 95
Harwood, K. V., 213
Hayes, S. C., 170, 184
health care, 46, 65, 89, 212, 240; public, 87, 148; and social work practice, 101–2; in U.S., 250. *See also* medicine
Health Care Financing Administration, 87
health maintenance organizations (HMOs), 87, 93
Heffner, J. E., 95
Henggeler, S. W., 161, 201
hero/heroine therapy, 199
hierarchical linear modeling (HLM), 180
Hillman, A. L., 99
Hippocrates, 101, 102
Hispanics, 195, 196, 197; and familism, 32, 33, 199, 203

HIV/AIDS, 63, 102, 202

Hoesch, Charles F., 148

Holland, L., 201

Hollon, S. D., 116, 117

Hooper-Briar, K., 263

Howard, Matthew Owen, 11, 83–104, 135, 170, 171, 218

hypotheses, 125, 277; and dose-effect relationship, 278; in research, 120, 121, 176, 177, 276

implementation: and accountability, 229, 233, 284; appropriate, 283–85; and development of guidelines, 123, 216; of EBP, 171, 228–29; and feedback, 276–77; of interprofessionalism, 261–63; of interventions, 120–21, 284; monitoring of, 229, 230, 232–33; of practice guidelines, 122, 124, 272; by practitioners, 223–33, 283–85

individual: behavior of, 6, 11; client as, 7–8, 37, 38, 48, 103; and community, 254; and culture, 197; interventions for, 63; in medicine, 158; and outcome, 173, 184; practitioner as, 174; and professional legitimacy, 244; in research, 177–78, 181; in society, 99, 157, 158

individualization: of decision making, 102; of EBP, 48, 52; and intervention structure, 66; *vs.* manualization, 172; of practice guidelines, 164, 170, 173–75, 224, 225; and social work practice, 161; and variability, 182

informed consent, 40, 41, 49, 50; in EBP, 43, 44, 52, 53

Institute for the Advancement of Social Work and Research, 103

Institute of Medicine (IOM), 84–85, 87, 91, 93, 94, 98, 224

institutional theories, 238–39, 245, 250

institutions. *See* organizations

insurance providers, 245, 264; and practice guidelines, 87, 98; reimbursement policies of, 98, 144, 208, 246, 248

interdisciplinary practice, defined, 256–57

International Classification of Diseases, 134

internet resources, 50, 51, 60, 96, 100. *See also* databases, electronic

interpersonal psychotherapy (IPT), 199

interprofessionalism, 253–66, 285; and collaboration, 261, 262; defined, 257; and EBP, 253, 261, 264; in education, 257, 258–59, 261, 262, 263–64; implementation of, 261–63; and knowledge, 257, 258, 259–61, 265; and legitimacy, 257, 263–64; and practice guidelines, 258, 259–61, 264; in research, 253, 257, 258, 259, 261, 262, 264

intervention research, 4–5, 10, 17–33, 153, 253, 272; and change, 21; and development of practice guidelines, 135; and effectiveness, 20, 24, 227–28; empirical, 59–71; and evidence, 26–27, 33; and knowledge, 21–22; limits of, 172–73; and outcomes, 112, 236; phases of, 27–28; and practice guidelines, 33, 271; priorities for, 275; in psychology, 88; strengthening of, 27–31; syntheses of, 104; and targets, 113, 156

interventions: adaptation of, 278, 284; approaches to, 3, 64–66, 129; arrays of, 109, 112–18, 122–23; brief, 211, 215–16; classification by, 150, 243; classification by targets of, 140–41; and creativity, 7–8; culturally-sensitive, 203; discrete, 114, 115, 122, 123; and *DSM*, 145; duration of, 63, 117; in EBP, 18, 19, 130, 131, 132, 171, 208–9; effectiveness of, 4, 59, 70,

interventions (*continued*)
169–88, 231; in effectiveness research,
178–79; empirically-based, 26, 88–89,
90, 115, 133; and epidemiological
research, 176; evaluation of, 10;
expectations of, 201, 202;
experimental, 70; family-centered,
30; frequency of, 117; and group-
specific commonalities, 6–7; in
guidelines development, 108–9,
117–18, 122, 123; home-based, 201;
implementation of, 120–21, 284;
improvisation in, 109, 120, 277;
intensity of, 117; interdisciplinary,
137, 182; and knowledge, 151;
manualized, 114, 116; medical, 93; for
mental illness, 65, 66, 68, 69, 185;
modalities of, 63, 110, 193, 236;
moderator variables in, 118–20, 146;
multisystemic, 161, 201; and
outcomes, 109–10, 118, 146, 276;
outcomes-focused, 255; particularization of, 109, 118–20; and PIE, 145;
and practice guidelines, 1, 43, 85, 102;
and practice knowledge, 243;
problem areas of, 63, 64; and
problem-based model, 110–11; and
problem identification, 142–45,
148–49; psychoeducational, 185; in
psychology, 90; relationship in, 67;
replicability of, 62; sequentially
ordered, 277; social-psychological,
117; and social work mission, 255;
standardized, 6–7, 284; structure of,
66–67, 70; and substance abuse, 163,
214; targets of, 9, 11, 109–21, 122,
140–41, 146–47, 149, 273; techniques
of, 67–69; testing of, 8, 122;
uncertainty in, 7, 8, 10; and
variability, 169–88, 231. *See also*
treatment
interventive programs, 62, 114–16, 120,
277, 278, 280; characteristics of,
63–69; definition of, 59; in guidelines
development, 122, 123;
interdisciplinary, 213, 214

Jenson, Jeffrey M., 11, 83–104, 170, 171,
218
Johns Hopkins University, 243
Joint Commission on the Accreditation
of Health Care Organizations, 87
*Journal of the American Medical
Association (JAMA)*, 96
journals, 40, 84, 112, 135, 216; and EBM,
96–97; and evidentiary standards,
133–34; interdisciplinary, 194, 195,
197; practice guidelines in, 87;
research in, 60, 83, 193, 218, 225
justice, 210, 244, 263, 265, 266; and social
work profession, 164, 255, 260

Kaegi, L., 91
Kanfer, F. H., 160
Karls, James, 145
Kazdin, A. E., 112, 131, 201
Kelly, J. T., 87
Kendall, P. C., 116
Kirk, Stuart A., 11, 83, 140–55, 271, 272,
275; responses to, 156, 157
Kleinbaum, D. G., 175
knowledge: abstract system of, 242;
academic, 242, 243–44; academic *vs.*
practical, 248; and agency culture, 50;
authority-based, 95–96; and best
practices, 265; and building-blocks,
273, 277, 280; censorship of, 44; and
change, 29–30, 233; classification of,
108, 141, 145–51, 161, 274–75;
codification of, 94; and critical
thinking, 260; development of, 2,
37–54, 84, 236–37, 256, 285; and
development of practice guidelines,
125, 135; and dissemination of
guidelines, 124; in EBP, 19, 20–24,
37–54, 227; empirically-tested, 1, 3, 10,

11, 59–71, 108; epidemiological, 20, 21, 22, 176, 182; ethical, 245–46; explanatory (etiological), 20–22, 24, 28–30, 33, 152–53; gaps in, 120–21, 229, 271, 279, 285; ideal, 119; inflated claims of, 48, 52–53, 54; and interprofessionalism, 257, 258, 259–61, 265; interventive (control), 10, 20–24, 140, 151; and interventive programs, 116; justification approach to, 41; legitimation of, 249–50; and legitimation of practice guidelines, 236–50; local, 22–23, 25, 29, 47, 161; and openness to criticism, 49; and outcomes, 110; and PAR, 263; practice, 7, 8, 10, 43, 231, 236–50, 285; *vs.* practice, 242–43; and practice guidelines, 226, 271; of practitioners, 227; practitioners' needs for, 108, 169; and process standards, 185; production of, 42, 275; professional, 3, 5, 108, 237–41, 239; and professional legitimacy, 241–46, 250, 259; reduction and metaphor in, 240; and research, 21–22, 24, 29, 122; scientifically-based, 172; in social work, 2, 8, 254; of social work-related professions, 9–10; synthesis of, 123; and target-based model, 150, 152–53; taxonomy of, 150; transmission of, 281–82; uncertainty in, 7, 8, 10, 43, 49, 50, 53, 109, 118, 285; utilization of, 1, 50, 249; of variability, 171
Koepke, Rick, 211
Kolko, D. J., 30
Krasnow, A. D., 281
Kupper, L. L., 175

Lambert, M. D., 135
latent growth curve analysis, 181
Latinos, 32. *See also* Hispanics
Lawson, H. A., 263
Lazarus, A. A., 187

Leape, L., 86, 91
learning theory, 65
Lee, V. L., 159
leeches, 95
legal issues, 47, 94–95, 135
legislation, 238, 240, 246
legitimacy: and accountability, 265; and culture, 244, 260–61; and interprofessionalism, 253, 257, 263–64; and knowledge, 241–46, 250, 259; of practice guidelines, 236–50, 260, 282; professional, 241–46, 250, 255, 257, 259, 260–61, 263–64; and theory, 249–50
Lehman, A., 184
Lewin, Kurt, 263
Littell, J. H., 180
Lomas, J., 92
Louis, Pierre, 95

McCracken, S. G., 184
McGuire, D. B., 213
McMahon, M. O., 276
McMaster University website, 100
Malgady, R. G., 198–99, 203
malpractice, 8, 87, 94
managed care, 12, 84, 200, 215, 217; and dose-effect relationship, 117; and *DSM*, 144; and EBP, 207–10; and monitoring of practice, 232–33; and practice guidelines, 87, 135, 137; reimbursement in, 208
Manning, P. R., 95
Marsh, Jeanne C., 12, 236–50, 259, 285
Mash, E. J., 274
Mattaini, Mark A., 11, 156–65
Mayden, R., 260
Mayo-Smith, M. F., 100
measurement: of change, 28–30, 32; culturally-sensitive, 26, 27, 28; and intervention research, 33; of outcomes, 52, 116, 209, 211, 233; in psychology, 89

Medicaid, 246

medical model, 130–31, 224, 240

Medicare, 93

medicine: brief interventions in, 215; classification in, 140, 142; clients in, 8, 91, 171; consequences of guidelines in, 94–95; cookbook, 94, 103; dose-effect relationship in, 117, 277; and EBP, 18, 187; effects of guidelines in, 91; errors in, 48; evidence-based (EBM) *vs.* authority-based, 37, 95–97; individual in, 158; practice guidelines in, 11, 33, 84, 85–87, 91–101, 109, 140, 170, 208, 224, 225, 253, 281; practice in, 92–94, 187; problem-based model in, 51, 110; and problem identification, 148–49; regional variations in, 86; research in, 102, 282; and social factors, 101–2; use of guidelines in, 171. *See also* health care

Mejía-Maya, L. J., 202

mental disorders, 46, 88, 136, 184, 223, 272, 285. *See also* depression; schizophrenia; substance abuse

mental health care, 63, 200–201, 202; and culture, 194–95; and *DSM*, 144, 152; and effectiveness research, 179–80; empirically-supported treatment in, 88; and evidentiary standards, 133–34; and interdisciplinary practice guidelines, 137; interventions in, 65, 66, 68, 69, 185; practice guidelines in, 104, 128, 173, 184, 208, 224, 225, 272; professional, 10, 53; and professional jurisdiction, 241; research in, 163, 170; and standardization, 210; standards of care in, 212; utilization of services in, 196. *See also* psychiatry; psychology

meta-analyses, 51, 60, 96, 173, 181, 279; and PPMD, 228; and practice

guidelines, 85, 92; and problem-based model, 110

method variance, 31, 32

Milford Conference (1929), 239

Miller, W. R., 215

Millman and Robertson (company), 98

mimesis, 29

minorities: and culturally sensitive measurement, 26, 27, 28; depression in, 174; and practice guidelines, 208; research on, 194; and standardization, 210; treatment models for, 198–200; and treatment relationships, 196–97; treatment termination by, 193–200. *See also* culture; ethnicity

Morgenstern, H., 175

Moseley, P. G., 42

Mullen, Edward J., 12, 212, 216, 223–33, 281, 282

National Alliance for the Mentally Ill, 285

National Association of Black Social Workers, 247

National Association of Social Workers (NASW), 17, 20, 103; Code of Ethics of, 261, 264; and development of practice guidelines, 135, 218, 247; and interdisciplinary guidelines, 136; and interprofessionalism, 264; and PIE, 131, 144–45; policy statements of, 212–13; and practitioner survey, 226; Press of, 25, 33, 245, 247; and professional legitimacy, 237, 238, 245; and standards of care, 212; substance abuse guidelines of, 215

National Comorbidity Survey, 196

National Federation of Societies for Clinical Social Work, 247

National Guideline Clearinghouse (NGC; website), 96, 100

National Health and Medical Research Council, 101

National Health Service (U.K.), 97; Research and Development Program of, 248

National Institute of Mental Health (NIMH), 17, 28, 180–81, 208

National Institute on Drug Abuse (NIDA), 17, 28

National Institutes of Health (NIH), 87, 174

Native Americans, 195

Nelson, K. E., 60

nursing, 135, 240; practice guidelines in, 33, 101, 208; standards of care in, 213–14

Office of Professional Development and Advocacy, 218

Office of the Forum for Quality and Effectiveness in Health Care, 96

organizational field, 239

organizations: accreditation, 87, 172, 245, 246, 248; community-based, 241; and development of practice guidelines, 217–18, 247, 286; governmental, 245; inflated claims of, 53; and interprofessionalism, 261, 263–64; and intervention research, 33; and legitimation of practice guidelines, 238–39; and outcomes, 236; participation in guidelines of, 216; professional, 12, 245, 285; and professional jurisdiction, 240–41, 242; service, 124; in social work practice, 2, 12; and standards of care, 212; and theories of professions, 238

Ottawa Hospital General Campus Library Evidence-Based Medicine and Practice Resources Website, 100

outcome-based model, 111–12

outcomes: assessment of, 1, 19, 86, 88; classification of, 112–14, 122, 273–75; and clients, 44, 157, 262, 274; collaboration on, 164; and creativity, 7; in EBM, 95, 97; and EBP, 19, 37; ephemeral, 6; and ethics, 49, 50; evidence for, 132, 134, 169; and experimental designs, 60; factors in, 137, 236; and individual diversity, 173, 184; intermediate, 114, 115, 116, 141; intermediate *vs.* ultimate, 276, 278; and interprofessionalism, 256–58, 259, 261; and interventions, 109–10, 118, 146, 276; measurement of, 52, 116, 209, 211, 233; and moderator variables, 118, 182–84; monitoring of, 185; positive, 62, 70, 94, 208; and practice guidelines, 94, 137, 224, 283, 284; priority of, 276; in research, 21, 26, 176, 178–79; research on, 69–70, 122, 172, 173, 208–9, 214, 227, 228; sequentially-ordered, 29–30, 114, 115, 116, 132, 277; social validity of, 274; in social work, 254, 272; and substance abuse, 163, 214; and supervision, 186; target, 9, 11, 109–10, 122, 158, 273–75; taxonomies of, 9, 11, 128–29; ultimate, 114, 115, 277; and variability, 3, 86, 173, 180

PAR. *See* participatory action research

Parker, C. W., 98

participatory action research (PAR), 263

Patti, R. J., 276

Paul, Gordon, 172–73

Peebles-Wilkins, Wilma, 11, 207–18

Perlman, Helen, 142–43, 146, 154

personalismo, 197, 199, 203

Personal Practice Model Development (PPMD), 216, 227–29, 231

Person-in-Environment (PIE) model, 129, 131, 140, 144–45, 152, 182–84

Persons, J. B., 172, 187

pharmaceutical industry, 39, 53, 154n6

pharmacotherapy, 101, 117

physicians, 92–94, 97, 98, 102–3, 130. *See also* practitioners

PIE model. *See* Person-in-Environment (PIE) model

Policy Statement on Alcoholism and Other Substance Abuse-Related Problems (NASW), 215

policy statements, 212; defined, 213

Popper, K. R., 41

PORT project, 184, 185

PPMD. *See* Personal Practice Model Development

practice: current, 274; interdisciplinary, 256–57; interprofessional, 257, 258, 261–63, 264; knowledge based on, 7, 8, 10, 43, 231, 236–50, 285; medical, 92–94, 187; monitoring of, 232–33; options in, 85; outcomes-oriented, 264; parameters of, 85; and research, 32, 120–21, 124, 171, 187–88, 260, 261–62, 265; target-based, 157–60; theory of, 52. *See also* evidence-based practice; practice wisdom; social work practice

practice guidelines: acceptance of, 12, 124, 282–83; adherence to, 236; bogus, 44, 48; broad *vs.* individual, 224, 225; components of, 109–21, 229; consensus-based *vs.* evidence-based, 136–37, 169, 213, 224, 226, 282; constructional, 162–65; and creativity, 7–8; defined, 1, 24, 42–43, 48, 84–85, 108, 213, 224, 236; development of, 11–12, 120–24, 128–38, 207, 211–17, 230, 247–49, 271–86; and empirically-tested programs, 59–71; in health-related professions, 83–104; initial development of, 214–16; institutionalization of, 94; interdisciplinary, 11, 136, 137; multidisciplinary development of, 91, 100, 128–38; particularization of, 161–62, 172–73; premature, 48; proliferation of, 86–91; research on

development of, 121–24; resistance to, 7, 116, 170, 223, 264, 283; revision of, 285–86; service-delivery factors in, 193–203; structure of, 108–25; and terminology, 207

``Practice Guidelines for the Treatment of Patients with Substance Use Disorders: Alcohol, Cocaine, Opioids" (APA), 216

practice research networks (PRNs), 120, 121, 274, 277, 280

practice wisdom, 7, 18, 40, 124, 276, 284; and culture, 196, 197; *vs.* research, 102

practitioners: acceptance of practice guidelines by, 124, 282–83; accountability of, 232; adherence of, 236; and applicability, 47; and attachment, 179–80; autonomy of, 52, 227, 233; behavior of, 92–93; biases of, 49; characteristics of, 184, 201–3; and clients, 157, 164, 196–97, 201–3, 231, 232; collaboration of, 230, 249; and consolidation of evidence, 280; critical appraisal skills of, 47; and culture, 193, 194, 195; decision-making needs of, 272; and development of practice guidelines, 93, 187–88, 218; diversity of, 5, 29, 118, 119, 174, 232; and EBP, 5, 18–19, 39, 229, 233; feedback from, 93, 121, 231, 280; implementation of guidelines by, 223–33, 283–85; and inter-professionalism, 261, 262; and interventive programs, 114; and knowledge, 42, 108, 169, 281; and managed care, 208; and monitoring of practice, 232–33; opinion leaders among, 282; and PIE, 145; and practice guidelines, 5–8, 85, 170, 212, 231; and practice wisdom, 276; and problem identification, 143, 149, 153–54; in psychology, 89, 91; and quality control, 186, 227; and research, 17–18, 46, 135, 174–75, 182–83, 231, 249, 274; resistance to practice guidelines of, 7, 116, 170, 223; as scientists, 17, 84, 88; self-improvement of, 39, 40; and supervisors, 211, 233; survey of, 225–27, 231; and target-based classification, 150, 152; and uncertainty, 40, 43, 49, 86; use of guidelines by, 12, 108, 171–73; use of research by, 40, 83–84, 212, 229, 249; and variability, 182, 186

prevention, 39, 157, 161, 175; and problem identification, 148–49

Preventive Services Task Force, U.S., 87, 97

problem-based models, 65, 140–55; classification in, 140, 142–45, 154n5, 193, 236; and guidelines development, 123, 140–41; of learning, 41, 45, 51; *vs.* outcome-based, 111–12; and practice guidelines, 162; in psychiatry, 110, 111, 144; in social work, 142–45; *vs.* target-based, 146, 149, 156–58, 161, 243

problem-reversal model, 111–12, 128, 129–30, 131, 148

problems: client, 101–2, 142–47; defining social, 254; health, 89; identification of, 143, 147–49, 153–54; and prevention, 157; and professional jurisdiction, 242. *See also* disorders

Proctor, Enola K., 1–12, 23, 42–43, 48, 108–25, 236; on intervention targets, 243; on moderator variables, 229; on outcomes, 224; on replicability, 284; on research agenda, 271–86; research reviews of, 60, 62; responses to, 128–38, 140–41, 146, 150, 157, 160; on standards, 231

``The Professionalization of Everyone?'' (Wilensky), 238

professions: authority-based, 37, 53, 95–97; *vs.* clients, 52–53; culture of, 193, 238, 244, 255; defining, 242; education for, 44, 45, 237, 243, 244; ethics in, 9, 237, 238, 244; health-related, 83–104; helping, 9–10; human-service, 253, 254; jurisdictional claims of, 239–41, 244–45, 247, 250, 265; knowledge in, 3, 5, 108, 237–41; legitimacy of, 241–46, 250, 255, 257, 259, 260–61, 263–64; licensing of, 238, 245; practice guidelines in, 11, 246–49; reduction and metaphor in, 240; relations between, 245; social work-related, 9–10, 121, 124, 182, 186, 211, 213–14, 225, 239, 271, 272, 277, 286; specialization in, 254, 255; stage theories of, 238; theories of, 12, 237–41; in U.S., 238, 245. *See also* interprofessionalism

protocols, 61, 70, 83, 85, 169, 248; defined, 213

psychiatry, 10; and culture, 194–95; diagnosis classification in, 140; knowledge base of, 182; practice guidelines in, 109, 128, 134, 135, 208, 224, 226, 246; problem-based model in, 110, 144; and professional jurisdiction, 241; research in, 227; standards in, 231

psychoeducational model, 29, 30, 65, 67, 184, 185

psychology, 10; brief interventions in, 215; clinical, 111, 112; EBP in, 88, 187; knowledge in, 182, 281; and minority clients, 194; practice guidelines in, 11, 33, 84, 87–91, 128, 134, 170, 172, 224, 225, 226, 246; problem-based model in, 110, 111; and professional jurisdiction, 241; research in, 17, 227, 276; and treatment manuals, 282; and variability, 173

psychopharmacology, 173
psychotherapy, 202
Public Health Service, U.S., 87
Puerto Ricans, 198–99, 203

quality control: and dissemination, 216, 229, 230–33; and implementation, 223–33; and managed care, 12; and practitioners, 186, 227; and standards, 207–18
quality filters, 49
quality of care, 207–10

race. *See* ethnicity
RAND Corporation, 87
random effects regression, 181
randomized clinical trials (RCTs), 4, 27, 42, 96; and *cuento* therapy, 198; and EBM, 97; and EBP, 51; in efficacy research, 176–78; and epidemiological research, 183; and evidence, 116, 132, 134, 279; and practice guidelines, 48, 94, 248; in psychology, 88, 89, 90, 276
reactivity, 30–31, 32
Red Jacket, 156
Reid, William, 10, 18, 24, 26, 27, 59–71, 110, 243
Reilly, B., 95
Rein, M., 243
Reisch, M., 276
relationships: social, 64, 199, 202–3; treatment, 67, 196–97
relevance, 202, 261, 262, 263
reliable change index (RCI), 137
replicability, 89, 132, 153, 280, 284; of research, 62, 69–70, 253, 277
research: on accessibility, 202; accessibility of, 1, 4, 43, 121; agendas for, 2, 108, 121–24, 271–86; assessment of, 33, 37, 42, 45–46, 53, 96; and behavior, 29, 175, 277; and best practices, 249; biases in, 46, 49,

69–70; on brief interventions, 215; building-blocks, 273–78; censorship of, 54; change-process, 177; and classification, 149, 151, 152–53; and clients, 46, 60, 83, 177–78, 179, 202; and Cochrane Collaboration, 46; *vs.* consensus, 226, 279; consolidation of, 273; critical thinking in, 174, 184–85; and culture, 26, 27, 32, 203; on development of practice guidelines, 121–24, 216; dissemination of, 46, 83, 84, 88, 90, 135, 273; and *DSM*, 128, 144; in EBM, 95–97; and EBP, 33, 182; education in, 84, 135, 182, 217, 229, 233; effectiveness, 11, 20, 24, 97, 120, 171, 178–81, 183–84, 227–28, 275–78, 280; efficacy, 4, 11, 20, 24, 175, 176–78, 278; on empirically-tested programs, 59–71; and empowerment, 263; epidemiological, 175–78, 183; and ethics, 246; evidence in, 26–27, 33, 282; experimental designs for, 60; explanatory, 21, 27, 32, 178–81, 184; falsifiability of, 41; feedback from practice in, 120–21, 124, 171; funding for, 20, 28, 46, 87, 180–81, 213–14; generalization from, 5, 278; hypotheses in, 120, 121, 176, 177, 276; idiographic, 170, 172, 176, 178; implementation of, 228–29; integration of, 45, 187–88; interdisciplinary, 23, 59, 125, 228, 254; interprofessional, 253, 257, 258, 259, 261–63, 264; and intervention targets, 9, 11, 109–10, 122; and interventive programs, 116; and legitimacy, 260; and manualized interventions, 116; medical, 97, 102, 282; methodologies of, 83; on minorities, 194; moderator variables in, 123, 125; multifactorial, 183; national center for social work, 103; nomothetic, 170, 172, 176, 184, 187;

and openness to criticism, 49; on outcomes, 69–70, 122, 172, 173, 208–9, 214, 227, 228; outcomes in, 21, 26, 176, 178–79; and particularized guidelines, 162; on personality, 172; pharmaceutical, 283; policy-related, 43, 45, 46, 51; and PPMD, 228; and practice, 32, 120–21, 124, 171, 187–88, 260–62, 265; and practice guidelines, 8, 10, 12, 123, 213, 224, 231, 247; practice-relevant questions in, 169, 170; and practitioners, 17–18, 46, 135, 174–75, 182–83, 231, 249, 274; practitioners' use of, 40, 83–84, 212, 229, 249; and problem identification, 153–54; and problem-reversal model, 130; and process standards, 185; in psychology, 17, 227, 276; published, 39; on quality of care, 208; RCTs in, 176–78, 183; replicability of, 62, 69–70, 253, 277; reviews of, 41, 42, 44, 45, 46, 49, 51, 53, 60, 92, 97, 104, 122, 136, 169, 170, 181, 279; on risk factors, 21, 26, 29, 32, 33, 175, 176, 178, 181, 182; scarcity of, 124; and scientific methods, 102; single-site, 181; on social agencies, 184; in social work, 23–24, 84, 248; and social work practice, 17–33, 153–54, 154n4, 169–71; in social work-related professions, 9–10; on substance abuse, 162–63, 170, 214; synthesis of, 122; and target-based model, 149, 151, 152–53, 158; and treatment decision alternatives, 169; in universities, 243–44; and use of guidelines, 223–24; utilization of, 3–5, 40, 83–84, 90, 124, 135, 212, 227, 229, 231, 249, 273, 281, 283; and variability, 173, 174, 176, 177–78, 182. *See also* intervention research; practice research networks
research and development model, 277, 280

Research in Social Work Practice (journal), 193, 218, 225
``Research Needs in Managed Behavioral Health Care in Massachusetts'' (Peebles-Wilkins), 208
resources, 47, 161; and EBP, 44, 50, 52; scarce, 45, 50. *See also* funding
Richmond, Mary, 142
risk factors, 49, 183; research on, 21, 26, 29, 32, 33, 175, 176, 178, 181, 182
Rivara, F. P., 103
Rogler, L. H., 198–99, 203
Rosen, Aaron, 1–12, 23, 42–43, 48, 108–25, 201–2, 236; on intervention targets, 243; on moderator variables, 229; on outcomes, 224; on replicability, 284; on research agenda, 271–86; research reviews of, 60, 62; responses to, 128–38, 140–41, 146, 150, 157, 160; on standards, 231; on utilization of research, 83
Rossell¢, J., 199, 203
Rothman, J., 27, 122
Rothwangl, J., 100
Russell, I. T., 93
Rutledge, R., 98

Sackett, D. L., 39, 40, 43, 47–48, 52, 95
Schefft, B. K., 160
Schilling, R. F., 276
schizophrenia, 173, 184, 185, 224
Schnitzer, P. K., 195
Schorr, 261
Schwartz, Arthur, 157
scientist-practitioners, 17, 84, 88
Scott, W. R., 245
Seligman, M.E.P., 112
service delivery systems, 213
Shahar, E., 51
Shaneyfelt, T. M., 100, 230
Sinclair, J., 232
single-case design, 84, 133, 185

single-system designs (SSD), 4, 7, 26, 60, 69, 134, 156, 285

skills, 2, 29, 114; cognitive-behavioral, 67; critical appraisal, 43–47, 49, 51–53; interpersonal, 187; and interprofessionalism, 257, 258, 259; as intervention technique, 67; professional, 237, 239; training in, 67, 68; and use of guidelines, 223

Social Casework: A Problem-Solving Process (Perlman), 142–43

social context: and behavior, 158, 159, 161, 164; and ethnicity, 195; and interprofessionalism, 255–58, 261; and PPMD, 228; in practice guidelines, 161, 162, 170; and research, 176, 177–78, 181; and target-based model, 158–60, 161; and variability, 173, 174

Social Diagnosis (Richmond), 142

social information processing theory, 27

Social Work Administration (Koepke), 211

social work practice: authority-based, 43, 47; constructional model of, 157, 161; contribution to guidelines development by, 103; cookbook, 187; culturally competent, 196; and culture, 203; ecobehavioral, 158, 159, 161; empirical, 41–42, 53; errors in, 48–49; flexibility in, 25; function of, 159, 160, 164; and health care, 101–2; idiographic, 184, 187; and individual, 161; interdisciplinary, 254; interpersonal skills in, 187; in interprofessional environment, 12; and intervention targets, 110; manualized, 114, 116, 172, 178; partnerships in, 255–56; premises of, 2–3, 5; published resources for, 19–20, 24; reform of, 17; and research, 3–5, 17–33, 120–21, 169–71, 187–88; *vs.* research, 153–54, 154n4,

170; in schools, 258; setting of, 236; and social context, 158–60; supervision of, 185–86, 211, 217, 233, 282; uncertainty in, 40, 43, 49, 86

social work profession: accreditation in, 87, 172, 232–33, 245, 246, 248, 250, 263; administrators in, 211; and allied fields, 121, 124, 182, 186, 211, 213–14, 225, 239, 271, 272, 277, 286; consultation in, 227, 229; culture of, 193, 260–61; and effectiveness research, 183–84; and inter-professionalism, 253–66, 258–59; jurisdiction of, 239–41, 244–45, 247, 250, 265, 272; and justice, 164, 255, 260; knowledge of practice guidelines in, 226; leadership in, 211; licensing in, 246, 248, 264; mission of, 255, 256; and PIE, 145; and practice guidelines, 8–10, 134–36; promotion of, 145; public mandate of, 2, 8; and scientific charity, 207; and social change, 250; and social context, 255–58; standards in, 8–9; supervisors in, 227, 229, 231, 282; terminology in, 211, 212, 218; and theory, 250; in universities, 248

society, 244, 250; and individual, 99, 157, 158

Society for Social Work Administration, 211

Society for Social Work and Research (SSWR), 18, 20, 103, 136; Outstanding Research Awards program of, 18, 23–24, 25

Society for Social Work Research, 218

Society of Clinical Psychology (APA), 88

Solomon four-group design, 31

Specht, Harry, 159–60

specialization, professional, 254, 255

standardization, 12, 83, 229; barriers to, 216; of interventions, 6–7, 284; and quality of care, 208–10 standards: of care, 212, 214; and CQI, 186; and dissemination of guidelines, 230–31; evidentiary, 131–34, 186, 230, 234n4; and flexibility, 230; legal, 95; legitimating, 263; length-of-stay, 98; of medical care, 94–95; in practice guidelines, 1, 85, 234nn3,4,5, 247; process *vs.* content, 184–85, 186; and professional jurisdiction, 240; in psychiatry, 231; and quality control, 207–18; and social work profession, 8–9; static, 94; uncertainty about, 95

Standards and Guidelines for Professional Nursing Practice in the Care of Women and Newborns, 214

Staudt, M. M., 23, 60, 62, 135, 284

Steketee, G., 218

Stoolmiller, M., 31

substance abuse, 63, 102; guidelines for, 104, 162–63, 215; and initial development of practice guidelines, 211, 214–16; interventions for, 66, 89, 163, 201, 214, 215–16; research on, 162–63, 170, 181, 214

Sue, S., 202

Swartout, J. C., 87

systematic planned practice (SPP), 7, 121, 284–85

systems theories, 66, 159, 238–39, 245

Tajima, E. A., 180

target domains, 112–14, 122, 123, 274, 275

targets: and autopoietic systems, 159; and building-blocks research, 273–75; classification based on, 140–41, 146, 149–53, 156–58, 161, 243; and constructional model, 156–65; definitions of, 151, 160, 165; guidelines based on, 140–55, 156–65; intervention, 9, 11, 109–21, 122, 146–47, 149, 273; outcome-based, 9, 11, 109–10, 122; practice based on, 2, 110, 157–61; *vs.* problem-based

models, 146, 149, 156–58, 161, 243; and problem identification, 147–48; and process standards, 185; and substance abuse, 214

task-centered approaches, 65, 239

Task Force on Promotion and Dissemination of Psychological Procedures (APA), 88, 90, 132–33

Task Force on Psychological Intervention Guidelines (APA), 116

Task Force on Social Work Research, 275–76

taxonomies: alternative, 131; disorder-based, 128, 129–30, 135, 243; of knowledge, 150; target-based, 9, 11, 109–10, 122, 128–29, 151, 274

technology: access to, 254; assessment of, 87, 96; information, 40, 228; and interprofessionalism, 262, 265; and practice guidelines, 125, 225, 227–29; and professional jurisdiction, 240–41, 242; and variability, 86, 119. *See also* databases, electronic; internet resources

television, 240

theory: of change, 262–63; coercion, 30; and consolidation of evidence, 280; in *DSM,* 144; grounded, 262; institutional, 238–39, 245, 250; and interventive programs, 114; learning, 65; and legitimacy, 249–50; and outcomes, 110; and PPMD, 228; of practice, 52; and practice guidelines, 124, 231; professions, 12, 237–41; social information processing, 27; systems, 66, 159, 238–39, 245

Thomas, E. J., 27, 122

Thyer, Bruce A., 11, 111, 128–38, 224, 243

time-series methods, 185

Toepp, K., 87

training, 41, 60, 229; community reinforcement, 163; in EBP, 44; insufficient, 45; in psychology, 90; in

training (*continued*)
research, 84; skills, 47, 67, 68; in social-service agencies, 225. *See also* education
transactions, 11; networks of, 159–60, 164, 165; and target-based practice, 158–60
transparency, 45, 49, 52, 230; and inflated claims, 53, 54; and pseudoscience, 51
treatment: for children, 89, 198–99, 203, 239; compliance with, 193–200; for depression, 88, 89, 199; empirically supported *vs.* validated, 89, 116; length of, 214; models of, 198–200; plans for, 114; relationships in, 67, 196–97; and research, 169; resistance to, 195–96; termination of, 193–201. *See also* interventions
treatment manuals, 24, 25, 33, 104, 281, 284; for community reinforcement training, 163; and dose-effect relationship, 117; and evidence, 26–27, 132, 133; in psychology, 89, 90, 282
Tyrrell, C. L., 179

Uman, G. C., 95
uncertainty: in implementation, 284, 285; of knowledge, 7, 8, 10, 43, 49, 50, 53, 109, 118, 285; in management, 49; and practice guidelines, 92, 108, 120–21, 124; and practitioners, 40, 43, 49, 86; and standards, 95
unilateral family therapy (UFT), 163
United Kingdom (U.K.), 97, 248, 282
United States (U.S.): health care in, 250; insurers in, 248; professions in, 238, 245; social work in, 246; universities in, 243–44
universities, 100, 227, 228, 245; and interprofessionalism, 258–59, 264; research in, 243–44; and social work profession, 248

University of Chicago, 227, 228, 244
utilization: barriers to, 47–48, 84, 201; and dissemination, 171, 231, 280–85; of knowledge, 1, 50, 249; of practice guidelines, 12, 108, 171–73, 184, 223–24, 249; of research, 3–5, 40, 83–84, 90, 124, 135, 212, 227, 229, 231, 249, 273, 281, 283; of services, 194, 195–96, 200–201; and target-based classification, 152. *See also* implementation
utilization review companies, 87

validity: of classification systems, 151; construct, 32–33; empirical, 89, 116; social, 274
variability: of attachment, 179–80; and clients, 118, 186; and EBP, 169, 186, 187–88; and effectiveness, 3, 86, 119, 169–88; and guidelines, 164; and interventions, 169–88, 231; knowledge of, 171; of needs, 255; of outcomes, 3, 86, 173, 180; and process standards, 185; and research, 173, 174, 176, 177–78, 182; typology of, 182–84
variables: agencies as, 184, 200–201; behavioral, 3, 6, 119; cultural, 173, 174; moderator, 118–20, 123, 125, 146, 182–84, 229; practitioners as, 182, 186
Vega, W. A., 32
Videka, Lynn, 11, 169–88, 243

Wagner, E. F., 32
Wandrei, Karin, 145
Ward, J. E., 101
Webb, L. Z., 93
Wennberg, J. E., 86
Wheelock College, 258–59
whistle-blowers, 49
White, S. H., 243
Whlie, B., 99
Whyte, William Foote, 263
Wilensky, H. L., 238

Witkin, S. L., 6
Wodarski, J. S., 111
``Working Statement on the Purpose of
    Social Work'' (1979), 156–57
Worrall, G., 94

Zane , N., 202
Zayas, Luis H., 11, 193–203, 202
Zeira, A., 276
Zigler, E. F., 202